Black Power in the Caribbean

UNIVERSITY PRESS OF FLORIDA

Florida A&M University, Tallahassee
Florida Atlantic University, Boca Raton
Florida Gulf Coast University, Ft. Myers
Florida International University, Miami
Florida State University, Tallahassee
New College of Florida, Sarasota
University of Central Florida, Orlando
University of Florida, Gainesville
University of North Florida, Jacksonville
University of South Florida, Tampa
University of West Florida, Pensacola

BLACK POWER
IN THE CARIBBEAN

Edited by Kate Quinn

UNIVERSITY PRESS OF FLORIDA

Gainesville / Tallahassee / Tampa / Boca Raton

Pensacola / Orlando / Miami / Jacksonville / Ft. Myers / Sarasota

This book may be available in an electronic edition.

First cloth printing, 2014
First paperback printing, 2015

Library of Congress Cataloging-in-Publication Data
Black power in the Caribbean / edited by Kate Quinn.
pages cm
Includes bibliographical references and index.
Summary: The first collection to explore the Black Power movement in its various
manifestations across the Caribbean.
ISBN 978-0-8130-4909-0 (cloth: alk. paper)
ISBN 978-0-8130-6188-7 (pbk.)
1. Black power—West Indies—History. 2. West Indies—Race relations. 3. Blacks—
West Indies—History. I. Quinn, Kate, 1975–, editor.
F1629.B55B55 2014
305.896'0729—DC23   2013029230

The University Press of Florida is the scholarly publishing agency for the State University
System of Florida, comprising Florida A&M University, Florida Atlantic University, Florida
Gulf Coast University, Florida International University, Florida State University, New College
of Florida, University of Central Florida, University of Florida, University of North Florida,
University of South Florida, and University of West Florida.

University Press of Florida
15 Northwest 15th Street
Gainesville, FL 32611-2079
http://www.upf.com

Contents

Acknowledgments

This project would not have been possible without the generous support of many people. I would like first and foremost to thank Brian Meeks and Rupert Lewis at the University of the West Indies, Mona, both for agreeing to co-convene the two conferences on 'Internationalising Black Power' out of which this book arose, but most importantly for their invaluable support, collaboration, and wise counsel throughout the long process of bringing this idea into print. I would also like to thank Tony Bogues for his input into shaping the conference agenda, and the staff at the Centre for Caribbean Thought, University of the West Indies, for hosting such a well-run and inspiring conference at Mona in February 2008. Special thanks also to Kimberly Springer (KCL) and to Olga Jimenez and staff at the Institute for the Study of the Americas, University of London, for their role in hosting the London conference in October 2007.

The book has also been made possible by a British Academy UK–Latin America and the Caribbean Link grant, which funded the two conferences in London and Jamaica; and by research and travel grants from the Central Research Fund, University of London, and the Institute for the Study of the Americas. I was helped enormously by staff in the National Archives (London), the Eric Williams Memorial Collection and University of the West Indies Library (St Augustine), University Archives (Mona), the National Archives and University of Guyana library (Georgetown), and the National Archives (Maryland). My research in Trinidad was facilitated by a great many people who went above and beyond the call of duty. I would especially like to thank Brinsley Samaroo, Raffique Shah, Wally Look Lai, Clive Nunez, and Earl Lovelace for so generously sharing their time and wisdom; also Bridget Brereton, Maarit Forde, Matthew Bishop, and Steve Cupid for making me welcome in Port of Spain. It was also a privilege to meet (among others) Khafra Kambon and Andaiye at the conference in Jamaica, who offered invaluable comments on my paper on Black Power in Guyana. In London, special thanks must go to Bill Schwarz who has offered unstinting support and advice from the beginning of the project; also Richard Drayton, James Dunkerley, Maxine Molyneux, Steve Cushion, Emily Morris, Dylan Vernon, and my colleagues at the Institute of the Americas, UCL, for their continued encouragement. I would also like to thank Peter Fraser, Neville Linton and others who have shared their memories of the period with me over the years.

Lastly, I would like to thank the team at University Press of Florida, particularly Meredith Babb and Michele Fiyak-Burkley for their patience, support, and expertise, as well as the two readers for their insightful reports. Robert Hill, Paul Buhle, and Selwyn Ryan were most generous in providing endorsements of the book. Special thanks to all the contributors to the book, and to my brother, Russell, for providing the cover art. I also of course owe a huge debt to friends and family; apologies for not naming all of you here.

Kate Quinn

Introduction

New Perspectives on Black Power in the Caribbean

KATE QUINN

February 2010 marked the fortieth anniversary of Trinidad and Tobago's Black Power uprising. To commemorate these events, a conference, "Black Power: Reflections, Relevance and Continuity," was held at the University of the West Indies–St. Augustine.[1] Many of the conference participants voiced despair about how little public knowledge and information there was on this period of Caribbean history, how Black Power continued to be viewed with suspicion and even hostility, and how young people—studying on the very campus where the sparks of Trinidadian Black Power ignited—knew so little about it. The conference ended with an urgent plea for the preservation of this history as some of those who were involved in the movement grow old and pass away and their personal archives lie unused. Similar sentiments were voiced at two "Internationalising Black Power" conferences, one held at the University of London in October 2007, the other at the University of the West Indies–Mona in February 2008.[2] These paired conferences sought to bring into comparative and international perspective events and ideologies of the Black Power era that are too often studied in isolation—a consequence, in part, of regional divisions within the academy that in many cases have separated studies of the United States from those of Africa, the Caribbean, and other diasporic locations where Black Power had resonance. By bringing together papers that engaged with Black Power across a number of geographic locations, including North America, the Caribbean, Africa, Latin America, and the United Kingdom, the conferences sought to gain a fuller understanding of the global contexts in which Black Power emerged, the transnational dimensions of the Black Power phenomenon, and the existence of and interactions between parallel and related movements outside of the United States.

At these conferences, it was evident that there were significant gaps and unevenness in the narrative of global Black Power. One such gap relates to the story of Black Power in the Caribbean, a region that experienced notable Black Power upheavals in the same period as its powerful northern neighbor. This book responds to the need to bring together the disparate threads of the Caribbean narrative—from the Bahamas in the north to the Guyanas in the south—as a contribution both to the wider, global story of Black Power and to the understanding of a significant period of Caribbean history whose legacies are still felt but have yet to be fully explored.

While scholarship and popular perceptions of Black Power have been dominated by the North American movement, the Caribbean has much to add to our understanding of the concept of "Black Power," its meaning in other contexts, and the extent to which it had resonance beyond the borders of the United States. Focusing on the turbulent decades of the 1960s and 1970s, this book offers an overview of Black Power in the Caribbean, outlining the particular national and international contexts in which it emerged, its local manifestations, and its relations with the movement in the United States. What did "Black Power" mean in the Caribbean context? What were its principal concerns? What commonalities and differences can be traced across the region? How might an analysis of Caribbean Black Power add to our understanding of Black Power in the global context?

The most famous definition of Caribbean Black Power is that provided by Guyanese academic and activist Walter Rodney, the foremost theoretician of the regional movement. Speaking on the Mona campus of the University of the West Indies in 1968, Rodney proposed that "Black Power in the West Indies means three closely related things":

(1) the break with imperialism which is historically white racist;
(2) the assumption of power by the black masses in the islands;
(3) the cultural reconstruction of the society in the image of the blacks.[3]

While the cultural message of Rodney's statement was common to most conceptions of Black Power in the region, its political implications were not embraced by all. As the chapters in this volume illustrate, definitions of Black Power in the Caribbean encompassed a broad spectrum of positions, from the "Jamesian insurrectionary socialism" of Antigua's ACLM to the religious conservatism of the Nation of Islam. One of the primary concerns of this volume is therefore to understand the different meanings and manifestations of Black Power within the diverse contexts of the Caribbean, a region characterized by wide variations in population, size, ethnicity, economy, and political status. In these diverse contexts, no one group could claim a "monopoly of understanding of the black predicament."[4]

That predicament, in the mid-twentieth-century Caribbean, was primarily a crisis of failed expectations. Whether this was the disappointments of "flag independence" in the former British colonies of Jamaica, Trinidad and Tobago, Barbados, and Guyana, or the limits of self-governance in territories such as Bermuda, the Dutch Antilles, Antigua, Dominica, and Grenada, the early optimism inspired by processes of decolonization and independence was replaced with a sense of increasing malaise focused on the region's continued dependency and social and economic inequalities, and the persistence of racial hierarchies and discrimination. In the late 1960s, demonstrations and strikes in Anguilla, Antigua, Bermuda, Curaçao, Guadeloupe, Jamaica, Suriname, Trinidad, and the Bahamas testified to a groundswell of discontent with conditions for the ordinary citizen in the Caribbean state. In 1970, popular agitation reached its climax in Trinidad and Tobago, where months of massive demonstrations culminating in a dramatic army mutiny constituted the first serious challenge to governance in the postindependence Anglophone Caribbean.

The Trinidad protests (dubbed the "February Revolution") explicitly invoked the language and symbolism of Black Power. Together with the October 1968 "Rodney Riots" in Jamaica, they hold a central position in the narrative and historiography of Caribbean Black Power. Yet as the contributions to this volume confirm, engagement with and mobilization around the concept of Black Power was not confined to these two states but occurred in multiple locations across the region as well as in transnational interactions within the region and beyond. While "organized" Black Power was primarily to be found in the English-speaking territories, exposure to the ideological currents of Black Power was region-wide. Even in the Hispanic Caribbean, where black mobilization had historically been channeled into other political and cultural affiliations, the relevance of Black Power was debated, not least in Cuba, which famously hosted prominent figures of the North American movement.[5]

While Black Power "as a concept if not a phrase"[6] might arguably be traced to the first slave rebellions on the soil of the New World, its definition here is limited to the "classic period" in the history of Black Power, spanning from the mid-1960s to the mid-1970s. "Black Power," in other words, does not refer here to black government (in the sense of Ivar Oxaal's *Black Intellectuals Come to Power* [1968]), early black labor organization (in the sense of W. F. Elkins's *Black Power in the Caribbean* [1977]), or to the intellectual and organizational Pan-Africanism of the first half of the twentieth century, although—as the contributions to this volume confirm—the phenomenon is impossible to understand without reference to these. For its proponents, Black Power was linked to all these historical moments as the latest stage in the region's long struggle for meaningful independence and black liberation.

Caribbean Black Power in Historiographical Perspective

U.S. Black Power and Black Power Studies

Scholarship on Black Power has been dominated by the North American story. After decades of scholarly neglect, the growth of "Black Power Studies" in the United States has revitalized the field, producing a plethora of new studies performing the work of historical recovery and revisionism, bringing important new insights to the analysis of the U.S. movement. This new scholarship has nuanced the understanding of North American Black Power in a number of important ways.[7] Firstly, by re-periodizing the struggle to include examples of radical black activism prior to the "classic period" of Black Power (1965–75), these new studies have reconceptualized the relationship between the civil rights and Black Power movements. Challenging the conventional narrative that viewed Black Power as a destructive and violent phenomenon that undermined the achievements of civil rights, the new scholarship has focused instead on the coexistence and common roots of both movements, paying attention to both their overlaps and strategic alliances as well as to their central differences. In this vein, Peniel Joseph argues that the "civil rights and Black Power era" should be viewed as "a complex mosaic rather than [as] mutually exclusive and antagonistic movements."[8] Secondly, recent scholarship has advanced a revisionist analysis of the major North American Black Power organizations, most notably in new works on the Black Panther Party and the U.S. Organization. These studies have complicated the binary analyses of "race" versus "class" and "political" versus "cultural" nationalism that had been encouraged by the tragic history of sectarian conflicts between these groups.[9] Thirdly, the new research has expanded the terrain of Black Power Studies to include previously overlooked local and grassroots organizations that "embodied the political imperatives, cultural sensibilities, and ideological commitments of the era."[10] As Joseph argues, this has led to a widening of the geographical lens beyond the urban centers of the northern states and to greater attention to local and municipal organization, a broadening of perspective that has given a space to women's groups, neighborhood community organizations, and working-class movements that had previously been obscured from the history of Black Power.[11] Exposing the gendered dimensions of the Black Power movement and the crucial role played by women activists has significantly enhanced our under-standing of the richness and complexity of the U.S. movement as well as its contradictions. Fourthly, studies of U.S. Black Power have begun to rethink its legacies and achievements, rejecting previous assumptions that its impact was confined to the domain of culture and identity. Notable successes in electoral politics at the municipal level, the groundwork that community organizing laid for future mobilizations, the development and consolida-tion of Black Studies programs, and the impact on later black feminist and antiapartheid campaigns, for example, all suggest that the Black Power era in the United States had a significant impact on American politics and society well beyond its presumed demise in the mid-1970s. For Joseph, Black Power must therefore be seen as an "integral [part] of a larger struggle for radical democracy in postwar America."[12]

Of most relevance to this volume is the new "international turn" in the de-veloping scholarship on Black Power. Central to the new Black Power Studies' agenda are a critique of the narrow domestic lens through which U.S. Black Power has been viewed and a call for greater attention to the international and transnational dimensions of Black Power. As Cedric Robinson argues, the "conventional narrative" that presented U.S. Black Power as an "autoch-thonous . . . national phenomenon" overlooked the important global contexts in which it emerged and the many ways in which the movement was affected "by events beyond American shores."[13] In a similar vein, Peniel Joseph has criticized the ways in which "narratives of both the Civil Rights and Black Power movements, with important exceptions, remain peculiarly *American* stories of domestic racial dissent."[14] By contrast, key proponents of U.S. Black Power ideology viewed the American struggle as intrinsically linked to the struggles of oppressed and colonized peoples across the developing world. Famously characterizing black communities as the "internal colonies" of the United States, Stokely Carmichael articulated a vision of a single struggle against the "common enemy" of U.S. imperialism, vividly imagined as a giant octopus with its tentacles reaching into every corner of the globe. While the tentacles were kept tied up by their comrades in Vietnam and Cuba, Carmi-chael argued, blacks in North America were taking the opportunity to put a knife in the eye of the octopus at home. "We understand that our destinies are intertwined," stated Carmichael. "Our world can only be the Third World, our only struggle, for the Third World."[15] This sentiment was affirmed again and again in the speeches and writings of black intellectuals and activists in the period. As James Forman stated, "the Black Power we are talking about in the United States has to become an international concept."[16]

Acknowledging this vision of an "imagined community" of black and Third World struggles beyond the United States, recent scholarship has begun to examine the international and transnational dimensions of the U.S. Black Power movement, exploring the material and ideological influences that shaped black internationalism in the period. This has included an evaluation of the internationalism evident in the political analyses of its progenitors (such as Robert Williams and Malcolm X) and that of Black Power organizations such as the African Liberation Support Committee, the Revolutionary Action Movement, and the Black Panthers, showing how they fused "a radical internationalist posture—anticolonialism, Third World solidarity, and opposition to U.S. imperialism—with an equally radical critique of U.S. society."[17] The new scholarship has also sought to understand how international events—the Bandung Conference, the Cuban Revolution, African liberation movements, the Vietnam War—shaped the emergence and ideologies of domestic U.S. Black Power. In this regard, examining the international travels of prominent African-American activists—such as Robert Williams in Cuba, Malcolm X in North Africa, and Julian Mayfield in Ghana—has proved a fruitful avenue for exploring the crosscurrents of influence that shaped politics in a number of key locations of the global black struggle.[18] Studies of African-American communities in postindependence African states have also underlined the centrality of Africa within the political imaginary of North American black activism as well as the significance of the transnational connections and networks that shaped the interactions, influences, and disagreements between African and African-American political struggles.

Despite the greater geographical proximity of the Caribbean, the circulation of Caribbean intellectuals within U.S. networks of black activism, and the profound ideological influence of great Caribbean figures such as Frantz Fanon and C.L.R. James, relations between North American and Caribbean black activism have received much less attention than have connections with the African continent. Significant exceptions can be found in Stephen Ward and Derrick White's articles on the Institute of the Black World (IBW), Fanon Che Wilkins's analysis of the Sixth Pan-African Congress, and David Austin's study of Caribbean student activism in Canada.[19] Both Ward and White have shown that Caribbean intellectuals were central to the "programmatic and ideological development" of the Institute of the Black World, an Atlanta-based independent black think tank formally launched in January 1970. C.L.R. James, for example, was involved with the Institute since 1969, when he delivered the inaugural W.E.B. Du Bois memorial lecture. Both he and Walter Rodney spent periods of residence there giving seminars, lectures, and interviews, while Robert Hill, considered to be "one of the Institute's key theorists," was appointed to its staff in spring 1970.[20] These Caribbean intellectuals—along with other visitors from the region, including Sylvia Wynter, Kamau Brathwaite, George Beckford, and St. Clair Drake—played a significant role in defining a "black perspective"[21] within the IBW that went beyond the specific domestic concerns of African Americans in the United States.

The interactions among African, North American, and Caribbean activists at a "critical turning point in the development of black internationalism"[22] are explored in Wilkins's examination of the organization of the Sixth Pan-African Congress (PAC), held in Tanzania in 1974. The idea for the Sixth PAC was mooted at the 1969 Black Power Conference (held in Bermuda) and was taken forward by Roosevelt Brown (Pauulu Kamarakafego), a central figure in the Caribbean Black Power movement, and SNCC activist James Garrett. Meetings of regional planning committees were held in the United States and in the Caribbean and, alongside North American members of SNCC and the Center for Black Education, included many of the Caribbean activists discussed in this volume—notably, James, Rodney, Kamarakafego, and Eusi Kwayana. As Wilkins argues, the congress and the international mobilization efforts that preceded it "exposed points of tension and unity between African Americans and the African diaspora" in their attempts to forge a discourse and practice of black internationalism that would challenge the colonial and postcolonial state.[23]

David Austin's analysis of black radicalism in Canada has expanded the geographical reach of Black Power Studies and offers a useful corrective to interpretations that view black mobilization elsewhere in the same period as an "outgrowth" of racial politics in the United States. Austin's article "All Roads Led to Montreal" paints a vibrant picture of emergent black radicalism in Canada through an examination of the Caribbean Conference Committee and of two seminal events that "temporarily transformed Canada and Montreal into the center of the Black Power Movement": the October 1968 Congress of Black Writers and the February 1969 Sir George Williams University Affair.[24] As Austin describes, Caribbean students in Canada were instrumental in bringing into contact and debate "a veritable 'Who's Who' of black political figures spanning multiple generations and countries,"[25] including influential figures of North American black radicalism and of the Caribbean "old" and "new" left. The Montreal conferences and the student protests at the Sir George Williams University "ignited the Montreal black community"[26] and had a profound impact on the development of Black Power in both Canada and the Caribbean.

All too often, however, the "international" or "transnational" paradigm that has begun to inform recent scholarship has tended to reinforce the centrality of the U.S. movement by focusing on how it was affected by engagement with the wider world, rather than exploring parallel or even related mobilizations elsewhere.[27] V. P. Franklin's assertion that "the movement for Black Power emerged in the United States in 1966 and eventually spread internationally to the Caribbean, . . . South America, . . . [and] South Africa"[28] exemplifies this tendency to view the movement from the perspective of a North American center. Without diminishing the huge significance of the U.S. movement and the influence it had, it should be said that such an approach can overlook the autochthonous conditions that produced parallel movements and the different roots (Rastafarianism, for example) and routes (Montreal to Port of Spain; Trinidad to Grenada) that fertilized Black Power outside the United States. In turning to the Caribbean, this volume seeks to give greater prominence to one axis of the black Atlantic triangle and to shed light on the different sources and directions of global Black Power.

Arguably the first serious attempt to examine the origins and mobility of Black Power in the international context is Jamaican scholar Locksley Edmondson's "The Internationalization of Black Power" (1974), which explores many of the themes now embraced by contemporary scholarship, including "the global themes in circulation in the movement, the international racial context within which black American racial assertiveness has evolved, and the initial dissemination of Black Power ideas beyond black America."[29] Decades before the concept of transnationalism came into vogue, Edmondson set out a three-point research agenda for the study of black internationalism that could still be usefully pursued today: (1) to examine "the evolution and significance of . . . global black nationalist ideologies"; (2) to undertake a "comparative study of their origin and transfusion"; and (3) to offer "transnational perspectives on the situations in black America, Africa, and the Caribbean" as a means of understanding the "internationalizing potentialities" of "pan-African" movements and ideological identifications.[30] Edmondson identified clear continuities between Black Power and earlier "pan-Negro" currents in the common themes of "African liberation and continental unity, . . . global racial solidarity, reflections on neo-colonialism, [and] the Garveyite 'Back to Africa' theme."[31] However, while acknowledging such continuities and the "infectiousness of the slogan beyond black America," Edmondson viewed Black Power as "a phenomenon basically indigenous to the United States." Contrasting its "origin and basic entrenchment in the realities of black American existence" with the profoundly transnational origins and outreach of Garveyism, Pan-Africanism, and the negritude movement, he concluded that Black Power was "limited in its potential as an internationalizing force."[32] Given that Edmondson's chapter was written before the major outbreaks of Black Power protest in the Caribbean, it is pertinent to revisit this argument while drawing inspiration from his comparative and international approach to Black Power.

Black Power Scholarship and the Caribbean

Despite the significance attributed to Black Power as the first serious challenge to West Indian governments of the postindependence era, scholarship on Black Power in the Caribbean has not acquired the same critical mass as that of its North American counterpart. The first wave of commentaries emerged in the wake of the October 1968 "Rodney Riots" in Jamaica and the 1970 Black Power revolt in Trinidad and Tobago and served first to document and then to offer explanations for the outbreak of Black Power disturbances in majority-black countries. The best documentary account from this period is Ivar Oxaal's *Race and Revolutionary Consciousness* (1971), which offered an "existential report"[33] on the 1970 disturbances in Trinidad and Tobago, collating primary sources to reconstruct the chronology of events and to reflect the diverse ideology of the movement. Nigel Bolland's 1969 paper "The Roots of Black Power in the West Indies" looked to the region's history of enslavement and plantation economies to explain the contemporary emergence of Black Power sentiment in the region, rooting it in the development of a social system in which race and class hierarchies had altered little since colonial times and in a corresponding history of West Indians' resistance to the conditions of their oppression. Such historical explanations have remained a constant theme of subsequent analyses of Caribbean Black Power, as has the narrative of continuity that locates 1960s Black Power within a longer tradition of West Indian struggle. As Bolland expressed it, "the movement known as Black Power which is now making such an impact throughout the West Indies is the most recent expression of black identity and solidarity in a long history of reaction against the economic, political, social, cultural, and psychological servitude imposed on black men by the white power structure."[34]

Many of the early analyses of Caribbean Black Power were written by firsthand witnesses to, and participants in, the events themselves. These accounts, such as James Millette's "The Black Revolution in the Caribbean" and William Riviere's *Black Power, NJAC and the 1970 Confrontation in the Caribbean*, sought to draw lessons from the apparent failures of the Black Power movement after the imprisonment of its leadership in Trinidad and the region-wide regrouping of the forces of the state. Their arguments are revealing of the diverse political positions that coexisted within the movement in the period. Riviere, who was himself incarcerated in Nelson Island, blamed tactics, not ideology, for the failure to sustain a mass movement. In criticizing "the extent to which the revolutionary consciousness of the masses had fallen short of that of the leadership,"[35] Riviere implicitly endorsed a vanguardist role for the intellectual that was not shared by all his colleagues at the University of the West Indies, where he was lecturing when the disturbances in Trinidad broke out. Riviere's position stands in notable contrast to Walter Rodney's Jamesian-inspired invocation that the black intellectual should become the "servant" of the masses. Rodney's *The Groundings with My Brothers* (1969), a series of speeches given in Jamaica and Montreal, remains the foundational text of West Indian Black Power by one of its foremost protagonists and theoreticians and was, along with works by Frantz Fanon and Malcolm X, required reading for any serious Black Power aspirant in the period.

In this period, too, many of the region's intellectuals, artists, and writers reflected on the rumblings of West Indian and global Black Power, from C.L.R. James's endorsement of Stokely Carmichael and "the enormous revolutionary potential" of Black Power to V. S. Naipaul's dissection of the movement's dark underbelly in his 1974 essay "Michael X and the Black Power Killings in Trinidad."[36] One of the most important works of contemporary analysis remains Rex Nettleford's collection of essays, *Mirror Mirror* (1970), a reflection on how the "three critical variables" of identity, race, and protest shaped the social realities of 1960s Jamaica. Alongside chapters on attitudes toward race in Jamaica and a pioneering analysis of the Rastafari as "the most authentic of Jamaican protesters," the third chapter, "Jamaican Black Power or Notes from the Horn," offered a nuanced and critical engagement with Black Power in Jamaica that rooted it firmly in the island's "tradition of black assertion."[37] Sensitive to the "textured complexities that characterize the Caribbean," "Notes from the Horn" examined both the strengths and the weaknesses of the appeal to Black Power in the Jamaican context, the extent to which its concerns echoed those of other groups (including nationalist governments), and the limitations that would constrain any attempts to go beyond its "polemical chronicling of [society's] ills."[38] Also of note is Orde Coomb's edited volume *Is Massa Day Dead? Black Moods in the Caribbean* (1974), a collection of essays by ten West Indian writers and intellectuals, including Kamau Brathwaite, Derek Walcott, Gordon Rohlehr, and Merle Hodge. Several essays, including those by Locksley Edmondson, James Millette, Timothy McCartney, and Eva Hodgson, directly addressed the theme of Black Power, the latter two offering rare studies of racial politics in the Bahamas and Bermuda.[39] Others reflected more generally on the political and economic realities of the region, the quest for a cohesive identity, and the relationship with the colonial past. Of these, Merle Hodge's chapter stands out for its attention to the gendered dimensions of inequality in the Caribbean. For Hodge, "Massa Day" would not be done until there was equality of the sexes—an analysis that was too often wholly absent from articulations of Black Power in the region.

Extended autobiographical accounts by the protagonists of the Black Power movement in the Caribbean are few and far between. The few examples include *X Communication* (1995), a selection of autobiographical essays by Belizean Black Power leader Evan X Hyde; *Me One: The Autobiography of Pauulu Kamarakafego* (2001); and *Mutiny: Ten Days at Teteron Barracks*, an account of the 1970 Trinidad Regiment mutiny by one of its central protagonists, Raffique Shah.[40] Raoul Pantin, then a twenty-seven-year-old journalist for the *Trinidad Guardian*, provided a lively memoir of the 1970 Black Power demonstrations in his *Black Power Day: A Reporter's Story* (1990), recording how "for fifty-five days . . . Trinidad and Tobago reverberated to the shuffle of thousands of marching feet and voices roaring, 'power to the people!'"[41] A recent documentary on these events contains invaluable archival footage and oral testimony from witnesses and participants on all sides of the confrontation.[42]

After a hiatus of almost two decades, the history of Caribbean Black Power returned to the academic agenda, inspired in part by significant anniversaries of the conflicts of 1968 and 1970. These works can be broadly grouped into those that examine Black Power as part of a wider history of Caribbean political thought and praxis and those country-specific studies that can be found scattered across journals and edited collections and as part of wider general histories. Several important studies have examined the intellectual and political contributions of significant protagonists of the period. Notable among them are Rupert Lewis's *Walter Rodney's Intellectual and Political Thought* (1998), the most comprehensive analysis of the life and thought of Guyana's outstanding intellectual-activist; Anthony Bogues's *Black Heretics, Black Prophets* (2003), which places Caribbean thinkers such as Rodney and C.L.R. James into a broader tradition of black radicalism encompassing Africa and the African diaspora; and Paul Buhle's *Tim Hector: A Caribbean Radical's Story* (2006), the only substantive study of Antigua's most remarkable public intellectual and the influences that shaped his activism and political thought. Khafra Kambon's political biography of Trinida-dian union leader George Weekes, *For Bread, Justice and Freedom* (1988), includes a valuable insider perspective on the critical relationship between radical labor and Black Power in the twin-island state.[43]

In the field of politics, Brian Meeks's two essay collections, *Radical Caribbean: From Black Power to Abu Bakr* (1996) and *Narratives of Resistance: Jamaica, Trinidad, the Caribbean* (2000), consider the Black Power events in Jamaica and Trinidad as part of a broader study of late twentieth-century Caribbean radicalism. In these books, Black Power is validated as part of a tradition of subaltern revolt in the region that "has been not so much an attempt to seize state power as it has been an endeavour to transform the hegemonic values which, with modifications, have dominated the Caribbean for four centuries."[44] These later studies—conducted by people who were themselves deeply influenced by the Black Power upheavals they describe—are profoundly colored by the events of the succeeding years. With the implosion of the Grenada Revolution and the subsequent U.S. invasion in 1983, the radical option in Caribbean politics had been dealt a crushing defeat. For Meeks, whose autobiographical "introspection" closes this volume, the "process of rethinking" brought on by the Grenada debacle inspired a new "philosophical approach that would depart from the hierarchical and closed confines of orthodox dogma" while preserving his "core concerns for human self-assertion and popular empowerment."[45] In the light of the Grenada tragedy, the heterogeneity of Black Power as well as its attention to factors of race *and* class took on a renewed appeal.

As the previous discussion indicates, scholarship on Black Power in the Caribbean has predominantly focused on Jamaica and Trinidad. On the latter, one of the most significant works is Selwyn Ryan and Taimoon Stewart's invaluable edited collection, *The Black Power Revolution 1970: A Retrospective* (1995). The product of the first major conference to engage with Trinidad and Tobago's Black Power upheavals, the collection sought to "record the views and recollections of [those] who were actively involved in the events of 1970" on the twentieth anniversary of their outbreak.[46] The conference generated heated debate on a number of contested issues that are now staples of the historiography on the Trinidadian case, including the government response to Black Power, the reactions of the Indian community, the role of lesser-known Black Power groups such as UMROBI and Young Power, and the movement's long-term achievements and failures.[47] The Trinidadian events and their ambiguous legacies have also been wonderfully captured in a number of works of literary fiction, most notably *The Dragon Can't Dance*

(1979) and *Is Just a Movie* (2011) by Earl Lovelace, himself a key participant in, and interpreter of, the period of political and cultural ferment that erupted so dramatically onto the streets of Port of Spain in February 1970.[48]

Analysis of Black Power in other Caribbean contexts is considerably less sustained. To date, the only book-length study of Caribbean Black Power outside of Trinidad is Quito Swan's *Black Power in Bermuda: The Struggle for Decolonization* (2009). Swan's study is unusual in focusing on a nonindependent territory, highlighting the anticolonial flavor Black Power acquired in that context and the actions the colonial authorities took to suppress it. Of the continental Caribbean, Guyana has received attention predominantly in analyses of one of its most famous sons, the radical scholar and activist Walter Rodney; however, David Hinds's work on the African Society for Cultural Relations with Independent Africa (ASCRIA) and Nigel Westmaas's study of the origins of the Working People's Alliance (WPA) have begun to broaden the lens on Black Power and other radical organizations in this mainland Caribbean context.[49] Much less work has been done on Black Power organizations in the smaller islands of the Eastern Caribbean. Rodney Worrell provides an overview of Barbados's People's Progressive Movement (PPM) in his *Pan-Africanism in Barbados* (2002), and Paul Buhle has examined the Antigua Caribbean Liberation Movement (ACLM) in his study of Tim Hector (2006), but the story of Black Power mobilization in places such as St. Kitts and Nevis, St. Vincent, St. Lucia, Dominica, and Anguilla has yet to be fully explored, despite the importance of the British invasion of Anguilla in arousing Black Power sentiment across the region. In short, while admirable work has been done, there is a need for a more holistic perspective that expands the narrative of Caribbean Black Power beyond Jamaica and Trinidad (and the talismanic dates of 1968 and 1970 associated with their respective Black Power protests) to examine the significance of Black Power across the region as a whole.

New Perspectives on Black Power in the Caribbean

This volume represents a contribution toward an expanded analysis of Caribbean Black Power, bringing together chapters on the upheavals in Jamaica and Trinidad with contributions on Antigua, Barbados, Bermuda, Guyana, the U.S. Virgin Islands, and the Dutch Caribbean. Comparative reflections open and close the book: Quinn's analysis assesses the heterogeneous meanings and manifestations of Black Power across the region and its relation to the movement in the United States; Meeks's conclusion provides a personal reflection on its regional legacies and its place within "the broader global wave of resistance of the late 1960s."

Part 1 of the book examines Black Power in the "big four" West Indian states that gained independence in the turbulent years of the 1960s: Jamaica (1962), Trinidad and Tobago (1962), Barbados (1966), and Guyana (1966). Independence transformed the legal status of the former colonies and brought into power a formidable generation of West Indian nationalist leaders—Alexander Bustamante in Jamaica, Eric Williams in Trinidad and Tobago, Forbes Burnham in Guyana, and Errol Barrow in Barbados. Political sovereignty alone, however, did not guarantee the transformation of social patterns embedded over hundreds of years of colonial rule. As the chapters in part 1 illustrate, the cry for "Black Power" that erupted less than a decade after independence can be viewed as "an interrogation of incomplete decolonization," marking a shift from one generation, whose primary goal was independence, to a new generation disillusioned with the "Afro-Saxons" of postcolonial government. In Drayton's terms (chapter 5), this was a transition from the politics of "primary decolonization"—the quest for political sovereignty—to those of "secondary decolonization," an internal struggle responding to the "inevitably partial and ambivalent victory" of independence.

Government responses to the challenge of Black Power were mixed. As the chapters in this section show, coercive measures, including surveillance, Public Order legislation, arrests, harassment, and intimidation, were deployed with varying degrees of severity by all governments of the newly independent Caribbean states. In Trinidad, as the contribution by Brinsley Samaroo outlines, the most brutal state repression was directed at the guerrilla organization NUFF (National Union of Freedom Fighters), eighteen of whose members were killed by state security forces. In Jamaica, suspected protesters were subject to arbitrary arrest and police harassment—vividly described in Rupert Lewis's chapter through the eyewitness testimonies of Rastafari and Black Power activists at the heart of the events of 1968. Even in Barbados, where Prime Minister Errol Barrow felt Barbadians were too "sensible" to be infected by the Black Power virus, precautionary security measures were taken, though, as Drayton's chapter shows, in these Barrow showed himself to be more lenient than his cabinet, who had pressed for a more stringent response to the "dangers" of Black Power.

Yet governments too were involved in their own projects of "secondary decolonization" that, as the chapters describe, might be framed as a form of moderate Black Power from above: a "complex response . . . in which the political leadership sought to assimilate the more radical currents and in self-conscious ways to extend the limits of decolonization."[50] This process was taken furthest in Guyana where, as Quinn (chapter 6) shows, the policies of Forbes Burnham's PNC government—including asylum for foreign black militants, the development of a cooperative sector of the economy, and the nationalization of key resources—were directly responsive to the demands of Black Power from below. In Trinidad, Samaroo argues, Black Power ushered in a "quiet revolution" as Prime Minister Eric Williams used the demonstrations to buttress his case to push through long-delayed reforms, while in Barbados Drayton identifies a leftward shift in Barrow's policies after 1968 that illustrates how the island's immersion in the wider currents of the age "quietly shifted the axis of that society away from its colonial location as 'little England.'" Even in Jamaica, where Hugh Shearer took a more hard line on Black Power, the repatriation of Marcus Garvey's body in 1964 and the visit of Haile Selassie in 1966 show, Lewis argues, that "the JLP government was concerned to promote its own version of moderate Black Power." All this suggests that, far from being an ephemeral moment in the political life of the postcolonial Caribbean, Black Power did have a perceptible impact in influencing moderate state reforms.

Part 2 of the book turns to the nonindependent Caribbean, covering examples of black mobilization in Antigua and Barbuda, Bermuda, the U.S. Virgin Islands, and the Dutch Antilles. In the era of Black Power, none of these territories enjoyed full political sovereignty. Under the Associated Statehood Act of 1967, Antigua, along with five other British colonies in the Eastern Caribbean, achieved full internal self-rule, but the powers of foreign policy, defense, and national security were left in the hands of Britain. A similar division of authority—with greater or lesser degrees of autonomy—applied in Bermuda, which remains a British Overseas Territory today; in the Dutch Antilles, defined in 1954 as internally autonomous countries of the Kingdom of the Netherlands; and in the U.S. Virgin Islands, an "unincorporated" U.S. territory since 1917.

In these contexts, it might be expected that black protest would have a strongly anticolonial dimension, but, as the chapters in this section show, the conflicts in these territories were more complex than a binary struggle of colony against metropolis. In Antigua, analyzed here in the contribution by Paget Henry, internal self-rule brought about "the sudden expansion of power and influence by a tiny (but almost entirely black) elite"[51] dominated by the charismatic figure of Vere Bird. As with its neighbors in the independent Anglophone Caribbean, the challenge of Black Power in the "tourist plantation" of Bird's Antigua was directed against the contradictions of black government and white economic power. In Bermuda and Curaçao, by contrast, protest was shaped in the context of white political domination in majority black societies, but had, as the chapters by Quito Swan and Gert Oostindie show, quite different emphases and outcomes. While in Bermuda Black Power emerged as "an anticolonial, revolutionary youth movement that aimed to dismantle British colonialism and the latter's support of the white oligarchy," in Curaçao, recognition of the "racial dimension to inequality" on the island did not translate into an anticolonial movement for independence. Local factors, these chapters suggest, were strongly in play. In Bermuda, the "South Africa of the West Indies," de facto segregation made the everyday experience of "white oppression and colonialism" peculiarly sharp. In Curaçao, the protest that broke out in May 1969 "did not target the Dutch government or Dutch neocolonialism per se" but was directed against targets closer to home: the hegemony of the (predominantly light-skinned) Democratic Party and specific labor grievances with Royal Dutch Shell. As in the U.S. Virgin Islands, discussed in depth in the contribution by Derick Hendricks, protesters in the Dutch Antilles did not push for "primary decolonization." In the former, as Hendricks shows, pro-independence currents existed alongside other, arguably more successful forms of black organization that chose to confront white hegemony by targeting specific symbols of racial hierarchy on the islands (for example, the foreign-owned tourist sector) without linking this to broader goals of political sovereignty. In both cases, the continued relationship with the metropolitan power brought ambiguous benefits as well as disadvantages.

As the contributions to this volume all suggest, this process of Caribbean self-assertion emerged as part of a much wider, global moment of antisystemic insurrection. While the connections with this wider, international context are discussed throughout the collection, so too are the local specificities of Caribbean Black Power. Attention to these local dimensions, as Nigel Westmaas's chapter reminds us, offers a corrective to narratives that validate only a particular kind of participation in global black internationalism. Analyzing the curious absence of Eusi Kwayana from the "pantheon of [global] pan-Africanist figures recognized in recent scholarship," Westmaas's chapter makes an important broader point about the "politics of knowledge production" and the exclusion of "organic intellectuals" from the "official texts and narratives of the pan-African and Black Power record." It is a point made implicitly in Anthony Bogues's emphasis on the importance of "subaltern intellectuals," such as Ras Dizzy, Ras Historian, and Jerry Small, in the making of a "radical black subaltern tradition" (chapter 3); in Rupert Lewis's assertion of the significance of Rastafari as "an existential and epistemic type of Black Power embedded in and arguing from within the mass of the population" (chapter 2); and in the attention paid throughout the collection to the role of popular music in articulating the consciousness of the age. The importance of the local and subterranean is there too in the contributors' emphasis on the strength of the native tradition on which Caribbean Black Power drew, nurtured as it was in a soil that had produced "multiple streams of resistance," including Garveyism, Ethiopianism, and Rastafari as well as the currents of radicalism in the labor rebellions of the 1930s. These connections with the "sufferers" were an integral part of organic Black Power in the Caribbean, something its more recognized protagonists such as Rodney clearly understood.

In a similar vein, the role of Caribbean women within regional expressions of Black Power has not been sufficiently recognized.[52] The contributions to this volume show that women were involved in all aspects of the movement, not only within spheres deemed to be traditionally "feminine," or "ancillary," but also in the front lines of the protests, including as active members of armed organizations, such as NUFF in Trinidad. Thus Derick Hendricks highlights "the major role that women played at both grassroots and leadership levels" of the Free Beach Movement and the Black Cultural Organization in the U.S. Virgin Islands; Paget Henry identifies the central contribution of Arah Weeks and other women in putting the issue of gender equality "high on the agenda" of the ACLM in Antigua; and Quito Swan shows how women were "highly active" in underground units of the Black Beret Cadre in Bermuda. Yet as Meeks argues in the concluding chapter, while women "were everywhere present in the 'struggle' . . . they were almost everywhere subordinate to the male leadership." All too often, issues of gender were overlooked or consciously excluded from masculinist conceptions of Black Power. Bogues, for example, notes that in its entire nine-month existence *Abeng* only once paid specific attention to the question of women's oppression, publishing "an eight-point program for women's liberation, including men sharing the 'burden of housework and child rearing,' equal pay for equal work, union rights, and rights of equal participation in the political process." As has been noted for the U.S. movement, the language of Black Power in the Caribbean context was heavily gendered, emphasizing the recuperation of black manhood and the assertion of black male power. As Anne Macpherson has argued elsewhere, in Belize, the "vigorous revindication of black manhood . . . embraced women as 'sisters' and celebrated black women's beauty but also insisted on the primacy of the male-led racial struggle as the path to liberation for all."[53] While some studies have begun to explore these gender dimensions, much research remains to be done to uncover the contributions of women to Caribbean Black Power and the crucial ways in which they challenged its shortcomings.

Lastly, analysis of Black Power in the Caribbean can broaden our understanding of racial mobilization in multiethnic and nonwhite majority contexts. As discussed in detail in chapter 1, in contrast to the binary constructions of race that informed the Black Power confrontation in the United States, Caribbean conceptions of Black Power were formed in black majority and multiethnic societies, where not all problems could be reduced to a conflict between "black" and "white." In the U.S. Virgin Islands, as Hendricks's chapter shows, rapid demographic changes associated with the development of the tourist industry produced a society in which the native-born black Virgin Islanders felt marginalized not only by the influx of white American "continentals" but also by the large numbers of immigrants from Puerto Rico and the West Indies. In the ethnically plural contexts of Trinidad and Guyana, any conception of Black Power had to confront the historic divisions between the countries' dominant African and Indian ethnic blocs. The Trinidadian Black Power leadership, as Samaroo's chapter outlines, consciously promoted an inclusive construction of "blackness" intended to embrace both ethnic groups. Though Indian identification with Black Power was limited, the "effort at unity so bravely attempted by the NJAC leadership" holds valuable lessons for a country where politics in the present day is still fragmented along ethnic lines. In Guyana, as the chapters by Quinn and Westmaas show, no such ethnic unity could be brokered under the aegis of Black Power. In a state dominated by the predominantly Afro-Guyanese PNC to the exclusion of the Indo-Guyanese majority, the concept of "Black Power" became too closely identified with sectional rather than national aspirations. Though many in the Caribbean did try to articulate an inclusive conception of blackness, in countries characterized by ethnic diversity, the appeal of the Black Power slogan was limited.

As the rest of this volume shows, the nature, significance, and legacies of Caribbean Black Power offer a rich mine of research that can deepen our understanding of black mobilization in the region and beyond. As the hotspots of Caribbean Black Power look back on fifty years of independence, much work on this vital period of regional history remains to be done.

Notes

1. The conference was organized by Dr. Jerome Teelucksingh and was held in the Department of History of the University of the West Indies–St. Augustine on 18–19 September 2010.

2. These conferences were organized by Kate Quinn in collaboration with Professors Brian Meeks and Rupert Lewis (UWI–Mona). Held in London (25–26 October 2007) and Mona (21–22 February 2008), the conferences were generously funded by a British Academy UK–Caribbean and Latin America Link Award.

3. Rodney, 38.

4. Nettleford, 115.

5. For reasons beyond the scope of this volume to discuss in depth, the Hispanic Caribbean did not have an equivalent concept of domestic *poder negro* (Black Power). This difference arises from the particular colonial and postcolonial histories of Cuba, Puerto Rico, and the Dominican Republic; the ethnic demographics and the particular concepts of national identity these histories have produced; and the bearings these have had on how ethnic identities have been negotiated and how ideas of black mobilization have been received. Broadly speaking, unifying concepts of *cubanidad, dominicanidad,* and *puertoriqueñidad* have emphasized "nation" above "race" and have provided an alternative to forms of identification and mobilization that directly invoke blackness. For an analysis of the dynamics of race and nation in the Hispanic Caribbean, see Dávila, *Sponsored Identities*; de la Fuente, "Race, National Discourse, and Politics in Cuba"; Sagás, *Race and Politics*; Howard, *Coloring the Nation*; and Eison Simmons, *Reconstructing Racial Identity*. On the interactions between U.S. Black Power activists and revolutionary Cuba, see Reitan, *Rise and Decline* and Sawyer, *Racial Politics*. There was, however, a significant relationship between the Hispanic Caribbean diaspora in the United States and the U.S. Black Power movement. Jeffrey Ogbar and Frank Moya Pons have noted examples in both the participation of Puerto Ricans and Dominicans in organizations such as SNCC, NAACP, and CORE and, in particular, the influence of and relations between the Black Panthers and urban Hispanic communities in the United States. See Ogbar, "Puerto Rico en mi corazón," and Moya Pons, "Dominican National Identity." Such interactions on U.S. soil and their impact back on the islands merit further research, as do the connections between political organizations in the Hispanic Caribbean and in the United States in the era of Black Power (Stokely Carmichael, for example, as leader of SNCC, visited Puerto Rico and made common cause with the *independistas*). If Black Power did not gain a foothold organizationally in the Hispanic Caribbean, it did make an impact on individuals and their sense of self and political consciousness.

6. Buhle, 37.

7. For a detailed historiographical analysis of New Black Power Studies, see Joseph, "Black Liberation without Apology," "Toward a Historiography," and "The Black Power Movement."

8. Joseph, "Toward a Historiography," 8.

9. See, for example, Van Deburg, *New Day in Babylon*; Jones, *The Black Panther Party Reconsidered*; Brown, *Fighting for US*; and Lazerow and Williams, *In Search of the Black Panther Party*.

10. Ward, 51.

11. Joseph, "The Black Power Movement," 765–66.

12. Ibid., 767.

13. Robinson, 565.

14. Joseph, "Where Blackness is Bright?" 111.

15. Carmichael, "The Third World, Our World," 18, and "Solidarity with Latin America," 101.

16. Forman, 148.

17. Spencer, 217.

18. See, for example, Tyson, *Radio Free Dixie*; Gaines, *African Americans in Ghana*; Mwakikagile, *Relations between Africans and African Americans*; and Markle, "'We Are Not Tourists.'"

19. Ward, "Scholarship in the Context of Struggle"; White, "An Independent Approach"; Wilkins, "'A Line of Steel'"; and Austin, "All Roads Led to Montreal."

20. Ward, 47–48.

21. White, 81.

22. Wilkins, 99.

23. Ibid., 98–105, 99.

24. Austin, 525, 529. On events in Canada, see also Eber, *Canada Meets Black Power*; Forsythe, *Let the Niggers Burn!*; and Mills, *The Empire Within*.

25. Austin, 524.

26. Ibid., 518.

27. The fall 2007 special issue of the *Journal of African American History*, titled "New Black Power Studies: National, International and Transnational Perspectives," is a case in point. With the exception of David Austin's article on radical Caribbean movements in Canada, all the articles explore U.S. movements and personalities in non-U.S. contexts (Africa, Asia, and the Caribbean). One book that takes a wider view is Nico Slate's edited collection *Black Power Beyond Borders* which includes chapters on Black Panther movements in India, New Zealand and Israel.

28. Franklin, 464.

29. Edmondson, 210, 212.

30. Ibid., 206.

31. Ibid., 221.

32. Ibid., 209, 211, 213.

33. A banner on the front cover frames the book as "an existential report on the 1970 Black Power revolt in Trinidad."

34. Bolland, "The Roots of Black Power in the West Indies."

35. Riviere, 54.

36. James, "Black Power." James had seen Carmichael speak at the Sir George Williams University and had been enormously impressed. Carmichael, he said, stood on the shoulders of Booker T. Washington, W.E.B. Du Bois, Marcus Garvey, George Padmore, Frantz Fanon, Aimé Césaire, and Malcolm X at "the high peak of thought on the Negro question which has been going on for over half a century." Naipaul's essay traversed London, Trinidad, and Guyana following the trajectory of Michael X (Abdul Malik) from petty criminal and debt collector in London to self-styled "Black Power" commune leader in Port of Spain. Malik was hanged in 1975 for his role in the murder of Gale Ann Benson and Joseph Skerritt.

37. Nettleford, vii, 10, 120.

38. Ibid., 169, 170.

39. See McCartney, "What Is the Relevance of Black Power," and Hodgson, "Bermuda and the Search for Blackness."

40. I am grateful to Raffique Shah for providing me with early drafts of this manuscript.

41. Pantin, 3–4.

42. See *'70: Remembering a Revolution*.

43. Kambon (formerly Dave Darbeau) and Weekes, head of the Oilfields Workers' Trade Union (OWTU), were leading figures in Trinidad's National Joint Action Committee (NJAC).

44. Meeks, 3.

45. Ibid., 6–7.

46. Ryan and Stewart, 2.

47. On the political impact of Trinidadian Black Power, see also Sutton, "Black Power in Trinidad and Tobago," and Ryan, *Eric Williams*, 381–404. On Indian engagement with Black Power in Trinidad, see Gosine, *East Indians and Black Power*, and Nicholls, "East Indians and Black Power," 61–80.

48. See also Lovelace's nonfiction commentaries on the period in Aiyejina, *Earl Lovelace*.

49. On Rodney, see, for example, Lewis, *Walter Rodney's Intellectual and Political Thought*, and West, "Seeing Darkly." On ASCRIA, see Westmaas, "Resisting Orthodoxy" and Hinds, "The African Society for Cultural Relations with Independent Africa."

50. Drayton, chapter 5 in this volume.

51. Buhle, 149.

52. Macpherson's work on Belize, *From Colony to Nation*, and Pasley's on Trinidad, "The Black Power Movement in Trinidad," have done much to confront the limitations of the existing scholarship. Pasley's article analyzes gender ideology and the participation of women in the Trinidadian Black Power movement. Both Pasley and Macpherson have established the connections between Black Power activism and the later emergence of Caribbean feminism.

53. Macpherson, 257.

Bibliography

Aiyejina, F. (ed.) *Earl Lovelace: Growing in the Dark (Selected Essays)*, Trinidad: Lexicon Ltd., 2003.

Austin, D. "All Roads Led to Montreal: Black Power, the Caribbean, and the Black Radical Tradition in Canada." *Journal of African American History* 92, no. 4, Fall 2007, 513–36.

Bogues, A. *Black Heretics, Black Prophets: Radical Political Intellectuals*, New York: Routledge, 2003.

Bolland, N. "The Roots of Black Power in the West Indies," West Indies Collection, University of the West Indies–Mona, 1969.

Brown, S. *Fighting for US: Maulana Karenga, the US Organization and Black Cultural Nationalism*, New York: NYU Press, 2003.

Buhle, P. *Tim Hector: A Caribbean Radical's Story*, Jackson: University Press of Mississippi, 2006.

Carmichael, S. "The Third World, Our World," *Tricontinental*, July–August 1967, 15–22.

———. "Solidarity with Latin America," in *Stokely Speaks: Black Power Back to Pan-Africanism*, New York: Random House, 1971, 101–10.

———. *Ready for Revolution*, New York: Scribner, 2003.

Dávila, A. *Sponsored Identities: Cultural Politics in Puerto Rico*, Philadelphia: Temple University Press, 1997.

de la Fuente, A. "Race, National Discourse, and Politics in Cuba: An Overview," *Latin American Perspectives* 25, no. 3, May 1998, 43–69.

Eber, D. *Canada Meets Black Power: The Computer Centre Party Part 1*, Montreal: Tundra Books, 1969.

Edmondson, L. "The Internationalization of Black Power: Historical and Contemporary Perspectives," in Orde Coombs (ed.), *Is Massa Day Dead? Black Moods in the Caribbean*, New York: Anchor Books, 1974, 205–31.

Eison Simmons, K. *Reconstructing Racial Identity and the African Past in the Dominican Republic*, Gainesville: University Press of Florida, 2011.

Elkins, W. F. *Black Power in the Caribbean: The Beginnings of the Modern National Movement* New York: Revisionist Press, 1977.

Forman, J. "The Concept of International Black Power," in Charles Hamilton (ed.), *The Black Experience in American Politics*, New York: Capricorn Books, 1973, 145–54.

Forsythe, D. (ed.) *Let the Niggers Burn! The Sir George Williams Affair and Its Caribbean Aftermath*, Montreal: Black Rose Books, 1971.

Franklin, V. P. "Introduction—New Black Power Studies: National, International and Transnational Perspectives," *Journal of African American History* 92, no. 4, Fall 2007, 463–66.

Gaines, K. *American Africans in Ghana: Black Expatriates and the Civil Rights Era*, Chapel Hill: University of North Carolina Press, 2006.

Gosine M. *East Indians and Black Power in the Caribbean*, New York: Africana Research Publications, 1986.

Hinds, D. "The African Society for Cultural Relations with Independent Africa (ASCRIA): A Short History," *Emancipation Magazine*, 4, 1996–97.

Hodgson, E. "Bermuda and the Search for Blackness," in Orde Coombs (ed.), *Is Massa Day Dead? Black Moods in the Caribbean*, New York: Anchor Books, 1974, 143–64.

Howard, D. *Coloring the Nation: Race and Ethnicity in the Dominican Republic*, Oxford: Signal Books Ltd., 2001.

Hyde, E. X. *X Communication: Selected Writings*, Belize City: The Angelus Press Ltd., 1995.

James, C.L.R. "Black Power," 1967. http://www.marxists.org/archive/james-clr/works/1967/black-power.htm.

Jones, C. (ed.) *The Black Panther Party Reconsidered*, Baltimore: Black Classic Press, 1998.

Joseph, P. "Black Liberation without Apology: Reconceptualizing the Black Power Movement," *The Black Scholar*, Fall 2001, 2–19.

———. "Where Blackness is Bright? Cuba, Africa and Black Liberation during the Age of Civil Rights," *New Formations* 45, Winter 2001–2, 111–24.

———. "Toward a Historiography of the Black Power Movement," in Joseph Peniel (ed.), *The Black Power Movement: Rethinking the Civil Rights-Black Power Era*, New York: Routledge, 2006, 1–26.

———. "The Black Power Movement: A State of the Field," *The Journal of American History* 96, no. 3, 2009, 751–76.

Kamarakafego, P. *Me One: The Autobiography of Pauulu Kamarakafego*, Canada: P.K. Publishing, 2001.

Kambon, K. *For Bread, Justice and Freedom: A Political Biography of George Weekes*, London and Port of Spain: New Beacon Books, 1988.

Lazerow, J., and Y. Williams (eds.) *In Search of the Black Panther Party: New Perspectives on a Revolutionary Movement*, Durham: Duke University Press, 2006.

Lewis, R. *Walter Rodney's Intellectual and Political Thought*, Barbados: University of the West Indies Press / Detroit: Wayne State University Press, 1998.

Lovelace, E. *The Dragon Can't Dance*, London: Andre Deutsch, 1979.

———. *Is Just a Movie*, London: Faber & Faber, 2011.

Macpherson, A. *From Colony to Nation: Women Activists and the Gendering of Politics in Belize, 1912–1982*, Lincoln: University of Nebraska Press, 2007.

Markle, S. "'We Are Not Tourists': The Black Power Movement and the Making of 'Socialist' Tanzania, 1960–1974," Unpublished Ph.D. thesis, New York University, 2011.

McCartney, T. "What Is the Relevance of Black Power to the Bahamas?" in Orde Coombs (ed.), *Is Massa Day Dead? Black Moods in the Caribbean*, New York: Anchor Books, 1974, 165–87.

Meeks, B. *Radical Caribbean: From Black Power to Abu Bakr*, Kingston: University of the West Indies Press, 1996.

Millette, J. "The Black Revolution in the Caribbean," in Orde Coombs (ed.), *Is Massa Day Dead? Black Moods in the Caribbean*, New York: Anchor Books, 1974, 47–67.

Mills, S. *The Empire Within: Postcolonial Thought and Political Activism in Sixties Montreal*, Montreal: McGill-Queens University Press, 2010.

Moya Pons, F. "Dominican National Identity and Return Migration," Centre for Latin American Studies, University of Florida, Gainesville, 1981.

Mwakikagile, G. *Relations between Africans and African Americans*, Dar es Salaam: New Africa Press, 2007.

Naipaul, V. S. "Michael X and the Black Power Killings in Trinidad," in *The Return of Eva Peron*, London: Andre Deutsch, 1980, 1–91.

Nettleford, R. *Mirror Mirror: Identity, Race and Protest in Jamaica*, Kingston: W. Collins and Sangster, 1970.

Nicholls, D. "East Indians and Black Power in Trinidad," in *Haiti in Caribbean Context*, London: The Macmillan Press, 1985, 61–80.

Ogbar, J.O.G. "Puerto Rico en mi corazón: The Young Lords, Black Power and Puerto Rican Nationalism in the U.S., 1966–1972," *Centro Journal* 18, no. 1, Spring 2006, 67–74.

Oxaal, I. *Black Intellectuals Come to Power: The Rise of Creole Nationalism in Trinidad and Tobago*, Cambridge, Mass.: Schenkman Publishing Company, 1968.

———. *Race and Revolutionary Consciousness: A Documentary Interpretation of the 1970 Black Power Revolt in Trinidad*, Cambridge, Mass.: Schenkman Publishing Company, 1971.

Pantin, R. *Black Power Day: The 1970 February Revolution, a Reporter's Story*, Santa Cruz, Trinidad and Tobago: Hatuey Productions, 1990.

Pasley, V. "The Black Power Movement in Trinidad: An Exploration of Gender and Cultural Changes and the Development of a Feminist Consciousness," *Journal of International Women's Studies* 3, no. 1, 2001, 24–40.

Reitan, R. *The Rise and Decline of an Alliance: Cuba and African American Leaders in the 1960s*, East Lansing: Michigan State University Press, 1999.

Riviere, W. *Black Power, NJAC and the 1970 Confrontation in the Caribbean, An Historical Interpretation*, Paper given to the University of Pittsburgh Annual Seminar on the Black Man in the Caribbean, 26 February 1972, St. Augustine: University of the West Indies, 1972.

Robinson, C. "Review: *Black Power in the Belly of the Beast* by Judson Jeffries," *The Journal of African American History* 92, no. 4, Autumn 2007, 561–66.

Rodney, W. *The Groundings with My Brothers*, London: Bogle L'Ouverture Press Ltd., 1990. First published 1969.

Ryan, S. *Eric Williams: The Myth and the Man*, Kingston: University of the West Indies Press, 2009.

Ryan, S., and T. Stewart (eds.). *Black Power Revolution 1970: A Retrospective*, St Augustine: I.S.E.R., University of the West Indies, 1995.

Sagás, E. *Race and Politics in the Dominican Republic*, Gainesville: University Press of Florida, 2000.

Sawyer, M. *Racial Politics in Post-Revolutionary Cuba*, New York: Cambridge University Press, 2006.

'70: Remembering a Revolution. Directed by Elizabeth Topp and Alex de Verteuil. 2012. Port of Spain, Trinidad: Pearl and Dean (Caribbean) Ltd. Film.

Shah, R. *Mutiny: Ten Days at Teteron Barracks*, Unpublished manuscript.

Sidanius, J., Y. Peña, and M. Sawyer. "Inclusionary Discrimination: Pigmentocracy and Patriotism in the Dominican Republic," *Political Psychology* 22, no. 4, Dec. 2001, 827–51.

Slate, N. *Black Power Beyond Borders: The Global Dimensions of the Black Power Movement*, New York: Palgrave Macmillan, 2012.

Spencer, R. "Merely One Link in the Worldwide Revolution: Internationalism, State Repression, and the Black Panther Party, 1966–1972," in Michael O. West, William G. Martin, and Fanon Che Wilkins (eds.), *From Toussaint to Tupac: The Black International since the Age of Revolution*, Chapel Hill: University of North Carolina Press, 2009, 215–31.

Sutton, P. "Black Power in Trinidad and Tobago: The 'Crisis' of 1970," *Journal of Commonwealth and Comparative Politics* 21, no. 2, July 1983, 115–31.

Swan, Q. *Black Power in Bermuda: The Struggle for Decolonization*, New York: Palgrave Macmillan, 2009.

Torres Saillant, S. "The Tribulations of Blackness: Stages in Dominican Racial Identity," *Latin American Perspectives* 25, no. 3, May 1998, 126–46.

Tyson, T. *Radio Free Dixie: Robert. F. Williams and the Roots of Black Power*, Chapel Hill: University of North Carolina Press, 1999.

Van Deburg, W. *New Day in Babylon: The Black Power Movement and American Culture, 1965–1975*, Chicago: University of Chicago Press, 1992.

Ward, S. "Scholarship in the Context of Struggle: Activist Intellectuals, the Institute of the Black World (IBW) and the Contours of Black Power Radicalism," *The Black Scholar*, Fall 2001, 42–53.

West, M. O. "Seeing Darkly: Guyana, Black Power and Walter Rodney's Expulsion from Jamaica," *Small Axe* 13, no. 1, 2008, 93–104.

White, D. "An Independent Approach to Black Studies: The Institute of the Black World (IBW) and Its Evaluation and Support of Black Studies," *Journal of African American Studies* 16, 2012, 70–88.

Wilkins, F. C. "'A Line of Steel': The Organization of the Sixth Pan-African Congress and the Struggle for International Black Power, 1969–1974," in Dan Berger (ed.), *The Hidden 1970s: Histories of Radicalism*, New Brunswick: Rutgers University Press, 2010, 97–114.

Worrell, R. *Pan-Africanism in Barbados*, Barbados: Prestige Printery, 2002.

1

Black Power in Caribbean Context

KATE QUINN

> . . . although the slogan Black Power originated with Stokely Carmichael
> in 1966, in ideological terms the struggle in the Caribbean has a
> history that is as old as the New World black experience itself.
>
> WILLIAM RIVIERE, *BLACK POWER, NJAC AND THE 1970 CON-
> FRONTATION IN THE CARIBBEAN, AN HISTORICAL INTERPRETATION*

The epigraph above captures both the broader and the narrower definitions of
Black Power: Black Power as the long historical struggle for black liberation
rooted in slavery and the transatlantic trade and Black Power as a particular
political movement whose origins are attributed to African-American activism in the mid-twentieth-century United States. This chapter is concerned
with Black Power as it was articulated in the turbulent decades of the 1960s
and 1970s, but its geographical lens is turned on the Caribbean, a region
that experienced notable Black Power upheavals in parallel with those of its
powerful northern neighbor. The potential for a Black Power movement to
take hold in the Caribbean occupied the minds of both British and American
authorities, who closely monitored events in the region for signs of political
backwash from black mobilization in the United States. In the wake of the
massive Black Power demonstrations in Trinidad and Tobago in 1970, both
the CIA and the Foreign and Commonwealth Office produced reports attempting to assess the strength of Black Power sentiment and organization
in the Caribbean.[1] Both recognized that conditions in the Caribbean played
a part in stimulating the growth of Black Power, the British conceding that
"the inequalities of social and economic standards" gave "much scope for agitators in several Caribbean countries," the Americans noting that "popular

grievances" were "often real and compelling."[2] To understand the nature of the movement these conditions produced, this chapter will first address the fundamental question of what "blackness" meant within Caribbean conceptions of Black Power. It will then assess the ideological content of Caribbean Black Power through a consideration of its political, economic, and cultural dimensions. Last, it will address the relationship with the North American movement as a means of highlighting both the local specificities of the Caribbean movement and its transnational dynamics.

Several Caribbean governments endorsed a moderate version of Black Power—publicly embracing its "legitimate" aspirations of black dignity, economic uplift, and cultural affirmation. This chapter, however, is concerned primarily with Black Power as it was articulated by groups and individuals outside of and most often in opposition to government and the mainstream political parties. In terms of "organized" Black Power, this includes the alternative or non-conventional political/radical groups that emerged in the late 1960s and early 1970s, such as the Afro-Caribbean Movement, later the Antigua Caribbean Liberation Movement (ACLM), in Antigua; the United Black Association for Development (UBAD), in Belize; the Black Beret Cadre, in Bermuda; the United Black Socialist Party, in Dominica; the Abeng group, in Jamaica; the Forum groups, in St. Lucia, St. Vincent, and Grenada; and the Black Panther Organization (BPO), the National Joint Action Committee (NJAC), the National Union of Freedom Fighters (NUFF), Pivot, Young Power, and the United Movement for the Reconstruction of Black Dignity (UMROBI), in Trinidad and Tobago. It also includes groups formed in an earlier period that came to identify strongly with Black Power, among these the African Society for Cultural Relations with Independent Africa (AS-CRIA), in Guyana, established in 1964, and the People's Progressive Movement (PPM), in Barbados, formed in 1965.

As this list implies, the term Black Power spread over "a wide matrix of ideas, activities, and . . . organizations" in the region.[3] Caribbean Black Power was not a singular ideology but a heterogeneous movement that encompassed a range of convergent and divergent political positions and concerns. In Trinidad, for example, NJAC consisted of a loose coalition of individuals and organizations, including students and lecturers from the University of the West Indies, radical trade unions, youth organizations, and cultural groups, all of whose members came into the alliance with different aims, political outlooks, and levels of engagement. Likewise, the Abeng group represented a number of different currents within the Jamaican political tradition, from those affiliated with the left wing of the People's National

Party to Garveyites and Rastafarians. In Belize, the Black Power organization UBAD "had one executive but three different directions": Black Muslim; "anti-Latin"; and "Malcolm X-Stokely Carmichael-Third World."[4] Such differences could lead to tensions and, ultimately, splits. In Belize, for example, the established Garveyites of the UNIA "chose to disassociate themselves" from UBAD once "the radical nature of [its] ideology became clear."[5] By contrast, in Jamaica, Garveyites actively supported local Black Power mobilization.[6] Such ideological diversity could be both a strength and a weakness. As Meeks argues, while Black Power was "always flawed, both organizationally and theoretically," it "brought with it an openness and diversity of political forms and politics" that was precisely part of its broad appeal.[7]

Manifestations of Black Power were not all formally organized. The street, or popular, element of Caribbean Black Power made itself evident in the large crowds that rallied to the mass demonstrations in Trinidad, in the urban rebellion of the youths of "Back a Town" in Bermuda, and in the spontaneous participation of Kingston's downtown "sufferers" in the Rodney demonstrations of October 1968. In Trinidad and Tobago, NJAC successfully channeled the energies of the street element for three months of mass mobilization, but when the leadership was imprisoned and a state of emergency imposed, this force was dissipated, and the post-1970 NJAC never again captured the same level of popular participation. In Jamaica, where Black Power was "decentralized, multipolar, and community based,"[8] it had a strong organic connection with the street and has survived in the continuing significance of Rastafari and Garveyism, indigenous currents with which it had deep connections. The Black Power mood was also strongly felt in the popular culture of the day: in poetry, art, and especially popular music; in the mushrooming of small publications such as *Abeng, Moko*, and *Blackman Speaks*; and in the work of the "subaltern intellectuals" of radical blackness,[9] whose contributions to the era remain to be written. To take Richard Drayton's phrase, organizational Black Power might thus be viewed as "merely the visible crest of a much larger wave."[10]

Defining Black Power in Caribbean Context

The primary contextual difference between Black Power in the United States and Black Power in the Caribbean is that the former emerged in a society in which blacks constituted a demographic minority while in the latter they were the overwhelming majority. In the Caribbean, therefore, the banner of Black Power was raised in protest against local governments whose members were primarily black. Given this black majority context, it has been argued that

black nationalism [in the Caribbean] could be articulated in anti-co-
lonial or majoritarian-democratic *political* terms to which a rigid racial emphasis was often subordinated. By contrast, in the conditions of
black American existence, black nationalism . . . inevitably involved a
pervasive racial emphasis in its political, socio-economic, and psychological dimensions."[11]

The specific racial regimes of the United States and the Caribbean thus
shaped the definitions and diagnoses of Black Power in each context. As
Lowenthal summarizes,

The long duration of formal colonial rule, the survival of a strong class
system, a general absence of industrial development, and, above all, the
presence of majority black populations mark the West Indies by contrast with the United States. Notwithstanding obvious resemblances,
borrowings, and interchanges, racial subjugation, accommodation,
and protest in the two realms reflect different types of oppression, different degrees of access to goals, and different divisions of race and
color.[12]

In the United States, where the "one-drop rule" produced a more rigid clas-
sification of "black" and "white," oppression and, by extension, resistance
took on a "racial" character that, with important exceptions, tended to de-
emphasize distinctions of class and color among the African-American population. In the Caribbean, where the particular patterns of colonial history
produced an intermediate and more privileged "colored" class, fine distinctions of shade, physical features, and economic standing became crucial in
locating a person's status in society, making class as well as shade important
markers of difference within the nonwhite population.

How then did these race-class formations play out, and what did "blackness" mean in Caribbean conceptions of Black Power? While there were a
variety of positions, here I will focus primarily on the radical left, whose
definitions of blackness had strongly political (not solely "racial") dimensions. There are three critical considerations here: first, how "blackness" was
defined against a global "white power" system into which the Caribbean was
inserted; second, how conceptions of "blackness" dealt with the existence of
a domestic black and brown middle class; and third, the extent to which definitions of "blackness" in the Caribbean context were inclusive of the region's
other ethnicities.

On the first consideration, radical Caribbean advocates of Black Power were clear that their struggle must be understood within a world-historical context in which imperialism, capitalism, and slavery had spawned racism, global divisions of labor, and the domination of the white over the nonwhite world. As Walter Rodney wrote, "the essence of White Power is that it is exercised over black peoples—*whether or not they are minority or majority* . . . in such a way that black people have no share in that power." Thus, "Black Power can be seen as a movement and an ideology springing from the reality of oppression of black peoples by whites within the imperialist world as a whole."[13] This international perspective shaped an inclusive definition of blackness that encompassed not only Africans and the African diaspora but also all "non-whites"—in essence, those of the developing world of Africa, Asia, and the Americas.[14] This interpretation is echoed in an undated issue of Trinidad's *Black Sound* in which the anonymous author states: "Black Power in the international sense refers to all people who are not white. Black men refers to all Africans, Indians, Chinese, Latin, Amerindian, etc."[15] Thus, although there was a clear racial dimension to the conception of "white power," the equation of whiteness with imperialism and capitalist exploitation gave an added ideological dimension to the definition of black and white. In this schema, anti-imperialists and revolutionaries such as Mao Zedong, Ernesto Che Guevara, and Ho Chi Minh could be incorporated as "Black Power heroes"[16] and, famously, Fidel Castro could be hailed as "the blackest man in the Americas."[17]

Caribbean conceptions of Black Power were also influenced by the particular dynamics of the multiethnic and black majority societies in which they evolved. In these contexts, the conceptualization of Black Power included a class dimension that took into account not only international and local "white power" but also the existence of a local brown and black middle class whose interests lay in preserving the status quo. The latter, the primary beneficiaries of decolonization and independence, occupied positions in government, the public sector, and white-collar professions such as law and medicine, enjoying standards of living worlds apart from those of the majority of the rural and urban poor. Heavily influenced by C.L.R. James's arguments on the ambivalent position of the West Indian middle class and by Frantz Fanon's critique of the role of the national bourgeoisie in colonial and postcolonial societies, radical advocates of Caribbean Black Power characterized the region's black and brown middle classes as agents of the international white power structure, fundamentally allied with the interests of capitalism and imperialism. In Rodney's analysis, this West Indian ruling class, "*irrespective of its racial or colour composition*," supported a social structure that kept the black masses at "the bottom of the social ladder."[18] From this perspective, black skin did not necessarily connote "blackness," nor did black government connote black power. Thus, for example, an anonymous pamphleteer in Trinidad could state, in typically gendered terms:

> A man may be black-skinned, but that does not automatically make him a black man. There are many black-skinned persons who behave white. He may feel no sense of togetherness with BLACK MAN. He may detest black people or at worst he may join white people in oppressing and suppressing BLACK MAN. SUCH MEN ARE NOT BLACK BROTHERS . . . BLACK GOVERNMENT IS NOT BLACK POWER.[19]

And in Barbados, Black Power advocate Leroy Harewood proposed that "[the] black bourgeoisie have nothing in common with the masses but the colour of their skin. It is they who are blowing up the myth about 'the rule of law,' 'freedom,' 'democracy,' and a 'multi-racial' society with blacks in power."[20] This attack on the myth of multiracialism was central to the Black Power critique of the race and class hierarchies operating in Caribbean societies. Highlighting the Jamaican case, Rodney condemned the "myth of a harmonious, multi-racial society" as a fiction perpetuated by the elite "to justify the exploitation suffered by the blackest of our population at the hands of the lighter-skinned groups." The role of Black Power, therefore, was to smash the myth of multiracialism and "proclaim that Jamaica is a black society."[21]

In this schema, blackness was thus both a cultural and a political identity. This political dimension (blackness as ideology) allowed for the inclusion of other ethnicities into definitions of Black Power and for the inclusion of the progressive bourgeoisie who aligned with the cause. As Rodney argued, "there is nothing in the West Indian experience which suggests that browns are unacceptable when they choose to identify with the blacks."[22] The prerequisite for middle-class participation was total identification with the black masses. Only by rejecting the privileges of their class and becoming "the servants of the black masses" could they be purged of their class origins and accepted on the side of the revolution.[23] Radical variants of Caribbean Black Power thus always had a class dimension.

The third, related definitional issue for Black Power in Caribbean context is the extent to which its conceptions of "blackness" could incorporate the region's many other ethnic groups. While this was of less concern in African-descent-majority countries like Jamaica, Barbados, and Antigua, it was critical in ethnically plural contexts such as Trinidad, Guyana, and Belize. In

Trinidad, where Indians made up 40 percent of the population, the leadership of NJAC took a decisive public stand after some Indian businesses were attacked in the early days of the Black Power mass demonstrations. Leading some 20,000 demonstrators on a solidarity march to the predominantly Indian area of San Juan where most of the violence had taken place, Makandal Daaga called for the "unity of all blacks—African and Indian"—a message later cemented by the historic march to the sugar lands of Caroni under the banner "Indians and Africans unite."[24] NJAC publications also sought to underline the "revolutionary solidarity" of the "two black races of Trinidad and Tobago," articulating a past and present of shared oppression and common struggle.[25] As Khafra Kambon recalls, "we [in NJAC] did not see 'Blacks' as Africans; we saw 'Black' as both Africans and Indians. . . . Black Power meant unity, self-consciousness, cultural revivalism, and harmony . . . between Africans and Indians . . . understanding that we have the same space to share."[26]

NJAC's reconceptualization of blackness to include both Africans and Indians constituted a direct challenge to the "carefully contrived division of political power"[27] in Trinidad and Tobago, in which political leaders on either side benefited from the continuation of ethnic cleavages. However, whether Indians identified with the designation "black" or were actively incorporated into the Black Power movement remains a matter of controversy. Certainly, Black Power in Trinidad did attract the support of significant individuals, such as Raffique Shah, the young leader of the Trinidad Regiment mutiny; Winston Leonard of the powerful Oilfields Workers' Trade Union (OWTU); and Chan Maharaj of the National Freedom Organization, an Indian group that for a time shared the NJAC platform. NJAC also made significant inroads into the heartlands of the rural Indian sugar community, finding common cause with a younger generation seeking to break from the stranglehold exercised by union boss Bhadase Maraj. Despite these efforts, most scholars contend that the majority of Indians simply did not identify with the term "black," did not actively participate in the movement, and openly questioned their place within its primarily "African" "symbolic universe."[28]

A similar pattern emerged in Belize, where the main Black Power organization, UBAD, operated in a society characterized by considerable ethnic diversity. Here, where "creoles" (Afro-Belizeans) made up about 40 percent of the population, "mestizos" 33 percent, Maya 9.5 percent, and Garifuna 7.6 percent, the leadership of UBAD likewise insisted that "black" "included all non-white people." However, UBAD's constituency, located mainly in Belize City, was primarily Afro-Belizean, and its "symbolic universe" reflected this affiliation: Belize, for example, was designated "Afro-Honduras"; the leader of

UBAD, Evan X Hyde, spoke of a "spiritual return to Africa." Thus, as Shoman argues, "despite the insistence that 'black' included all nonwhite people, it was especially difficult for non-Africans to identify with UBAD. . . . The fact is that in Belizean society at the time black meant black, not 'black, brown, red and yellow' as the movement leaders declared."[29]

Both these examples highlight the distinction between Black Power as an ideology and Black Power as a movement in the multiethnic context of the Caribbean. Reflecting on NJAC's experience in Trinidad, Khafra Kambon asserts that while the Black Power ideology "fully incorporated the Indian experience," the Black Power movement "was more significant for Africans."[30] Thus, although the leadership articulated a conception of blackness that could include nonwhite ethnicities, the face of the street movement was overwhelmingly Afro-Caribbean. In these multiethnic contexts, there was an ultimately irreconcilable tension between Black Power as a political identification and Black Power as a cultural identification—that is, between the inclusive definitions of blackness (embracing Indians, mestizos, Maya, et al.) and the exclusive cultural identification with Africa. It was precisely the contradictions involved in mobilizing around ideas of blackness that contributed to the decline of Black Power in the Caribbean context.

Black Power and Politics, Economics, and Culture

Black Power and "Conventional Politics"

The upsurge of Black Power in the Caribbean in the late 1960s can be viewed as a crisis of political legitimacy—in essence, a response to the failures of the existing political system to deliver substantive change and fulfill the expectations raised by the processes of decolonization and independence. Central to this political critique was an attack on "conventional politics," which in the Anglophone context meant the trappings of Westminster, the "tweedledum and tweedledee" politics of the entrenched two-party system, and the detachment of "mimic men" politicians from the realities of the masses.

In Trinidad, the most extensive articulation of this critique was outlined in NJAC's pamphlet *Conventional Politics or Revolution?*, published after the high-water mark of the mass demonstrations. NJAC's "total rejection of conventional politics" was based on the belief that the problems confronting Caribbean societies could "not be solved within the conventional system" but were in fact inherent within a system that acted as a "rubber stamp for the white power structure."[31] NJAC's claim that "the people" had rejected conventional politics found some justification in the results of the 1971 election in which Eric Williams's People's National Movement (PNM) party was returned to power in an election boycotted by almost all parties and in which only 32 percent of the electorate turned out to vote. But while NJAC advocated the total rejection of the system, it was, like many other Black Power groups, less clear on what should replace it. *Conventional Politics or Revolution?* envisaged an organic process—given life by the experiences of the "February Revolution"—in which "fundamentally different political institutions [would] emerge out of the conscious struggle of black people for complete liberation." The "People's Parliaments" convened by the Black Power protesters in Woodford Square had shown the way, embodying, NJAC argued, a new conception of people's participation whose "[forms] and procedures" had evolved "according to the demands of the people and as their ideological consciousness developed."[32] Notable here is the extent to which NJAC anticipates some of the arguments later put forward by the New Jewel Movement (NJM) in Grenada, with which it had strong connections. NJAC's critique of political participation as limited to casting a vote once every five years was later echoed in the NJM's scorn of "five-second democracy," while its search for new forms of people's participation later found concrete manifestation in the Grenadian experiment with "people's assemblies."

While the majority of Black Power groups opposed the incumbent governments, the case of ASCRIA in Guyana provides an interesting exception. In the specific political and ethnic constellations of Guyana, ASCRIA at first supported the ruling People's National Congress (PNC) party (under Forbes Burnham), a predominantly Afro-Guyanese party in a majority Indo-Guyanese state. In effect, ASCRIA, positioning itself as the "critical consciousness" of the government, constituted the radical left wing of the PNC and had a significant impact on its policies.[33] Only later did ASCRIA break with the PNC, subsequently becoming one of the founding members of the interethnic Working People's Alliance (WPA), who entered "conventional" politics by establishing themselves as a political party (as opposed to a pressure group) in 1979.

As the case of ASCRIA illustrates, there was wide variation in the extent to which different Black Power groups were prepared to engage with the "conventional" political system, with a spectrum of positions ranging from those who rejected it altogether (such as some Rastafarians) to those who sought to participate in formal electoral politics (such as the PPM in Barbados and the United Black Socialist Party in Dominica) to the minority who engaged in guerrilla activities against the state (such as NUFF in Trinidad and the Black Beret Cadre in Bermuda). In Curaçao, as Oostindie shows, the disturbances of May 1969 gave birth to a new political party, the *Frente Obrero i Liberashon 30 di mei 1969*, which scored a notable success in the elections that year, resulting in a coalition government comprised of the new party of the "revolution" and the establishment party against whom their criticisms were aimed.[34] In the postindependence Anglophone Caribbean, however, those groups that entered the political fray via the conventional methods of electoral politics, had little success: in Barbados, for example, the Black Power/Marxist-oriented PPM garnered just thirty-three votes in the by-election of 1969, while in Belize, UBAD's single candidate, Evan X Hyde, notched up only eighty-nine votes in the elections of 1974. Alternative parties, such as the PPM in Barbados, the ACLM in Antigua, NJAC in Trinidad (when it entered electoral politics in the 1980s), and the WPA in Guyana, simply could not overcome the entrenched divides of two-party politics, nor could they compete with the patronage the established parties could offer. Grenada aside, the political impact of Caribbean Black Power is thus mainly to be found in its influence on the mainstream political parties: in the co-option of its rhetoric, symbols, and in some cases personnel, and in moderate reforms that clearly responded to the Black Power agenda.

Black Power and the Economy

Black Power's strongest suit was its critique of the distorted and inequitable nature of Caribbean economies. It is worth noting that Black Power emerged as a force in the region not only in countries that suffered below-average growth or per capita income levels but also in those that performed well by such measures of development. All Caribbean territories, however, shared the experience and perception of socioeconomic inequality, whether in income, distribution of land, or in ownership of national resources. In Jamaica, for example, the economy experienced high levels of growth in the 1960s, but the inequalities in its income distribution were among the worst in the world. The U.S. Virgin Islands, undergoing a tourist boom in the same decade, had very high average per capita incomes, but this was of little comfort to local fishermen pushed out of their fishing areas by the construction of large resorts. In Dominica, patterns of land distribution also reflected gross inequalities: in 1961, the census found that just 1.4 percent of farmers occupied 56.4 percent of the land, consigning the rural peasantry to squatting "the most inaccessible crown land."[35] Levels of unemployment and underemployment added to the hardships faced in the region. This was often particularly acute among the young, who were beneficiaries of increased access to education but victims of economies that could not absorb the new generation of school and university graduates. In Trinidad, for example, unemployment was "concentrated in the urban areas of black population, and largely among the young," with 20 to 25 percent of 20- to 24-year-olds without work.[36] Such statistics help to explain the very youthful face of Black Power in the Caribbean.

The economic critiques of Black Power advocates were central to their analyses of "black powerlessness" in the Caribbean: both the powerlessness of Caribbean governments operating within a global economic system favoring metropolitan interests ("a black man ruling a dependent State within the imperialist system has no power") and the powerlessness of the ordinary Caribbean citizen within a social structure that "ensures that the black man resides at the bottom of the social ladder."[37] The Black Power critique of Caribbean economies centered on two fundamental issues: foreign ownership and control of major resources and the domination of the local economy by minority local elites, who were mostly lighter-skinned. This analysis was strongly influenced by the economic theories of the New World Group, in particular by Best and Levitt's conception of the plantation model, with its emphasis on dependency and the distortions of export-oriented economies that existed to service metropolitan needs.

Foreign ownership of major resources—a common condition of all Caribbean economies except revolutionary Cuba—took different forms across the region, and these differences were reflected in the specific targets of Black Power protest in each context. For example, in Trinidad, protesters' anger was directed at such companies as Texaco, Fed-Chem, and Tate and Lyle, major players in the dominant oil and sugar industries, while in Dominica it was channeled against the British-based multinational Geest Industries, which monopolized marketing and distribution in the banana and citrus industries. In small, tourist-dependent islands where land ownership was a major issue, protests focused on particular symbols of exclusion (the Mount Irvine Golf Club and Pigeon Point in Tobago; Sapphire Beach and Bolongo Bay in the U.S. Virgin Islands) and even on particular individuals (expatriate landowner Lord Brownlow in the case of Grenada). As Hendricks illustrates, tourism and the ills it brought in its wake (foreign ownership of prime land, de facto segregation, visible economic and racial disparities) were deeply sensitive issues in places where formerly agricultural societies were being rapidly transformed by the development of the new tourist economy.[38] While in St. Thomas protests took the creative form of beach-ins and swim-ins led by the Free Beach Movement, in Tobago Black Power demonstrators took a more direct approach to the hated symbols of privilege and exclusion, smashing the golf club's windows and tearing down the British flag.[39] Not for nothing did Forbes Burnham, in a country with negligible tourism, "[raise] his glass to toast 'Guyana's muddy waters.'"[40]

Black Power also exposed fundamental inequalities in the domestic economy, focusing in particular on the domination of business and commerce by predominantly light-skinned (often Jewish, Syrian, Lebanese, or Chinese) local elites and on discriminatory employment practices in some private sectors, such as tourism and banking. The existence of such racial/occupational hierarchies was confirmed by a number of studies in the period. The Commission of Enquiry into Racial and Colour Discrimination, conducted in Trinidad in 1970, found "a state of racial and colour imbalance" in the private sector, and Acton Camejo's 1971 study found that Trinidad's business elite were 53 percent "white," 15 percent "off white," and just 4 percent "African."[41] Such analyses reinforced the notion that the government rhetoric of national unity and development served to mask the reality that economic status and opportunity were still, over a century since emancipation, closely aligned with color.

Cultural Identity and the Reclamation of Selfhood

At its most fundamental level, Black Power is about reclaiming the power to define the self and the world in one's own terms. As Rodney stated, "the road to Black Power . . . must begin with a re-evaluation of ourselves as blacks and with a redefinition of the world from our own standpoint."[42] For many, the validation of self meant first coming to terms with the "psychic disintegration" wreaked by centuries of social conditioning and the historic denigration of blackness:

> In a slave society and in a post-slavery society in which advancement has been determined by how nonblack the blackest of men can be, a sense of yourself as black has to be achieved before a sense of yourself as being a full man can ever be approached. Freedom and black consciousness, therefore, go together.[43]

Psychic liberation would therefore be achieved by taking pride in blackness and breaking from the symbolic universe in which the powers of definition had belonged to whites. "Such a redefinition of the world," NJAC affirmed, "is the essence of the Black Revolution."[44] Many Black Power–oriented organizations therefore saw education as central to black empowerment and the reclamation of black history, culture, and identity. Publications such as *Abeng, Blackman Speaks, Black Star,* and *The Black Revolutionary,* study groups and "liberation schools," lectures and "groundings," and the informal circulation of "subversive" texts were all central to the re-educative efforts of

Black Power, giving voice to the struggle and providing spaces in which the heterogeneous positions of the movement were debated and shaped.

The construction of a new symbolic universe included the Africanization of names, campaigns for black dolls for children, attacks on the cultural bias towards European norms of beauty, the wearing of dashikis and Afros, campaigns to replace "imperialist" statues and street names, lobbying for the teaching of African history and languages, protests against the white iconography of the Christian church, and interpretations of Caribbean history that emphasized a continuous tradition of resistance. In its drive to decolonize Caribbean culture and identity, Black Power shared many of the concerns of earlier traditions of anticolonialism and cultural nationalism. Indeed, many nationalist governments of the postindependence era voiced similar preoccupations with the recuperation of national histories, the validation of folk cultures, and the creation of education systems appropriate to the needs of the new nations. These same governments were happy to endorse the cultural (if not the political) aspirations of Black Power, arguing that the goals of black dignity, cultural pride, and consciousness were "perfectly legitimate and in the interests of the community as a whole."[45] However, most governments, especially those in ethnically heterogeneous contexts, were reluctant to embrace constructs of cultural identity that emphasized "blackness." Instead they promoted an explicitly nonracial vision of creole cultural nationalism embodied in the appeal to ideas of "one people, one nation" and "all o' we are one."

The call for the "cultural reconstruction of society in the image of the blacks"[46] was interpreted in various ways. Some turned to folk traditions as examples of authentic cultures of the people born in the conditions of the Caribbean; others turned to Africa, seeking to connect to the ancestral continent through African history, languages, forms of dress, and cultural practices. However, in searching for cultural "roots" Black Power exposed some of the tensions inherent in the quest for self and cultural identity in Caribbean societies formed through slavery, colonialism, and the transplantation of peoples from Europe, Asia, and Africa. For Rex Nettleford, writing on the Jamaican case, the emphasis some Black Power advocates placed "on African history, even at the expense of West Indian and Jamaican history" revealed a basic contradiction between the imperatives of black nationalism and those of Jamaican nationalism. Nettleford warned against "the tyranny of a black culturalism" that risked imposing a new set of narrow cultural parameters without due sensitivity to the region's history of cultural cross-fertilization.[47] In a similar vein, Guyanese writer and artist Denis Williams viewed Black Power's emphasis on racial ancestry as "destructive . . . , inhibiting us from facing up to . . . the mongrel condition which is the first reality of this region and which is the foundation of our uniqueness." Williams criticized the Africanization elements of ASCRIA's "cultural revolution" as limiting and divisive: "Strive as we may to maintain the image of such a relationship we can never again become Indians or Africans or Chinese or Europeans. . . . We are peoples of the New World."[48] Such critiques of the "black culturalist" elements of Black Power hint at the limitations of an appeal to blackness in the plural contexts of the Caribbean.

Caribbean Black Power and North American Black Power: Influence and Interactions

Witnessing the proliferation of the symbols, styles, and rhetoric of Black Power on the streets of Kingston, Nassau, and Port of Spain, many observers at the time dismissed Caribbean Black Power as an American import of little relevance to Caribbean society. As one columnist for the *Trinidad Guardian* wryly observed, "newspaper editorials, hitherto insensitive to our neo-Americanism, deplored the borrowed rhetoric of the Black Power movement."[49] Timothy McCartney, describing the increased visibility of Black Power slogans, phraseology, and style on the streets of the Bahamas, noted that visitors to the islands, "some of them black Americans, . . . have said that as they walked through some of our 'over the hill' streets they wondered whether they were at 125th Street in Harlem."[50] However, to characterize the Caribbean movement as merely imitative does justice neither to the local dimensions of Caribbean Black Power nor to the transnational contexts in which it emerged.

The relationship between North American Black Power and Caribbean Black Power can only be understood with reference to the profound linkages that existed across the black world. These connections, reflected, for example, in the entangled Caribbean and North American heritages of many of the most visible members of the U.S. movement,[51] in the circulation of Caribbean and North American Black Power activists within the same geographical spaces, and in the identification of common cause within a global black struggle, demonstrate the falsity of conceptualizing Caribbean Black Power as "another alien importation to the West Indies."[52] However, despite asserting the underlying commonalities of their struggle, there were also very significant cultural and ideological differences between the U.S. and Caribbean movements, as became apparent in the experiences of some North American activists who visited the region.

There is no doubt that the U.S. movement had tremendous inspirational and symbolic appeal in the Caribbean. The actions of the civil rights and Black Power movements were widely covered in the region's media, most prominently in the newly emerging Black Power publications, such as *Moko*, *Abeng*, and *Black Star*. While many Caribbean governments sought to in-oculate their populations against such influence by banning the entry of both publications and people associated with the U.S. movement, the black American struggle nevertheless resonated strongly in the region, inspiring many future Caribbean Black Power leaders. Raffique Shah, one of the young officers who led the Regiment Mutiny in Trinidad in April 1970, writes of this influence as a central part of his own radicalization while training at Sand-hurst Royal Military Academy, the very heart of the British establishment:

> As young men in search of knowledge far beyond what was taught in the lecture rooms and on the training fields, we questioned [the] stereotyping of [our formal political education]. We looked to the lega-cies of Nasser in Egypt, Sukarno in Indonesia, Nehru in India, Tito in Yugoslavia. We were fascinated by what Fidel Castro and Che Guevara had achieved in Cuba. . . . Most of all, and maybe closest to our hearts, were the Civil Rights Movement in the USA and its more pro-active successor, the Black Power movement. We admired Martin Luther King Jnr., but we found common ground with Stokely Carmichael, . . . a Trinidad-born American who had all but set that country ablaze with an aggressive battle for basic rights for Afro-Americans. We read vo-raciously, . . . [devouring] books like *The Autobiography of Malcolm X*, Eldridge Cleaver's *Soul on Ice*, and Mao Zedong's *Little Red Book*.[53]

This political education was later replicated in the barracks of the Trinidad Regiment, where informal study groups "discussed neo-colonialism, Black consciousness, [and] imperialism" and "books like *The Autobiography of Malcolm X* and Walter Rodney's *Groundings with My Brothers* made the rounds until they became worn."[54]

Similarly, many Caribbean students studying at universities in the United States and Canada were exposed not only to the particularities of North American racism but also to the political and cultural currents animating black movements on the continent. Evan X Hyde, who founded UBAD in his native Belize in February 1969, was a student at Dartmouth College, where he saw Stokely Carmichael and Amiri Baraka speak on campus. Hyde's au-tobiographical essay "North Amerikkkan Blues" (1971) describes how he was politicized by his student years in America, both through the negative ex-periences of prejudice and through positive experiences of witnessing and participating in the political and cultural "black renaissance" of the times, remembered by Hyde as "the explosion of a people awakening." Hyde's portrayal of the black movement in the United States was not uncritical: observing the "strife and bickering" among the various black organizations in America gave him an early lesson in the importance of black unity.[55] The influence of the U.S. movement was tangibly felt in Caribbean locations with strong historic linkages with the "mainland," including Bermuda, the Bahamas, and the U.S. Virgin Islands. In the latter, as Hendricks shows, many of those involved in the Free Beach Movement were graduates of Morgan State University who had participated in the campus protests of the 1960s and directly transferred the tactics learnt in the United States to the beach protests of the 1970s. In Bermuda, the strong connections maintained by individuals on the island with the U.S. Black Panthers heavily influenced the formation, manifesto, and even uniform of the Bermudan Black Beret Cadre.[56] As Oostindie notes, returning graduates were also significant conduits linking local and international struggles in the Dutch Caribbean, bringing back to Curaçao "the spirit of the sixties that was alive in the universities of Europe and the United States."[57]

But it was events in two Canadian universities that are most famously connected with watershed moments in the history of Caribbean Black Power: the October 1968 Congress of Black Writers, organized by black students from the Sir George Williams University and McGill University, and the occupation and destruction of the computer center at the Sir George Williams University in February 1969. As is well known, while Walter Rodney was attending the Congress of Black Writers in Montreal, the Jamaican government banned him from returning to Jamaica, where he was lecturer in the History Department of the University of the West Indies. The decision to ban Rodney ignited the so-called Rodney Riots in Kingston, marking a defining moment in the politics of postindependence Jamaica, while in Trinidad, the NJAC-led demonstrations initially linked to the Sir George Williams University affair ultimately escalated into the three-month Black Power "revolution" that came close to toppling Prime Minister Eric Williams. In both cases, West Indian students were central to the events on the Canadian campuses, notably those involved with the Caribbean Conference Committee (CCC), which included such figures as Rosie Douglas (Dominica), Robert Hill (Jamaica), Franklyn Harvey (Grenada), Alfie Roberts (St. Vincent), Anne Cools (Barbados), and Tim Hector (Antigua). As David Austin has shown, members of the CCC were instrumental in bringing into contact key figures of the U.S. Black Power movement with established and emerging names of the Caribbean left, including Stokely Carmichael, James Forman, C.L.R. James, and Walter Rodney, all of whom spoke at the Congress of Black Writers.[58] This Congress, and the subsequent Hemisphere Conference to End the War in Viet Nam, which took place in Montreal in November 1968 and was chaired by Barbadian PPM leader Glenroy Straughn,[59] "[increased] racial and political consciousness . . . to unprecedented heights,"[60] setting the scene for the 1969 confrontation at the Sir George Williams University. Here, West Indian students, pressing the administration to deal with charges of racist treatment by a member of the faculty, catalyzed the two-week occupation of the computer center by some two hundred students that ended with the arrest of ninety-seven people. Among the arrested were members of the CCC (Anne Cools and Rosie Douglas were seen as the instigators of the protest), members of the West Indian Society (among whom were Trinidadians Teddy and Valerie Belgrave), and students from across the Caribbean, including eleven Trinidadians, several Jamaicans and Grenadians, and Cheddi Jagan Jr., the son of the Guyanese opposition party leader.

From the Caribbean perspective, these events are significant for several reasons. Firstly, they provided a political training ground for a number of West Indians who would contribute significantly to emergent black organizations in the region: notably for example, Tim Hector, who joined the Afro-Caribbean Movement on his return to Antigua; Robert Hill, founding member of Jamaica's Abeng movement and editor of its eponymous newspaper; and Rosie Douglas, a central figure in Dominican radical politics of the 1970s and ultimately Prime Minister of Dominica.[61] These students went on to play significant roles in transmitting Black Power ideas back to the Caribbean—Douglas, for example, doing "much to stir up anti-Canadian sentiments both in Canada and in the rest of the Caribbean, which he toured extensively before the trial of the West Indian students began in Montreal."[62] Secondly, they contributed to a sense of a regional Caribbean black consciousness both among the various West Indians based in Canada and between that diaspora and their sympathizers back in the Caribbean, who protested their treatment in acts of solidarity both large (Trinidad) and small (Barbados, Guyana, Antigua, and St. Kitts). The formation of NJAC, as is well known, was directly linked to the Sir George Williams events. As Valerie Belgrave recalls, the leaders of NJAC visited Montreal to see how they could assist the arrested students, while in turn they "assisted [NJAC] even to the point of helping [them acquire] their first loudspeaker system."[63] It did not require a great leap to link Canadian racism abroad to Canadian exploitation at home: Canadian banks, insurance companies, mining interests, and even the Canadian Governor-General himself were targeted by Black Power protesters in the Caribbean. Thirdly, as much as the Canadian events fed into the wider currents activating Black Power sentiment and organization in the Caribbean, they also alerted Caribbean governments to the dangers of a regionally linked, homegrown Black Power movement. While several governments paid the fines and legal fees incurred by their nationals arrested in Montreal (in part to assuage growing Black Power restlessness at home), others added the student leaders to growing immigration stop lists: Rosie Douglas and Grenadian Frederick Kennedy (also among the accused in Montreal) found themselves listed as "undesirable immigrants" in a number of Caribbean territories, obstructing their plans for a regional speaking tour.[64]

The Canadian events underline the transnational dimensions of Black Power activism, first in demonstrating that the ripple effects of the conferences and student protests were felt far from Canadian shores and materially affected events in the Caribbean, and, second, in revealing an interconnected network of activists (some loosely, some strongly connected) operating across a variety of geographical spaces, engaged in cognate struggles in which local and international concerns intersected. The activities of the CCC and the conferences organized by black students at McGill and Sir George Williams provided forums where figures from across different generations and locations of black political activism debated the terms of a black liberation agenda.

Another such forum was the First Regional Conference on Black Power, held in Bermuda in July 1969.[65] This conference was the fourth in a series of Black Power conferences held between 1966 and 1969, but was the first one to be held outside the United States. The first three, held in Washington, D.C. (1966), Newark (1967), and Philadelphia (1968), were designated national conferences, but the Bermuda conference was the first to bring together participants from both the United States and the Caribbean in a regional conference on Black Power. As such, it might be seen as symptomatic of the new internationalist currents of a U.S. movement that had begun to look beyond the framework of the domestic struggle to encompass the wider black world. As Swan shows, the selection of Bermuda for the first international conference owed much to the work of Pauulu Kamarakafego (then Roosevelt Brown), appointed regional Black Power coordinator for the Caribbean area, and his strong personal connections with activists in the U.S. movement. While the Bermuda conference attracted, in the estimates of the British, between thirteen hundred and fifteen hundred participants, only eight attendees were from the rest of the Caribbean.[66] While this may be attributed partially to cost, distance, and difficulty of travel, it was also due to the extensive use of immigration stop lists by the British authorities on the island. The success of this policy and the subsequent banning of the proposed Second Regional Black Power Conference, scheduled to be held in Barbados in July 1970, limited the impact such gatherings might have had on the broader Caribbean movement. However, for Bermuda, as Swan shows, the conference was instrumental in raising black consciousness on the island and directly led to the formation of the Black Beret Cadre.

The visits of U.S. Black Power activists to the Caribbean region also shed light on the dynamics in the relationship between U.S. and Caribbean variants of Black Power. Perhaps the best known example in the narrative of U.S. Black Power is that of African-American engagement with (and often exile in) revolutionary Cuba, including the experiences of Robert Williams, Stokely Carmichael, Eldridge Cleaver, and Assata Shakur.[67] While there were significant points of convergence in the political positions of black militants from the United States and their Cuban hosts, there were also crucial points of divergence, not the least with respect to the Cuban analysis of Black Power in the U.S. context, their approach to racial issues within their own society, and their rejection of race-based mobilization in favor of the unifying imperatives of revolutionary socialism. These differences were apparent in the otherwise mutually appreciative speeches of Fidel Castro and Stokely Carmichael at the Conference of the Organization of Latin American Solidarity (OLAS), held in Havana in August 1967. While Castro gave a class-based analysis of black militancy in the United States, Carmichael was clear that "[his] analysis of [the United States] and of international capitalism begins with race."[68]

Carmichael's sojourn in Guyana offers a vivid example of the potential tensions between definitions of Black Power based on the particular circumstances of the United States and those of the Caribbean. Carmichael's explicit definition of Black Power as "African Power" and his call for separate racial organization was rejected not only in the ethnically polarized context of Guyana but also in Trinidad, where NJAC consciously sought to define Black Power as inclusive of all nonwhite peoples. The *Trinidad Guardian* used the opportunity of Carmichael's controversial visit to Guyana to warn against "the dangers of importing foreign concepts and ideologies to deal with the existing social and economic problems in our society," noting that:

[Carmichael's] latest utterances have proved that his "stateside" sojourns have alienated him from the society in which he was born and from which he is banned. Stokely's vituperations have pointed up a narrow racist rancour which no West Indian society can tolerate. As far as we can make out, his view of Black Power is not shared by either the Black Power movement in Trinidad nor by the ruling PNM.[69]

Thus, while there is no doubt that the U.S. Black Power movement had a tremendous symbolic appeal in the Caribbean, this did not result in the Americanization of Caribbean Black Power. Each movement was responsive to local contexts, borne of particular historical experiences that gave rise to differing conceptions of race and racial politics. Analyses that gave primacy to race, as was the case with some U.S. variants of the cause, did not readily translate to Caribbean contexts. The tensions outlined above highlight just some of the conflicts that fragmented internationalist visions of Black Power. They also demonstrate that the currents of influence between U.S. and Caribbean Black Power operated in both directions. The Caribbean experiences of Carmichael, Cleaver, and others contributed to shaping their thinking about the international dimensions of the black struggle beyond the borders of the United States.

Conclusions

The Caribbean Black Power movement of the late 1960s and early 1970s stands as a significant moment in the history of the colonial and postcolonial Caribbean. For its proponents, it represented the latest stage in the region's long struggle for black liberation and meaningful independence stretching back to the first revolts on the slave ships as they left the coasts of Africa. Like many of the movements that preceded it, its local concerns were articulated with reference to a global black struggle with which it claimed solidarity.

The lessons to be drawn from the achievements and failures of this movement are yet to be fully weighed. Looking across the region reveals that the impact of Black Power was mixed. On the one hand, the ideological currents of Black Power flowed into the broader stream of leftist thinking in the Anglophone Caribbean in this period and significantly influenced political development in the region. This influence might be seen in the co-option of radical figures into leftist governments (as in Jamaica), the eventual electoral success of political alliances including Black Power figures (as in Dominica), and in the role it played as midwife to the Grenada Revolution. The Rat Island meeting of Caribbean black left nationalist groups in late 1970 was a "direct product" of the Black Power movement and marks a crucial moment in the evolution of leftist strategy in the region.[70] On the other hand, Grenada excepted, the Black Power critique did not translate into substantive reforms of the political system, nor, arguably, to a transformation of the dominant political culture, given the persistence of clientelist practices and other markers of the "conventional" politics it opposed.

In exposing the widespread social and economic inequities of the colonial and postcolonial Caribbean, Black Power did help to create a climate in which Caribbean governments had to be seen to be redressing the grievances at the heart of the movement's critiques. Evidence of this pressure toward reform might be seen in the land reforms and aviation taxes in Barbados, the part-nationalizations and business levies in Trinidad, and in the legislation on price controls in St. Lucia, all enacted in the wake of the ferment of 1970. Likewise, businesses in the private sector felt pressured to address visible signs of discrimination, opening employment opportunities to a broader segment of the population. Ironically, the very success of Black Power mobilization on this front may have helped contribute to its demise: the consolidation and expansion of the black middle class was not conducive to further radicalization. In this light, Mark Figueroa, then dean of the Faculty of Social Sciences at the University of the West Indies–Mona, has questioned "the extent to which we should persist with the Black Power concept when its beneficiaries have not been black people." Figueroa's comment was made in relation to the "racial filter" he perceived on the Mona campus, where, he believed, lecturers, students, and service workers could still be identified by shade.[71] In a similar vein, Ethelbert Wilson, speaking at the February 2010 Black Power Conference in Trinidad, noted that thirty-five years after NJAC stormed the bastions of tourist apartheid in Tobago, a security guard shot a local man deemed to be trespassing on the resort of Pigeon Point.[72] Such incidents have furnished the argument that in the nexus of race and class in the Caribbean "the line of power" has been "blurred but [remains] essentially intact."[73] If anything, these observations suggest that the criticisms raised by Caribbean Black Power have far from exhausted their validity.

The emphasis that Black Power placed on the validation of self and cultural identity, its quest for cultural decolonization, and its pride in the region's African heritage did much to raise black consciousness in the era and can be viewed as one of its most significant contributions to the search for cultural, spiritual, and psychological liberation in the "postcolonial" Caribbean. However, here too there have been tensions, both within the broad spectrum of Black Power and between its proponents and critics. As in its North American counterpart, some of the fractures within Caribbean Black Power emerged around the question of culture, specifically over the perceived dangers of so-called "black culturalism" and the extent to which this could be manipulated by the black ruling class. Critics warned against "a view of Black Power more in line with a nebulous ideology of cultural nationalism" in which culture was equated with "song and dance, . . . clothes and slogans, . . . and other symbols disconnected from the hard economic/political/social violence of our existence."[74] In this view, the appeal to "blackness" was of limited utility in understanding and confronting the nature of oppression in Caribbean societies, which has both class and racial dimensions. As is well known, a more "orthodox" class analysis came to dominate the radical leftist groups of the Caribbean in the 1970s. The subsequent failure of the orthodox option (embodied in the implosion of the Grenada Revolution) may suggest that the contribution of Black Power to theorizing the dynamics of both race *and* class in Caribbean societies needs to be revalorized.

The fundamental questions it raised—questions of power and in whose hands it was vested—are still of critical significance in the present day.

Notes

1. The CIA intelligence memorandum "Black Radicalism in the Caribbean" was commissioned at the request of President Richard Nixon, who wished to ascertain whether there were any relations between the Caribbean Black Power movement and Black Power in the United States. The FCO's "Black Power in the Caribbean" summarizes the situation in the British and formerly British Caribbean.

2. "Black Power in the Caribbean," 2; "Black Radicalism in the Caribbean," 2, 3.

3. Nettleford, 118.

4. Hyde, 30.

5. Shoman, 190.

6. See Lewis, chapter 2 in this volume.

7. Meeks, 210.

8. Ibid., 198.

9. Bogues, chapter 3 in this volume.

10. Drayton, chapter 5 in this volume.

11. Edmondson, 213. On the historical differences between racial categorization in the United States and that in the Caribbean, see also Lowenthal, "Post-Emancipation Race Relations," and Franklin, "Caribbean Intellectual Influences on Afro-Americans in the United States."

12. Lowenthal, "Black Power in the Caribbean Context," 116.

13. Rodney, 26; my emphasis.

14. Rodney, 25–27.

15. *Black Sound* was published from the St. Augustine campus of the University of the West Indies.

16. "Black Power in the Caribbean."

17. The quote by Stokely Carmichael is repeated in Rodney's *Groundings*, 42. Not everyone

agreed with Carmichael's assessment. For a contrary view, see Riviere, *Black Power, NJAC and the 1970 Confrontation in the Caribbean*, 52, and Lewis, chapter 2 in this volume.

18. Rodney, 20, 74; my emphasis.

19. "Black Power," *Black Sound.*

20. Harewood, 13.

21. Rodney, 40, 41, 75.

22. Ibid., 40.

23. Ibid., 43.

24. "March to San Juan an Apology for Kiralpani Fire." The atmosphere of the march to Caroni is wonderfully captured in Raoul Pantin's *Black Power Day.*

25. NJAC, *Black People Are a Winner.*

26. Millington interview with Khafra Kambon, *Black Power*, 90.

27. Millette, "Politics of Succession."

28. Samaroo, chapter 4 in this volume. See also Nicholls, "East Indians and Black Power in Trinidad," and Gosine, *East Indians.*

29. Shoman, 192, 194, 196.

30. Millington interview with Khafra Kambon, *Black Power*, 91.

31. NJAC, *Conventional Politics or Revolution?*, 1–3.

32. Ibid., 30, 33–34.

33. On ASCRIA's influence on PNC policies, see Quinn, chapter 6 in this volume.

34. See Oostindie, chapter 11 in this volume.

35. Christian, "In Times Crucial."

36. Millette, "The Black Revolution in the Caribbean," 60.

37. Rodney, 27, 74.

38. See Hendricks, chapter 10 in this volume.

39. American Embassy Port of Spain to Department of State, "Black Power Demonstrations."

40. Richie, British High Commission, Georgetown, to Sewell, Caribbean Department, FCO, 25 April 1970.

41. Dennis Pantin, 668, 670.

42. Rodney, 45.

43. Small, v.

44. NJAC, *Slavery to Slavery*, 1.

45. Williams, E., 6.

46. Rodney, 38.

47. Nettleford, 154, 155.

48. Williams, D., 7, 8, 18.

49. Observer, "Black Power: Stirrings of an Integrative Society."

50. McCartney, 166.

51. Stokely Carmichael (Kwame Ture) was born in Trinidad and lived there until he was eleven years old. Malcolm X was born to a Grenadian mother, Louise Norton, who was an active member of the Montreal chapter of the UNIA, where she met Malcolm's father, fellow Garveyite Earl Little. Edmondson notes that at least four prominent members of SNCC and CORE had Caribbean connections: Lincoln Lynch, associate director of CORE, and Ivanhoe Johnson, director of the New York branch of SNCC, were born in Jamaica; Roy Innis, chair-

man of the Harlem branch of CORE, was born in the U.S. Virgin Islands; and Courtland Cox, SNCC field secretary, had lived in Trinidad (Edmondson, 239).

52. Bolland, 1.

53. Shah, 9.

54. Ibid., 13.

55. Hyde, 180–81, 182, 183.

56. See Hendricks (chapter 10) and Swan (chapter 9) in this volume.

57. Oostindie, chapter 11 in this volume.

58. Austin, "All Roads Led to Montreal."

59. "Black Power in the Caribbean," 6. The PPM hosted Stokely Carmichael when he traveled to Barbados in May 1970; Carmichael was banned from speaking in public.

60. Belgrave, 124.

61. That the students themselves saw the computer room occupation as part of their political training is suggested by English professor Henry Beissel's account to Dorothy Eber. Beissel related that he had warned the West Indian students that they were in danger of exposing themselves to deportation. Their response, he says, was "that doesn't matter; this is training for us—we'll go back and do the same thing at home" (Eber, 100–101).

62. "Black Power in the Caribbean," 11. Douglas was chairman of the February 11th Defence Committee.

63. Belgrave, 130.

64. *Saint Vincent Government Gazette* 25, 17 April 1970, 195.

65. See Swan, chapter 9 in this volume and chapter 4 of his *Black Power in Bermuda* (77–94) for an analysis of this conference and its ramifications.

66. "Black Power in the Caribbean," 11.

67. On African-American engagement with the Cuban Revolution, see Rietan, *Rise and Decline.*

68. Carmichael, 89.

69. "No Room Here for Stokely Since He Preaches Racism," *Trinidad Guardian*, 7 May 1970.

70. Lewis, "Black Power: Engaging Plantation Legacies and Urban Realities."

71. Figueroa, "Opening Remarks."

72. Wilson, "Tobago before 1970."

73. Sankeralli, "1970 or the 70's."

74. Ibid.

Bibliography

American Embassy Port of Spain to Department of State, "Black Power Demonstrations," 9 April 1970. Box 2629, NARA, Maryland.

Austin, D. "All Roads Led to Montreal: Black Power, the Caribbean and the Black Radical Tradition in Canada," *The Journal of African American History* 92, no. 4, Autumn 2007, 518–22.

Belgrave, V. "The Sir George Williams Affair," in Selwyn Ryan and Taimoon Stewart (eds.), *The Black Power Revolution 1970: A Retrospective*, St Augustine: University of the West Indies Press, 1995, 119–31.

"Black Power," *Black Sound*, n.d. University of the West Indies Library, St. Augustine.

"Black Power in the Caribbean," June 1970, FCO 63/380, TNA, London.

"Black Radicalism in the Caribbean," 6 July 1970, CIA Directorate of Intelligence Intelligence Memorandum, NARA, Maryland.

Bolland, N. "The Roots of Black Power in the West Indies," West Indies Collection, University of the West Indies–Mona, 1969.

Carmichael, S. "The Dialectics of Liberation," in *Stokely Speaks: From Black Power to Pan-Africanism*, New York: Random House, 1971, 77–100.

Christian, G. "In Times Crucial: Radical Politics in Dominica 1970–1980," Accessed 7 June 2012. http://www.da-academy.org/radpol.html.

Eber, D. *Canada Meets Black Power: The Computer Centre Party Part 1*, Montreal: Tundra Books, 1969.

Edmondson, L. "The Internationalization of Black Power: Historical and Contemporary Perspectives," in Orde Coombs (ed.), *Is Massa Day Dead? Black Moods in the Caribbean*, New York: Anchor Books, 1974, 205–31.

Figueroa, M. "Opening Remarks," Internationalising Black Power 2 Conference, 21–22 February 2008, University of the West Indies–Mona.

Franklin, V. P. "Caribbean Intellectual Influences on Afro-Americans in the United States," in Alistair Hennessy (ed.), *Intellectuals in the Twentieth-Century Caribbean Vol. 1*, London: Macmillan, 1992, 179–90.

Gosine, M. *East Indians and Black Power in the Caribbean*, New York: Africana Research Publications, 1986.

Harewood, L. *Black Powerlessness in Barbados*, Bridgetown, Barbados: Black Star Publications, 1968.

Hyde, E. *X Communication: Selected Writings*, Belize City: The Angelus Press Ltd., 1995.

Lewis, R. "Black Power: Engaging Plantation Legacies and Urban Realities," Internationalising Black Power Conference, Institute for the Study of the Americas, London, 26 October 2007.

Lowenthal, D. "Post-Emancipation Race Relations: Some Caribbean and American Perspectives," *Journal of Interamerican Studies and World Affairs* 13, no. 3/4, Jul.–Oct. 1971, 367–77.

———. "Black Power in the Caribbean Context," *Economic Geography* 48, no. 1, Jan. 1972, 116–34.

"March to San Juan an Apology for Kiralpani Fire," *Express (Trinidad)*, 7 March 1970.

McCartney, T. "What Is the Relevance of Black Power to the Bahamas?" in Orde Coombs (ed.), *Is Massa Day Dead? Black Moods in the Caribbean*, New York: Anchor Books, 1974, 165–87.

Meeks, B. "The Rise and Fall of Caribbean Black Power," in Michael O. West, William G. Martin, and Fanon Che Wilkins (eds.), *From Toussaint to Tupac: The Black International since the Age of Revolution*, Chapel Hill: The University of North Carolina Press, 2009, 197–214.

Millette, J. "The Politics of Succession," *Trinidad Express*, 9 June 1970.

———. "The Black Revolution in the Caribbean," in Orde Coombs (ed.), *Is Massa Day Dead? Black Moods in the Caribbean*, New York: Anchor Books, 1974, 47–67.

Millington, M. "Black Power: The Case of Trinidad 1970" (includes a 29 June 2007 interview with Khafra Kambon), Unpublished B.A. thesis, University of the West Indies–St. Augustine, 2007.

Nettleford, R. *Mirror Mirror: Identity, Race and Protest in Jamaica*, Kingston: William Collins and Sangster Ltd., 1970.

Nicholls, D. "East Indians and Black Power in Trinidad," in *Haiti in Caribbean Context*, London: The Macmillan Press, 1985, 61–80.

NJAC. *Slavery to Slavery: NJAC on the Economic System*, Belmont: NJAC Education and Research Department, n.d.

———. *Black People Are a Winner*, NJAC pamphlet, University of the West Indies Library, St Augustine, n.d.

———. *Conventional Politics or Revolution?* Belmont: The Vanguard, 1971.

"No Room Here for Stokely Since He Preaches Racism," *Trinidad Guardian*, 7 May 1970.

Observer. "Black Power: Stirrings of an Integrative Society," *Trinidad Guardian*, 21 March 1970.

Pantin, D. "The 1970 Black Power Revolution: Lessons for Public Policy," in Selwyn Ryan and Taimoon Stewart (eds.), *The Black Power Revolution 1970: A Retrospective*, St Augustine: University of the West Indies Press, 1995, 663–89.

Pantin, R. *Black Power Day, the 1970 February Revolution: A Reporter's Story*, Santa Cruz: Hatuey Productions, 1990.

Richie, K. G., British High Commission, Georgetown, to Tom Sewell, Caribbean Department, FCO, 25 April 1970. FCO 63/463, Black Power in Guyana, TNA, London.

Rietan, R. *The Rise and Decline of an Alliance: Cuba and African American Leaders in the 1960s*, East Lansing: Michigan State University Press, 1999.

Riviere, W. *Black Power, NJAC and the 1970 Confrontation in the Caribbean, An Historical Interpretation*, University of the West Indies–St. Augustine, 1972.

Rodney, W. *The Groundings with My Brothers*, London: Bogle L'Ouverture Press Ltd., 1990. First published 1969.

Saint Vincent Government Gazette 25 (17 April 1970).

Sankeralli, B. "1970 or the 70's," Pamphlet distributed at the conference Reflections, Relevance, and Continuity: Caribbean and Global Perspectives on Black Power, University of the West Indies–St. Augustine, 24 August 2010.

Shah, R. *Mutiny: Ten Days at Teteron Barracks*. Unpublished manuscript.

Shoman, A. *A History of Belize in 13 Chapters*, Belize City: The Angelus Press Ltd., 2011.

Small, R. Introduction to *The Groundings with My Brothers*, by Walter Rodney, London: Bogle L'Ouverture Press Ltd., 1990, iv–viii.

Swan, Q. *Black Power in Bermuda: The Struggle for Decolonization*, New York: Palgrave Macmillan, 2009.

Williams, D. "Image and Idea in the Arts of Guyana," Edgar Mittelholzer Lecture 1969, Georgetown: National History and Arts Council, Ministry of Information, 1969.

Williams, E. "Nationwide broadcast delivered by Dr. the Right Honourable Eric Williams, Prime Minister of Trinidad and Tobago, Prime Minister's Television Broadcast," 23 March 1970. Eric Williams Memorial Collection, University of the West Indies–St Augustine.

Wilson, E. "Tobago before 1970," Reflections, Relevance and Continuity: Caribbean and Global Perspectives on Black Power Conference, University of the West Indies–St Augustine, 18–19 September 2010.

PART I

Black Power in the Postindependence Anglophone Caribbean

2

Jamaican Black Power in the 1960s

RUPERT LEWIS

This chapter traces the particular manifestations of Black Power in the Jamaican context. In this analysis, the origins of Black Power can be traced to the ongoing legacies of the transatlantic trade and the plantation system, which gave birth to specific manifestations of racism and inequality as well as specific forms of anticolonial black mobilization. Thus while the Black Power movement in Jamaica is linked to the student and youth demonstrations in Kingston on 16 October 1968, the protests had far deeper roots. As Rodney proposed, the slogan of Black Power was new, but it was "really an ideology and a movement of historical depth."[1] In Jamaica this historical depth was rooted in social movements, especially among the urban poor, working class and lower-middle class that drew heavily on the ideas of the Garvey movement and the worldviews of Rastafari. This chapter explores how these currents fed into the Black Power movement of the 1960s, the nature of Black Power mobilization in the period, and the response of the Jamaican state, before reflecting on its repercussions and relevance in the present day.

The Jamaican Context

Black Power activists engaged a Jamaican state marked by colonial legacies that included a head of state, the Governor-General, who represented the Queen; a Prime Minister, who functioned with a constitution that had been arranged between the British government and the leaders of the two main parties without the input of the people; and a judiciary, civil service, and police system engineered in the era of colonial rule to serve British and sugar-plantation interests. By the 1960s, these institutions were being taken over by brown (mulatto) and black Jamaicans. The Jamaica Labour Party (JLP), whose leader, Alexander Bustamante, emerged as a hero of the 1938 labor

revolt, led Jamaica to independence in 1962. Bustamante's successor and protégé, Hugh Shearer, was Prime Minister when the Black Power protests broke
out in 1968.

In Rodney's analysis, the main beneficiaries of the 1938 labor revolts were
those of "a narrow, middle-class sector whose composition was primarily
brown, augmented by significant elements of white and other groupings,
such as Syrians, Jews and Chinese." In a statement issued after the Shearer
government had banned him from reentering Jamaica on 15 October 1968,
Rodney noted that, "Of late, that local ruling elite has incorporated a number of blacks in positions of prominence. However, irrespective of its racial
or colour composition, this power-group is merely acting as representatives
of metropolitan-imperialist interests. Historically white and racist-oriented,
these interests continue to stop attempts at creative social expression on the
part of the black oppressed masses."[2] Rodney was also highly critical of the administration of justice, particularly police violence against citizens. Between
August 1967 and April 1968, thirty-one people were shot by the police, sixteen
of them killed.[3] Social and economic inequalities and deeply held racial prejudices against the black majority persisted in postindependence Jamaica.

The independent Jamaican state, like the colonial state before it, saw black
nationalism as culturally and politically subversive. Between 1955 and 1962,
when the People's National Party (PNP) was in government, 128 people were
banned from Jamaica; ninety-one more were banned by the subsequent JLP
government in the years 1962 to 1968.[4] Not all of these bans were on political
radicals, but they did become targets, especially in the Cold War climate of
the late 1940s. In this climate, publications as well as people were targeted
for exclusion from the Jamaican state. In a letter to Amy Jacques Garvey, the
Jamaican socialist W. A. Domingo noted that a "formidable list of publications" had been banned from entry into Jamaica. By this act, he wrote,

> . . . the government simply reveals its fears. Colonial peoples have
> a double problem. They have to fight their own reactionaries as well
> as the naturally reactionary government of the controlling power. The
> situation is worse when the two elements fuse and work against the
> masses, one openly as the agent of an alien over-lord and the other
> concealed as the friends of the people of whom they are a part. The
> question that the people should ask: of what are the rulers afraid?[5]

The JLP government, however, did not only respond to black mobilization
by recourse to repressive methods. The repatriation of Marcus Garvey's body
from London to Kingston in 1964, the official visit of Emperor Haile Selassie

to Jamaica in 1966, and the award of the Marcus Garvey Prize for Human Rights to Martin Luther King, received by his widow, Coretta Scott King, show that the JLP government was also concerned to promote its own version of moderate Black Power.

Jamaican Black Power, however, had multiple streams of resistance to British colonial legacies and to the neocolonial rule of the independence era. These streams drew on Garveyism, Rastafarianism, aspirations for social and economic mobility, and strong identification and solidarity with Africa. As Rex Nettleford has shown, Jamaican Black Power was a vigorous effort to correct the prejudices against black Jamaicans, the negative stereotyping of Africa, and the internalization of self-hate.[6] Thus the struggle was not only against a white Jamaican elite or propertied racial minorities, nor was it only against a black political elite that protected the interests of the propertied class; it was also a struggle against the thinking of black Jamaicans who felt themselves inferior to their white and light-skinned compatriots. Black Power also struggled to change the material conditions that held black Jamaicans in poverty. Issues of race and class were thus inseparable in Black Power discourse of the 1960s.

Influences and Antecedents

Garveyism

For the early twentieth century, Marcus Garvey represented the foremost thinker and mass leader of people of African descent. His Universal Negro Improvement and Conservation Association (UNIA) was organized in more than forty countries through approximately twelve hundred divisions in Africa, Australia, Europe, and the Americas. Garvey's core ideas of racial self-determination and black nationalism were set out in the Declaration of Rights of the Negro Peoples of the World, adopted at the 1920 UNIA Convention. Unlike ideas of white supremacy, Garveyites did not preach the subjugation of whites or of any other peoples.

Garvey's original vision encompassed multiple locations across the black world, and his influence was felt across Africa, the Caribbean, and the United States. His impact on the rise of African nationalism has been documented in two volumes of Robert Hill's compilation of Garvey papers, which illustrate the activities of the UNIA and African Communities League (ACL) on the African continent.[7] Among the pioneering group of African independence leaders, Kwame Nkrumah was Garvey's staunchest disciple and became a powerful symbol of Pan-Africanism from the 1940s until the early

1970s.[8] In the United States, the civil rights and Black Power movements can be traced of course not only to Garveyism but also to other movements, such as the National Association for the Advancement of Colored People (NAACP), intellectuals such as Dr. W.E.B. Du Bois, and a wider canvas of Pan-Africanists that includes George Padmore and Malcolm X. As the recent biography of Malcolm X by the late Manning Marable shows, Malcolm's parents, Earl and Louise Little, were organizers for the Garvey movement in Omaha, Nebraska, as well as in Milwaukee, Wisconsin.[9] In turn, U.S. Black Power and the civil rights movement were to have a considerable impact on the Caribbean, especially among youth. Caribbean Black Power, however, was not an imitation of its northern equivalent. Daily engagement with white racism did not exist in the same way as it did for the African-American minority; there was also a greater sense that black Jamaicans belonged in the Jamaican environment and could shape it, notwithstanding the repatriation-to-Africa trend in Jamaican Black Nationalism.

The return of Garvey's body to Jamaica in 1964, and his subsequent designation as an official national hero, was an important moment in the discussions about Jamaica's national identity, prompting debates over Garvey's significance and the role of majority and minority groups within concepts of Jamaican nationhood.[10] Rodney's comment that they had "brought Garvey's bones but not his philosophy" resonated with many people.[11] Thousands turned out to witness his interment in what became known as National Heroes Park. Many veteran Garveyites were still a part of the political landscape; some were active in the trade union movement, political parties, and community organizations, and others tried to revive the UNIA. Most prominent among them was Garvey's widow, Amy Jacques Garvey, who assumed a greater public presence in the 1960s and became a strong critic of the JLP government. Jacques Garvey spoke at Black Power meetings on the University of the West Indies (UWI) campus, contributed articles to Black Power publications, and spoke out publicly against the ban on Walter Rodney in October 1968.

Marcus Garvey Jr. was also involved in establishing his own organization, the African Nationalist Union (ANU), in 1969. The ANU publication, *The Blackman*, which described itself as the "authentic voice of Garveyism in Jamaica," emphasized a version of Black Power described as "African National Socialism"—an attempt to merge the African Nationalism of his father and the African Socialism of Kwame Nkrumah and Julius Nyerere. Garvey Jr. argued that Black Power consisted of four concepts: first, black awareness, or pride in African heritage; second, pride in being black; third, that "the only salvation for the black man lies in black institutions under black leadership"; and fourth, the forging of national and international black unity. He contended that the "fifth concept of Garveyism, which the modern black power advocates have not so far stressed . . . is the concept of the United States of Africa."[12] This fifth point is a distinguishing feature in that some interpretations of Black Power focused on the struggle for equality in a national context without reference to Africa. For Garveyites and Rastafarians, for whom Africa was the motherland, the focus on a free and united Africa was cardinal. Repatriation to Africa therefore became the clarion call.

Rastafarianism

Garvey is seen as the prophet of the emergence of Ethiopian leader Ras Tafari as Emperor Haile Selassie in November 1930. A group of Jamaicans came to identify Ras Tafari as their king and god, articulating a philosophy that was not only critical of the British monarchy but also switched allegiance to the Ethiopian king and gave him godlike status. They also asserted the right of repatriation to Ethiopia. These subversive ideas were never accepted by the majority of the African-Jamaican population, most of whom were loyal to the British monarchy. Rastafari was therefore a profound act of alienation from colonial Jamaica with its slave and colonial legacies. Gaining many new recruits after Italy invaded Ethiopia in 1935, Rastafari became part of a wider anticolonial movement against European colonialism.[13] Perceived by the authorities and by large segments of the middle class as a dangerous sect, Rastafarians were subject to stringent measures of repression and humiliation, including prison sentences for minor offenses such as the smoking of marijuana, placement in the lunatic asylum for public utterances deemed seditious, the cutting of sacred hair locks, and whipping with the cat-o'-nine-tails.[14]

One of the leading figures in the early Rastafari movement was Leonard Howell, who attracted hundreds of supporters from the 1930s to the 1950s. In the 1950s and 1960s, adherents of Rastafari grew "locks," or matted hair in the style of the Kenyan Mau Mau fighters. By the 1960s, Ras Planno in West Kingston and Ras Negus in East Kingston were among the most influential leaders. They were to play important roles in the awakening of black consciousness among youth, and particularly among musicians and singers: Ras Planno, for example, had a significant influence on Bob Marley's Rastafarian outlook and consequently on his music.

Part of the appeal of Rastafari was its delegitimizing of the colonial system and critique of the continuation of that system in the period after political independence. In designating the colonial system and modern capitalism as

"Babylon," Rastafari offered an anti-systemic critique of modern capitalism and developed its own type of postcolonial thought. It delegitimized the Christian God, deified "I and I" (the self), and provided an alternative "livity," or way of living. Being among the people in their daily life, especially within the poorest rural and urban communities, Rastafarians have been able to challenge fundamental premises of human existence derived from the colonial period, such as the innate inferiority and subhuman status of people of African descent. They have also engaged their fellow citizens in dialogues about what they eat and drink, how they dress, who they worship, and how they live. Rastafari therefore became an existential and epistemic type of Black Power embedded in and arguing from within the mass of the population. Rastafari also challenged the hegemony of the church, which adherents argued was based on the theology of the Church of England and the Pope of Rome, instead purveying a different hermeneutic of the Bible that highlighted the importance of Ethiopia in early Christianity. However, while Rastafari developed this new type of spirituality, there was some reluctance to engage in politics. Debates on political activism frequently took place, with some Rastafari withdrawing from all aspects of political life, while others emerged as political activists, especially during the turbulent months of 1968.

The decade of the 1960s saw the growth of Rastafarianism as an important social force. Rastafarians' contribution was a vision away from Jamaica, like Garvey looking to Africa, but simultaneously creating an indigenous black consciousness movement that would reshape Jamaican spirituality, language, aesthetics, and music.

Reverend Claudius Henry

Fear of Rastafari subversion was strong, as exemplified by the severity of the state response to the killing in 1963 of a gas station owner, allegedly by Rastafarians, in the community of Coral Gardens just outside Montego Bay. The state responded with ferocity, killing three Rastafarians and detaining hundreds in neighboring parishes. Jamaican political and business elites, along with the middle class, feared that the Rastafarian movement, if politicized, could pose a serious threat to the state. Reverend Claudius Henry posed just such a threat, and as such was a marked person throughout the 1960s. A spiritual leader in the heretical and prophetic tradition of black radicalism, Henry established contacts with the Rastafari, came to believe that Haile Selassie was "earth's returned Messiah," and advocated repatriation to Africa.[15] In 1960, Claudius Henry and his son Ronald were involved in an attempt to challenge the Jamaican state by force of arms. Naively, they had appealed to Fidel Castro, writing him a letter, which was found during the subsequent police raid on Henry's headquarters. The letter read in part:

> We wish to draw your attention to the conditions which confront us today as poor, underprivileged people which were brought from Africa by the British slave traders over 400 years ago to serve as slaves. We now desire to return home in peace, to live under our own vine and fig tree, otherwise a government like yours that gives justice to the poor. All our efforts to have a peaceful repatriation has [sic] proven a total failure. Hence we must fight a war for what is our rights [sic].[16]

Ronald Henry and a group that included African Americans launched a guerrilla campaign in the hills of St. Catherine and were captured by the police. Ronald was sentenced to hang for murdering one of his supporters, and his father was sentenced to ten years. On his way to the gallows, Ronald is said to have declared his commitment to the ideas of Marcus Garvey.

In 1966, Claudius Henry organized the International Peacemakers Association, which established headquarters in the district of Green Bottom in the parish of Clarendon. The economic mainstay of this enterprise was the entrepreneurial fish vendor Edna Fisher, who became Henry's wife. She developed the business activities of the commune, which included a bakery, a church, a school, vehicles, a farm, and a shop, block- and tile-making works, and an electrical plant. Through her work, the idea of self-reliance became a central part of Henry's evangelical Black Power.[17] When I traveled with Walter Rodney in the summer of 1968 to visit Reverend Henry, the church was packed. Sabbath was marked on a Saturday, the congregation was disciplined, and nyabinghi drumming by the Rastafarian brethren punctuated the singing. The rituals and the centrality of biblical hermeneutics were Christian, but Henry's Afrocentric message, Rastafarian following, and prison record meant that he was seen as subversive by the Jamaican state. Soon after Rodney was barred from reentering Jamaica, *Bongo-Man* reported that Henry had spoken to a large crowd on the second anniversary of his release from prison. The description of this meeting hints at the encounter between the various currents of black radicalism in the Jamaican context:

> Conscious Conscious! Marcus Garvey hymns. Pictures of Black Christ. Black Mary. Emperor Haile Selassie. Drums! Original chants & Black Christmas. [Henry] spoke of Dr. Rodney's lectures on African History and Marcus Garvey and of his son Trevor whom they hanged.[18]

Rodney's presence at Henry's church in rural Jamaica was ill regarded by Special Branch, and was later used by Shearer as evidence that Rodney was planning subversion.

Plantation Legacies: Rural Poverty and Urban Realities

While Black Power has primarily been understood as an urban phenomenon, it is crucial to grasp the importance of rural poverty and its impact on the movement. The Jamaican economist George Beckford insisted on this point in his classic work *Persistent Poverty* (1972). Beckford's work points to the rural dimensions of Black Power in its focus on the plantation economies of the world and in its observation that the "greatest concentration of plantation economies is to be found in the Caribbean." More importantly, he contended that some 130 years since Emancipation, the Jamaican peasantry had still not managed to secure much of the country's agricultural land and other resources. Beckford also identified the racial structure of the plantation system as laying the foundation for ongoing racism, so that persistent poverty and persistent racism were different sides of the same coin. In this vein, he noted that "the predominant social characteristic of all plantation areas of the world is the existence of a class-caste system based on differences in the racial origins of plantation workers on the one hand and owners on the other. . . . In every instance, the system was introduced by white Europeans who had to rely on non-white labor for working the plantations. Race, therefore, was a convenient means of controlling the labor supply."[19]

Rural impoverishment led to rural-urban migration and the consequent development of slums. By 1951, there were four large squatter settlements, in West Kingston, Trench Town, Dung Hill, and Kingston Pen, otherwise known as Back O'Wall.[20] In the 1960s, these locations, especially Trench Town, became the source of Jamaican popular music, as well as contested areas between rival gangs connected to political parties, with housing schemes built by the two main parties being allocated to their respective supporters. This laid the economic foundation for "garrison politics," where party support is guaranteed and where violence is used to enforce political control of an area.[21] Impoverishment impacted both on the nature of party politics and on the appeal of Black Power. As Jamaican political scientist Carl Stone observed,

. . . evidence of strong feelings of black solidarity within the black working and lower classes in urban Jamaica is not surprising in a society which has given birth to the Garvey and Rastafari movements. The ideological thrust of these movements have attempted, with some manifest success, to counter the history of black denigration that is rooted in the plantation slave history of the Caribbean, in spite of the fact that residues of these historical forces persist. The fundamental obstacle to the elimination of these residues . . . is not the absence of appropriate black racial ideologies but black poverty and white affluence.[22]

Black Power Activism and the State Response

In 1967, a Black Power group was formed at the Mona campus of the University of the West Indies, loosely structured around the four Halls of Residence that formed the core of campus life. Its aims, as outlined in an early pamphlet, were: "1. To create an awareness of what it means to be black; 2. To mobilize and unify Black people to act in their own interest; 3. To reject white cultural imperialism; 4. To seek to ensure the rule of Blacks in a black society."[23] Among those associated with this group were students from across the Anglophone Caribbean, including Peter Phillips, Garth White, Keith Noel (based at Irvine Hall), Bernard Marshall, Arnold Bertram, Edwin Jones (Chancellor Hall), Jackie Vernon, Maureen Stephenson (Mary Seacole Hall), Wyck Williams, Marva Henry, and John Dowie (Taylor Hall). A subset of this group, which included Peter Phillips, Jerry Small, Garth White, and Minion Phillips, connected the UWI campus with inner-city Afrocentric cultural and political activism.[24] This network facilitated lecturer Walter Rodney's "reasonings,"[25] especially in poor communities in Kingston. No single grouping, however, can claim the movement, which was broad and amorphous, not coalescing around any one group or individual.

Jerry Small and a group of young men who had been students at Jamaica College were some of the most active Rastafarian-influenced Black Power activists in Kingston, and theirs was among the most articulate and politically aware youth group with which Walter Rodney worked. Small was one of the organizers of a strike at Jamaica College in 1964, called in solidarity with a strike at the newly developed Jamaica Broadcasting Corporation (JBC). A product of the black middle class, Small broke with the tradition of higher education and professional advancement to become a Rastafarian and engage in the risky activities surrounding Black Power activism. The Jamaica College group included Garth White, Peter Phillips, John Davis, and Poco Morgan, all of whom went on to study at the University of the West Indies. Moving in the wider circles of the Rasta movement in the city, the group had a passion for reading about the history and contemporary realities of Africa. Rodney's expertise on this topic made him sought after by many groups as his reputation spread by word of mouth.

Rodney knew Jamaica well from his days as a student from 1960 to 1963. When he returned in 1968 with a PhD in African history from the School of Oriental and African Studies and the willingness to speak at schools, churches, communities of the poor, and Rastafarian gatherings, he developed a following. His return to UWI followed a period of teaching and political activism at the University of Dar es Salaam between 1965 and 1966, where he had taken part in discussions about Julius Nyerere's radical agrarian reform and established links with Southern African liberation movements. Moreover, he had also been to Cuba, placing him firmly on the watch list of the Special Branch, which feared his "[charisma] at the grass-roots level and . . . following among young intellectuals."[26] Soon after his arrival in Jamaica in January 1968, Rodney offered his services to the newly formed African Studies Association of the West Indies (ASAWI) and was elected its treasurer. The president of ASAWI was the Trinidadian linguist Mervyn Alleyne, and on the executive council were Amy Jacques Garvey and the young Jamaican sociologist Orlando Patterson, whose 1964 novel *Children of Sisyphus* depicted the ethos of hopelessness of the urban poor and captured the growth of Rastafarian influence among them. This was also the period when poet-historian Kamau Brathwaite joined the history department at Mona and the appearance of his trilogy *Rights of Passage* (1967), *Masks* (1968), and *Islands* (1969) bore testimony to the awakening of a Pan-African consciousness.

It was not easy, however, to transfer this level of growing black consciousness into an organization. For instance, Small cites the Rastafarian fear of forming organizations, arguing that "Rastaman always wary of organizations; and . . . because of the history of Marcus Garvey, plenty people feel that organization is a readymade way for a betrayal to formalize itself."[27] Nevertheless, in January 1968 the group decided to publish a magazine, *Blackman Speaks*, with articles on Africa, speeches by Haile Selassie, and sections of the U.N. Human Rights charter. Small recalls how he met Walter Rodney:

> I remember Peter Phillips . . . told me that there was this young history teacher just come from Africa who . . . had a lot of personal contact with the liberation struggle in Africa . . . who would like to help us in the work that we were doing . . . [and could get us] in personal contact with the OAU. . . . They arranged for me to meet him. . . . I was struck you know, the smallness of his size and the pleasantness of his features,

almost a kind of little boy look, not looking really hard and tough and aloof . . . [28]

Rodney put Jerry Small in touch with the OAU Liberation Committee based in Dar es Salaam. Observing Rodney's revolutionary outlook, Small recalls:

I remember coming down to McGregor Gully and Walter kind of want to revolutionize things more, you know . . . because you know Rasta more deal with repatriation, human rights on a local level, but him did really want [to] get the man them to address the problem of the political situation in Jamaica, and to . . . confront the system here and now. I remember him suggested to the man them one time that the paper [*Blackman Speaks*] should be edited from week to week by [different groups of us]. . . . It wasn't really a practical way of editing a publication, but in that time of revolutionary experimenting and wanting to democratize, we approve, we say alright go on. . . . I remember [one] edition [edited by Rodney, Ruddy, and Ras ID] did cause some commotion . . . on the back page them put a picture of Fidel Castro, and a quotation by Castro which is very powerful and relevant . . . "The exploitation of man by man must be dug out by the roots." But now I remember one of the main man who used to take the most amount of them was Prince Buster. . . . When [he] saw the picture of Fidel Castro he asked "what this man a do on *Blackman Speaks*" and he dumped the entire consignment.[29]

Small's interpretation of Prince Buster's rejection of the image is that the singer feared being targeted by the authorities for subversive activities. Another possibility is that Buster did not approve of a white person, revolutionary or not, being featured in the magazine.

Among those Rodney met through Small's group were Ras Single (from McGregor Gully), Frank Hasfal (Bull Bay), Ras Negus (Dunkirk, East Kingston), Count Ossie (Wareika Hills), Ras Planno (West Kingston), and Ras Dizzy, Ras ID, and Ras Historian (Laws Street). Other connections were Neville Howell, who was close to elements in the Young Socialist League attached to the PNP in Trench Town, and persons in Ghost Town, a PNP garrison community known as Concrete Jungle. What did Rodney see in Rastafari? In Small's view, it was the African sentiment, the strong element of fearlessness and resistance, and the articulateness and ability to communicate with the rest of the population: "although Rasta is a minority . . . like many articulate minorities, they can speak for the rest of the population and both interpret things for the rest of the population when the rest of the population don't feel to really examine things too closely for themselves."[30] Rodney, however, did not accept Selassie's divinity—a view he articulated in some circles but not in others, where it would not have been politic to do so.

Rodney's talks at the university, schools, and in poor communities took place in a climate of state intimidation, with intense police surveillance and repressive measures against Black Power activists brutally enforced by the police. Rodney himself was under constant surveillance. As Small recalls,

> Walter's car would be tailed day and night by more than one car of the Special Branch. They [activists] would borrow cars from family members, especially the mothers, and rotate their use to dodge Special Branch detection. . . . more than one car would have to leave town in different directions . . . and at some point later on you would pick up the person and proceed to where you going, but you would have to use some tactics to get them off your tail.[31]

One of the places in rural Jamaica that Rodney visited regularly was the home of Dr. D. K. Duncan, a young dentist recently returned from studying in Montreal and very active in the Black Power movement. Duncan lived in Brown's Town some two hours' drive from Kingston. Small recalls that one night the police sealed off all exits leaving the town. "We was down at Duncan yard and some of us leave to go buy some herb [marijuana]. When we coming back through, them block off every road and search the whole place . . . them take away all literature from us . . . and them all want to frame we with herb and gun."[32] This was the climate when Rodney left the island in 1968 to attend a Black Writers Conference in Montreal.

The Riots

On 15 October 1968, the Shearer government banned Rodney from reentering Jamaica. On hearing the news, students at the University of the West Indies campus gathered at a meeting organized by Ralph Gonsalves, then president of the UWI Students Guild. His description of the events is worth recounting:

> The aircraft which brought Rodney back from Montreal where he was attending a Congress of Black Writers landed at 2.20pm on Tuesday 15th October. However, it was not until 9.00pm that the students learnt that he was refused re-entry and confined to the aircraft. Immediately,

the Guild President contacted the Vice-Chancellor for his reaction but the latter declined to comment until he knew the facts. Soon thereafter a meeting of students on the campus was advertised for 11.00pm in Mary Seacole Hall. The meeting of some 900 students unanimously accepted a resolution to march the following day on the offices of the Minister of Home Affairs and the Prime Minister to deliver two petitions. To this end Messrs McCauley were contacted to provide the necessary transportation but when they failed to turn up at the agreed time (7.00am) on Wednesday 16th the students decided to proceed on foot.[33]

That evening, Arnold Bertram and I went to neighboring August Town to discuss how to respond. We supported the student mobilization, and the word was spread through the grounding networks of the student march. In Small's assessment, prior to the ban on Rodney, "most of the people on campus at the time" had been "antagonistic" toward Rodney and the Black Power grouping, but were outraged by the ban and decided to show solidarity.[34] Soon after the march started from the campus, the students were met by policemen armed with guns and tear gas and were broken up, but the students regrouped. "At Jamaica House, a tear gas canister was thrown at the feet of Pat Rodney, pregnant wife of the banned lecturer," further enraging the demonstrators. Marching in their scarlet gowns to distinguish themselves from others, the students' protest "gathered support on the streets as they marched to the offices of the Minister of Home Affairs." By this time "the crowd . . . had grown to over 2,000—a number of unemployed youths, workers and Rastafarians having joined the protest."[35] Black Power activists from the student body issued leaflets protesting the ban, and many noncampus people joined the march, but the vast majority had their own agendas, and the demonstration provided a pretext for their actions against the state, especially the police.

On their way to the Prime Minister's office, the demonstrators had to pass the headquarters of the Bustamante Industrial Trade Union, the union affiliated with the ruling JLP. "[A] clash ensued in which stones, bottles and miscellaneous missiles were flung . . . A detachment of the police intervened with batons and tear gas to disperse the crowd. A few people were injured in the process including a policeman. Several cars were destroyed."[36] According to Gonsalves, the violence outside the BITU headquarters was not instigated by the students but by workers belonging to a rival union associated with the opposition People's National Party. Thus the student protest was the match that lit the fire for wider protests in downtown Kingston. In the evening, commercial Kingston was shut down by rioters who emerged to loot business places and smash cars. The students made their way to George VI Memorial Park, where George Beckford urged nonviolence; however, the police continued to use their batons and throw tear gas. The student march was thrown into disarray as they found their way back to the campus. Meanwhile, the University of the West Indies was surrounded by the military, and access to its compounds was highly restricted.

While the conservative *Gleaner* emphasized the "widespread vandalism" caused by "hooligan gangs [taking] charge of many areas of the city,"[37] Gonsalves' account focuses instead on the social causes:

> . . . unemployed youth and workers gave the events a new turn. For them the protest was not so much about a lecturer who was banned—however influential he might have been—but about the inequalities stemming from the class and racial oppression in the country. More than likely criminal elements also took advantage of the commotion to loot and plunder . . . Big businesses, both foreign and local, were attacked. They included Canadian Imperial Bank of Commerce, Bank of London and Montreal, Pan American, Air Jamaica, Kingston Ice and Commodity Service, Woolworth, North American Life and Bata Shoe Store. On Orange Street Marzouca's Building was damaged; Royal Bank of Canada's Manchester Square Branch was stoned and so was the Jamaica Public Service Station at Gold Street. Significantly, 53 JOS [Jamaica Omnibus Service] buses were burnt or otherwise damaged and this was clearly related to the fact that the fare had been increased recently . . . Looting continued at many stores in the city and on Spanish Town Road throughout the night of October 16th. . . . Three persons were reported killed in incidents related to these disturbances.[38]

From the perspective of the Jamaican government, Prime Minister Shearer sought to justify his actions on the grounds that Rodney was a threat to national security. Shearer claimed that the exclusion order was prepared without the knowledge that Rodney had left the country, but when it was discovered that he had, and was due to return on 15 October, they decided to ban him from reentering. Defending this action to the Jamaican Parliament, Shearer stated that Rodney was banned not for his attendance at the Black Writers Conference, but for his "destructive anti-Jamaican activities in Kingston, St. Andrew, Clarendon and St. James."[39] In this the Prime Minister was relying on Special Branch reports identifying locations where Rodney had visited or given talks. His visit to Claudius Henry's compound in Clarendon, for example, was taken as evidence that he was planning a violent overthrow of the government. Shearer therefore argued that the government had "acted to save the nation from a Castro plot"—citing Rodney's attendance at a students congress in Leningrad and two visits to Cuba in 1962 as evidence of his extreme communist views. Shearer claimed that when Rodney returned to Jamaica to take up an appointment as lecturer in the Department of History, he "lost little time in engaging in subversive activities":

> He quickly announced his intention of organizing revolutionary groups for what he termed . . . "the struggle ahead" and then closely associated himself with groups of people who claimed to be part of the Rastafarian Movement and also with Claudius Henry who was convicted in 1960 of Treason Felony as a result of activities which required the use of armed force. . . . He openly declared his belief that as Jamaica was predominantly a black country all brown-skinned mulatto people and their assets should be destroyed. He consistently told the groups with whom he associated that this could only be achieved by revolution and that no revolution had ever taken place without armed struggle and bloodshed. This resort to violence was the recurrent theme of all his discussions with these groups as was his condemnation of the democratic system of government in Jamaica.[40]

The Prime Minister and the island's leading newspaper, the *Daily Gleaner*, also blamed non-Jamaicans for the events of 16 October, pointing to the fact that Rodney was from Guyana and that several of the leaders of the UWI Students Guild were not Jamaican, including the Guild president, Ralph Gonsalves, who was from St. Vincent; the first vice president, who was from Trinidad; and the second vice president, who was from England. Only the treasurer was Jamaican.[41]

However, the assessment of the U.S. Embassy in Kingston provides an interesting divergence in opinion as to the reasons for the protests. The Embassy reports assessed that the protests were "spontaneously generated," and no evidence was found of involvement by the Rastafarians, Rev. Henry's group, or the Nation of Islam, nor did the Americans find "any real connections between the Jamaicans who rioted and UWI students and teachers," despite the presence at the university of a "core of radical intellectuals . . . working to incite the Jamaican masses."[42] This assessment is closer to the truth, as the core of students and academics at UWI did not have the capacity to stage these protests.

The Jamaican Aftermath

On 17 October, Maxwell Carey, a member of parliament who represented the PNP in the South Eastern Westmoreland "seized the Mace, the symbol of authority of Parliament . . . and walked with it towards the door of the chamber" in protest of the banning of Rodney without giving him the opportunity to see his wife and child. The same day, Roy McNeil, the Minister of Home Affairs, imposed an order banning all marches and meetings in the corporate area. This was symptomatic of the increasingly repressive measures taken by the state in the immediate aftermath of the Rodney demonstrations. UWI students were confined to campus, and "units of the Jamaica Defence Force and the police took up positions at the entrances to the University, allowing students to enter but not to leave."[43] While Shearer did not have much evidence to indict the Black Power core and students on campus, a leaflet entitled "Tactics! Tactics! Tactics!" that was produced on the morning of the demonstration, played into the hands of the government, as it called on demonstrators to "provoke the police, don't argue with them! Insult them, ridicule them, goad them, let them attack you! And reveal the true nature of the system." It also encouraged the making of Molotov cocktails, called on students to close the university, to advocate for student representation on university committees and for solidarity with workers, ending with the invocation "Burn UWI . . . Burn UWI . . . Burn UWI."[44]

The *Gleaner* went on the offensive, determined to secure more intelligence about radical groups and to urge the use of more force to quell protests: "As the party in office, the party in opposition, the professors, the politicians and the public settle down in the next few days and weeks, clearly they all must come to the cold and chilling conclusion that there has been a change in the national climate. There has now come to live with us a fearsome shadow— a new stark dimension—the imminence of instability, awaiting which are ready-made agents of evil, gulled and trained to throw fuel on the flame of national calamity." The editorial called for "more and more money to buy information for the state's protection . . . more and more money to recruit, train and arm the brave and patriotic personnel who guard the ramparts of secret information . . . so as to forewarn the country of hostile plans of iniquity and revolt."[45]

After the ban on Rodney, a respondent in Small's group recalls that he stayed on the campus for four days before going to his home in August Town. On the night of his return,

... 'bout 60 soldiers and police in about 8 vehicles come down the August Town Road and them stop in front of the University playing field. ... The yard where them stop in front of is my brethren yard, a bredder name Dippy. ... So him tek a short cut behind and run come down and tell we say, bwoy, a whole heap of soldier and police up the road deh and them a come fe we. So when we hear them coming we just finish smoking what we ah smoke, and sweep out all like little herb and little herb seed what was in the house and sit down there and wait on them. And after about 10 minutes we hear the brakes, you know them big Bedford truck, you always hear the brakes a squeal a come down the road. We sit tight man, everybody nervous but we clean still ...

The group had put up Jamaican flags and images of the Prime Minister, and when the police entered with guns and ordered, "Don't move a rass . . . ," the soldiers and police rushed through the front door, and "when him see Shearer picture and see Jamaica flag . . . the Commanding officer said 'The Prime Minister wrong to rass, man' . . . Anyway them search, them tear open the ceiling, search up and down and turn over the bed, and mash up everything in the place, and them a look for prohibited literature and them find some little book by Martin Luther King and Special Branch man them a tek down name of book." Not finding any herb, the police sent someone to buy a quarter ounce, and when the man returned with the herb they were charged with it. Four males and two females, high school youths who were drawn to Rastafari, were put in the police truck and beaten.[46] Later on, among the prominent activists harassed was Marcus Garvey Jr., who was arrested while participating in a demonstration on 24 May 1970 in solidarity with the liberation movements in Africa. Members of his organization were beaten by the police. About his arrest, he wrote:

When I was arrested I was first taken to Hunt's Bay Police Station and then afterwards spirited off to Matilda's Corner Station. The intention was to keep me incommunicado for as long as possible so that a good period of solitary confinement would dampen my revolutionary ardor. The police lied to my mother and other relatives when they came to bail me . . . They pretended that they did not know where I was. . . . On orders from their white superior officers—the pigs—you can be sure. I have seen white power at work in Jamaica. I have seen at first hand the brutality of Shearer's bully boys from Harmon Barracks. I know now where the sufferers go, every day, every week. . . . Black power for black people! Down with the pigs![47]

Political and Cultural Repercussions

While the demonstrations met with state repression, they also helped to catalyze the growing political and cultural consciousness around Black Power. In the wake of Rodney's expulsion, a number of new radical publications appeared across the Anglophone Caribbean. Jamaica's *Abeng* newspaper, founded in 1969, was part of a regional awakening that included new publications, such as *Moko*, *Pivot*, and *East Dry River Speaks* (Trinidad), *Black Star* (Barbados), *Outlet* (Antigua), and *YULIMO* (St. Vincent), that appeared alongside existing publications, such as Jamaica's *Impact* (1967–1968) and *Bongo-Man* (1968–1972), Trinidad's *Tapia*, and Guyana's *Ratoon*.[48] Like other periodicals of the period, its name was chosen for its local significance, the "abeng" being the horn used by the Maroons for communication in the mountains of Jamaica. The Abeng group was a political matrix for the Black Power movement, socialists, the independent trade union movement, Rastafarians, supporters of the opposition People's National Party, and others disaffected with the two main political parties. The *Abeng* newspaper, whose editors included Robert Hill (a graduate student at the University of the West Indies), George Beckford (a UWI lecturer), Rupert Lewis (a UWI graduate student), and Trevor Munroe (a UWI lecturer), became a focal point of critique and activism against the ruling Jamaica Labour Party and a harbinger of the radicalism in Jamaica in the 1970s. Almost every issue included articles taken from Marcus Garvey's Jamaican newspapers *The Blackman* (1929–1931) and the *New Jamaican* (1932–1933), which were reprinted alongside articles on Jamaican history.[49] Other manifestations of the vibrant political-cultural consciousness that flowered in Jamaica in the era of Black Power can be traced in the development of more West Indian–focused curricula at the University of the West Indies, the Afrocentric reorientation of performance poetry and dance, and, mostly obviously, in the black-conscious messages of the popular music of the day.

The radical journalism represented by *Abeng*, the mobilization of young people, the linkages between middle-class and community activists, between elements on the campus and the urban population of "sufferers," and the development of connections with the working class that bore fruit in the formation of the University and Allied Workers Union in 1971, were to contribute to strengthening the electoral prospects of Michael Manley as Prime Minister of Jamaica. As leader of the PNP since 1969, Manley had actively campaigned to win over activists from the University of the West Indies and the wider Black Power movement. In 1969, Manley visited Ghana, where he received a plaque from Dr. Busia, the Ghanaian Prime Minister. Such public acknowledgement of Jamaica's African heritage—indicative of the impact of the Black Power movement on the mainstream political parties—played a part in gaining Manley support from within the movement. Claudius Henry, for example, chose to support Michael Manley after he embraced some of the tenets of Black Power, such as support for African Liberation movements and reorienting the educational system to valorize the African heritage of the Jamaican people. Key activists of the Black Power group of the UWI campus also opted to support Manley, including Arnold Bertram and Dr. D. K. Duncan, the latter subsequently becoming the General Secretary of the PNP and the leading figure of the left wing of that party. The Black Power movement was therefore the prelude to the most radical period in twentieth-century Jamaican political history with the electoral victory of Michael Manley in 1972 and his party's adoption of "democratic socialism" from 1974 to 1980. It was also the harbinger of the broader Caribbean regional left-wing movement that culminated in the Grenada Revolution of 1979 to 1983.

Some proponents of Black Power, however, rejected the political system as a whole. Marcus Garvey Jr., for example, was implacably opposed to the two main political parties and their leaders. Responding to his arrest in 1970, Garvey Jr. noted that "[the] experience makes me more determined than ever to fight against Shearer, Seaga, Michael Manley, McNeil, Coore and all the other puppets and jokers of the two party system who work to keep the whites, Chinese and Mulattoes in power in their black, African country of Jamaica."[50] The Rastafarian movement also remained outside of party politics, with one new group, the Twelve Tribes, continuing a strong focus on repatriation to Africa.

Conclusion

The political agenda articulated through Black Power in the 1960s and 1970s has been only partially accomplished. The Black Power demonstrations and activism had a profound impact on the political climate in Jamaica, brought intense pressure to bear on the Shearer administration, and helped to shift political support to Michael Manley's PNP, which systematically recruited many activists into the party after Manley's huge electoral victory in 1972. The Black Power movement therefore acted as yeast to assist in the realignment of relations between the state and the people in a particular historical moment. However, the need to address socioeconomic deprivation—a key demand of the popular movement—remains an ongoing issue. Economic challenges still exist, as Afro-Caribbean participation in corporate life continues to be restricted, although this is being challenged by a younger generation of entrepreneurs. The black middle classes have been the main beneficiaries of a less racialized society with wider opportunities, particularly in education and politics. The grandchildren of the rude boys of the 1960s, however, have had their social base considerably expanded with the growth of the black lumpen-proletariat and the emergence of transnational gangs. While structural racism has been eroded in the traditional plantation sense, the world economy has reinvented itself, and capitalism remains globally dominant. In today's global economy, migrants to the industrially developed countries from Africa and the Caribbean, locked into low-wage jobs and new ghettoes, encounter twenty-first-century racism. However, while the legacies are mixed, the themes of Black Power deserve to be revisited, in order to understand the role it played in the formidable task of remaking the colonial and postcolonial world.

Notes

1. Rodney, *Groundings*, 21.
2. Ibid., 12.
3. Ibid., 14.
4. Editorial, *Bongo-Man*, 2.
5. "Historical Letters of Marcus Garvey, W. A. Domingo and George Padmore," *Bongo-Man*, 22.
6. See Nettleford.
7. Hill, *The Marcus Garvey Papers*.
8. See Jacques Garvey, 168.
9. Marable, 20–23, 27, 28.
10. Nettleford, 19–37.
11. Rodney, "Message to Afro-Jamaica Associations," 15.
12. Garvey Jr., "The American Scene: An Interview with Marcus Garvey," 13–17.
13. Lewis, 145–58.
14. Simpson, 219.
15. Bogues, 12–13, 166–74.
16. Chevannes, 277.
17. Bignall, 8.
18. Editorial, *Bongo-Man*, 3.
19. Beckford, 15, 23, 67.
20. Clarke, 139.
21. See Gray, Sives, and Hutton.

22. Stone, 112.

23. Mimeographed leaflet in Rupert Lewis's "Black Power in the 1960s" personal collection.

24. Peter Phillips became General Secretary of the People's National Party and served as minister in the administrations of Michael Manley, P. J. Patterson, and Portia Simpson-Miller. Garth White is a noted authority and writer on Jamaican popular music. Keith Noel is an educator and former principal of St. Jago High School. Trinidadian by birth, he has lived in Jamaica since the late 1960s. Bernard Marshall hailed from St. Vincent and was a historian and lawyer. Arnold Bertram is a prominent historian and former minister in the administrations of Michael Manley and P. J. Patterson. Edwin Jones is a distinguished academic in public administration. Wyck Williams is Guyanese and has published a novel. Jerry Small was a public intellectual long before the term was known, with a unique narrative style drawing on Rastafarian argot and his own native intelligence. He now has his own radio talk show.

25. "Reasonings," known in the Rastafarian language as "groundings," were informal gatherings where discussions took place. The location might be a gully bank where squatters lived, a camp of Rastafarians, a school, a church, a trade union hall, or any place where ordinary people could meet and discuss issues of interest. In many instances, Rodney listened, and at other times he gave talks.

26. Davis, interview with Rupert Lewis. Davis worked in Special Branch.

27. Small, 16.

28. Ibid., 18.

29. Ibid., 32.

30. Ibid., 59.

31. Ibid., 33–34.

32. Ibid., 35.

33. Gonsalves, 1–24. Dr. Ralph Gonsalves is presently the Prime Minister of St. Vincent and the Grenadines.

34. Small, 40.

35. Gonsalves, 6–7.

36. "Campus Row Brings Out Vandals."

37. Ibid.

38. Gonsalves, 9.

39. "Shearer Tells House of Guyanese's 'Castro Plot.'"

40. Ibid.

41. West, 34–35.

42. "Shearer Tells House of Guyanese's 'Castro Plot.'"

43. Ibid.

44. Ibid.

45. "Chilling but Real."

46. Small, 44–45.

47. Garvey Jr., "Mwalimu Marcus Garvey Speaks," 1.

48. This period is dealt with at length in Lewis, chapter V.

49. See Bogues's chapter in this volume.

50. Garvey Jr., "Mwalimu Marcus Garvey Speaks," 1.

Bibliography

Beckford, G. *Persistent Poverty: Underdevelopment in Plantation Economies of the Third World,* New York: Oxford University Press, 1972.

Bignall, M. "The Construction of a Self-Reliant Community in Jamaica: Claudius Henry's Peacemakers Association," Research report, Masters in Social Work, Faculty of Social Sciences, University of the West Indies, Mona, 2012.

Bogues, A. *Black Heretics, Black Prophets: Radical Political Intellectuals,* New York and London: Routledge, 2003.

"Campus row brings out vandals, marches, fires, thugs on rampage menace capital," *The Daily Gleaner*, 17 October 1968.

Chevannes, B. "The Repairer of the Breach: Reverend Claudius Henry and Jamaican Society" in Frances Henry (ed.), *Ethnicity in the Americas*, The Hague: Mouton, 1976, 263–90.

"Chilling but Real," *The Daily Gleaner*, 18 October 1968.

Clarke, C. *Kingston, Jamaica: Urban Development and Social Change, 1692–2002*, Kingston: Ian Randle Publishers, 2006.

Davis, F. Interview with Rupert Lewis, 3 June 1991.

Editorial, *Bongo-Man*, No. 1, 1968.

Garvey Jr., Marcus. "The American Scene: An Interview with Marcus Garvey," *The Blackman*, 2: 1, 1970.

———. "Mwalimu Marcus Garvey Speaks," *The Blackman*, 2: 5, 1970.

Gonsalves, R. "The Rodney Affair and Its Aftermath," *Caribbean Quarterly*, 25: 3, 1979, 1–24.

Gray, Obika, *Demeaned but Empowered: The Social Power of the Urban Poor in Jamaica*, Mona: University of the West Indies Press, 2004.

Hill, R. *The Marcus Garvey and Universal Negro Improvement Association Papers*, Berkeley and Los Angeles: University of California Press, Volume 1, 1983, Volume 2, 1983, Volume 9, 1995, Volume 10, 2006.

"Historical Letters of Marcus Garvey, W. A. Domingo and George Padmore," *Bongo-Man*, No. 1, 1968.

Hutton, C. "Oh Rudie: Jamaican Popular Music and the Narrative of Urban Badness in the Making of Postcolonial Society," *Caribbean Quarterly*, 56: 4, 2010, 22–64.

Jacques Garvey, A. *Garvey and Garveyism*, New York: Macmillan, 1963.

Lewis, R. "Marcus Garvey and the Early Rastafarians: Continuity and Discontinuity" in Nathaniel Samuel Murrell et al. (eds), *Chanting Down Babylon: A Rastafari Reader,* Philadelphia: Temple University Press, 1998, 145–58.

———. *Walter Rodney's Intellectual and Political Thought*, Kingston and Detroit: University of the West Indies Press and Wayne State University Press, 1998.

Marable, M. *Malcolm X: A Life of Reinvention*, New York: Viking, 2011.

Mimeographed leaflet in Rupert Lewis's "Black Power in the 1960s" personal collection.

Nettleford, R. *Mirror, Mirror: Identity, Race and Protest in Jamaica,* Kingston: William Collins and Sangster Ltd., 1970.

Rodney, W. *The Groundings with My Brothers* [1969], London: Bogle L'Ouverture, 1996.

———. "Message to Afro-Jamaica Associations," *Bongo-Man*, No. 2, 1969.

"Shearer Tells House of Guyanese's 'Castro Plot,'" *The Daily Gleaner*, 18 October 1968.

Simpson, G. E. *Religious Cults of the Caribbean: Trinidad, Jamaica, and Haiti,* Rio Piedras: University of Puerto Rico, 1970.

Sives, A. *Elections, Violence, and the Democratic Process in Jamaica, 1944–2007,* Kingston: Ian Randle Publishers, 2010.

Small, J. Interview with Rupert Lewis, 1989, Typescript.

Stone, C. *Class, Race and Political Behaviour in Urban Jamaica,* Mona: Institute of Social and Economic Research, University of the West Indies, 1973.

West, M. "Walter Rodney and Black Power: Jamaican Intelligence and U.S. Diplomacy," *African Journal of Criminology and Justice Studies,* 1: 2, 2005, 1–50.

3

The *Abeng* Newspaper and the Radical Politics of Postcolonial Blackness

ANTHONY BOGUES

> Black Power. I believe that this slogan is destined to become
> one of the great political slogans of our time. Of course, only Time
> itself can tell that. Nevertheless when we see how powerful an
> impact this slogan has made it is obvious that it touches very
> sensitive nerves in the political consciousness of the world today.
>
> C.L.R. JAMES, "BLACK POWER"

The political slogan "Black Power" reverberated in North American society and found wings in the Caribbean.[1] It was not the first time in the twentieth century that a radical black political idea had found motion, moving across the black world. One cannot think of twentieth-century black radicalism without grappling with political ideas that may have begun in one locale of the black world and worked their ways into different parts of the black diaspora. From Garveyism to Pan-Africanism to the radical black politics of George Padmore, there exists a long history of black political practices and thought that has been both transnational and internationalist. This internationalism has had two dimensions. In the first instance, it seeks to gather Africans and African-diaspora populations into a form of programmatic unity, and while oftentimes operating at a locally specific level, pays serious attention to transnational forms of political solidarity. Secondly, this form of politics, depending on the context of its practice, is antiracist, anticolonial, and anti-imperial. Thus Black Power in the Caribbean and Jamaica should be located within a historical trajectory in which it is understood as an anticolonial and anti-imperial instantiation of twentieth-century radical black politics reconfigured in a juridically postcolonial site. With this historical injunction in mind, we turn to the *Abeng* newspaper, founded as part of a radical political moment in the history of postindependence Jamaica.

In twentieth-century radical politics, the newspaper has been both a tool of communication and a vehicle that creates and affirms critical consciousness while organizing and mobilizing significant social forces into action. Thus, typically radical political newspapers were interventionist political entities. They exposed fault lines in society, advocated clear political positions, and did so in order to facilitate the emergence and growth of a social and political movement. Historically, in some instances radical newspapers were the direct outgrowth of a movement already in motion. In others, the newspaper was both the expression and the organizer of the movement, with its primary role being to make possible the creation of organizational structures. In such a context, the radical newspaper, while giving form to the movement in motion, performs a double role: it is a bearer of critical consciousness and an organizer of social groups. It is important here to distinguish between the newspaper that attempts to create critical consciousness and engages in various forms of criticism while "speaking truth to power" and the newspaper that emerges out of social/political action and considers itself expressing the mood of the times while seeking to be that movement's organizing tool. The *Abeng* newspaper belonged to this latter type, and its brief, explosive growth and then demise is an important story of a specific moment in postcolonial Jamaican politics. The folding of the newspaper in October 1969 was followed a few years later by the formal liquidation of the Abeng group as a political grouping, whose demise marked a specific moment of radical black independent politics in postcolonial Jamaica.

The Context of Abeng

The *Abeng* newspaper operated for nine months in 1969. It began publication in a period of social and political maelstrom in postcolonial Jamaica. In 1962, Jamaica had formally achieved political independence through the process of constitutional decolonization. This form of political independence occurred within the global context of the historical and political demise of colonial empires in the second half of the twentieth century. The post–World War Two end of colonial empires wrought changes within global politics, with the newly independent nation-states enlarging the terrain of international politics. However, these former colonies achieved nationhood during the Cold War and under the long shadow of preeminent U.S. power—factors that were crucial in influencing the shape of postindependence politics and society in the Anglophone Caribbean. Thus, for example, in 1961, with political independence for the Caribbean in the air, there was discussion in the U.S. National Security Council about the formation of a Caribbean Security Agency, which would act to make sure that the region remained tied to the "free world."[2] All this was of course in sync with the analysis of radical intellectual Frantz Fanon. In 1961, the year before Jamaica's political independence, Fanon noted in his conclusion of *The Wretched of the Earth* that "a former European colony decided to catch up with Europe. It succeeded so well that the United States of America became a monster."[3] For many Caribbean countries, therefore, political independence was achieved under the shadow of American power. This would have profound consequences for any attempt to transform the processes of political independence into a decolonizing one.

Another factor shaping the character of political independence in the English-speaking Caribbean was the political nature of the dominant anticolonial nationalism of the independence moment. I have argued elsewhere that while the region-wide labor rebellions of the 1930s shook colonial power, the formal institutional political process that emerged was one in which a creole anticolonialism became the ideological bedrock of the anticolonial moment.[4] One consequence was the construction of a hegemony in which black nationalism was placed on the back burner or elided altogether in the deployment of the main nationalist narrative. This created a state hegemony in which blackness was replaced by the conception that Jamaica was a creole nation. The difficulty with this conception of creoleness was that it was primarily defined as a form of mixed hybridity that subordinated blackness, thus paying scant attention to Africa as part of the cultural and historical memory of the majority of Jamaicans. It is not that Africa was not recognized by creole nationalist narratives but rather that this recognition, when it occurred, framed Africa and African-derived practices as less "civilized" elements of Jamaican social and cultural life. Creole nationalist state hegemony attempted to elide questions of race and color in early postcolonial Jamaica and fostered a national myth about racial matters. The late Rex Nettleford, writing in 1970, eight years after political independence, noted that "The trouble with this solution to our race differentiation problems is that if the hybrid is the norm, then the vast majority of pure blacks must be the aberration. It therefore invests the mixed-blood idealization with a middle-class unction which is unacceptable to lower-class blacks."[5]

All hegemonies nestle themselves within a set of economic and political relationships. In the Jamaican case, these relationships in the early postcolonial period rested upon the domination of the economy by imperial power through foreign ownership; a set of laws and social customs that actively discriminated against the Afro-Jamaican; and a political process in which the question of self-determination had been reduced only to the right of political equality, that is, to the right to vote. So glaring were these issues—particularly those of economic power and the legacies of colonial domination—that a 1970 Central Intelligence Agency report on the Caribbean, written by Richard Helms, noted the following: "political independence in Guyana, Trinidad-Tobago, Jamaica and Barbados . . . has [not] significantly altered their socioeconomic structures. In many ways, the social patterns that developed in the plantation economies during the days of colonialism persist today."[6] In such a situation, the hope of Jamaican political independence joyously expressed in Derrick Morgan's song "Forward March" was, within four years, shattered by the Ethiopians' biting observation in their hit song "Everything Crash."[7]

Two other elements are critical in our thinking about the conditions for the emergence of Black Power in Jamaica and of the *Abeng* newspaper. The first is historical and pertains to the different currents of Jamaican political thought, and the other is the immediate context of the paper's birth. Twentieth-century Jamaican political thought has had many streams of black political thinking, ranging from Garveyism, Rastafari, and various forms of Ethiopianism. Indeed, one could easily argue that early-twentieth-century Jamaican political history was littered with groups and newspapers that espoused different currents of Black Nationalist and Pan-Africanist ideologies.[8] Recent scholarship on the strikes and labor rebellions points us to the profound influence of not only the local Garvey movement but also to the role of the Rastafari movement.[9] In this period, individuals like Stennet Kerr-Coombs[10] and others wrote and advocated a radical, anticolonial politics, which drew its ideological sources from the black internationalism of the early twentieth century. This black anticolonial politics was discursively expressed alongside a preoccupation with reforming the economic system and some understanding of what could broadly be called socialism. It is of some importance to grasp that black radicalism in twentieth-century Jamaica has roots in a political genealogy that has been overshadowed by the dominant form of creole nationalism. Thus, in examining the Black Power movement of the postindependence period, we might want to see this as a second historical attempt in twentieth-century Jamaica in which a politics of radical blackness attempted to gain some foothold in the island's political landscape. Again, it is important to note that this radical black politics and its ideas are connected to various forms of black internationalism and therefore constitute part of a larger terrain of African diasporic politics and radical thought. To think about twentieth-century radical black political thought is to grapple with how political ideas have traveled throughout Africa and its diaspora during this period. So, while specificities are crucial to the local character of political ideas, so too is an understanding of how political ideas moved within these spaces. Thus, any attempt to ascribe authenticity to one conception of Black Power over another is to mistakenly privilege one African or diasporic site over another. This is not to say that radical postcolonial blackness in Jamaica had its precursor in early-twentieth-century African diasporic politics; rather, it may be that while the former drew some of its sources from the latter, within the context of Caribbean decolonization, new political questions were placed on the agenda.[11]

This point is of some importance in order to discern the character of the *Abeng* newspaper as a radical newspaper that emerges from the motion of a movement and social groups. Postcolonial Jamaica was not only a society in which the structural legacies of British colonial power were intact, but it was one where among the subaltern groupings there were significant rumblings during this period. The late Carl Stone, one of the leading political sociologists of postindependent Jamaica, observed in 1973 that "strong feelings of black solidarity within the black working and lower classes in urban Jamaica [were] not surprising in a society which had given birth to the Garvey and Rastafari movements. The ideological thrust of these movements attempted to . . . counter the history of black denigration . . . poverty, unemployment, low educational opportunities, and the hopelessness and parasitic paternalism they breed in political life . . ."[12] But there was more than black solidarity in the 1960s. The decade had opened with the Henry Rebellion, and then there was the Coral Gardens incident of 1963 and the 1965 anti-Chinese riots.[13] In addition, there was the visit of Haile Selassie and the fillip that this gave to Rastafari.[14] These events were illustrative of the class-race structure of Jamaican society and indicative of profound dissent about the form of political independence. All of these events, along with the explosion of small radical publications, such as *Blackman Speaks, African Youth Move,* and *Our Own,* made up the ingredients of a black-consciousness stew of the period.

Oftentimes in radical politics it takes an occasion for disparate currents that circle around similar grounds to combine their activities. In the Jamaican case, it was the event of the Rodney Riots of October 1968 and their aftermath that created the precise moment for the emergence of the *Abeng* newspaper.[15]

The Emergence of *Abeng*

In reviewing the initial phases of *Abeng*, we want to keep in mind the distinction between the newspaper, its editorial board, and the political grouping that coalesced around the newspaper. The newspaper's editorial board was broad-based, and for the first couple of issues, the names of the board members were not published. In the fourth issue, the newspaper published the names of those on its editorial committee. These were Rupert Lewis, Robert Hill, George Beckford, and Horace Levy.[16] Lewis recalls that the editorial board was politically mixed and made up of "disaffected elements in Jamaican society from the left through to the center of Jamaican politics."[17] Included in this initial grouping, according to Lewis, were individuals close to the left wing of the People's National Party (PNP)—for example, Vernon Arnett[18] and the human rights lawyer Dennis Daley, who continued to be part of Abeng until its 1974 demise. Part of the grouping included black-nationalist individuals involved in business, such as Vin Bennett. Additionally, there were young Rastafarian figures like Jerry Small. However, although the founding group was broad, thereby constituting itself as a wide ideological spectrum, from its inception, the newspaper's politics struck a radical chord.

The first issue of the paper proclaimed that it would be a national weekly. The front page editorial notes: "We are a very distinctive people with a very distinctive history. But we know very little of our own past and the struggles of our forefathers who survived the horrors of slavery."[19] This is, of course, a nationalist, anticolonial position, but what concerns us here is why the paper took such a position just a few years after constitutional decolonization. Explaining the choice of name for the paper, the front-page editorial states that "The Abeng was used by the Maroons and other Jamaicans in bygone days to communicate with one another in a very precise and special way."[20] Thus, the intention of *Abeng* was to have a "particular call . . . for each and every Jamaican," to convey "particular ideas about the state of the society—what is wrong with it and why" and to "invite the views of everyone," thereby transmitting a multiplicity of ideas.[21] Examining this editorial alongside the rest of the stories on the front page, which focused on the current news items of the day, one might initially deduce that *Abeng* intended to carve a space for itself as a tool of communication and an instrument to expose the ills of Jamaican society. Inside the paper, however, another editorial, entitled

"Bread, Work and Human Dignity," posited a different narrative. It made it clear that *Abeng's* preoccupations would be explicitly radical-political and that this was therefore a newspaper with a different point of view in postcolonial Jamaica—unlike, for example, the *Daily Gleaner*, which had emerged as the island's most powerful newspaper and was conservative in stance. The editorial continued by exposing the island's political independence as meaningless for the majority, noting that:

> The cry for bread, work and human dignity—30 years after the revolt of 1938—still goes unheard in Jamaica. Thirty years later, dispossession is still the lot of the vast majority of our Jamaican people. But this is what 1938 precisely set out to end, once and for all. . . . The society, as presently organized, seems only able to meet the crisis with the suppression of popular demands . . . in spite of the formidable problems of making these changes everywhere our people show daily signs of their readiness. It will demand an even greater mobilization of popular energies to get this gigantic effort started.[22]

There are a few things to note about this editorial. First, it marks the 1938 rebellion as a watershed in Jamaica's political history: an event that challenged colonial power as ordinary Jamaicans attempted to create new grounds for politics and life. Secondly, it argues that the aspirations of 1938 had been thwarted and suggested that new attempts to create a different form of society were under way, but that greater efforts and mobilization were required. How was this mobilization to occur? It is here that we see *Abeng* functioning as a newspaper that saw itself both as a transmitter and as an organizer of this critical consciousness. Thus, for example, the first issue of the newspaper proposed to establish editorial committees across the island to record the "attempts which our people are making daily to break out of the continuing oppressive system." Gathering around it "fresh efforts to fashion a free Jamaica," the newspaper would thus be part of the necessary task of creating a new society.[23] Thus, the editorial argued that *Abeng* would serve as a recording journal that gathered struggles already under way. It would not lead these, but by making them public would create circles of engagement in which political conversations and joint action could be possible.

At the level of political ideas, the conceptions driving such a political outlook were shaped by the thought of C.L.R. James, the influential Caribbean political theorist.[24] James's political ideas about the role of a newspaper in the Caribbean, as outlined in his 1962 book, *Party Politics in the West Indies*, conceptualized the radical newspaper as organizer, educator, and reporter on the new society, which the masses, in moments of crisis, shaped.[25] *Abeng* seemed to have had an initially contradictory position, in which the front-page editorial proclaimed that it would be a voice of communication, exposing society's ills, while the inside editorial made an explicit political call to organize. This contradiction might suggest that there was early tension among the editorial board members about the newspaper's political directions, generated in part by the loose coalition that formed around the paper. However, by the second issue, the tension seems to have settled, and a clear, radical stance was now enunciated—one in which the issue of blackness was central. This was blackness not as a cultural construct or what some have called a "black culturalist" position, but rather a preoccupation with blackness as a signifier of radical political potential. In such a frame and given the times, Black Power quickly became the newspaper's rallying call and a political slogan with an implicit program of social change.[26] To sustain this claim, I will review below some of the newspaper's key columns and articles.

Radical Blackness as Ideology

In explicating the revolutionary black political ideology of the newspaper, we should begin with some of the political terms it often deployed. One term that appears in the first edition is *sufferer*. This is a self-referential term used by the Jamaican oppressed in this period to draw attention to their social and economic condition. *Sufferer* denoted the hardships that an oppressed person had to endure. To be a sufferer was not to be a victim of oppression but to be adversely affected by its consequences, making oppression and domination an active process. *Abeng* quickly picked up this term, and sufferer became an all-embracing notion inclusive of different social groups, including workers, the unemployed, and small farmers. The deployment of this term and the attention paid to language in the newspaper illustrates that the radical politics of *Abeng* was about the *expression* of critical consciousness rather than *producing* such a consciousness. In this regard, many issues of the paper ran a regular column called "Sufferers Diary," in which ordinary Jamaicans told stories about their lives as sufferers. In the first column, an individual recounted part of his life in four parts: his birth; his days as a sugar worker in different parishes; his leaving to work at the shipyard at the U.S. Naval Base at Guantánamo Bay in Cuba; and finally how he was seized by the police and sent back to Jamaica. In this brief narrative of about a quarter page can be discerned a sense of the migratory processes of the ordinary Jamaican in the early twentieth century. "Sufferers Diary" was not a letters page in the conventional sense, but rather was about putting within the public domain examples of the ordinary lives of Jamaicans. It was also a venue for poetry as an expressive mode of storytelling, illustrated, for example, in an early issue that carried a poem dedicated to the remarkable Ras Dizzy, who wrote a regular column for the paper. In perhaps one of his most provocative columns, Ras Dizzy attempted to dissect the sociocultural phenomena at the time of the "Rude Bwoys." He writes: "The Rudies are searching for that hidden share which is truly belonging to them . . . the way they drink beer and then dance to the beat of the blues show that they are sophisticated human beings searching for freedom and recreational facilities free from the fear of force."[27] The diary gave meaning to the newspaper's bold banner, a quotation from Marcus Garvey, which appeared in the second issue and remained there permanently. The banner read "We Want Our People To Think For Themselves." This suggested a political practice that situated the oppressed and their movements in a different relationship to the conventional understanding of the political and to other social forces, particularly the intelligentsia. In this political perspective, the intellectual did not act from any vanguardist position but rather his/her function was to record, report, and encourage a movement already in motion. From such a frame, radical intellectual work became one of knitting together, linking local and isolated activities into a broader network.[28] For the *Abeng* newspaper, the creation of such a broader network was a critical dimension of its work. Indeed, as one reads all of the issues of the paper, it is clear that, for the editors, the creation of a network of vendors, readers, writers, and correspondents was central if the newspaper was going to be successful in reporting on and facilitating the birth of a new society.

If the newspaper was going to be an instrument of special communication, then ways had to be found to sustain this. The editorial committees were to provide such a mechanism. These committees were to be established at the parish and village levels and were conceptualized as a way to sustain the newspaper as an "organ independent of existing political parties and commercial interests."[29] One editorial notes that "the Editorial Committees will make it possible for the NEWSPAPER to recognize and record all the attempts which our people are making to break out of the continuing oppressive system of colonial control of our resources."[30] Politically, we should observe here that the editorial makes charges about the continuities between colonial and postcolonial Jamaica, arguing that one key feature of this was economic power. Another important feature of the newspaper was the way it supported and was supported by sections of the growing Jamaican musical personalities. Prince Buster took out advertisements in the paper, along with the recording artist Clancy Eccles.[31] Popular music was the terrain on which ordinary Jamaicans attempted to carve out a space for their voices and aspirations. Within the black diaspora, black music has been laden with political and social import. Recognizing this, *Abeng* paid special attention to the venues where dances where held and welcomed advertisements for these dances. One particular advertisement ran like this:

Nite of Black Harmony
With the Mighty Stereo From Spanish Town.[32]

The newspaper also advertised a series of discussions about Jamaican music under the title "Cosmic Series in Musical Groundings: The Years of Freedom Sounds."[33]

Two main figures formulated the political/theoretical positions of the newspaper in its initial stages: Robert Hill and George Beckford. The latter was an economist by academic training and a central member of the New World Group.[34] Hill contends that there was a transformation in Beckford's political outlook when he began to work with the newspaper, arguing that Beckford's work with *Abeng* made him a part of "a revolutionary intellectual tradition of dread thought in the Caribbean."[35] There is, I think, some accuracy to this claim. Beckford, or "G Beck," as he was called, was deeply shaped by the stirrings of radical blackness in Jamaica during this period.[36] This radicalism was expressed in a two-part article, "Why We Are Dispossessed," published in the second and third issues of the newspaper.

The article begins with the claim that the crisis in Jamaican society was "the sour fruit of seeds planted over 130 years ago" and then posits that a great deal of the crisis could be located in foreign ownership of the economy. It noted, "Because of foreign control of our economy, the masses of our people were outcasts in 1838. They were outcasts in 1938. And today, despite seven years of 'Independence,' they are still outcasts."[37] The article was organized around nodal moments in Jamaica's political history and argued that, at each moment, the majority of Jamaicans had been marginalized. Referring to the post-1938 period, Beckford noted that after the uprising, there was "little change in the social order. Black men were still uneducated, had no vote and little or no proper health care. During this time the ruling class began accepting some black men who followed its thinking into its ranks."[38] The import of the final point was Beckford's attempt to begin to define a postcolonial radical blackness. In other words, Beckford was asking how could one now define Black Power in a society where many elements of the political elite were themselves black? To grapple with this point, Beckford in the second article argued that political independence was a myth, since "real power was in the hands of foreign white people who own our basic resources. The social structure is still white on top, brown in the middle and black at the bottom. Black people still have no economic power. White culture still reigns supreme."[39] From Beckford's perspective, two things operated in postcolonial Jamaican society that required a political response of radical blackness: control of economic power by local and foreign whites, and the dominance of Eurocentrism in the hegemonic cultural values of the country. These two elements became bedrock ideas for the advocacy of Black Power in Jamaica and marked its distinctiveness from the various ways in which, as an ideological configuration, it appeared in some other sites of the black diaspora. In the Jamaican case, although political equality had been achieved and issues around formal liberal political representation were still outstanding, there was a native black political elite. What was pressing was the control of the economy, sometimes called the question of economic independence. However, there was also the issue of culture—that is, how the Jamaican symbolic order had been constructed. Whiteness and so-called fair skin in Jamaica was not just representative of economic power but was also cultural power. One of the common features of Black Power everywhere, even when specificities emerged, was that it created in various ways a cultural and symbolic ground for an affirmation of black humanity. This affirmation has been a historic contribution; we recall that both the black colonized and the black in the Americas were constructed as figures of "non-being" by colonial and racial power.

The next few issues of the paper carried articles on Black Power by Marcus Garvey Jr., followed by Walter Rodney's essay on the relevance of Black Power to the Caribbean. From its second issue, the paper regularly carried a column in which, under a drawing of Marcus Garvey, editorials from Garvey's various newspapers were printed. In the third issue, the newspaper carried a two-part series titled "Why Black People Have No Work." By the fifth issue, the paper was proposing a platform for economic development. This nine-point program was based on a national plan, which included: proposals for turning bauxite into alumina and aluminum; irrigation of the parishes of St. Elizabeth, Westmoreland, Trelawny, and St. James; the creation of industries; and the integration of industry, agriculture, tourism, and aluminum into a "vast programme for rural construction."[40] Interestingly, on the very same page, the newspaper carried a program for the liberation of women. The preamble to this program reads: "Abeng stands for complete liberation of the female in our society." The newspaper then promulgated an eight-point program for women's liberation, including men sharing the "burden of housework and child rearing," equal pay for equal work, union rights, and rights of equal participation in the political process. The program also noted that "women are not sexual objects. They are whole and complete human beings. Women's bodies are not commodities for cheap shows and cheap pleasure."[41] This specific attention to the question of the oppression of women in Jamaican society should be noted, since the newspaper did not in its short life return to this issue in any frontal way. The paper also made it clear that, in its view, the two main political parties in Jamaica were tied to the neocolonial project. In its report on the internal PNP leadership elections, the newspaper proclaimed: "The PNP will choose a new leader on Sunday. The choice is between Vivian Blake and Michael Manley . . . [yet] many PNP-ites seem to feel that to choose between Vivian Blake and Michael Manley is being forced to choose between 'black dwag and monkey.' And they are right." Arguing that this was a contest about personalities, not ideas, the article ended with a long quotation from Marcus Garvey reminding people not to trust those who placed themselves "in authority and through selfishness arrogate to themselves all that is good . . . to the exclusion of those who suffer and who place them in their positions of trust."[42]

At the level of black international politics, *Abeng* was attentive to African liberation struggles and carried extensive reports on these in a column called "African BattleLine" written by Omo Ogun (who we know today was the English political scientist Ken Post, who taught African politics at the University of the West Indies–Mona).[43] The newspaper also covered the Black Power movement in the United States, with articles on the Black Panthers and other movements and figures, framing all of these as part of a global black movement for liberation. It carried articles by Huey P. Newton and Amilcar Cabral; a short interview with Stokley Carmichael on Black Power, in which he advocated for a close relationship between African-American and Third World struggles; and an article celebrating the Cuban Revolution. Walter Rodney also published an essay on socialism in Tanzania. It is safe to argue that the clearest ideological statement on Black Power and its meanings for the Caribbean can be discerned from the article published by Walter Rodney in the sixth issue of the paper. In this article, entitled "The Rise of Black Power in the West Indies," Rodney noted that the "West Indies have always been a part of the white capitalist society. We have been the most oppressed section because we were a slave society and the legacy of slavery still rests heavily upon the West Indian black man." Rodney then details the history of the region, paying attention to slave emancipation, the 1865 revolt in Jamaica, and the development of the indentured labor system in the colonial Caribbean. The essay ended with Rodney's now famous definition of Black Power in the Caribbean:

> *Black Power in the West Indies means three closely related things:*
> 1. The break with imperialism which is historically white racist
> 2. The assumption of power by the black masses in the islands
> 3. The cultural reconstruction of the society in the image of the Blacks.[44]

These explicit positions, I would argue, marked a different conception of decolonization from that of constitutional decolonization. They demanded a radical break with colonial power. Rodney was of course at that time operating within the tradition of twentieth-century black radicalism, of which James, Padmore, Fanon, Claudia Jones, and others were central figures. He had embodied within his person this tradition, studying with James in London while being a profound scholar of African history.

Within this context, it was clear to official circles in the United States that Black Power in the region was an important radical movement. Major American newspapers reported on the Caribbean movement, such as the *New York Times* article of 25 April 1970 entitled "What Caribbean Black Power Means." This article identified Black Power as belonging to a "range of radical thought" within the region. Moving from island to island, the article made an attempt to identify some of the key figures and movements. In Trinidad it singled out Geddes Granger, James Millette, and Lloyd Best. In Grenada, it was Lincoln Charles; in Antigua, Tim Hector; and in Jamaica, Dr. Abeng Doonquah and Trevor Munroe (the latter had completed his studies at Oxford and joined *Abeng* on his return.)[45]

All Caribbean progressive groupings at the time were impacted by Black Power and the emergence of this radical movement of blackness. The New World Group, which had been formed earlier, recognized the influence of *Abeng*. Norman Girvan, who was the chair of the Jamaica New World Group at the time, wrote in the *New World Quarterly* that "many New World members have switched their activity to *Abeng* . . . Prior to *Abeng* the New World Group provided an outlet for the energies of people who were interested in engaging in social protest. . . . Now *Abeng* is doing this but doing much better."[46] Lloyd Best, recognized as the driving force behind New World, paid tribute to the African-American call for Black Power in a Black Power Special Issue of the *New World* journal, and noted that within the Caribbean, "Black power therefore expresses itself in large part as a demand for economic power."[47] Critically, the New World editorial in the special issue noted that one possibility of Black Power was that it would be "the development of a NEW MAN, capable of building a new society on the ashes of the old, of not only using the tools left to us by slavery and indentureship, but of fashioning new ones out of our own collective . . . imagination."[48] I think that these examples suffice to make the claim that within the Caribbean, Black Power became for a short while the political banner under which segments of the society felt that full decolonization could be achieved. The demise of that movement therefore marked a watershed in Jamaica's and the region's postcolonial political history.

The Demise of *Abeng*

After thirty-five issues, the newspaper ceased publication in October 1969. A few months before, its printing press had partly burned down; its vendors had been harassed; and many of its "sufferer" supporters had been beaten by the police, and so the newspaper folded and began to reorganize. From its ashes emerged a political grouping whose explicit purpose was to revive the newspaper and develop itself as a group. As a political grouping, Abeng continued a publishing program, with perhaps its most important pamphlet being Joseph Edwards' "Unions versus Menegment."[49] This pamphlet was an outgrowth of the shift by many members of the group to explicit political work with the island's independent trade union movement at the time. As a political grouping, Abeng lasted until April 1974. By the time the group folded, independent radical black politics outside the two-party system in Jamaica had become fragmented as a radical current in Jamaican postcolonial politics.[50] The demise of the group was one sign that the various ideological currents that had gathered into Abeng, first as a newspaper and then as a political grouping, had now been replaced by other conceptions of radical politics. The historical evidence illustrates that the demise of the group Abeng occurred when different currents, ignited by various conceptions of radical black politics, began to consolidate themselves into other political organizations outside the framework of radical black politics. It is important here to define what I think the radical blackness of the period meant. The political ideas of radical blackness circled around the following: first, a politics in which the history of slavery and colonialism in Jamaica and the Caribbean was understood as being explicitly dominated by class and race, and that in post-independence Caribbean societies both race and class were coeval. Secondly, that Afro-Jamaicans belonged to an African diaspora and thus the struggles against imperial power in postcolonial Jamaica were an integral part of an international black struggle. Thirdly, that the political party system and the main political parties were neocolonial in character with a special element of "political tribalism." Fourthly, that issues of what we may loosely call human culture, music, religion, art, and so on were important terrains in which ordinary black people attempted to humanize themselves. Finally, that the intellectual sources for political ideas and action were to be found in a Caribbean and black radical intellectual tradition in the twentieth century. These positions were clearly articulated in the *Abeng* newspaper. However, as the paper collapsed and the group began to splinter into different political currents, various political groupings emerged. So, for example, by 1972, one stream that had worked for a while with the *Abeng* newspaper found itself a political home inside the People's National Party, and by 1974 would be recognized as the PNP left. Other streams congealed into Marxist organizations.[51] This, however, is not to say that independent black politics was totally replaced by either the Marxist-Leninist option (represented by the Workers Party of Jamaica and other groups) or the radical democratic socialist option (represented by the PNP). In particular, Rastafari (for example, the Rastafari Movement Association)[52] and other black nationalist groupings strove mightily to keep alive a tradition of radical postcolonial blackness that had been represented by the *Abeng* newspaper.

Rupert Lewis, one of the founding members of *Abeng* the newspaper and Abeng the political group, has argued, in relation to the origins of the Workers Party of Jamaica, that the fragmentation of Abeng as a political group led to the creation of Leninism in late-twentieth-century Jamaican politics.[53] It did more than that. It signaled a decisive shift in the contours of Jamaican radical postcolonial politics in two ways. First, it opened a political-epistemic space, in which the categories of political analysis about the newly independent nation were now taken from an orthodox and, in many cases, crude reading of Marxism-Leninism, primarily influenced by the theoretical writings from the then Soviet Union. This meant that although there was great attention to concrete Jamaican conditions and many individuals bravely confronted local power, they did so on terms far removed from the symbolic universe of the ordinary Jamaican. Thus, as is often the case in radical politics when there is a clash between courage and analysis, political tragedy occurred. The second matter is that the growth of Leninism, while politically courageous and attractive to many, collapsed post-1983 after the implosion of the Grenadian Revolution. This, along with the defeat of the reformist left in the PNP in the 1980 election, created the conditions where the promise of radical politics quickly became a distant horizon in Jamaica. To fill out the contextual picture, one should of course point to the emergence and rapid consolidation of neoliberalism as an economic model and an ideological system that limited options for social transformation and change and, importantly, framed political discourse around only market possibilities. This in turn created the grounds for both the collapse of creole-nationalist hegemony as well as subaltern configurations that advocated for social transformation on the island.[54] In the end, it may be plausible to argue that the flowering of *Abeng* represented one possibility of certain kinds of radical politics and that, from a historical perspective, its demise meant the closing of a historical trajectory for an explicitly radical politics of blackness in Jamaica for some time.

Notes

Epigraph source: This speech was first published in the Caribbean in *New World (Black Power Special Issue)* Vol. 5. No 4. 1971.

1. The Black Power slogan was first proclaimed by Willie Ricks, a field secretary of the Student Non Violent Coordinating Committee (SNCC) in 1966. The slogan was then popularized by Stokely Carmichael, when he declared to a crowd of some six hundred persons at a mass rally in the Mississippi Delta in the summer of 1966, "We want Black Power."

2. See National Security Action Memorandum No. 44.

3. Fanon, 313.

4. Bogues, "Nationalism and Jamaican Political Thought."

5. Nettleford, 25–26.

6. Intelligence Memorandum, "Black Radicalism in the Caribbean." The report was written in response to a request from the White House for an intelligence study on the relationship between black radicalism in the United States and the Caribbean.

7. There is no doubt that one archive for Jamaica's political history is popular music. Indeed, I would argue that any subaltern history of Jamaica has to be very attentive to this archive, not as a complement to other archives but as a possible way to begin to grapple with the consciousness of the subaltern.

8. For a useful brief discussion of black nationalism in the region in the early twentieth century, see Elkins, *Black Power in the Caribbean*.

9. In particular, I am referring to the forthcoming doctoral thesis of Louis Moyson at the University of the West Indies–Mona and his work on the birth of the Rastafari movement and the story of its founder, Leonard Howell, titled "Leonard Howell and the Rise of RastaFari."

10. Stennet Kerr-Coombs can be seen as representing the Jamaican subaltern intellectual. For a while he was on the editorial committee of that amazing Jamaican radical newspaper of the early twentieth century, *The Jamaica Labour Weekly*. There is a great deal of work to be done unearthing these subaltern intellectuals that litter Jamaican and Caribbean political history.

11. In this regard, the work of Walter Rodney is crucial in representing this current of postcolonial blackness.

12. Stone, 112.

13. For discussions of the Henry Rebellion, see Meeks, *Narratives of Resistance*, and Bogues, *Black Heretics, Black Prophets*. On the Coral Gardens incident and anti-Chinese riots, see Lewis, *Walter Rodney's Intellectual and Political Thought*.

14. For a discussion of this visit, see chapter 5 of Lewis, *Walter Rodney's Intellectual and Political Thought*.

15. For a discussion of the Rodney Riots, see Lewis, *Walter Rodney: 1968 Revisited*.

16. All of these individuals are important in Jamaican and Caribbean postcolonial radical politics and intellectual life. Hill was deeply influenced by the work of C.L.R. James while studying in Canada and is today James's literary executor and a renowned Garvey scholar. Lewis is also a renowned Garvey scholar, as well as the driving force of the recent establishment of Liberty Hall in Jamaica; the late Beckford could be considered one of the region's seminal political economists, and his work in the late 1970s on a non-IMF program for Jamaica remains a nodal moment in popular economic planning; Levy is today one of the most important figures in Jamaican public life, and his intellectual and community work around violence in Jamaica today is seminal.

17. Scott, "The Dialectic of Defeat," 98.

18. Vernon Arnett is one of the least known and yet extraordinary figures in twentieth-century Jamaican politics. For years, he was the general secretary of the PNP. A committed left-wing political figure, he maintained a deep personal and political integrity. In the early 1960s, he was supportive of the Young Socialist League and its relationship to the PNP at the time. His story is in dire need of telling.

19. Editorial, "Why Abeng," 1.

20. Ibid.

21. Ibid.

22. Editorial, "Bread, Work and Human Dignity," 2.

23. Ibid. It should be noted that it does not seem that the editorial committees were very successful and sustainable. They would have needed to be based more firmly on a form of political organization, rather than what seem to have been ideas about loose groupings. Also, there would have been the difficulty of organizing these committees and operating the newspaper simultaneously, unless there was a fairly substantial organization in place. Some of this difficulty I think may have led to the set of articles in the newspaper written by "Blackman," the political alias then used for Trevor Munroe. The theme of these articles was "Time Now to Work Out the Politics of Movement." See, in particular, the article in Vol. 1, No. 30, 2 August 1969.

24. This is not surprising, since the editorial was probably written by Robert Hill, who had been politically shaped by James's political ideas. The ideas are very much in tune with James's conceptions of the role of the newspaper and the emergence of a new society. See James, *Party Politics*.

25. These ideas were further elaborated in James, *Facing Reality* (1958), his study on the 1956 Hungarian Revolution.

26. It is not an accident that the Rodney Riot of October 1968 is sometimes referred to as the Black Power Riot and that the movement up until the PNP's electoral victory in 1972 is seen by many as the Black Power period in Jamaican radical politics. In this period and after the riots, the then Prime Minister, Hugh Shearer, made attempts to define Black Power for the

Jamaican context. The leader of the PNP, Norman Manley, did the same. What is clear is that Michael Manley, who was elected leader of the PNP in 1969, understood that there were serious currents of rebellion in Jamaican society at the time and made an effort to integrate many elements of what was then known as the Black Power movement. These elements included D. K. Duncan and Arnold Bertram, who were included in the party as key figures. The former became the General Secretary of the party and the major figure of the PNP's left in the 1970s. The latter was a critical ideological figure in the formulation of the 1974 program on democratic socialism.

27. "Why Rudies Got to Be Ruder," *Abeng*. Ras Dizzy was an extraordinary poet and painter in Jamaican society. Some of his artwork is in the permanent collection of Jamaica's National Gallery. During 1969 he was sent to prison for nine months.

28. This idea resonates very much with C.L.R. James's position on the relationship between the oppressed social groups and the intellectuals. Among his numerous writings on this subject, see his essays published in Glaberman (ed.), *Marxism for Our Time*.

29. Editorial, "Bread, Work and Human Dignity," *Abeng*, 2.

30. Ibid., 2.

31. For a good discussion of Jamaican music and some of the leading figures, see Bradley, *Bass Culture*.

32. "Cosmic Series in Musical Groundings," *Abeng*.

33. Ibid.

34. For a discussion of the history and ideas of the New World Group, see Meeks and Girvan (eds.), *The Thought of New World*, 2010.

35. Hill, "From *New World* to *Abeng*," 2.

36. For an excellent summary of George Beckford's ideas, see his "Caribbean Man and the Land," 1986.

37. Beckford, *Abeng*, 3.

38. Ibid.

39. Ibid.

40. *Abeng*, 8 March 1969, 2.

41. Ibid.

42. *Abeng*, Vol. 1, No. 2, 8 February 1969.

43. For a discussion of some of Post's writings in *Abeng* on Jamaican history, see Bogues, *History, Decolonization and the Making of Revolution*. For an important discussion of Post's role in radical Jamaican politics, see David Scott's interview with him in *Small Axe*.

44. Rodney, 3.

45. It is interesting that the article paid no attention to the 1969 conference on Black Power in Bermuda. Attended by more than 1,000 delegates, this conference marked a very important moment in the Black Power movement internationally. It was due to the activities of this moment that efforts emerged to host the Sixth Pan-African Congress in Tanzania in 1974. This conference, the first Pan-African conference to be held on the African continent, was a seminal one in the political history of twentieth-century Pan-Africanism. For a discussion of this important conference and Black Power in Bermuda, see Swan, 2009. Some of the figures mentioned in the article had disagreements with each other, but the point of the article was to provide in broad strokes the issues and personalities that the author thought were central to radical Caribbean politics at that moment. Of course, one figure should be singled out, and

that was Tim Hector, who had been deeply influenced by C.L.R. James and was a key figure in the student Black Power movement in Canada.

46. Girvan, 3.

47. Best, "Black Power and the Afro-American."

48. Editorial Statement in *New World Black Power Special Issue,* 1.

49. *Abeng* pamphlet, No. 1, October 1971.

50. The formal dissolution of the Abeng political group occurred on 30 April 1974 in a meeting in which some members of the group presented a statement calling for the group's dissolution. The four members who presented this statement were Trevor Munroe, Rupert Lewis, Richard Byles and the late Michael Kelly. Defining themselves as the "Marxist-Leninists in Abeng Group," these individuals argued that the Abeng group consisted of "petty-bourgeois revolutionary democrats. . . . petty-bourgeois democrats and petty-bourgeois liberals." This political appellation followed a line of thinking about the character of national liberation struggles that had been posited by the Soviet Union and popularized by the Soviet theorist Ken Brutens. These four individuals' statement ended by arguing that "Staying together on the basis of publishing a revolutionary democratic newspaper retards the development of the democratic and Marxist-Leninist trends and therefore precludes the possibility of doing so." All citations taken from "Statement to Abeng Group," April 1974, a document in the author's possession.

51. The individuals who prepared the previously described statement formed the nucleus of what later became the Workers Party of Jamaica (WPJ). Other members of the group went in different directions: one member, Paul Robertson, joined the PNP; others—Dennis Daley, Richard Small, and Ronald Thwaites—went into legal and political work around human rights; others also joined the WPJ over time (Mark Figueroa, Peter Figueroa, and Horace Levy), while others (Anthony Bogues) attempted to form a Marxist grouping (the Revolutionary Marxist Collective, later to be the Revolutionary Marxist League), which was influenced by the Caribbean radical political tradition, particularly the writings of C.L.R. James.

52. This grouping was one of the most important explicitly political Rastafari groupings of the period. It was led by Ras De Silva, who was an active trade unionist and leader of an independent workers union at the time, and Ras Historian, who as a figure represents a long history of Jamaican subaltern intellectuals who publish small booklets and journals and actively seek to keep alive a radical black subaltern tradition.

53. Lewis, "The Fragmentation of Abeng."

54. For a discussion of the collapse of both hegemony and subaltern radical frames in Jamaica, see Meeks, *Narratives of Resistance,* and Bogues, "Politics, Nation and Postcolony," 1–30.

Bibliography

Beckford, G. "Why We Are Dispossessed," *Abeng,* Vol 1. No. 2, 8 February 1969.

———. "Caribbean Man and the Land," *Transition* (Institute of Development Studies: University of Guyana), Issue 14, 1986.

Best, L. "Black Power and the Afro-American in Trinidad and Tobago" in *New World, Black Power Special Issue,* 1971, 3–33.

Blackman. "Time Now to work out the Politics of Movement," *Abeng*, Vol. 1, No. 30, 2 August 1969.

Bogues, A. "Nationalism and Jamaican Political Thought" in K.E.A. Monteith and G. Richards, *Jamaica in Slavery and Freedom: History, Heritage and Culture*, Kingston: University of the West Indies Press, 2002, 363–87.

———. "Politics, Nation and Postcolony: Caribbean Inflections," *Small Axe*, No. 11, March 2002, 1–30.

———. *Black Heretics, Black Prophets: Radical Political Intellectuals*, New York: Routledge, 2003.

———. "History, Decolonization and the Making of Revolution: Reflections on Writing the Popular History of the Jamaican Events of 1938," *Interventions* Vol. 12 (1), 2010.

Bradley, L. *Bass Culture: When Reggae Was King*, London: Viking, 2009.

"Cosmic Series in Musical Groundings: The Years of Freedom Sounds," *Abeng*, Vol. 1, No. 21, 21 June 1969.

Dizzy, Ras. "Why Rudies Got to Be Ruder," *Abeng*, Vol. 1, No. 27, 2 August 1969.

Editorial, "Bread, Work and Human Dignity," *Abeng*, Vol. 1, No. 1, 1 February 1969.

Editorial, "Why Abeng," *Abeng*, Vol. 1, No. 1, 1 February 1969.

Editorial Statement, *New World Black Power Special Issue*, 1971.

Edwards, J. "Unions versus Menegment," Abeng pamphlet, No. 1. October 1971.

Elkins, W. F. *Black Power in the Caribbean*, New York: Revisionist Press, 1977.

Fanon, F. *The Wretched of the Earth*, New York: Grove Press, 1963.

Girvan, N. "Mona New World Report: Abeng, Moko and New World: A Review," *New World Quarterly*, Vol. 5, Nos. 1&2, 1969, 1–4.

Glaberman, M. (ed.) *Marxism for Our Times*, Jackson: University Press of Mississippi, 1999.

Hill, R. "From *New World* to *Abeng*: George Beckford and the Horn of Black Power in Jamaica, 1968–1970," *Small Axe*, 11: 3, October 2007, 1–15.

Intelligence Memorandum, "Black Radicalism in the Caribbean," Directorate of Intelligence CIA: Washington DC, July 1970.

James, C.L.R. *Facing Reality*, Detroit: Correspondence Committee, 1958.

———. "Black Power," *New World (Black Power Special Issue)* Vol. 5. No. 4, 1971, 8–14.

———. *Party Politics in the West Indies*, San Juan, Trinidad: Imprint, 1984 (reprint).

Lewis, R. *Walter Rodney: 1968 Revisited*, Kingston: Canoe Press, 1994.

———. *Walter Rodney's Intellectual and Political Thought*, Kingston: University of the West Indies Press, 1998.

———. "The Fragmentation of Abeng and Its Consequence: The Case of the WPJ as a Variant of Jamaican Radicalism," unpublished paper, 1998.

Meeks, B. *Narratives of Resistance: Jamaica, Trinidad, the Caribbean*, Kingston: University of the West Indies Press, 2000.

Meeks, B. and Girvan, N. (eds.) *The Thought of New World: The Quest for Decolonization*, Kingston: Ian Randle Press, 2010.

National Security Action Memorandum, No. 44, April 25, 1961 (Declassified, 4 September 1976).

Nettleford, R. *Identity, Race and Protest in Jamaica*, New York: William Morrow, 1972.

Rodney, W. "The Rise of Black Power in the West Indies," *Abeng*, Vol. 1, No. 5, 8 March 1969.

Scott, D. "No Saviour From On High: An Interview with Ken Post," *Small Axe*, 4, September 1998, 85–157.

———. "The Dialectic of Defeat: An Interview with Rupert Lewis," *Small Axe*, 5: 2, September 2001, 85–178.

"Statement to Abeng Group," document in author's possession, April 1974.

Stone, C. *Class, Race and Political Behaviour*, Kingston: Institute of Social and Economic Research, 1973.

Swan, Q. *Black Power in Bermuda: The Struggle for Decolonization*, New York: Palgrave, 2009.

4

The February Revolution (1970) as a Catalyst for Change in Trinidad and Tobago

BRINSLEY SAMAROO

The February (or Black Power) Revolution in Trinidad and Tobago can be defined as the efflorescence of a movement in which thousands of citizens revolted against the status quo and demanded substantive changes in governance. The view among those who challenged the existing system was that the black-led government of the People's National Movement (PNM) had concentrated on capturing the administrative machinery of power but had left economic control in the hands of the colonial (European) and neocolonial (North American) capitalist classes and the local comprador bourgeoisie. Lloyd Best, of Trinidad's Tapia House group, viewed the events of February 1970 as the beginning of a revolution, expressive of a powerful renewal of democracy in Trinidad and Tobago:

> What you will notice right here, right under our noses, is being created a new and exciting form of democracy. Five, ten, fifteen, twenty thousand citizens have been marching to the bugle call: power, power, to the people. Young men rush to sell political newspapers, old women rush to buy them. As the militants demand the power, even the little children take up the chant: power to the people! Everywhere the people are holding their heads high in confidence, tall in hope . . . what we have had in the last few years is revolution, nothing less.[1]

This chapter traces the emergence of the Black Power movement in Trinidad and Tobago, locating it as part of a long historical struggle for meaningful participation that has its roots in the nineteenth century. It argues that for all of its warts, the February Revolution changed the course of Trinidad and

Tobago's development in a number of discernible ways. In assessing this impact, three areas will be highlighted here: (a) the emergence of armed Black Power in the form of the National Union of Freedom Fighters (NUFF); (b) the effect of the Black Power movement on the country's Indian population; and (c) the response of Prime Minister Eric Williams, and how he used the revolution to push through long-delayed reforms. In all of these areas, the events of 1970 and beyond played a significant role in shaping the contours of politics and development in postindependence Trinidad and Tobago.

Background to Revolution

In 1962, Trinidad and Tobago gained its independence after a long period of Crown Colony governance, instituted since the beginning of the nineteenth century. From the 1830s, there began a long struggle for the opening up of that system, but those requests came primarily from the small white elite that constituted the merchant and planter oligarchy. For this elite group, representative government meant increasing their power to enhance their investments in the colony. By the early twentieth century, the black and brown working classes started to assert their presence in the movement toward representative government through organizations such as the Workingmen's Association, founded in 1897 and reorganized in 1907. Under the leadership of Captain Arthur Andrew Ciprani (1875–1945), who emerged as leader during the 1920s, the association morphed into the Trinidad Labour Party (TLP) in 1932. Five years later, the working-class movement, under the new leadership of Tubal Uriah "Buzz" Butler (1897–1977) and Adrian Cola Rienzi (1905–72), had developed sufficiently to bring the economy to a halt and to win significant concessions from the colonial regime. The labor uprisings of 1935 to 1937, which began in the sugar and oil belts of southern Trinidad, soon enveloped the whole island and spread to Tobago. These disturbances became an example to the rest of the Caribbean, from Belize to the Guyanas, and compelled the British government to send the Moyne Commission in 1938 to make recommendations for the restoration of tranquility so that the colonies could continue as safe havens for European investments.

In addition to a rapidly developing trade union movement in the Caribbean region, there were other forces at work providing information and inspiration to Caribbean peoples. There was, for example, the New Negro Movement, whose Caribbean manifestation was Marcus Garvey's Universal Negro Improvement Association (UNIA), founded in Jamaica in 1914.[2] The period of the First World War (1914–18) was a major early catalyst in further stirring up the West Indian imagination. Black West Indians in the theaters of war suffered racial discrimination to the extent that they could not be deployed in warfare against white soldiers but could only bring up the rear in cleaning toilets, carrying weapons, and digging trenches. Their presence in Europe during the Russian Revolution of 1917, and their observance of syndicalism in France, sharpened their intellects, leading them to take active leadership roles upon their return to the Caribbean. This heightened consciousness meant that Garveyism took deep roots in the Caribbean, even after Garvey's departure for the United States in 1916. During and after the First World War, the Trinidad Workingmen's Association maintained close links with the Garveyite movement, whose activities were regularly featured in the association's publications *The Argos* and *Labour Leader*. In 1937, Garvey visited Trinidad at the invitation of his adoring followers, but his movements were very restricted by the colonial administration, which understood well the implications of the visit.[3] These limitations to Garvey's activities, however, did not squash the movement in Trinidad and Tobago or in the rest of the Caribbean. In the postindependence period, this underground movement would emerge with renewed vigor in the form of Black Power.

The post–World War Two period enabled the Caribbean and indeed the wider world to breathe easier. Under strict orders to maintain the peace because of wartime conditions between 1939 and 1945, trade unions and Garveyites held their fire while they organized behind the scenes. With the end of the war, everyone came into the open, demanding change. New leaders arose, such as Marryshow in Grenada, Jagan and Burnham in Guyana, Manley and Bustamante in Jamaica and, in 1956, Eric Williams in Trinidad and Tobago. These leaders gave hope to colonial Caribbean people who dreamed of owning their oil, sugar, bauxite, cocoa, and bananas. They envisioned their children seeking education and aspiring to employment in the higher echelons of service from which they had hitherto been barred, and they believed that under the new dispensation they could freely inhabit the recreational spaces in their homelands. But independence during the 1960s did not bring these desired changes.

In Trinidad and Tobago, the upsurge of dissatisfaction came earlier and was more intense than in the rest of the Caribbean. One explanation for this lies in the nation's relatively wealthier status by comparison with the rest of the region. In this context, the contrast between the small wealthy class and the large mass of poor workers was at its starkest. Inequalities based on ethnicity were likewise more visible than in other Caribbean states. The ostentatious life of the wealthy remained a constant taunt to the majority of citizens.

This is sharply depicted in Monique Roffey's 2009 novel, *The White Woman on the Green Bicycle*, whose main character remembers the pampered life of her French-born mother and English father, who came to Trinidad in 1956 and remained there during and after the events of 1970. The following extract depicts the discrimination that was evident, even after independence, at the Trinidad Country Club, a traditional watering hole for expatriates:

> At the country club whites played, blacks worked. No one asked questions. Neither knew nor cared about each other. Unnatural but accepted; the rules had been written long ago, in blood, in sweat. An aloofness existed in the club's atmosphere, a keep your eye averted code of conduct prevailed. The large Indian community were absent; they neither worked nor played at the club. An official colour bar existed: no black human was allowed membership. But the black staff, in their own silent way, made us pay for this.[4]

It is no surprise that the country club, which was besieged and looted during the February Revolution of 1970, was one of the first targets of Trinidad's Black Power protests.

The year 1969 witnessed the coming together of many streams of protests. In February 1969, West Indian students at the Sir George Williams University in Montreal, frustrated by the alleged discriminatory marking practices of a biology professor, occupied and set fire to the university's computer center. In January 1970, ten Trinidadian students stood among a group that was brought to trial in Canada. The charges included arson, which carried a possible penalty of life imprisonment.[5] In 1969, the National Joint Action Committee (NJAC) was formed, partly in response to the events in Canada. NJAC was spearheaded mainly by undergraduates at the St. Augustine campus of the University of the West Indies, and as it took shape in early 1970, there were regular discussions on the campus, during which information and analysis were provided by activists of the Tapia House movement, by young lecturers on the campus, and by activists from outside the university. Significantly, deliberate efforts were made to include East Indian students and lecturers on the campus. After this initial mobilization, NJAC took the action beyond the walls of the university. Groups of activists went out into the communities "rapping" with disillusioned youths in San Fernando (where Young Power was vibrant), in the hills of Laventille and Morvant, and with the brethren in Sangre Grande. When, in late 1969, Canadian Governor-General Roland Michener sought to enter the St. Augustine campus, NJAC organized a massive protest, preventing Michener and his host, Prime Minister Eric

Williams, from entering the campus. The leaders of NJAC were mainly the children of working- and middle-class parents who had supported the ascendancy of Williams's People's National Movement since 1956. Among these leaders were Makandaal Daaga (then Geddes Granger), who was pursuing a degree in the social sciences in 1970, Khafra Kambon (then Dave Darbeau), Carl Blackwood, Aiyegoro Ome, Kelshall Bodie, and Russell Andalcio. In preventing Michener from entering the campus, the demonstrators made it clear that they stood in solidarity with the arrested Caribbean students in Montreal. The Sir George Williams confrontation thus was the trigger for the uprising in Trinidad and Tobago.

The 1970 Crisis

The chronology of the February Revolution has been extensively recorded elsewhere and hence will not be detailed here.[6] However, some major events will be remembered, since these form an important part of this narrative. On 26 February 1970, NJAC mounted a demonstration in support of the students on trial in Canada. This first demonstration took place at the premises of the Royal Bank of Canada, from whence the demonstration moved to the Roman Catholic Cathedral a short distance away. One day later, nine of the leaders were arrested; these arrests set in motion a wave of public protests, which continued until the end of April, by which time the state had gained the upper hand through a carrot-and-stick approach. March and April marked the height of the revolution. On 3 March, for example, NJAC conducted well-attended meetings in Curepe, St. James, and San Fernando; similar meetings continued at other venues in Trinidad and in Tobago. On 12 March 1970, NJAC was able to organize the first of two decisive marches to the county of Caroni, the heartland of the Indian sugar belt. Some six thousand marchers left Port of Spain, and four thousand additional persons had joined them by the time the march reached Caroni. The second march, now led by thousands of sugar workers, started in Couva on 20 April, with the intention of reaching Port of Spain the next day. This march met with considerable police opposition and was finally squelched by the declaration of a state of emergency on the evening of 21 April. The significance of these attempts to forge unity between the two major ethnic groups will be discussed below.

Throughout March, the movement gathered strength, extending its reach to Diego Martin and Arima, where NJAC held large meetings on 24 and 28 March, respectively, followed by another at Mayaro in the southeast of the island on the 29th. While Williams and his advisers sized up the situation on a daily basis, the protests escalated. On 1 April, NJAC met with the Association of Steelbandsmen, ardent erstwhile supporters of the ruling PNM, while on 4 April, more large marches took place from Port of Spain to Maraval and from the city center to Belmont. On that day too, the powerful Oilfield Workers Trade Union (OWTU) came out in support of the revolution. At the same time, Tobago erupted into mass demonstrations. On 6 April, the confrontation worsened when Basil Davis, a young NJAC activist, was shot dead by a policeman. His funeral on 9 April drew some thirty thousand mourners, who followed the procession from Port of Spain to San Juan, commanding the police to give way as the procession crossed Morvant Junction on its eastward cortege. By this time, other civic groups had joined the protest. The Tapia House group held its first meeting at its Tunapuna parliament, Auzonville Park on 19 March, and James Millette took his newly formed United National Independence Party (UNIP) to a public meeting in Woodford Square, now christened the People's Parliament, on 12 April. At the same time, radical groups in San Fernando mobilized their forces.

The movement gained further momentum when, on 13 April, a leading member of Williams's cabinet, A.N.R. Robinson, resigned from the government (prompting his former PNM colleagues to brand him Another Negro Rebel, after his initials). Public anger deepened on 15 April, as the state ordered that no airlines should carry Stokely Carmichael (who was due to visit neighboring Guyana) to his Trinidad homeland. It was during this period of heightened unrest that the leaders of NJAC, in collaboration with the university-based Society for the Propagation of Indian Culture (SPIC) announced the proposed march to Caroni and back to Port of Spain over the two days of 20 and 21 April. The fact that this second march was supported by East Indians and that a large meeting was held in the sugar town of Couva on the first day signaled to Williams that the matter had gone too far. On that very evening, he called a state of emergency and arrested the leaders, incarcerating them at Nelson Island off Trinidad's northwestern peninsula—the very place where Uriah "Buzz" Butler, a national hero of the labor struggle, had been jailed in 1937. The arrest of the leaders of the Black Power movement and the declaration of emergency powers put an end to the overt, generally peaceful stage of the revolution.

The Rise of the National Union of Freedom Fighters

Despite the incarceration of NJAC and other Black Power leaders, a small group of youthful revolutionaries decided to continue the struggle by violent means. Comprised mainly of disenchanted middle-class youths, the National Union of Freedom Fighters (NUFF) felt that the February Revolution had fallen far short of national expectations. In their view, the structural violence of the status quo and the persistence of a hierarchical system of inequality remained unchanged, despite the months of protest. About three dozen of these youths took to the hills of the northern range, from whence they waged guerrilla warfare against the establishment in the mode of the maroons, who had resisted slavery by escaping into the hills and carrying out raids on the plantations.[7] NUFF's deployment of guerrilla tactics was therefore not without historical precedent. In the context of the twentieth-century Caribbean, such precedents included the Henry Rebellion in Jamaica[8] and of course the Cuban Revolution, fought from the Sierra Maestra—so similar, as Fidel Castro later remarked, to the hills and valleys of Trinidad's northern range.

There are two major sources of information on the activities of NUFF. The more balanced one is the bravely researched account by David Millette, who was present when NUFF attacked from the hills. Subsequently, he interviewed a number of participants who were still alive after their leaders' violent deaths. Subsequent to Millette's account, a former Commissioner of Police, Eustace Bernard, gave an insider's view of the uprising, drawing from police records as well as his own familiarity with the events. Bernard's account underlines the manner in which Williams was kept constantly informed about the activities of the Black Power marches of 1970. At one stage, Bernard recounts, the Prime Minister intervened to secure the admission of a former NUFF activist to a British university in order to protect her from erstwhile colleagues who regarded her as a police informant.[9]

According to Millette, the major ideological point of difference between NJAC and NUFF was the latter's belief that NJAC had lost its effectiveness and that the organization was only talking.[10] The high rate of unemployment persisted, foreign domination of the economy was rampant, and police brutality, unleashed in 1970, was on the increase. Despite these critiques, the two organizations continued to interact during the period of violence. Many NUFF members had regularly attended "rap sessions" organized by NJAC since late 1969 and continued to relate to that body. When NUFF leader Guy Harewood was killed by police, NJAC arranged a colorful Black Power funeral for the fallen hero.[11]

The ideological leanings of NUFF might also be traced in the wide range of mainly leftist literature discovered by the police on their raids on NUFF compounds. This included *Guerrilla Warfare* by Che Guevara, *A West Indian State* by the Guyanese socialist leader Cheddi Jagan, Nelson Mandela's

No Easy Walk to Freedom, and the Trinidad-based United Revolutionary Organization's *Victory for the Left*. NUFF held regular talk sessions, at which its members discussed ways of radically reforming society and, from my personal experience, maintained regular contact with lecturers and activists at the University of the West Indies, regularly collecting copies of the student magazine *Embryo*.

In the end, however, NUFF failed in its mission to engineer a mass uprising, because the level of deprivation in the nation was not as widespread as it had believed. Despite the inequalities, there was enough for the majority of the population, particularly with the continued export of oil and natural gas. Most people believed the state's propaganda that these were communists bent on violent overthrow of the country, and many believed that NUFF's activities were more criminal than revolutionary. Thus there was no popular protest as eighteen young persons were killed by the police, who themselves lost three of their colleagues. As Millette argues, NUFF's energies were ultimately smothered by constant police harassment and by the rise of the United Labour Front (ULF), which absorbed some of the left-leaning elements and energies.[12] Eric Williams's analysis of NUFF will be discussed below.

East Indians in the February Revolution

Conscious efforts to include the Indian community within the Black Power movement had been initiated before the historic Caroni marches, as NJAC began to organize itself on the St. Augustine university campus. However, the effort at unity so bravely attempted by the NJAC leadership confronted substantial institutional barriers. For one thing, in Trinidad, as in South Asia, Cyprus, West Africa, and other parts of the Caribbean, European colonialism had pursued a deliberate policy of divide and rule, with lasting consequences for Afro-Indo relations. This policy was re-created after the 1857 Indian revolt, when Hindus and Muslims had united and nearly overthrew the British Raj. In Trinidad and Guyana, the presence of two major ethnic groups provided an ideal objective situation for the operation of divisive politics. For example, in the postmortem to the 1884 Mohurram Massacre, when some sixteen celebrants were killed by police and dozens more seriously injured, the ruling class warned that there had been a dangerous degree of black ("creole") participation in this "coolie" commemoration. The official report of inquiry spoke ominously of a possible reenactment in Trinidad of the 1857 Indian revolt.[13] Eighty years later, brutal suppression was again deployed against the 1937 labor uprising, when sugar and oil came together under the joint ethnic leadership of Tubal Uriah Butler and Adrian Cola Rienzi. After 1937, determined efforts were made by the colonial regime to keep the races apart.

Independent Trinidad and Tobago emerged out of this fractured framework, which found expression in the emergence of, on the one side, the African-dominated People's National Movement, and, on the other, the Indian-dominated People's Democratic Party (PDP) and its successive reincarnations. While the maximum leadership of both those parties took pains to deny their ethnic bases, the reality was different. The year 1970 therefore saw the two ethnic leaders, Williams and Bhadase Sagan Maraj, cooperate to preserve their respective turfs.[14] Against this background, one can understand the cautious, often ambivalent Indian response to Black Power.

Some Indians, however, did show enthusiasm for the new movement. At the St. Augustine campus, the Society for the Propagation of Indian Culture (SPIC) became actively involved in the February Revolution, assisting in the organization of the Caroni marches. This student support was buttressed by widespread dissatisfaction among the sugar workers, who were particularly angry that their union, under the leadership of Maraj, was dragging its feet in negotiations with the British-based owners of the industry. Sugar workers were eager to rumble! For these reasons, there was no hostility demonstrated toward the NJAC-led foray into Caroni on 12 March, nor for the massive meeting held in Couva on 20 March. The significance of this historic attempt to link up the mainly Afro-Trinidadian urban movement with the rural population of Indian sugar workers was not lost on Prime Minister Williams. Ken Parmasad, a leading light in SPIC and one of the organizers of the Caroni marches, contends that the second aborted march to and from Caroni was the major reason for the government's declaration of a state of emergency after two months of demonstrations: "When on April 21st, 1970 the state of emergency was declared and the full might of the state was to be unleashed against the people, a fairly large contingent of Indian sugar workers were already mobilized to begin a march to Port-of-Spain. The state obviously saw the dreadful implication of this scenario and moved quickly to squash it."[15] Sensing the seriousness of the rapidly escalating movement, Williams sought and obtained the help of Maraj in suppressing the Caroni marches. Williams subsequently thanked Maraj publicly for that support.

While some Indians were sympathetic to the Black Power movement, they also questioned their place within what they regarded as its primarily "black" symbolic universe. As I wrote at the time, "The Trinidad Indian feels hardly welcome in a power demonstration when he knows that the clenched fist is really borrowed from the Black Panthers in the U.S., a purely Negro group, or when he sees the local advocates of power wearing their dashikis, a symbol of identification with Africa."[16] There was also the recurring problem, still unresolved, that Indian-Trinbagonians do not consider themselves as black. During the intense debates of the 1970s, most black activists could not understand the Indian's unwillingness to identify with blackness, and this proved to be a major break within the movement.[17] Eric Williams also inadvertently contributed to the Indian's reluctance to embrace Black Power. His repeated references to the term "Black Power" in speeches of the 1970s, coupled with his frequent claims of assistance to black enterprises, caused further alienation of Indians, who saw the Prime Minister as a black leader pushing a black agenda. Williams no doubt interpreted black empowerment as applying to the entire nonwhite sector, but in the context of the time, that admonition was narrowly interpreted. The debate about broadening the political definition of black is as alive today as it was in April 1970. While the debate continues, the calypsonian Valentino, a genuine voice of the people, keeps up the refrain of ethnic unity:

> But we must all try to bridge the gap
> My Indian and Afro brother
> Remember one hand could never clap
> So let we unite at once and come together.[18]

In placing the discourse of blackness at the forefront of national debate, the February Revolution has had another profound effect on the Indian-Trinbagonian community. The search for and debate about black identity, which was a major element of the revolution, stimulated a strong response from this group. Ken Parmasad has argued that this pride in Indian ancestry was present well before 1970. Divali celebrations, for example, were belatedly allowed on the St. Augustine campus after intense agitation by SPIC during 1968 and 1969.[19] Religious organizations such as the Sanatan Dharma Maha Sabha, the Arya Prathinidhi Sabha, the Trinidad Muslim League, and the Anjuman Sunnat-al-Jamaat Association had also been promoting their heritage for at least two decades before 1970. The 1950s had witnessed a burgeoning of Hindu and Muslim schools, breaking the hegemony of the Presbyterians. The bold assertion of Black Power as part of the February Revolution gave an added boost to the assertion of an Indian-derived identity. This was a source of deep disappointment to Afro-Saxons such as Eric Williams, who had chastised the American anthropologist Morton Klass for his assertion that the Indian identity was increasing rather than declining in the age of independence.[20] Williams's social engineering was geared toward the melting-pot amalgamation of all cultural streams. The East Indian agenda from the 1970s has been characterized by a host of identity markers, such as a return to meaningful Indian names, increased attendance at Hindi and Urdu classes, an increasing number of Indian radio and television stations, pride in Indian dress and cuisine, the search for ancestral roots, and a greater turn toward India for business and education. India's recent ascendancy, alongside China, as an economic force, has strengthened those inspirational ties. Because of the religious nature of Indian culture, this regeneration has been particularly expressed in the widespread support for a large number of religious organizations in Trinidad and in Tobago. There are frequent visits by South Asian missionaries, religious groups, and cultural delegations, and we are seeing the establishment of new venues for religious and cultural activities. In this way, Trinidad and Tobago has become a model for the peaceful coexistence of many cultural streams.

Williams's Response to the February Revolution

It is instructive to examine Williams's handling of the turbulence of 1970. Selwyn Ryan claims that after 26 February 1970, Williams built a wall around his house and isolated himself for a full month before he finally spoke to the nation.[21] The strategy, Ryan believes, was to wait until the Black Power movement had either exhausted its welcome, or overreached itself and thereby provoke a backlash to his benefit. Others contest the view that Williams isolated himself. There is evidence that Williams always relied on a coterie of "grassroots" supporters who alerted him about the movement on the ground. This informal group, whose members changed over the years, became one of the institutions of PNM governance, created by Williams and later taken up by his successors. To the observant politician, members of this informal group could be easily spotted standing next to Williams at public meetings, appearing to engage him in conversation so as to keep the masses and their myriad problems away from "the Chief." During the February Revolution of 1970, Williams was in touch with the trade union and political leader Bhadase Maraj, who saw it as his duty to protect the "Indian" community from the advocates of Black Power. Another member of this advisory group was the veteran politician Ferdie Ferreira, now eighty, an ardent supporter of Williams since the 1960s. In his public statements, as well as in an interview with me on 25 July 2010, Ferreira recounted that from late February 1970,

Williams regularly met with a group consisting of Ivan Williams, Carl Tull, Carlton Gomes, Irwin Merritt, and Bertie Ballantyne. This group walked among the protestors collecting pamphlets, gathering information about future events, and seeking those leaders who could be bought out.[22] In this way, the Chief was able to find out what was taking place on the ground. He could therefore avoid the frantic advice of most of his ministers who saw the communist bogey or wanted him to call an immediate state of emergency. In June 1970, Commissioner of Police Eustace Bernard returned to his post after a leave. His recollection of Williams's grasp of the situation is instructive: "In July 1970 and throughout the remainder of the State of Emergency, the Prime Minister knew as much about matters pertaining to the security of the State as the Commissioner of Police. In fact he was even more informed than the Commissioners as he had private sources not available to me."[23] The existence of such nonofficial information-gathering bodies is supported by the late economist and political activist Dennis Pantin, who wrote of the simultaneous existence of two cabinets since 1970: "The first is the official, publicly announced cabinet consistent with the constitution. The second and real cabinet tends to be made up of trusted lieutenants of the prime minister."[24] By these means of intelligence-gathering, Williams was able to frame his public responses appropriately, appearing conciliatory at times, even when action on the ground was otherwise. In this way too, he was able to influence the course of events—for example, in persuading an intermediary to dissuade the Roman Catholic archbishop from his intention to join the African-Indian solidarity march to Caroni on 20 April.

An examination of Williams's immediate responses to the February Revolution during March and April 1970 reveals that, for all his condemnation of the uprising, he was pleased that such public protestation had taken place. In fact, the protests gave Williams the opening he needed to implement a wide range of reforms that he considered necessary but that he had been prevented from enacting by a host of constraints. Indeed, it was Williams's view that he had already done much to liberate his people from the thralldom of colonization; thus he felt that there was considerable ingratitude in these demonstrations of dissatisfaction. On 23 March, in his first public broadcast in response to the demonstrations, Williams highlighted a long list of his government's achievements and questioned why, after all of these, there was still dissatisfaction:

We have consciously sought to promote Black economic power. We have in five years created 1,523 Black small farmers over the country;

we have encouraged small businesses in manufacturing and tourism . . . We have brought free secondary education within the reach of thousands of disadvantaged families who could not dream of it in 1956 . . . Our Public Service, at all levels, is staffed almost entirely by nationals mainly Black . . . We have created no fewer than 68,200 new jobs between 1956 and 1969.[25]

The Prime Minister then provided his interpretation of the reasons for the protests. Firstly, he argued, there "was a political element seeking to use the legitimate demonstrations for its own ends . . . nothing in Trinidad and Tobago is complete without our unsuccessful politicians, who sought to jump on the bandwagon."[26] Secondly, there was not sufficient public awareness of government policy or of its implementation—an information void the government would now take steps to correct. Thirdly, public anger was blamed on the slow pace of change: "administrative procedures," Williams lamented, "are slow and bureaucratic."[27]

In this first address, Williams's tone was very conciliatory. The demands of the demonstrations for black dignity, black consciousness, and black economic power were, he said, "perfectly legitimate and are entirely in the interest of the community as a whole. If this is Black Power, then I am for Black Power."[28] On 3 May, Williams again gave a nationwide broadcast, seeking, he said, to give a clearer picture of what had really transpired. He strongly reemphasized the difference between the young idealists who had legitimate grievances and what he saw as the other bunch, comprised of trade unionists, university lecturers, students, and some politicians who wanted to take over the government by "unconstitutional means and armed revolution."[29] He claimed that plans were afoot for the beginning of a series of strikes among sugar workers, water supply workers, oil workers, and others in the public service. In order to forestall this calamity, he had advised the acting Governor General to call a state of emergency on 20 April 1970.[30] In Ferdie Ferreira's opinion, a major factor in Williams's decision to call the emergency was the shooting of Basil Davis by the police on 6 April. The size of Davis's funeral and the fact that the leaders of the march had ordered the police to desist from blocking the procession—events reported by Williams's men on the ground—hastened his decision.[31]

In his address of 3 May, Williams also spoke publicly of the mutiny that had taken place at the army base at Teteron on the Chaguaramas peninsula, in the wake of the emergency. In order to quell this uprising, the government had accessed arms from the United States and Venezuela. The mutiny had been suppressed and charges laid against the mutinous officers. Having established the seriousness of the events, Williams then used the rest of the speech to list a number of initiatives that were now to be undertaken by his government. These included the reconsideration of the role and function of the defense force, aid to various Black Power enterprises, such as the steel band movement, the establishment of cooperatives, the setting up of a workers' bank, and other similar projects.[32] The civil service was to be reorganized and an ombudsman appointed. As a final sop, Williams announced the lifting of the curfew in the rural areas. One week later, on 10 May, Williams again addressed the nation, this time concentrating on cabinet changes and reform of the public service. He used this opportunity to remove a number of nonperforming cabinet ministers ("millstones," as he called them) and bring in persons from outside the parliament who were then made senators. Significantly, he added to his already extensive portfolio a new Ministry of National Security and a National Security Council, of which he was chair; he took on responsibility for External Affairs and Tobago Affairs, adding to his previous positions as Minister of Finance, Planning, and Development, as well as Community Development and Youth Affairs. He would also chair a weekly meeting of the Civil Service Advisory Committee. The demonstrations of 1970 thus gave the prime minister the opportunity to recentralize government, focusing power in his hands. The leader of the Maha Sabha, Bhadase Maraj, was rewarded with the privilege of nominating an appointee to the Senate.[33]

For the rest of 1970, Williams concentrated on warning the youths against being misled by power seekers in pursuing their legitimate aspirations and in giving publicity to past and proposed measures aimed at controlling the commanding heights of the economy. Addressing the Caribbean Cane-Farmers Association on 17 August 1970, he reminded his audience that in 1968 the government had bought out the Orange Grove sugar estate and had made a decision to take the majority holding in Trinidad's largest sugar estate, Caroni: "Thus the national take-over of the sugar industry in Trinidad and Tobago and the substitution of local for external decision-making represent the total reversal of four centuries of Caribbean history."[34] Up to the end of 1970, Williams demonstrated an eagerness for reconstruction, now buffeted by the popular demands of the February Revolution. In his Independence Day address to the nation, on 31 August 1970, he proclaimed that "we have to redefine our relations with foreign capital" and emphasized the need to utilize the "accumulated experience" and the entrepreneurial talent possessed by the local business sector. In order to give effect to the "power to the people" slogan, the Prime Minister now promised financial and technical assistance to entrepreneurs and a workers bank to make loans for "participation in the economy of the ordinary people, through small businessmen." From henceforth, he said, indigenous art and culture would be promoted as the nation tried "to throw off the insidious penetration of North American materialist values." In his concluding remarks, Williams emphasized three areas to which the nation should direct its urgent attention: (a) recognition by youths of the contribution of older members of the society; (b) recognition by the elders of the idealism and creative capacity of the youths; and (c) the development of a national cohesion, which did not exist.[35]

In the meantime, other sectors of society reacted in diverse ways. The majority of white creole society, known locally by the misnomer "French Creoles," were very scared by the implications of Black Power—a fear that was translated into strong support for the PNM and its law-and-order stance. Ferdie Ferreira believes that funds for the 1976 elections were collected from this group.[36] These funds were not urgently needed for the 1971 elections, when the PNM won all the seats in an uncontested poll. Many "French Creoles" and Chinese chose migration as a means of escape, and exclusive neighborhoods now became open to middle-class black and brown nationals. Those who migrated took considerable sums out of the country. Those who remained took heed of events and changed their employment practices, hiring black and brown youths in banks, business places, and in the professions. This objective had always been high on Williams's agenda; now events were hastening the process. A quiet revolution had taken place.

Williams's Post-Event Analysis

Our final consideration focuses on how Williams later analyzed the February Revolution and NUFF's decision to engage in violent revolution. By 1976, Williams had completed what was to be his last testament, namely a manuscript entitled *The Blackest Thing in Slavery Was Not the Black Man*. This manuscript was never published, despite an announcement of its impending publication by the London publisher Andre Deutsch. Having successfully prevailed over what was undoubtedly the most serious threat of his long rule (which had started in 1956), he now sought to justify his actions. With the benefit of hindsight and with his position in power firmly reconsolidated, Williams took the historian's long view of events as he sought to contextualize the protests in Trinidad and Tobago against a backdrop of worldwide restlessness. While as a black historian he was sympathetic to the assertion of Black Power, as an administrator he could not have allowed such an assertion to rock the ship of state. Less than a decade after barring Stokely Carmichael from entry into Trinidad, Williams's manuscript carried a chapter entitled "Black Power," which was prefaced with the phrase "Black is Beautiful"—a phrase popularized by Carmichael. Williams's analysis of Carmichael's activities in the Caribbean, however, was critical. Writing on Carmichael's controversial visit to Guyana in May 1970, Williams noted:

> In this explosive situation, Stokely Carmichael . . . explicitly stated that Black Power was not something for the Indian population which must develop its own solution. This naturally aggravated the existing racial antagonism. The Black Power movement in Trinidad and possibly also as a consequence sought to define black as including both Africans and Indians. Their slogan "Indians and Africans unite" has met with apparently little success so far.[37]

Later in the chapter, Williams drew attention to the international dimensions of the country's 1970 disturbances, noting that they had originally broken out as a protest against the trial of West Indian students in Canada, who had been protesting racial discrimination at the Sir George Williams University. He observed that the Black Power activists in Trinidad and Tobago had been strongly influenced by black American hairstyles, dashikis, attacks on the establishment and white power structure, designation of police as "fuzz" and "pigs," and the rejection of "conventional politics." Subsequent to the declaration of emergency, Williams recalled, there were massive protests against the emergency powers, the detention of the principal agitators, and proposed legislation against the possession of arms. Among the more serious aspects of the unrest were "demands for nationalization of oil, sugar, and the banks."[38]

Whereas Williams was mild in his criticism of the Black Power movement, with whose objectives he sympathized, his attitude to the NUFF was decidedly harsh: "A group of young people generally well educated (reminiscent of the unrest among affluent students in United States) are taking to the hills and forests, robbing banks, holding up paymasters, attacking isolated police stations, shooting policemen, while their well-wishers declaim against 'police brutality' when a shoot-out occurs."[39] Williams believed that unlike the Chinese under Mao or the Vietnamese in their anti-French or anti-American struggles, the local guerrillas lacked a clear-cut ideology. They were irrelevant in Trinidad, he wrote, because there was no foreign or colonial aggressor, the mass of the population had not been alienated, and there was no significant and legitimate political dissatisfaction. The difference in Williams's attitude to these two groups, Black Power and NUFF, was reflected in the treatment of the respective participants. The Black Power leaders were released after a short detention on Nelson Island; the members of NUFF were relentlessly pursued, and most of them were shot during brutal police encounters.

Conclusion

Like the strikes and disturbances that convulsed the Caribbean during the period of 1935 to 1937, the February Revolution of 1970 had local as well as wider Caribbean repercussions. It was more than a Black Power revolution in that it involved issues other than blackness, bringing to the fore issues such as foreign domination of the economy and of the media, ethnically biased employment practices, local politicians in government but not in power, and the morphing of the two-party system into ethnic enclaves. Williams as a historian understood this changed mood and trimmed his sail to suit to the wind, using the arguments of activists to buttress his case for change. Had he insisted on the heavy hand of the law, things might have turned out differently. Unlike Eric Gairy in Grenada, he did not seek to counter dissent by creating a counterforce of repression, nor did he take counsel from those members of his cabinet who saw the communist bogey everywhere. More often than not, he correctly gauged the popular movements and played his cards to suit.

In the small Caribbean Sea, the February Revolution had repercussions among neighbors. Tim Hector's Antigua Caribbean Liberation Movement, for example, drew inspiration from its southern neighbor.[40] In Grenada and Guyana, the vibrations were stronger. Indeed, both the New Jewel Movement (NJM) in Grenada and the Working People's Alliance (WPA) in Guyana had strong connections with Black Power activism in Trinidad and Tobago. Maurice Bishop was in Trinidad at the height of the ferment in 1970, and thereafter would visit from time to time to discuss strategy with fellow NJM leader Bernard Coard, then a lecturer at St. Augustine; others would join them in the Senior Common Room from time to time prior to the Grenada Revolution of March 1979. In like manner, Walter Rodney was always in close contact with his colleagues in Trinidad and Tobago and was once deported from the airport in Trinidad, having arrived to do some lectures at St. Augustine. In Guyana, Rodney sought to duplicate the African-Indian camaraderie that NJAC had initiated previously. His success in that venture was the cause of his undoing. After his death in 1980, Guyana reverted to its ethnic mold, despite the best efforts of the WPA.

The February Revolution of 1970 was indeed a catalyst for positive change in Trinidad and Tobago as in the wider Caribbean. It occurred without the scale of bloodshed that characterized the French or Russian or Chinese revolutions, but it was a major part of the struggle for West Indian emancipation—a struggle that continues today, under changed circumstances.

Notes

1. Best, 2.

2. Martin, 284.

3. Ibid., 287.

4. Roffey, 213.

5. For an account of this incident, see Belgrave.

6. See, for example, Oxaal, *Race and Revolutionary Conciousness*; Raoul Pantin, *Black Power Day*; and Meeks, "The 1970 Revolution."

7. In Trinidad, such maroon settlements existed in places like Brigand Hill on the east coast and at La Seiva in the northern range, overlooking the fertile Maraval Valley.

8. The Henry Rebellion in Jamaica was led by the Rastafarian leader Reverend Claudius Henry and his son Ronald, who attempted through violent means to effect a large Rastafarian repatriation to Ethiopia and a relief program for Jamaica's poor. The rebellion was put down by a force of one thousand troops and police. Claudius Henry was convicted of treason and jailed, and Ronald was hanged for the death of British troops. See Lewis, chapter 2 in this volume, and Martin, 313.

9. Bernard, *The Freedom Fighters*, 89.

10. Millette, 628.

11. Bernard, *The Freedom Fighters*, 270.

12. Millette, 651.

13. Norman Commission report cited in Singh, 9.

14. Bhadase Sagan Maraj was leader of the Hindu religious organization Sanatan Dharma Maha Sabha, leader of the Democratic Labour Party until 1960, and leader of the All-Trinidad Sugar Estates and Factory Workers Union until his death in 1971.

15. Parmasad, 309.

16. Samaroo, "East Indians and Black Power."

17. Samaroo, "Indians and Politics."

18. Cited in Constance, 21.

19. Parmasad, 313.

20. Williams, Public lecture, San Fernando, April 1965. Attended by author.

21. Ryan, 384.

22. Interview with Ferdie Ferreira, 2010.

23. Bernard, *Against the Odds*, 189.

24. Dennis Pantin, 682.

25. Williams, *Nationwide Broadcast*, 23 March 1970, 4.

26. Ibid., 4.

27. Ibid., 5.

28. Ibid., 6.

29. Williams, *Nationwide Broadcast*, 3 May 1970, 3.

30. Ibid., 3.

31. Interview with Ferdie Ferreira, 2010.

32. Williams, *Nationwide Broadcast*, 3 May 1970.

33. Williams, *Nationwide Broadcast*, 10 May 1970.

34. Williams, *Address to Canefarmers*.

35. Williams, *Independence Day Message*.

36. Interview with Ferdie Ferreira, 2010.

37. Williams, *The Blackest Thing in Slavery Was Not the Black Man*, 417.

38. Ibid., 418.

39. Ibid., 418.

40. On the ACLM, see Paget Henry chapter 8 in this volume.

Bibliography

Belgrave, V. "The Sir George Williams Affair" in Ryan and Stewart (eds.), *The Black Power Revolution 1970: A Retrospective*, St. Augustine: I.S.E.R., University of the West Indies, 1995, 119–31.

Bernard, E. *Against the Odds*, Port of Spain: Imprint Caribbean, 1991.

———. *The Freedom Fighters*, Trinidad: Imprint, 2000.

Best, L. *Black Power and National Reconstruction: Proposals following the February Revolution*, Tunapuna: Tapia, 1970.

Constance, Z. *Valentino: Poet and Prophet, Blues and Rebellion*, San Fernando: Z. O. Constance, 1984.

Ferreira, F. Interview by B. Samaroo, Trinidad, 25 July 2010.

Martin, T. *Caribbean History: From Pre-Colonial Origins to the Present*, New Jersey: Pearson Education Incorporated, 2012.

Meeks, B. *Radical Caribbean: From Black Power to Abu Bakr*, Barbados: University of the West Indies Press, 1996.

Millette, D. "Guerrilla War in Trinidad 1970–1974" in Ryan and Stewart (eds.), *The Black Power Revolution 1970: A Retrospective*, St. Augustine: I.S.E.R., University of the West Indies, 1995, 625–60.

Oxaal, I. *Race and Revolutionary Conciousness: A Documentary Interpretation of the 1970 Black Power Revolt in Trinidad*, Cambridge, Mass: Schenkman Publishing Company, 1971.

Pantin, D. "The 1970 Black Power Revolution: Lessons for Public Policy" in Ryan and Stewart (eds.), *The Black Power Revolution 1970: A Retrospective*, St. Augustine: I.S.E.R., University of the West Indies, 1995, 663–89.

Pantin, R. *Black Power Day: The 1970 Revolution—A Reporter's Story*, Santa Cruz: Hatuey Productions, 1990.

Parmasad, K. "Ancestral Impulse, Community Formation and 1970: Bridging the Afro-Indian Divide" in Ryan and Stewart (eds.), *The Black Power Revolution 1970: A Retrospective*, St. Augustine: I.S.E.R., University of the West Indies, 1995, 309–17.

Roffey, M. *The White Woman on the Green Bicycle*, New York: Simon & Schuster, 2009.

Ryan, S. *Eric Williams: the Myth and the Man*, Kingston: University of the West Indies Press, 2009.

Ryan, S. and Stewart, T. (eds.) *The Black Power Revolution 1970: A Retrospective*, St. Augustine: I.S.E.R., University of the West Indies, 1995.

Samaroo, B. "East Indians and Black Power," *Vanguard*, San Fernando, 21 March 1970.

———. "Indians and Politics," *Tapia*, 20 December 1970.

Singh, K. *Bloodstained Tombs: The Muharram Massacre 1884*, Basingstoke: Macmillan Caribbean, 1988.

Williams, E. Public lecture, San Fernando, April 1965. Author's lecture notes.

———. *Nationwide Broadcast*, 23 March, 3 May, and 10 May 1970. Port of Spain, Trinidad: Government Printery, 1970.

———. *Address to Canefarmers*, 17 August 1970, Eric Williams Collection, University of the West Indies Library, St. Augustine, File 1961.

———. *Independence Day Message*, 31 August 1970, Eric Williams Collection, University of the West Indies Library, St. Augustine, File 1961.

———. *The Blackest Thing in Slavery Was Not the Black Man*, unpublished manuscript, Eric Williams Collection, University of the West Indies Library, St. Augustine, File 158.

5

Secondary Decolonization

The Black Power Moment in Barbados, c. 1970

RICHARD DRAYTON

I

The problem of the "postcolony," of the persistence of a colonial order after the acquisition of constitutional sovereignty, has been addressed implicitly or explicitly at least since Fanon explored the "pitfalls of national consciousness."[1] Caribbean novelists and poets, even before "independence" in the 1960s, asked how that burden of experience would be undone, particularly by political leaders who were the products of the imperial plantation.[2] Kamau Brathwaite's 1969 poem "Negus" reminded that:

it
it
it
it is not

it is not
it is not
it is not enough
it is not enough to be free
of the red white and blue
of the drag
of the dragon[3]

But the region's historians, who have tended to think of independence celebrations as magic thresholds separating slavery radically from freedom, have yet provided few descriptions of how "the drag/of the dragon" restrained

Caribbean experience after the 1960s, and of how, and with what success, some struggled against it.[4]

In the historiography of periods of imperial conquest, we have distinguished between "primary" and "secondary resistance"—that is, the initial period of violent resistance to European invasion, and the period that follows, characterized by the emergence of challenges to the colonial order mounted by those who were in part its products.[5] Might a distinction between "primary" and "secondary" decolonization not prove equally useful for mapping the end of the imperial experience? Primary decolonization might be seen as the climax of secondary resistance, with a later moment of response to that inevitably partial and ambivalent victory. The struggle for sovereignty—cast in the Anglophone Caribbean context as the passage from the political awakening of the 1930s to the acquisition of flags and nominal sovereignty in the 1960s—led to a new kind of internal struggle. The black men in frock coats who shook the Governor's hand at midnight found themselves facing opposition both within their societies and within their own ambivalent consciousnesses.

What is clear is that the extended 1970s were a period of seismic cultural and social change in the once British West Indies, a moment in which the remains of colonial order in general—and the unusual privileges of whites, and the subordination of civil society to Britain in particular—became challenged in a hitherto unimaginable way. In Jamaica, the Rodney Riots of 1968 led into the political awakening of the Manley period of the 1970s, for which the anthems were Max Romeo's "Let the Power fall on I / give I justice, peace, and love Far-I" (1972) and Peter Tosh's apocalyptic "Downpressor Man" (1977). In Trinidad, Eric Williams spent his last decade coping with the legacies of the Black Power revolt of 1970, and the political upheaval and guerrilla insurgency it bequeathed. In Guyana, the Burnham regime from 1970 sought to profit from the rising tide, but found itself in conflict with the young lions of the Working People's Alliance (WPA). In Grenada, the New Jewel Movement emerged in opposition to Gairy's repression, and seized power by force of arms in 1979. Around the region, the dreadlocks sprouted on and in the heads of the young.

This 1970s political and cultural moment grew out of the experience of what we may call the Bandung generation: those who had come to political consciousness when European imperialism was in crisis, and the American Civil Rights movement and the Cuban Revolution were in motion. Their political optimism—the sense that it was possible to change the world—was combined with a sense of urgency, sharpened by Sharpeville, the murders of

Lumumba, Malcolm X, and King, and the apparent consolidation of white minority rule in South Africa and Rhodesia. There was a visible Third World insurrection, marked by the meeting of the Organization for African and Asian Solidarity in Conakry five years after Bandung, followed in 1966 by the Tricontinental Conference in revolutionary Havana. For many young, educated Caribbean people, the realities of their societies after independence were seen through the lens of this global struggle, for which Algeria, Vietnam, and the opposition of a tropical New Left to neocolonial regimes were key symbols. The Black Power movement in the United States claimed this location, with the expatriate Trinidadian Stokely Carmichael beginning his manifesto with a chapter that presented the African-American condition as "colonial," and affirmed, "There is only one place for Black Americans . . . and that is on the side of the Third World."[6] When the slogan was reimported to the Caribbean, it meant an interrogation of an incomplete decolonization and a claim to participation in this wider international shift. It is the purpose of this chapter to suggest that even those who did not use the slogan were moved by both aims.

Barbados, with its reputation as the conservative of the region, has never been understood as having been part of this post-1968 awakening.[7] But this conservatism has always been more mask than reality. Barbados, after all, exported Hubert Critchlow and A. A. Thorne to British Guiana, Clement Payne and George Padmore to Trinidad, and Richard Moore to the United States. And its relative internal tranquility concealed powerful currents of anger at the (neo)colonial order, even among apparent conservatives. This chapter seeks to explore how Barbados participated in that global and regional moment for which "Black Power" was the emblem. It asserts that the very few Barbadians who used the slogan were merely the visible crest of a much larger wave, which quietly shifted the axis of that society away from its colonial location as "Little England." Since in Barbados, as elsewhere in the region, few postindependence government documents have been released, it uses the reports of British diplomats and colonial and security officials before and after independence to illuminate, from an oblique angle, how secondary decolonization opened up in Barbados in the decade after 1966. The chapter examines how the political leaders that emerged from the end of empire responded to the pressures from below and found themselves making a stronger break with the colonial past than they had quite likely envisioned at midnight when the new flags were unfurled. Across the twentieth century there were always two convergent de facto "Black Power" movements: one, from above, which wanted black men to share in, or replace, white men in positions of power; and another, from below, which sought a radical transformation of the character of social power. With Shearer's Jamaica in 1968 and Gairy's Grenada in 1970, one kind of Black Power did battle with the other, but in Barbados, as in Guyana, and indeed in Manley's Jamaica after 1972, a more complex response unfolded, in which the political leadership sought to assimilate the more radical currents, and in self-conscious ways to extend the limits of decolonization.

II

To understand the political moment circa 1970, it is necessary to understand the underwater life of Barbadian politics in the decades before the Democratic Labour Party (DLP) came to power in 1961 and took Barbados to independence in 1966. The political location of the DLP was complex, since it contained within it both radical opponents of Grantley Adams and his Barbados Labour Party, and a mixture of patriotic businessmen and ambitious young men. Its leader was the unusual figure of Errol Walton Barrow.

Barrow was born in 1920 to a proud and propertied black middle-class family. His father was a churchman with Pan-African identification. His uncle was Charles Duncan O'Neale, who brought Keir Hardie's socialism to Barbados after the First World War. But he had always been identified socially with order and respectability; he liked to say he was born in a plantation great house, not a tenantry, and as a schoolboy was entrusted with a rifle in the suppression of the 1937 riots and dispatched to guard the white suburb of Worthing. He had a distinguished career in the Royal Air Force during World War II and then, via the London School of Economics (LSE) and Middle Temple, returned to a legal and political career in Barbados. He was self-confident, larger than life, a classic Weberian charismatic leader. A British diplomat commented:

> Barrow . . . is to be seen everywhere in the country. . . . one day he is aqualunging with the underwater boys, and then he is attending their annual dinner. Next morning we can be "buzzed" by the Prime Minister flying himself on a tour of inspection of Barbados. Sometime during the week he may be either buying or selling a cow; and he will certainly be driving himself around in a Vauxhall Viva or an 1100, shunning chauffer and ceremony . . . At 5.30 in the morning he can, on occasion, be seen riding down Broad Street on his bay mare . . . or

shooting duck. He will perhaps lunch at the American Businessmen's Club. He will have appointments all the morning, will often work late in the office over the weekend, and will take time off to visit his extra-mural companion.[8]

He was the sometime lover of Nina Simone, who dedicated "The House on a Hill" on her last album to Barrow. He had the ability to communicate with all social classes, and sought always to achieve compromise between different interests. He was pulled in a conservative direction by friends such as J. Cameron Tudor and his many business contacts. He succeeded in wooing funding for the DLP from both the local Jewish and Lebanese businessmen, leading his opponent, "Tom" Adams, to quip that he had "succeeded where the United Nations have failed, in bringing Jews and Arabs together."[9] But he had had his own experiences with race in Barbados and Britain. He had returned home from London with an anticolonial consciousness and the idea that he was something called a West Indian. It is striking that he announced his break with Adams with a bill in the House of Assembly to nationalize Barbados Rediffusion in 1952.

The DLP is usually understood in Barbados as a party formed by angry young men, such as Barrow and Tudor, who broke from Grantley Adams and the Barbados Labour Party for essentially personal reasons in the early 1950s. This was certainly the view from Government House, which feared that its protégé Adams "shared the gift of Sir Robert Walpole for driving young men into opposition."[10] But the DLP was also the refuge for those who hoped for a more fundamental change in Barbadian society. From 1940 to 1961, Adams had at all times resisted any political movement that went beyond what was acceptable to the British. He saw himself as the colonial partner of the British Labour Party, and the colonial governors, from Bushe in 1944 onward, assisted him in engineering moderate social reforms, with which he could build his political base. In exchange, Adams marginalized political trouble-makers, pushing into the wilderness the working-class troublemakers of the 1930s, and regularly purging radicals from his Barbados Workers Union (BWU) and Labour Party. Among these were veterans of Marcus Garvey's UNIA, who had returned after seasons in Panama, Cuba, Trinidad, and the United States—men and women who had brought home a Pan-African consciousness and dreams of social reform and revolution. All of these elements became critical to the rise of the DLP.

The most important radical political force underlying the DLP was the Congress Party of Wynter Crawford (b. 1910), its direct ancestor as the vehicle for the opposition to the Barbados Labour Party. It was not merely that Crawford and his lieutenants, in particular Edwy Talma (Deputy Prime Minister in 1971), moved to the DLP. If one looks at the electoral geography of Barbados, it is evident that from the 1946 elections, the first to see real party politics, the parishes of St. Lucy, St. Philip, and St. John had emerged as anti-BLP strongholds, which they continued to be through 1961 and even today. But Congress was a far more radical party than its successor, demanding, for example, in 1946 that Barbados nationalize its sugar estates, just as the "mother country" had nationalized its industries. The British believed that Crawford was "in close contact with the state and national headquarters of the Communist Party in New York City."[11] He was certainly, as his choice of "the West Indian National Congress" as his party's name made clear, in conscious solidarity with the Indian and African National Congresses, a decade before Bandung, and with a pan-Caribbean identification. The West Indian National Congress had a strong working-class base, to which Crawford appealed directly, announcing at a mass meeting in Queen's Park that he was quite different from Adams: "Adams belongs to the big whites and does not care anything about the masses." In 1945, the *Barbados Observer*, Crawford's organ, announced the demand: "Bring Socialism to Barbados." While Adams defended the virtues of the British Empire to the United Nations in November 1948, Crawford in 1953 denounced the "repressive measures" used in Kenya against Mau Mau rebels.[12] It was perhaps in order to weaken Crawford, and to close off the political option he represented for Barbados, that Bushe in 1945 did his best to help Adams.[13]

The early 1950s are the critical turning point in the political history of primary decolonization in Barbados. The newspapers told of the jailing of Nkrumah, the consolidation of apartheid, and the Seretse Khama affair, while Adams continued to declare his faith in Britain. Meanwhile, at home, Adams alienated young men like Barrow within his party, while launching a witch hunt to remove what he called the "iron curtain element" from the Barbados Workers Union. In 1953, Adams rushed to defend Britain when it abruptly removed from power the People's Progressive Party (PPP) in the same year it had won the first election by universal suffrage in British Guiana.[14] He accepted London's charge of a Communist conspiracy, not least because he (and Norman Manley of Jamaica) were locked in a struggle to exclude "communists," in particular the PPP's leader Cheddi Jagan, from the Caribbean labor movement.

Adams underestimated how his political opponents in Barbados identified with both British Guianese nationalism and radical politics in the wider Caribbean. Barrow had been a close friend at the LSE of Forbes Burnham, a key figure in the PPP. Ulric Grant, one of the political leaders of the 1937 riots, was in correspondence with the Jamaican Richard Hart, secretary of the Caribbean Labour Congress, from whom, the Special Branch alleged, he was "receiving quantities of Communist literature."[15] When, in September 1953, Martin Carter, a PPP minister, stopped off in Barbados—with Lennox Pierre of Trinidad—on his way to the Youth Congress in Bucharest, Crawford took them to see the BLP dissident T. T. Lewis, and they had a discreet conversation while bathing in the sea. Dudley Holder and Norman Layne, two of the unionists expelled from the BWU, were in correspondence with Quentin O'Connor and T. U. Butler in Trinidad. On 28 October 1953, a debate at the Press Club, during which Fred "Sleepy" Smith (like Barrow, a young lawyer and BLP dissenter) and Ulric Grant denounced the British, led to blows with Frank Walcott (then Adams's lieutenant in the BWU). On 13 November 1953, there was a public meeting of the Caribbean People's Alliance at the house of J.E.T. Brancker, where the widow of Marcus Garvey asserted, to loud applause, that the PPP's only crime was that it had "exposed the poverty in British Guiana." In her wake in Speightstown, the island's second city, a Caribbean Women's Alliance briefly flourished in association with the Caribbean Women's League of Trinidad.

In September 1953, the radicals Ulric Grant and Carlton Gill met with Cameron Tudor and raised with him the idea of forming a new political party with Barrow, "Sleepy" Smith, Brancker, and the Congress. Two years later, in 1955, in the same week that, on the other side of the world, the Bandung Conference collected the energies of the global anticolonial movement, the Democratic Labour Party was launched in Barbados. It was from its origins a nationalist and reformist party, with radicals like Grant agreeing, as they had a generation earlier with the BLP, to yield leadership to more respectable (and conservative) figures. The DLP succeeded in that goal that so many successful parties have of being "left"—having a less compromising attitude to white and British power—and, at the same time, keeping friendly relations with business interests and the planter and merchant elite. To Adams's shock, while he was in Trinidad as the first Prime Minister of the Federation of the West Indies, the DLP swept the polls in 1961. When the Federation collapsed a year later, and Jamaica, and then Trinidad, took independence, the road was open for Barrow to take Barbados across the threshold in November 1966.

III

In the early years of independence, the DLP regime continued to fly with both its left and right wings. It expanded the scale of the free public education system it had created after 1961 and public health care. Cabinet took the decision, at the moment of independence, to recommend to Her Majesty that the Barbados Yacht Club, with its exclusively white membership, be stripped of the title "Royal."[16] Yet most of the de facto segregation of private and recreational life on the island continued. At the same time, the DLP attempted to imitate Puerto Rico's "industrialization by invitation" economic model and to attract foreign capital. Many in the cabinet retained close connections with the British High Commission, with Tudor leaking information happily.[17] Barrow continued to position himself publicly as a friend of every interest in society, even if it was perceived that "since the 1966 Independence Conference he has become somewhat disillusioned with Britain."[18] In 1970, the *Democrat*, the official organ of the party, was described as publishing views "to the right of those expressed in the columns of the *Beacon*, the organ of the BLP." Yet, it is difficult not to see a change of course of the DLP in the era after 1968, and to see a repositioning in response to external example and the opportunities of power.

In 1969, a number of small gestures indicated the shift in Barrow's policy. In 1969, the Anglican Church, which since 1627 had been the official church, was disestablished. In response to an apparent racial incident at Sandy Lane Hotel, where the wife of Sir Lionel Luckhoo was treated with discourtesy, Barrow threatened to terminate the work permits of all the expatriate staff if there was no apology. British diplomats reported that, in general, the High Commission, BOAC, and Cable and Wireless all had problems obtaining work permits for expatriate staff, "related to government policy that these technical and managerial tasks should be undertaken by Barbadians." Barrow declared that he felt no gratitude for the preferential access that Barbadian sugar exports enjoyed in Britain, arguing that this was "a debt due by the British Government, who, over the years, have witnessed plantation owners exploit the peasants."[19]

Since 1966, the DLP had been criticized from the Left by the People's Progressive Movement, a small political group with a Pan-African identification—as indicated by the Garveyite name of its newspaper, *Black Star*.[20] But external events were also pressing in, with rumors of revolution passing through the region silently from several directions—the assassination of King in 1967, burning cities in the United States, student riots in Paris and at Berkeley and Cornell universities, Carlos and Smith giving the Black Power salute at the Olympics in Mexico. The fuse of the Black Power movement in the Anglophone Caribbean lit from two directions. First, the 1968 riots in Jamaica, in which students protesting the banning of Walter Rodney were tear-gassed by the police, sparked outrage among students at the other two campuses of the University of the West Indies. Second, the February 1969 rebellion of West Indian students at Sir George Williams University in Canada sent shock waves through the region, including Barbados, where Sally Cools, one of its leaders, had roots. While in Barbados there was no equivalent to Trinidad's National Joint Action Committee (NJAC)—the key Black Power organization formed in February 1969 in solidarity with the Canadian disturbances—the impact was powerful nonetheless. In August 1969 Roosevelt Brown, the Bermudian politician and one of the region's foremost Black Power advocates, visited Barbados to sound out the possibility of holding a pan-Caribbean Black Power conference the following July. There were several unsolved incidents. Two homemade bombs exploded in September 1969, and both of the two main department stores in Bridgetown, Cave Shepherd, on 10 December 1969, and Fogarty, on 19 January 1970, burned to the ground.

IV

Then, in early 1970, the news of the Trinidad uprisings came. In February 1970, while Port of Spain marched, the Students Guild of the Cave Hill campus of the University of the West Indies recorded its "firm solidarity with former West Indian students of the Sir George Williams University now facing trial before the Canadian courts . . . [and] called on all West Indian governments to set up an investigation into the incident."[21] In March 1970, students at Cave Hill blockaded an administration block barring the principal and other administration staff from entering the building, in solidarity with Jamaican colleagues at Mona. A letter to the *Advocate* advised that while there was no Black Power movement on campus, "there are many here who believe in its philosophy." Meanwhile, at Codrington College, on 22 March, the theological students donned their gowns and stood in line at the entrance to the chapel under the sign "a Black God for a Black Priest." On 14 April, Frank Walcott, leader of the Barbados Workers Union, declared at a public meeting that "The Union intended to demonstrate what power meant to the economic advancement of the black masses," while other union speakers attacked "the economic structure of the island and the system of private enterprise," which one speaker described as "the official system of exploitation."[22] Protesters also took to the streets of Bridgetown, with one public meeting on 22 April 1970 attracting a crowd of more than five hundred people to hear speeches from "Bobby" Clarke, Calvin Alleyne, and visitors from the Rattoon group of Guyana, cheering calls for the nationalization of the Anglican Church, the telephone company, and Barbados Light and Power "under the first revolutionary law." The British speculated, too, that "a possible future leader of more moderate nonrevolutionary Black Power, concentrating on black culture and black dignity," might be Mr. Elton Mottley, under the general aegis of the (refurbished) Barbados Labour Party. Mottley had organized a series of "Black Nights" to celebrate African culture, each of which attracted hundreds of people.

While all of this took place close to home, in the early months of 1970 there was an incident in Britain that must have reminded Barrow of the underside of his own experience across the water.[23] At 3:40 a.m. on 8 February, a car driven by Peter Simmons, then 27 years of age and a junior in the Barbados High Commission, was stopped by the police in Southall.[24] They lifted Simmons from the car and threw him on the road, arresting him and his brother David Simmons, then age 29 and a lecturer in law at West London College. When Branford Goddard of the Barbados High Commission asked for information at the police station, "a plainclothes officer viciously assaulted Mr. Goddard by punching him in the chest." After appeals were lodged, the police began a campaign of harassment of Simmons, stopping him twice a week over the succeeding months, and sending police cars to call at his house frequently on various pretexts. The court case, in which Barrow's British representatives were fined £20 with £10 costs for obstructing the police, came to its climax in early April just as events crested in Trinidad.[25]

Whatever the causes, Barrow's response to the upheavals of the early 1970s was tolerant and even in part responsive, a world away from the repressive reactions of Shearer in Jamaica or Williams in Trinidad. In April 1970, the Trinidadians Geddes Granger (now Makandal Daaga) and Clive Nunez, leaders of NJAC, planned to visit Barbados. At a party on 15 April to celebrate the opening of the new Tamarind Cove Hotel, Sir Theodore Brancker (the Speaker of the House), together with Springer (the Deputy Commissioner of Police and the head of the Special Branch) told a British diplomat that these troublemakers would not be admitted. While Barrow was away from the island, the cabinet made a decision on 17 April to this effect. But, that very day, when Barrow heard of it in Jamaica, he sent back a telegram demanding the revocation of the order, and, on the threat of his own resignation, insisted that they publish his denunciation of their decision: "No West Indian shall be prevented from entering Barbados as a visitor."[26] Members of the cabinet claimed to have considered resignation, "however in the event the fruits of office proved more attractive than the bitter fruits of political exile," and on 18 April, the order prohibiting the entry of NJAC's leaders was officially rescinded.[27]

Barrow was certainly viewed by conservative elements in Barbados as unreliable, and they turned, treasonously, to outside powers to put pressure on him. Sydney Martin, principal of the Cave Hill campus, lobbied the British High Commission to help him resist any pressure that the government of Barbados might exert to urge him to allow university buildings to be used for any Black Power conference. In May 1970, Cameron Tudor telephoned the High Commission for advice on the impending visit of Stokely Carmichael, promising that Carmichael would be banned from visiting. At the same time, Crowson, the Security Liaison Officer at the British High Commission (the local representative of the British intelligence community) wrote to Donald G. Allen in the Caribbean Department of the Foreign and Commonwealth Office about his secret lunch meeting with Wilfred Farmer, whom he described as "the (white Barbadian) Commissioner of Police."[28] Farmer told him that he had given his domestic help the day off so that they could meet in confidence, and had asked the British diplomat to come without a chauffeur. Farmer then proceeded to share what the Special Branch knew about the situation with the foreign power: he advised that all of the members of the cabinet were in favor of banning Stokely Carmichael's imminent visit, except for Barrow. Farmer's disloyalty to the government of an independent Barbados was not, perhaps, uncharacteristic of many segments of society.

Barrow had compelled his colleagues to allow Carmichael's entry, but on 10 May agreed that this would be conditional on his not being allowed to speak in any public context. Carmichael, on landing, was handed a court order, which advised him that he was admitted as a visitor to Barbados, on the condition that he avoid all involvement in political activities while he was there. Carmichael asked, jocularly, whether they wished for him to sign the document. On being told yes, he took the paper and added to it the phrase "In order to free our land we will have to kill," and then, with a smile, affixed his signature. As Carmichael stepped into a waiting Dear's Garage taxi, which had been chartered by his hosts, he was challenged by the independent taxi men at the airport: "Why are you who stand up for the coloured man, traveling in a white-owned car?" He was taken to the home of Lucius Cools in Brighton. The Police Commissioner, in a panic, sent three riot squads to stand by at Independence Square to conduct mass arrests if Carmichael arrived to speak to an ongoing People's Pressure Movement meeting. But he waited indoors, receiving later a group of perhaps eighty people from the meeting who returned to speak with him. The British diplomat claimed that the Police Commissioner had alleged that his Special Branch informant at the meeting had heard a variety of threats from Carmichael and others to kill public figures (including Barrow), and to take over CBC, the telephone company, and Cable and Wireless "when the revolution" took place. Carmichael was alleged to have demanded that Bobby Clarke coordinate the seizure of Central Police Station, and that "he wanted action this summer" since "Barbados was the stumbling block in . . . the total revolution of the Caribbean."

This absurd and implausible declaration reminds us that security reports are often used to manipulate politicians. It may be that Barrow was moved by what he was told by his security advisers, local and foreign. What is certain is that he then tacked to the right, and moved to enlarge the repressive powers available to the state. Even in March, perhaps with an eye to events in Trinidad—or perhaps on the example of the Guyana Defence Force of his friend Forbes Burnham—Barrow announced to the House of Assembly his plans for a Barbados Defence Force.[29] The *Financial Times* reported in early May that he had "launched a verbal broadside on black power militants in the island."[30] On 12 May he met with Roosevelt Brown, and his companions Robert Carson and John Hickman, and advised them that he denied permission for a Black Power Conference to be held in Barbados in 1970. At the end of the month, Barrow presented to the House of Assembly the Public Order Bill, which by June made it an offense to preach violence or racial hatred.[31] In October 1970, "Bobby" Clarke was fined $250 under this act for "inciting any person to kill any other person while at a public meeting."

The Police Special Branch, presumably with Barrow's support, went into overdrive. The Police Commissioner took an overheated view of the radical threat, and was convinced that the basement of a house in the exclusive suburb of Highgate, owned by a chemist called Smith working for Banks Breweries, was a factory for Molotov cocktails or explosive devices; that a certain Pierre, who was the son-in-law of the Governor-General, was a "black power fanatic"; that an English visitor called Arthur Bowen, who had been expelled from Grenada as a prohibited immigrant, was "a revolutionary" funneling Cuban funds to Barbados; that Bobby Clarke was up to no good, although the commissioner admitted he had absolutely no evidence to support his assertion; Glenroy Straughan was "a dangerous man," the leader of the "revolutionary element of the PPM"; and "Tom" Adams was described as "a bastard," as he had been responsible for the BLP's decision not to support the Public Order Act.

And yet the passage of the act did not end either Barbados's or Barrow's response to the contemporary currents. In June, Suzanne and Sally Cools, Bobby Clarke, and Eric "Fly" Sealy demonstrated outside of Parliament under the banners "No Police Power" and "No White Power." In the same week that Elton Mottley published a Black Power manifesto in the *Advocate News*, Barrow stood up in the House of Assembly on 15 July to warn, to the shock of British diplomats, referring to Britain's imminent arms deal with South Africa, that "it should not be difficult for the Commonwealth nine years later to promote the exclusion of any other one of its members."[32] On 8 December, Barrow decolonized Barbados's aviation, with the House passing a bill revoking the power of the U.K. government to set airline fares.

It was also in 1970 that Barrow announced his plans for a Central Bank of Barbados, and for a sovereign currency that would no longer be tied to sterling. This caused great anxiety in London, where throughout the period of decolonization it had been assumed that former colonies would continue to prop up sterling with their foreign reserves in perpetuity. They sternly "advised" Barrow that such action would be "retrograde," to which he responded that the status quo, by which 97 percent of Barbados's reserves were in sterling, was "unbalanced," considering the shape of the economy.[33] Jack Dear, a senior BLP politician, secretly approached the British High Commissioner in November 1970 to promise that if his party was returned to power in 1971 it would "repeal such a Central Bank."[34] But the BLP did not win, and two years later Barrow announced that he would follow through with his decision, as "Barbados had a surplus with the hard currency areas of North America," and it should not be tied to the British economy.[35]

V

The global Black Power revolution passed through Barbados in 1970, even if there were only a few visible crests above the surface. As before in the 1930s, external fires and small clouds of domestic smoke prompted rapid defensive accommodation. The British High Commissioner wrote in 1971:

> More and more of the old white Barbadian commercial families are coming to accept—however reluctantly—that their economic future depends on their ability to accept the realities of the present and to forget the pleasant past in which the black man accepted his subor-

dinate status. . . . The perceptible progress in Barbados is probably, in some part, due to the Trinidad troubles, which have brought home to the white Barbadian population the problems they will face if they are unwilling to come to terms with the aspirations of the large majority of the population.[36]

It would take another two decades before Hilary Beckles's challenges would lead to the inclusion of significant numbers of darker-skinned people on corporate boards, but the first steps followed 1970. This was, however, the least of the outcomes.

In 1971, Barbados's relations with Britain entered into a crisis, which was the deepest and most public that has yet been seen in the postcolonial period. Barrow had become convinced, or at the least had decided to make public his belief, that Britain and the United States were lending assistance to the opposition Barbados Labour Party prior to the imminent general election, and that they had—in gratitude for the BLP's Cold War loyalty under Grantley Adams—intervened in 1966, lending "moral and other support" to the BLP in its opposition to independence, in the hope that it, rather than the DLP, would control a sovereign Barbados.[37] On 25 June 1971, Barrow called a press conference, at which he accused the United States and the United Kingdom of "meddling in the internal affairs of Barbados," and said that if evidence of further meddling arose, he would "take steps to ask for the peaceful withdrawal of the citizens of the country in question," declaring at the same time that the government had turned down a $7 million loan offer from the United States because "the terms attached smacked of imperialism or neo-colonialism."[38] In July 1971, he confronted the United States Ambassador: when she threatened him that the U.S. government might feel impelled to deny the allegation, Barrow coolly responded that if they did, he would produce documentary evidence in his possession about their interference.[39] When she told him that there were no CIA operations in Barbados, he looked at her with an expression of open disbelief. The British High Commissioner confirmed that Barrow's suspicions were not unreasonable: "a depressing series of telegrams from Trinidad makes it clear that the U.S. Embassy here is not fully briefed about CIA operations (or perhaps, to be fair, has just not fully hoisted in the nature of their operations) and makes me wonder (a) what has been going on that we do not know about, and (b) more importantly, how many more cards does Barrow hold in his hand. At the moment he seems to be playing stud poker with the Americans and the Opposition."[40]

Barrow won his game, winning a third term in office in the 1971 elections. The next year, he joined Manley, Burnham, and Williams in opening diplomatic relations with Cuba, in defiance of both the United States and the Organization of American States.[41] In 1972, he discreetly rebuked Cameron Tudor, who opposed this step, dismissing him as Minister of External Affairs and sending him, pointedly, to London as High Commissioner. Barrow, in the late 1970s, frequently complained that his government in Barbados faced the same kind of destabilization from the United States as Manley's government in Jamaica. Perhaps, again, he did not exaggerate, since from 1975 Cuban planes used Barbados's airport, quite possibly with Barrow's tacit consent, to supply the Caribbean troops fighting beside the MPLA in Angola against South African- and CIA-backed insurgents. The relations between Barbados and the United States warmed somewhat when "Tom" Adams defeated Barrow in the 1976 elections, climaxing with Barbados's "invitation" to the United States to invade Grenada in 1983.

The echoes of the post-1968 crisis, however, continued into and beyond the Adams period. There were some small violent ripples: in 1978, the ritual burning of "Mr. Harding" on the Garrison Savannah at the end of the first Kadooment march led to a riot in which the surrounding crowd pelted this giant effigy of a white planter with stones and bottles, while on 13 March 1979, the morning when news of the Grenada Revolution had come over the radio, a crowd at Kensington Oval closed play with volleys of bottles, wood, and iron. But it was mainly as culture—the flowering of the Barbadian calypso, sound systems playing dub, the taking of African names, new energies going into drama and the visual arts—that the impact of 1970 was most enduring. Rastafarianism spread like a cane fire among the youth, even when dreadlocks were known to lead to police harassment. Barbadians, who so often had held themselves above their West Indian neighbors, began to borrow happily from the cultural riches of Trinidad and Jamaica.

The experience of Barbados, thus, on close inspection, appears more similar to that of Jamaica, Trinidad, or Grenada than has usually been assumed. And there, as elsewhere in the region, secondary decolonization in the 1970s coincided with a period in which American imperialism extended its interests in the Anglophone Caribbean. Perhaps, then, the most striking recent political echo came in 2003, when Barbados led the entire fifteen-nation bloc of CARICOM states in refusing to bow to American and British pressure to support the attack on Iraq. Prime Minister Owen Arthur, who had spent a formative period during the Manley period in Jamaica, declared, in a speech that could have come from Errol Barrow's mouth, to the House of Assembly on 17 March 2003:

> We do not need any tutelage in relation to the conditions under which we should support international engagement with sovereign states . . . We do not support the precept nor the practice of regime change. We believe that every country has the right to self-determination. We do not believe in the practice of unilateralism, no matter how powerful the country that seeks to practice it may be. . . . we also find very disturbing the precept of pre-emption as the basis of self-defense as practiced by nations.[42]

The struggle for (secondary) decolonization goes on.

Notes

A note on unpublished sources:

The chapter turns on sources from the Foreign and Commonwealth Office files on events in, and relations with, Barbados after it became independent in 1966. Since the Government of Barbados has not released its own records of the period to the Barbados Archives, this collection in London is the best public archival source we have for the history of independent Barbados. These are cited in full in the notes under the rubric TNA, with a reference to the CO, FCO and PREM series in which the documents may be found.

Newspapers:

> *Barbados Observer*, 26 June 1971.
> *The Democrat*, 25 June 1971.
> *Financial Times*, 3 May 1970.
> *The Guardian*, 4 April 1970.
> *Morning Star*, 7 December 1967.
> *The Nation* (Barbados), 18 March 2003.
> *The Times*, 4 April 1970.

> 1. Fanon, *Wretched of the Earth*; Mbembe, *On the Postcolony*.
> 2. On this George Lamming was persistently acute. See, among other interventions, the essays of *The Pleasures of Exile*; his description of the dangerous alienation between the political classes and the energies of the "Forest Reserve" in *Season of Adventure*; and his contrasting of the despotisms of European *conquistadores* and postcolonial political *caciques* in *Natives of My Person*.
> 3. Brathwaite, 222.
> 4. See Scott, *Conscripts of Modernity*, and Meeks, *Radical Caribbean* and *Narratives of Resistance*.

5. Ranger, 631–41.

6. Carmichael and Hamilton, xiii. H. Rap Brown wrote to U. Thant at the United Nations that same year, offering to send a "Black American International Brigade" to liberate South West Africa (*Morning Star*, 7 December 1967).

7. Although see Worrell, *Pan-Africanism in Barbados*, and Drayton, "The Problem of the Hero(ine) in Caribbean History," 32.

8. "Black Power in Barbados" [undated essay], The National Archives, London [cited henceforth as TNA]: FCO 63/443.

9. British High Commission, Bridgetown to T.R.M. Sewell, Caribbean Department, Foreign and Commonweath Office, 15 May 1970, TNA: FCO 63/449.

10. "Barbados Political Report for October 1953," TNA: CO 1031/131.

11. C.M.C. Henderson to Bushe, 22 February 1946, TNA: CO 537/1682.

12. "Barbados: Political Situation 1949," TNA: CO 537/4890.

13. For their anxiety about Crawford, see Sir G. Bushe to Secretary of State for the Colonies, 21 February 1945; C.M.C. Henderson (Senior Defense Security Officer, Caribbean Area), 22 February 1946; the reports of T. Walker Paton (Security Officer); and other correspondence in "Strikes and Other Labour Disputes," TNA: CO 537/1682 and "Intelligence and Political Situation Reports," TNA: CO 537/2247, 4890, 6126, 7371.

14. On the British Guiana crisis, see Drayton, "Anglo-American 'Liberal' Imperialism."

15. Grant was described as part of "the local Communist group," Monthly Political Reports, 5/8, October 1953, TNA: CO 1031/131.

16. For the controversy surrounding the Barbados Yacht Club, see "The 'Royal' Barbados Yacht Club and the Loss of the 'Royal' Title," TNA, FCO 23/28.

17. The High Commissioner exulted at Tudor's holding of the Foreign Affairs portfolio, "This should be to our advantage since Tudor . . . has more affinity to the United Kingdom." D. A. Roberts minute, October 1971, TNA: FCO 63/703, f. 10.

18. "Personality Note: Visit of Errol Barrow, Prime Minister of Barbados, to UK," 17 July 1972, TNA: PREM 15/572.

19. "Barbados: Annual Report for 1969," TNA: FCO 63/441.

20. Central Intelligence Agency, "Black Power Organizations in the Western Hemisphere," CIA Report, 1971.

21. "Political Parties in Barbados," 1 January 1970, TNA: FCO 63/590.

22. "Intercept of a Broadcast on Radio 610," 14 April 1970, TNA: FCO 63/590.

23. "Relations between Barbados High Commission in London and Her Majesty's Government," 31 December 1970, TNA: FCO 63/451; *The Guardian*, 4 April 1970; *The Times*, 4 April 1970.

24. Peter Simmons was, thirty-eight years later, the High Commissioner of Barbados to London, while his brother David became Chief Justice of Barbados.

25. The High Commissioner wrote to London, complaining of attempts to minimize the significance of the incident: "It is a matter of interest to the whole Caribbean." J. S. Bennett to Mayall, 17 August 1970, TNA: FCO 63/451.

26. J. S. Bennett to Mayall, 21 April 1970, TNA: FCO 63/444.

27. "Annual Report of Barbados in 1970," TNA: FCO 53/700.

28. R. B. Crowson to Allen, 15 May 1970, TNA: FCO 63/443.

29. "Armed Forces in Barbados," TNA: FCO 63/447.

30. "An Army for Barbados," *Financial Times*, 3 May 1970.

31. "Barbados: Annual Review for 1970," 1 January 1971, TNA: FCO 53/700.

32. "Barbados Monthly Review, July 1970," TNA: FCO 63/451.

33. "Central Bank of Barbados," TNA: FCO 63/446.

34. Minute of J. S. Bennett, 20 November 1970, TNA: FCO 63/446.

35. "Visit of Errol Walton Barrow to the United Kingdom," 17 July 1972, TNA: PREM 15/572.

36. "Annual Report of Barbados in 1970," TNA: FCO 53/700.

37. "Political Relations between the United Kingdom and Barbados," TNA: FCO 63/705; for the 1966 period, see Cox Alomar, "An Anglo-Barbadian Dialogue," 671–90.

38. *The Democrat*, 25 June 1971, and *Barbados Observer*, 26 June 1971.

39. D. A. Roberts, Barbados High Commission to C. S. Roberts, Caribbean Department of the Foreign and Commonwealth Office, 12 July 1971, TNA: FCO 63/705.

40. Ibid.

41. On this period, see Phillips, 69–102.

42. *The Nation* (Barbados), 18 March 2003.

Bibliography

Beckles, H. *Chattel House Blues: Making of a Democratic Society in Barbados From Clement Payne to Owen Arthur*, Kingston: Ian Randle, 2004.

Brathwaite, K. *The Arrivants: A New World Trilogy*, London and New York: Oxford University Press, 1973.

Carmichael, S. and Hamilton, C. *Black Power: The Politics of Liberation in America*, New York: Random House, 1967.

Central Intelligence Agency. "Black Power Organizations in the Western Hemisphere," CIA Report, 1971, Thompson-Gale: *Declassified Documents On Line*, Document No. CK3100352539.

Cox Alomar, R. "An Anglo-Barbadian Dialogue: The Negotiations Leading to Barbados's Independence, 1965–6," *The Round Table*, 93, 2004, 671–90.

Drayton, R. "Anglo-American 'Liberal' Imperialism: British Guiana and the World since September 2011" in Roger Louis (ed.), *Yet more Adventures with Britannia: Personalities, Politics and Culture in Britain*, London and New York: I.B. Tauris, 2005, 321–42.

———. "The Problem of the Hero(ine) in Caribbean History," *Small Axe*, 15: 1 (34), 2011, 26–45.

Fanon, F. *The Wretched of the Earth*, [1961] London: Penguin Books, 1990.

Lamming, G. *Season of Adventure*, London: M. Joseph, 1960.

———. *Natives of My Person*, New York: Holt, Rinehart and Winston, 1971.

———. *The Pleasures of Exile* [1960] Ann Arbor: University of Michigan Press, 1992.

Mbembé, A. *On the Postcolony*, Berkeley: University of California Press, 2001.

Meeks, B. *Radical Caribbean from Black Power to Abu Bakr*, Kingston: University of the West Indies Press, 1996.

———. *Narratives of Resistance: Jamaica, Trinidad, the Caribbean*, Barbados: University of the West Indies Press, 2000.

Phillips, D. "Defense Policy in Barbados, 1966–1988," *Journal of Interamerican Studies and World Affairs*, Vol. 32, No. 2, Summer 1990, 69–102.

Ranger, T. O. "Connexions between 'Primary Resistance' Movements and Modern Mass Nationalism in East and Central Africa," *The Journal of African History*, Vol. 9, No. 4, 1968, 631–41.

Scott, D. *Conscripts of Modernity: The Tragedy of Colonial Enlightenment*, Durham: Duke University Press, 2004.

Worrell, R. *Pan-Africanism in Barbados*, Washington DC: New Academia Publishing, 2005.

6

"Sitting on a Volcano"

Black Power in Burnham's Guyana

KATE QUINN

The Rodney Riots in Jamaica (October 1968) and the February Revolution in Trinidad and Tobago (February–April 1970) have been seen as watershed moments in the history of the postindependence Anglophone Caribbean. Symptoms of a region-wide upsurge of popular discontent with economic and social conditions in the postcolonial Caribbean state, these two episodes delivered an unsettling message to political leaders in the Caribbean. Popular protest—once channeled into grievances against the colonial state—was now clearly directed at local governments condemned as puppets of the neocolonial order. News of the disturbances in Trinidad broke the same week that Guyana celebrated the founding of its Co-operative Socialist Republic.[1] What began in Trinidad as a protest against the arrest and trial of West Indian students in Canada (the Sir George Williams University affair) quickly escalated into large-scale demonstrations protesting local conditions, foreign exploitation of Trinidad's economy, and the perceived failure of Eric Williams's PNM government to deliver meaningful change. The February Revolution, led by an organized opposition under the banner of Black Power, was quelled under a state of emergency after months of demonstrations, the mass mobilization of organized labor, and a mutiny by a section of the Trinidad Regiment. Notably, the key disturbances of 1968 and 1970 both had Guyanese connections: Cheddi Jagan Jr., son of the opposition People's Progressive Party leader, was among the West Indian students whose arrests in Canada had catalyzed the formation and early demonstrations of the National Joint Action Committee (NJAC) in Trinidad. More significantly, the Jamaican protests of 1968 witnessed the emergence of Guyanese academic and activist Walter Rodney as a powerful figure capable of galvanizing the political energies of a cross-class opposition of students, intellectuals, and the urban unemployed.

The lessons of Jamaica and Trinidad were not lost on Guyana's Prime Minister, Forbes Burnham, who perceived in these events a "direct challenge to the whole establishment." Returning from the Caribbean Heads of Government Conference in Kingston, Burnham was "depressed" by the complacency of his regional colleagues, observing, "We are all sitting on a volcano."[2] This chapter will explore the implications of this "volcano" for Guyana, first examining the complex relationship between the government and domestic Black Power organization ASCRIA (the African Society for Cultural Relations with Independent Africa) and the impact this relationship had on Burnham's domestic and regional policies. Burnham's strategy toward this potentially volatile ally was one of containment and compromise, a "bargaining process"[3] through which he sought to mollify Black Power elements by granting certain policy concessions—explored here through an analysis of Burnham's response to the crisis in Trinidad; policies of cooperative socialism; and issues of political asylum. The chapter then assesses local interactions with U.S. Black Power, focusing on the presence in Guyana of a significant community of African-American exiles/émigrés. The conflicts that erupted when variants of U.S. Black Power ideology were transplanted to the Caribbean context highlight both the contradictions within Burnham's stance on domestic and external Black Power, and the tensions and fragmentation within the imagined community of the "black international."[4]

In analyzing the dynamics of Caribbean Black Power, Guyana offers a different perspective to other cases in the region where relations between Black Power movements and the state were mutually antagonistic. Burnham was unique in the Anglophone Caribbean in the extent of his public declarations of support for Black Power; in the welcome he accorded to high-profile Black Power activists banned elsewhere in the Caribbean (with the notable exception of Rodney); in actively courting relations with black militants from the United States; and in providing material support for liberation movements on the African continent. Addressing the Seminar of Pan-Africanists and Black Revolutionary Nationalists (held in Georgetown to coincide with Guyana's inaugural Republic celebrations), Burnham declared that his government "was not hostile to Black Power, was not afraid of Black Power, and thinks that Black Power has a contribution to make, especially here in the Caribbean."[5] Partly as a result of this stance, and partly as a result of Guyana's ethnically divided politics, Burnham was also unique in the support—initially at least—that he levered from internal and external Black Power elements, notably, ASCRIA, and a number of North American black activists circulating in Guyana and the wider region in the period. Whereas elsewhere in the region, the "enemy of Black Power [was] the regime . . . political leaders who [were] themselves black,"[6] in Guyana Burnham for a time successfully depicted the regime as the vehicle through which the goals of Black Power could be most readily achieved. Thus the Seminar of Pan-Africanists (hosted by ASCRIA and attended by African-American delegates) praised Burnham as "the only militant black governing leader in this hemisphere" and pledged full support for the new Co-operative Socialist Republic as "a revolutionary concept worthy of encouragement."[7]

Engagement with Black Power was considerably complicated by the particular alignments of ethnic and party politics in the Guyanese context. Memories of the country's devastating ethnic violence of 1963–64 were fresh when Burnham's PNC party took the country to independence in 1966, after elections and an independence settlement widely perceived to have been designed to keep Cheddi Jagan's Marxist-oriented People's Progressive Party (PPP) out of power. From the 1968 elections onward, Burnham's predominantly Afro-Guyanese PNC was kept in power through fraudulent means in a country with a majority Indo-Guyanese population (50 percent compared to 44 percent Afro-Guyanese in 1966). There were, therefore, considerable anxieties about the implications of Black Power in the Guyanese context. In all of this, Burnham had to walk a difficult political tightrope, balancing, on the one hand, the desires and aspirations of his black constituency and erstwhile Black Power allies, and, on the other, the unifying imperatives of Guyana's official national motto: One People, One Nation, One Destiny. With the examples of Jamaica and Trinidad before him, Black Power was a force that Burnham was keen to contain.

ASCRIA and the PNC: Early Relationship

Discussing the Trinidad upheavals with the British High Commissioner to Georgetown, Burnham was scathing in his assessment of his political counterparts in the Caribbean, who, he believed, had been "slow to recognise" the threat posed to "the whole establishment" by the recent upsurge in black radicalism. While he believed that "the situation in Guyana [was] less threatening than . . . elsewhere," he insisted that this was only because he was "taking steps all the time to preempt those who could make serious trouble."[8] The troublemakers to whom Burnham referred were not the main opposition party—Cheddi Jagan's People's Progressive Party (PPP)—but a segment of his own supporters: namely, Eusi Kwayana's ASCRIA.[9]

Founded in 1964, ASCRIA was the creation of Sydney King, who changed his name to Eusi Kwayana as part of his campaign for Afro-Guyanese people to embrace the African dimensions of their ancestral heritage.[10] Although born during Guyana's difficult period of interethnic violence, ASCRIA's founding was not based on narrow claims of ethnic defensiveness but on the desire to instill a positive sense of identity and self-worth among the Afro-Guyanese, giving them the same cultural confidence as other groups whose greater retention of identity, values, and cultural norms was viewed as advantageous. Primarily, ASCRIA sought to promote the economic and cultural uplift of the Afro-Guyanese: the first to be achieved as part of a broader push for economic independence (discussed below), and the second through a "cultural revolution" to overturn the cultural distortions of colonialism and celebrate black achievements, history, and heritage. While ASCRIA did not describe itself as a Black Power organization (and was founded before the term was popularized), its aims and sympathies were wholly consistent with the concept, and it was viewed both internally and externally as the most significant and influential Black Power group in the country. At ASCRIA's third annual convention, held in 1969, Kwayana stated: "We have not in ASCRIA seen fit to use the slogan of Black Power as our mode of struggle. But we want it to be understood that so long as Black Power means the overthrow of white power by non-whites, by black men and brown men and yellow men, we identify ourselves with it completely and without reserve."[11]

Although ASCRIA membership was initially relatively small (U.S. Embassy reports estimated some four hundred participants at its inaugural convention; later reports spoke of about one thousand "hard-core" members), it had many sympathizers within the Afro-Guyanese population. Kwayana's personal reputation and ASCRIA's relationship with the ruling party made it the most significant black organization outside the PNC. The main base of its support was drawn from Kwayana's stronghold of Buxton, a village about twenty miles east of Georgetown, where he commanded the loyalty of almost all of the two-thousand-strong population. It was also influential among a number of constituencies of interest to the PNC, including Georgetown's black working class and unemployed, and the younger and more militant members of the PNC, with notable support within the party's youth wing, the Young Socialist Movement, and the Guyana Mine Workers Union in Linden (Wismar-MacKenzie), traditionally a PNC stronghold.[12] Indeed, as U.S. Embassy reporters observed, ASCRIA sympathizers were to be found not only among the party rank and file, but also within the government (in the Ministry of Economic Development), the state sector (the head of the National Co-operative Bank), and even within the cabinet: the poet Martin Carter (Minister of Information) was named as one of a handful of cabinet members for whom it was suspected that ASCRIA's "Africanism and left wing socialism [had] a certain appeal."[13]

Hence, though ASCRIA and the PNC were never formally allied, there were significant overlaps and connections between the two (both personal and political) in the early years of ASCRIA's existence. Kwayana, who had served as General Secretary of the PNC from 1958 to 1961, was considered to be "personally close" to Burnham, and although he was no longer a party member, his position as chairman of the state-controlled Guyana Marketing Corporation placed him to some degree within the shadow of the state. The perception of a friendly alliance was reinforced by Kwayana's travels with Burnham, both inside Guyana and on his visit to Central and East Africa in late 1970; Burnham's addresses to ASCRIA-sponsored seminars and rallies; and ASCRIA's statements endorsing the principles of cooperative socialism. This impression was further encouraged and perpetuated by the opposition press, which sought to discredit both organizations by painting them as hand in glove.[14]

Burnham's stake in this relationship was undoubtedly the desire to keep ASCRIA's constituency of disaffected black youths and urban unemployed within the orbit of the PNC. While Kwayana was viewed as a "problem [to be handled] gingerly," the government was conscious of the value of his support, and there is some evidence to suggest that it sought to secure this support during the 1964 and 1968 elections by "providing some jobs" to ASCRIA's members.[15] While too close an association with ASCRIA presented Burnham with a number of problems—not least undermining his projection of a multiethnic government of national unity—at least in the early years of his rule, he calculated that it would be unwise to alienate an organization whose support for his government had some political utility.

For ASCRIA's part, relations with the PNC were partly motivated by the expectation that an Afro-Guyanese government would be receptive to their program of social and economic reforms. As ASCRIA member Sase Omo recalls, their hope was that a black government "would . . . put social and economic structures in place to soften the impact of underdevelopment."[16] ASCRIA therefore publicly endorsed the government's position on a number of occasions, including, in contrast to radical black organizations elsewhere in the Caribbean, aligning themselves with the government's own definition of Black Power. At the ASCRIA congress of 1969, Kwayana stated: "We are glad to hear the Prime Minister of Guyana, our brother Forbes Burnham, declare . . . that for him and his government, Black Power meant the consolidation and strengthening of the rule of the black man and brown man over the resources and destinies of Guyana. . . . This is a concept with which ASCRIA has no quarrel."[17] However, ASCRIA's relationship with the ruling party was never uncritical or unconditional, and its public statements endorsing PNC policy were invariably accompanied by demands for more radical reforms. As Kwayana told journalist Ricky Singh in 1965, "just as [ASCRIA] had opposed the PPP, [so too] it would oppose the PNC if that party failed the people."[18] ASCRIA's anticorruption campaigns of 1970, while "quietly [angering] the ruling party," cemented its role as "the conscience and the critic" of the PNC, as well as Kwayana's reputation for personal incorruptibility and political independence.[19] ASCRIA's "growing strength, self-confidence and influence" thus marked it as a potential threat long before its split with the PNC in October 1971.[20]

ASCRIA, the PNC, and Regional and Domestic Policies

The pressures of domestic and regional Black Power mobilization were one among many factors that shaped the environment in which government policies were made. At home, Burnham faced criticism not only from the avowedly Marxist-Leninist PPP, but also from radical academics based at the University of Guyana, who, like Kwayana, wished to see reforms pushed in a more radically leftward direction. Abroad, Burnham had to balance relations with Western powers, which were significant investors in Guyana (in particular, the United States, Britain, and Canada) against his commitment to an agenda of Third World internationalism, in which he sought to play a leading role. In this context, the PNC's shift to the left, which accelerated after 1970, must be viewed as part of a broader strategy to outmaneuver the leftist opposition at home and to project (and genuinely pursue) a progressive image abroad. However, there is substantial evidence that among the constellation of factors influencing PNC policy, the upsurge of an antigovernment Black Power protest movement in neighboring Trinidad and the existence of an increasingly vocal Black Power group at home played a significant part in Burnham's policy calculations in a number of key areas. Most notable among these is how Burnham responded when fellow Caribbean leader Eric

Williams in Trinidad found himself in serious jeopardy from an opposition movement mobilized under the banner of Black Power.

The Crisis in Trinidad

From the early days of the crisis, Burnham was "keeping a very close watch on things" in Trinidad, with "deep anxiety about the situation [there] and the effects it may have in Guyana."[21] Toward the end of April 1970, Burnham's anxieties were to be confirmed, as events in Trinidad took a more serious turn. On 21 April, the Williams government declared a state of emergency in response to a proposed march on the capital, Port of Spain, by an alliance of the Black Power movement, NJAC, and militant labor, including the dreaded combination of (Afro-Trinidadian) oil workers and (Indo-Trinidadian) sugar workers, and a threatened general strike. Despite the arrest and incarceration of the Black Power leadership, groups of rioters continued to smash shop windows in downtown Port of Spain, defying the efforts of the police—armed with batons and tear gas—to enforce the dawn-to-dusk curfew. Much more ominous, however, were the events unfolding that same morning at the army barracks at Teteron, west of the capital, where two young lieutenants, Raffique Shah and Rex Lasalle, led a mutiny of a section of the Trinidad Regiment just as it was being mustered to enforce the state of emergency. In light of this dramatic turn of events, Prime Minister Williams turned to his regional colleagues, sending urgent requests to the governments of Jamaica and Guyana for troops and weaponry to confront the potential uprising. Such an event was unprecedented in the postindependence Anglophone Caribbean and did little to dispel the impression that the government was teetering on the edge of collapse. Indeed, one of Burnham's first reactions to the news was to wonder if he should "back a loser."[22]

It is in this context that Burnham called an emergency cabinet meeting on how to respond to Williams's request for military assistance. While cabinet members were "adamant" that Guyana should not send troops, Burnham initially hesitated on the question of sending some token weapons. According to the observations of the British High Commissioner, Burnham's reluctance "primarily concerned . . . the very strong reactions which could be anticipated here by black power advocates."[23] On the question of weapons, "Burnham actually felt obliged to consult the President of ASCRIA privately [on the issue] and received a sharp reaction."[24] All but one of the PNC cabinet voted against sending assistance to Williams. Two days into Trinidad's state of emergency, Burnham sent a hand-carried letter to Williams, stating in effect that his hands were tied not only by a lack of resources but also by "internal political factors."[25]

Burnham was deeply perturbed both by the "possibility that Williams might fall" and by "his inability to send assistance,"[26] highlighting as it did, the degree of influence that could be exerted by the "troublesome" elements of domestic Black Power. However, the events in Trinidad also reaffirmed to him that his strategy of preemptive policy concessions was "absolutely right." In Burnham's eyes, Williams had failed to "heed the warning signs that he himself [had] heeded for a long time past,"[27] and while it was "hard for him to turn his back on [a] beleaguered . . . colleague," in this instance domestic interests prevailed over regional solidarity—a political calculation also made by Hugh Shearer in Jamaica, who likewise failed to provide military aid. As the U.S. Ambassador inferred, "[To have provided] material assistance in putting down [the] black power movement in Trinidad would [have] undercut Burnham's own strategy of containing [Black Power] in Guyana by establishing himself as a leading proponent of change."[28]

Cooperative Socialism

The main vehicle for projecting this vision of change was the establishment of the Co-operative Socialist Republic, officially inaugurated on 23 February 1970, the same week that demonstrations in Port of Spain marked the first salvos of Trinidad's February Revolution. The founding of the republic marked a symbolic break from Guyana's colonial past, removing the British monarch as titular head of state and terminating the relationship with Britain's Privy Council, now replaced by a local court of appeal. It also provided a platform to consolidate the policy of "cooperative socialism": a development strategy that proposed to effect the decolonization of the economy by making cooperatives the dominant sector, increasing local ownership and control of the nation's resources, and pursuing policies of import substitution, all framed in a discourse of "self-help."

Cooperative socialism was the product of many factors relating to the particular constellations of local, regional, and international politics in the period. Besides the genuine desire to increase local control over Guyana's economic resources, more instrumental rationales were at play, including the desire to outmaneuver the PPP and other opposition critics on the left. But it is also clear that the government was responding to discontent from within its own quarters, and in particular from ASCRIA, whose members were critical of the PNC's economic strategy, and who were now exerting "powerful pressures [on the government] to secure a radical improvement in the economic situation of the Afro-Guyanese community."[29] It is quite clear that the very fundamentals of cooperative socialism responded precisely to the grievances articulated by the Black Power movement both at home and in the wider Caribbean.

ASCRIA had long pushed for "economic power" and had tempered its statements of support for the PNC with demands for more radical economic reforms. Strongly influenced by Nyerere's concept of *ujaama* in Tanzania, its earliest manifesto proposed cooperatives as the principal basis for economic development; subsequent declarations called on the government to estab-lish a "collectivist economy," with proposals including the "decolonization of commercial banks," the organization of cooperatives for savings, agricul-ture, forestry, mining, and small businesses, and the nationalization of Guy-ana's key industries, bauxite and sugar.[30] In a position statement in March 1970, ASCRIA made clear that "We are for nothing less than a thorough non-capitalist revolution." While the statement credited the Co-operative Republic as providing "an instrument" to achieve that end, it also pushed for assurances that "reconstruction will not exclude any sector and will include the so-called commanding heights of the economy."[31] Economic grievances were also at the heart of Black Power agitation in the wider Caribbean, as was evident in the attacks on major symbols of foreign and local capital in both the Jamaican and Trinidadian demonstrations. Burnham was not slow to make this connection, and in his private conversations he chastised his Caribbean colleagues for their apparent failure to recognize that the price of their political survival was economic reform.

At the height of the troubles in Trinidad, Burnham made a speech that strongly emphasized a leftward turn in PNC policy. Addressing the party faithful at the April 1970 Congress of the PNC, Burnham demanded the elimination of the "metropolitan presence" in the Caribbean; denounced foreign aid, private investment, and foreign banks; reiterated the govern-ment's intention to develop Guyana's economy through cooperatives; an-nounced a policy of state control over imports; made a strong critique of racism in Britain and the United States; and embraced Black Power as part of the "socio-economic revolution" being forged, it was claimed, under the auspices of cooperative socialism.[32] It is not difficult to see Burnham's brand of economic nationalism as a counter to precisely the criticisms made by radical black movements both at home and elsewhere in the Caribbean. In-deed, Burnham made this connection explicit both in private conversations, in which he repeatedly cited Black Power pressures as a factor in his drive for reform, and in public speeches, in which, deploying the same rhetoric as the radicals, he sought to project PNC policy as the solution to the problems they identified. Addressing the Seminar of Pan-Africanists and Black Revolutionary Nationalists, Burnham declared "we do not yet own our country, we do not yet control our economy, and it is in this context that the emphasis on co-operatives . . . must be understood."[33] These policies were pushed through despite anxieties within Burnham's own cabinet. Indeed, in a conversation with the British High Commissioner, Attorney-General Shridath (Sonny) Ramphal complained that "in his handling of Black Power elements here, Burnham had gone too far in making concessions to Eusi Kwayana. In doing this . . . Burnham thought he was controlling Kwayana but in fact the boot was on the other foot. Far too much internal policy reflected Kwayana's demands."[34]

However, it is also evident that Burnham was able to manipulate Black Power agitation for his own ends. The threat of "another Trinidad" served as political leverage in asking the Americans to try to persuade the Canadian government to drop the trials of the West Indian students involved in the Sir George Williams University affair in Montreal, Burnham warning that "things could get out of hand in the Caribbean if the trials continue."[35] More significantly, Burnham also used the excuse of Black Power pressures as justification for pushing ahead with nationalization plans for Guyana's bauxite industry. In this endeavor, he could capitalize on anti-Canadian feelings and demonstrations in Guyana and the wider Caribbean to pressure "Canadian . . . and other Western financial interests," including the Canadian bauxite company DEMBA, which was purchased by the government in 1971.[36] Behind the scenes, Burnham told the British High Commissioner that his move on the bauxite companies was motivated by Black Power pressures, poverty and the risk-taking it encouraged, and the desire not to retire before he was 55—"[which] is what would happen if he doesn't get on with radical policies."[37] Publicly, the message was much the same. Discussing government proposals for majority control of the bauxite companies in an interview with the New York Times, Burnham stated that: "People tell me that a corporation like ALCAN can break me, but I say it is better to be broken by a corporation like ALCAN than it is to be broken by *your own people*."[38]

It was precisely these economic policies that Burnham repeatedly deployed to undermine the idea that Black Power—understood as a movement of opposition—was necessary in the Guyanese context. In the same speech outlining his leftward turn, Burnham stated:

> Some Black Power advocates . . . look upon the movement as an op-
> position movement against all governments. . . . In Guyana where the
> black man has achieved political and social gains . . . and is striving to-
> wards economic power, Black Power as an opposition is self-defeating.
> Its role . . . is to strengthen and support the social and economic revolu-
> tion that is taking place here.[39]

Hence, in a veiled warning to domestic Black Power elements, Burnham consigned Black Power to a supportive role to consolidate the achievements claimed for his own government, thus shifting the locus of guardianship of Black Power from ASCRIA to the PNC.

These policies (and the asylum policy, below) were a means of contain-ing any threat that might be posed by domestic Black Power, as well as other critics on the left, including the Ratoon Group and the PPP. With regards to ASCRIA, Burnham was, at this stage, relatively successful. AS-CRIA had significant ideological leverage with regards to PNC policy, but Burnham was not one to tolerate competitors. On several occasions, Kway-ana was pressed to rein in potentially embarrassing demonstrations (such as a protest directed at the United States the day that representatives from the Rockefeller mission were visiting Georgetown),[40] and he was strongly discouraged from attending a "teach-in" on Black Power held at the Uni-versity of Guyana, at which he had been billed to speak. In the view of the British High Commissioner, "it [was] abundantly clear that Kwayana did not appear because he had been told by Burnham that he had bloody well better not."[41] The real success, however, was in eliciting voluntary state-ments of support. At the height of the crisis in Trinidad, ASCRIA, echo-ing Burnham's own position, issued a statement that Guyana had no need to emulate the Trinidadian protesters. "Our solidarity with the Trinidad movement is unquestioned," they declared, "but it does not mean that we have to do here what our brothers there have felt forced to do. In Guyana things are rather more advanced along the road of real power . . . We con-sider that the government backed by the people has created the conditions for an economic revolution and that the revolutionary potential of the Co-operative Republic is boundless."[42]

Asylum

One of the more controversial policies to have been influenced by ASCRIA was that of offering asylum to "freedom fighters" in the global black strug-gle—a policy in stark contrast to governments elsewhere in the Anglophone

Caribbean that had imposed bans on various North American and Caribbean proponents of Black Power. At the third annual convention of ASCRIA in 1969, Kwayana congratulated Burnham "for steering clear of the anti–Black Power hysteria that has got hold of Jamaica, Trinidad and Surinam" but at the same time "[demanded] that the Guyana government . . . make it known that it will give sanctuary to all black liberators in trouble in their land of residence."[43] In February 1970, Burnham announced just such an asylum policy at the Seminar of Pan-Africanists and Black Revolutionary Nationalists, making explicit reference to "freedom fighters from the continent of Africa" as well as the United States.[44]

The 1970 announcement gave expression to a process that had already been under way since the late 1960s. As Richard Helms noted in his report on black radicalism in the Caribbean, "the greatest amount of travel by U.S. blacks has been to Guyana." Helms specifically mentioned the meeting of Pan-Africanists and Black Revolutionary Nationalists, noting that a follow-up meeting was held in New York in March and that plans had been discussed for a permanent secretariat to be established, as well as a Pan-African journal linked with the Center for Black Education in Washington DC.[45] It was through such transnational connections, and in particular through contact with Eusi Kwayana, that Guyana came to be seen as an attractive destination for African Americans seeking models of black governance beyond the boundaries of the United States.

It is difficult to ascertain how many took up Burnham's offer, partly because Guyanese immigration statistics list only nationality, not ethnicity. However, one exile, Larry Watani Stiner, a Black Power activist who escaped from San Quentin prison and fled to Guyana, describes joining a "bustling refugee community" on his arrival in Georgetown in May 1974. Stiner viewed Guyana at that time as "one of the centers of international Black Power."[46] In the late 1960s, the *Guyana Graphic* makes reference to the existence of a "Black Power . . . settlement" comprising American Black Muslims on the East Bank of the Berbice River at Bradwagt Sari (East Berbice-Corentyne); in all probability, this is the same community referred to by the U.S. Ambassador, who notes that the PNC government had given permission to "about three dozen U.S. Black Muslims to immigrate to Guyana and occupy an abandoned rural land settlement."[47] This settlement came to the attention of the newspapers after three of its "disciples" were shot in an incident between a local "Black Power advocate" and members of the U.S. Black Muslim community, who had "recently come to Guyana to spread the gospel of 'Black Power' and were addressing a meeting of prospective . . . followers." The article goes on:

... the Guyanese "Black Power" leader accused the American of mis-
leading and attempting to fleece the Guyanese people. A heated argument arose and during the disorder that followed, the bearded men,
attired in their African shirts, were shot and wounded. Among those
questioned by the Ruimveld Police yesterday were several other American "Black Power" advocates who came to Guyana late last year to help
establish the local movement on a firmer footing.[48]

As the local press correctly affirmed, such a settlement could not have existed "without the tacit approval of the authorities."[49] Indeed, members of the
Guyanese government were directly involved in facilitating the entrance of
several dubious characters who came in under the aegis of the asylum/im-
migration policy, including Abdul Malik (Michael X), who was arrested in
Guyana for the murder in Trinidad of Gale Ann Benson; Rabbi Washington
(David Hill), whose House of Israel organization was used by the state to
terrorize the opposition (discussed below); and the "Reverend" Jim Jones,
whose People's Temple cult gained notoriety after the mass suicide/murder
at Jonestown, Guyana, in 1978.[50]

The image of Guyana as a model of progressive black government also
attracted a handful of African Americans who found jobs in the Guyanese
government, most often with the Ministry of Education (as teachers) or
in the bureaucracy of the Ministry of Information and Culture. Significant
among these was writer and activist Julian Mayfield, who came to Guyana
in October 1971. Mayfield was attracted by the reports he received from fellow U.S. artist and activist Tom Feeling, who was employed as a planning
officer in the Ministry of Education, who wrote in praise of Burnham's pro-
gressivism, self-help schemes, and financial contribution to African liberation movements.[51] Mayfield's move to Guyana was characteristic of his long
search for alternative ways of living in an international black community
outside the confines of the white-majority society of the United States. In
the 1950s and 1960s, as Kevin Gaines has shown, Mayfield and his fellow
expatriates sought just such an alternative in Kwame Nkrumah's Ghana.[52]
By the early 1970s, Burnham's policies and overt appeals to Pan-African
solidarity put Guyana on the map as a destination for those who, like Mayfield, saw themselves as part of a supranational black community, "[as] much
at home in Georgetown as in New York or Dar-es-Salaam."[53] In Guyana,
Mayfield was soon employed as a communications specialist in the Ministry of Information and Culture, and as a senior special assistant in the
Office of the Prime Minister, roles that essentially involved selling a posi-

tive vision of Burnham's Guyana both to the Guyanese electorate and to the international black community. However, a shift in the relationship between ASCRIA and the PNC would soon plunge the American expat community into the mire of Guyanese domestic politics, forcing them to choose between competing versions of black emancipation polarized around the two figures of Burnham and Kwayana.

The PNC–ASCRIA Split and Fallout

Mayfield may have come to Guyana in search of black solidarity, but his arrival there coincided with important shifts in the political landscape that fragmented Afro-Guyanese allegiances. As is well known, the relatively benevolent relations between ASCRIA and the PNC were short-lived. Kwayana was a thorn in Burnham's side, and Burnham was not long in finding ways to undercut someone he saw as a potential rival. In October 1971, after the attempted shooting of University of Guyana lecturer and Ratoon group member Joshua Ramsammy, ASCRIA issued a statement recanting its backing of the PNC:

> The radical groups in the Caribbean, the USA and elsewhere were assured by ASCRIA that the Guyana Government not only supported black nationalist and revolutionary organizations but also believed in socialist-co-operative people's democracy. It would seem that we now have to withdraw those assurances.[54]

ASCRIA's stance on corruption (establishing watchdog committees in government departments and calling two high-ranking PNC ministers to account on corruption charges) and its involvement in the bauxite strikes of 1971 ultimately made its association with the PNC untenable, leading to direct conflict with the ruling party. By 1973, they were in open opposition. ASCRIA released a position paper in June that year affirming that it had come "to a definite break with the PNC." Criticizing what it called the philosophy of "Burnhamism," the paper stated that the PNC had "betrayed the wishes and interests of the African people, and has engaged in a vicious betrayal and exploitation of manual workers, farmers and brain workers and of all true revolutionary principles." "Burnhamism," the paper went on, "has done nothing to liberate the descendants of African slaves from their economic bondage" but operated instead as "the political vehicle of a middle class bent on establishing itself as a bourgeoisie . . . while maintaining control of the working masses and deceiving them with slogans of equality."[55]

This shift from an exclusively Afro-Guyanese agenda to a new emphasis on class analysis facilitated new alliances that cut across Guyana's ethnic divides. As early as 1970, ASCRIA had initiated a phase of intense internal debate on African-Indian relations, concluding with the decision that "there could be no revolution of one race" in Guyana.[56] The most significant example of this new interethnic approach to struggle was the January 1973 land rebellion on East Coast Demerara, which saw ASCRIA lead an occupation of disused sugar lands by African and Indian sugar workers against the powerful Bookers Company. While the government forcibly evicted the squatters, it shortly announced that the state would take possession of all disused sugar lands, to be redistributed for the purposes of agriculture and housing.[57] Actions such as the land rebellion helped to lay the foundation for the birth of the Working People's Alliance (WPA) in 1974, marking "a new chapter in ethnic politics and ethnic relations in Guyana."[58] Founded to create a new political culture that would break with the old politics of racial division in Guyana, the WPA was formed as an alliance of ASCRIA, with a number of leftist opposition groups, including the Indian Political Revolutionary Associates (IPRA) led by Moses Bhagwan, with whom ASCRIA had jointly campaigned in the sugar lands occupation; the university-based Ratoon group; the Working People's Vanguard Party (WPVP); and the Movement Against Oppression (MAO). When Walter Rodney joined the WPA on his return to Guyana in 1974, the scene was set for a serious confrontation with the state.

The split between ASCRIA and the PNC had serious repercussions, both for the organization itself and for those émigrés viewed to be closely associated with it. ASCRIA's 1971 statement recanting its backing of the PNC alleged that "[the] security police and immigration officials show openly that they have received new orders about ASCRIA and other black organizations."[59] By 1973, the PPP's *Mirror* newspaper was reporting an "intolerable degree" of pressure on the organization: while Kwayana was singled out for constant harassment by the regime, ordinary members found their jobs under threat; even those schooled in ASCRIA classes, it was alleged, found it increasingly difficult to obtain employment in the state sector.[60] Burnham's willingness to persecute his former allies in ASCRIA—not least through intimidation by such dubious groups as the House of Israel—underlines the opportunism of his engagement with Black Power.

The exile and expatriate community also found itself targeted by the authorities. Those perceived to be closely connected to Kwayana were harassed and in some cases deported, as was the case with two African-American teachers, Shango Umoja and Mamadou Lumumba, deported to the United

States after a dawn raid on their homes by immigration officials in January 1973. Larry Watani Stiner, who had escaped from San Quentin prison in 1974, fled from Guyana after being threatened by the Minister of Home Affairs. As Watani Stiner recalls, his attendance at a WPA meeting incurred the ire not only of the Guyanese government but also of the exile community:

> I was informed that the government was considering turning me over to U.S. authorities as an example to other exiles who dared to flirt with, or participate in activities opposed to the PNC regime. . . . I was criticized by the African American exile community for being "naïve" and "ungrateful" to Burnham after he granted us sanctuary in his country . . . My "political excursions" were putting everyone at risk.[61]

This conflict spilled over into the pages of the international black press. While deportees Umoja and Lumumba "raised hell" in articles calling on all Pan-Africanists to reject the "fascist . . . PNC government," Julian Mayfield, in his role as communications specialist in the Burnham government, mounted a counterpropaganda campaign to depict his employers as "the most progressive black government in the hemisphere" and to discredit Eusi Kwayana, who he now privately viewed as "a political enemy."[62] In these endeavors, Mayfield visited the United States to give his version of events in Guyana to such figures as Maya Angelou, Angela Davis, and David Dubois, asking the latter to provide "good exposure" in the *Black Panther* newspaper to counter the allegations circulated by Umoja and Lumumba and give positive press to Burnham.[63] He also placed articles in the *Black Scholar* condemning "the mystique called Kwayanism . . . which is being vigorously promoted in Pan-African circles outside the country" and accusing Kwayana of race betrayal because of his refusal to support Burnham in the 1973 elections.[64]

In his contention that if the PNC lost the elections, "all African people everywhere will have lost,"[65] Mayfield essentially endorsed Burnham's position that the primary facilitator of real Black Power was the government. This "race first" position went well beyond anything that Burnham could have publicly espoused. Mayfield's conception of Black Power did not include the Indo-Guyanese, who were depicted in his unpublished hagiography, *Burnham of Guyana*, as "the enemies of all things politically and culturally African" and as the primary aggressors in Guyana's ethnic conflict of the early 1960s.[66] In this version of black solidarity, Mayfield was at odds with many Caribbean variants of Black Power that explicitly included all nonwhites, and with the class analysis being adopted by Kwayana, Rodney, and other black radicals in the wider Caribbean.

Conclusions

In the context of the wider Caribbean, the Guyanese case is unusual, both in Burnham's approach to Black Power and in the relationship between domestic Black Power and the ruling party. While Burnham was not the only Caribbean leader to try to co-opt elements of Black Power rhetoric and policy, he recognized the potential threat earlier, went further in responding to Black Power demands, and was initially more successful than his counterparts in deflecting opposition from those quarters. In contrast to Williams in Trinidad and Shearer in Jamaica, Burnham initially managed to achieve a modus vivendi with domestic Black Power in the form of ASCRIA, deploying a two-pronged strategy of preemptive reforms that, on the surface at least, responded to Black Power demands, while behind the scenes he maneuvered to pressurize and neutralize so-called troublemakers. Shearer, who had taken a hard line on Black Power in Jamaica, and Williams, whose moderate economic reforms and cabinet reshuffles were seen as too little too late, were unable to cast off the image that they were black overseers facilitating the white exploitation of their countries. Burnham, on the other hand, quite consciously sought to differentiate himself from his regional colleagues, precisely to avoid their fate. Cooperative socialism, nationalizations, and a radicalized foreign policy allowed Burnham to position himself more successfully to both a foreign and a domestic audience as a progressive leader willing to push through a radical program of change.

This approach was not without risks. Fail to push reforms far enough and he risked losing the support of the radicals; push the reforms too far and he risked alienating his core constituency as well as foreign benefactors. In this sense, Burnham's statement that he would rather be broken by ALCAN than by his own people highlights the wider dilemma faced by Caribbean leaders in this period, caught between the powerful economic interests of the West and the demands of their own people for change.

Although Burnham had a greater degree of success than his Caribbean counterparts in managing the perceived threat of black radicalism, he was also less likely than them to be faced with a genuine threat of an internal black rebellion, such as that which had been seen in neighboring Trinidad. This is partly because of the policy concessions described, but primarily because of the nature and strength of ethnic and party politics in Guyana in the period. The PNC was an Afro-Guyanese government in a majority Indo-Guyanese state, and, as is widely accepted, from 1968, maintained its position in power through fraudulent means. So long as ethnic and party allegiances coalesced; so long as the PNC was identified as aligned with black interests and the Indo-Guyanese PPP viewed as a threat to those interests; and so long as there was no viable alternative, the Afro-Guyanese were unlikely to bring down Burnham. The Guyanese political context was therefore not conducive to the successful establishment of an opposition movement mobilized around the concept of Black Power; indeed, the issue of Black Power divided the opposition, driving a deeper wedge between ASCRIA and the PPP.

As the 1970s progressed, it became increasingly evident that cooperative socialism was not delivering the economic liberation it promised, but was instead the instrument of a ruling class distributing its benefits to an ever-shrinking elite. ASCRIA's break with the PNC marked a fundamental shift in Guyanese politics, splitting the allegiance of the Afro-Guyanese and opening the gateway for new alliances that began to cut across Guyana's ethnic divides. ASCRIA's eschewal of a primarily black agenda for a new multiethnic alliance reflected a wider shift in Caribbean politics in the period, with many of those who had been profoundly influenced by Black Power moving toward analyses that were more firmly rooted in the concept of class relations. In Guyana, it was the new multiethnic alliance in the shape of the WPA that constituted a far greater threat to the administration than the Black Power movement, whose criticisms Burnham had been able to absorb and contain. When the volcano erupted in Guyana, hence, it was not in the form of Black Power. The real tremors came when Guyanese of different ethnicities, social classes, and political persuasions took to the streets in the late 1970s to protest the iniquities of Burnham's rule. It is to the credit of ASCRIA and groups like Ratoon that they diagnosed those iniquities so early on, at a time when many in the Caribbean and beyond chose to look the other way.

Notes

1. Guyana's Co-operative Socialist Republic was inaugurated on 23 February 1970, the date chosen to mark the anniversary of the Cuffy slave rebellion of 1763. The symbolic "invasion" of Port of Spain cathedral by National Joint Action Committee protesters in Trinidad took place on 22 February 1970.

2. K. G. Richie, British High Commission, Georgetown, to T.R.M. Sewell, Caribbean Department, Foreign and Commonwealth Office, 25 April 1970.

3. Ibid.

4. The term is used by Michael O. West, William G. Martin, and Fanon Che Wilkins in their edited volume, *From Toussaint to Tupac: The Black International Since the Age of Revolution*.

5. American Embassy Georgetown to Secretary of State, Washington DC, 16 March 1970.

6. Knowles, 40.

7. "Pan-Africanists Pledge Support for Burnham," *Sunday Graphic*.

8. Richie to Sewell, 25 April 1970.

9. Ibid. Burnham was also referring to "those he described as the gentlemen of the university," i.e., the Ratoon Group of intellectuals centered at the University of Guyana.

10. "ASCRIA's Cultural Revolution," *Guyana Graphic*.

11. Kwayana, "ASCRIA's Plan for Guyana," *Sunday Graphic*.

12. American Embassy Georgetown to Secretary of State, Washington DC, "ASCRIA Influence," 15 March 1971.

13. American Embassy Georgetown to Secretary of State, Washington DC, "Black Power in Guyana," 3 April 1969. See also American Embassy Georgetown to Secretary of State, Washington DC, "ASCRIA Influence," 15 March 1971.

14. "In High Places," *Weekend Post and Sunday Argosy*; Jagan, "ASCRIA's Balancing Act," *Mirror*.

15. American Embassy Georgetown to Secretary of State, Washington DC, "Black Power in Guyana," 3 April 1969. In an interview with African-American writer Julian Mayfield, who worked for the PNC government, Burnham also alleged that he had given Kwayana backing at the bank and paid his brother's scholarship fees (Mayfield interview with Forbes Burnham, Julian Mayfield Papers).

16. Omo, telephone interview with author, 9 September 2002.

17. Kwayana, "ASCRIA's Plan for Guyana," *Sunday Graphic*.

18. Kwayana, *The Morning After*, 113.

19. Westmaas, "1968 and the Social Foundations of the WPA," 10; Latin America Bureau, *Guyana: Fraudulent Revolution*, 50.

20. American Embassy Georgetown to Secretary of State, Washington DC, "Black Power in Guyana," 3 April 1969.

21. British High Commission Georgetown to Foreign and Commonwealth Office, Telegram No. 241, 22 April 1970.

22. Ibid.

23. Ibid.

24. British High Commission Georgetown to Foreign and Commonwealth Office, Telegram No. 245, 24 April 1970.

25. American Embassy Georgetown to Secretary of State, Washington DC, "Reaction to Trinidad Developments," 23 April 1970.

26. Ibid.

27. Richie to Sewell, 8 May 1970.

28. American Embassy Georgetown to Secretary of State, Washington DC, "Williams Request for Guyanese Assistance," 22 April 1970.

29. Richie to Sewell, 25 April 1970.

30. Kwayana, "ASCRIA's Plan for Guyana," *Sunday Graphic*.

31. American Embassy Georgetown to Secretary of State, Washington DC, "Reaction to Trinidad Disturbances," 16 March 1970.

32. Central Intelligence Agency, *Central Intelligence Bulletin*, 8 April 1970.

33. American Embassy Georgetown to Secretary of State, Washington DC, "Reaction to Trinidad Disturbances," 16 March 1970.

34. Richie to Sewell, 2 May 1970.

35. American Embassy Georgetown to Secretary of State, Washington DC, "Burnham Urges Halt to Canadian Prosecution WI Students," 25 March 1970. ASCRIA and (separately) the PPP and "militant leftist and black power elements of the University of Guyana staff organization" picketed the Canadian High Commission and the offices of the Canadian bauxite company DEMBA in Georgetown (American Embassy Georgetown to Secretary of State, Washington DC, "Support for Black Power Demonstrations in Trinidad," 9 March 1970).

36. Ibid. Burnham entered discussions with Reynolds and DEMBA (the Demerara Bauxite Company, a subsidiary of the Canadian company ALCAN) in May 1970. The nationalization of DEMBA in 1971 was the first in a series of nationalizations that took place over the next five years, culminating in 1976 in the hugely symbolic nationalization of Bookers.

37. Richie to Sewell, 9 May 1970.

38. Cited in Knowles, 47 (her emphasis).

39. "What the PM Thinks about Black Power," *New Nation*. Burnham originally made this point in his speech to the PNC Annual Congress in 1969 and quoted this segment again in his speech to the PNC Congress the following year.

40. American Embassy Georgetown to Secretary of State, Washington DC, Telegram, 27 May 1969.

41. Richie to Sewell, 14 March 1970.

42. Ibid.

43. Kwayana, "ASCRIA's Plan for Guyana," *Sunday Graphic*.

44. Burnham's speech to the Seminar of Pan-Africanists and Black Revolutionary Nationalists cited in Manley, 90–91.

45. CIA Directorate of Intelligence, Intelligence Memorandum "Black Radicalism in the Caribbean," 6 July 1970.

46. Watani Stiner and Brown, 545.

47. "3 Black Power Disciples Shot at 'Scheme' Meeting," *Guyana Graphic*; American Embassy Georgetown to Secretary of State, Washington DC, "Black Power in Guyana," 3 April 1969.

48. "3 Black Power Disciples Shot at 'Scheme' Meeting," *Guyana Graphic*.

49. "Riding the Tiger of Black Power," *Islamic Guardian*.

50. On Abdul Malik, see Naipaul, "Michael X and the Black Power Killings in Trinidad." On Rabbi Washington and the House of Israel, see Morrison, "Birds of a Feather." On Jonestown and the People's Temple, see Lewis, *Gather with the Saints at the River*.

51. Feeling to Mayfield, Julian Mayfield Papers, 22 April 1971.

52. Gaines, "From Black Power to Civil Rights: Julian Mayfield and African American Expatriates in Nkrumah's Ghana, 1957–1966."

53. Mayfield to Minister McDavid, "African-Americans Employed by Ministry of Information and Culture and Ministry of Education," Undated memo, Julian Mayfield Papers.

54. "Politics of the Gun Condemned," *Weekend Post & Sunday Argosy*.

55. "ASCRIA Has Definitely Broken with the PNC," *Sunday Graphic*.

56. Kwayana, "The Masterminds Have Made Buxton-Friendship a Human Wasteland."

57. American Embassy Georgetown to Secretary of State, Washington DC, "Government of Guyana Statement on Squatting Issue and Editorial Reaction," 24 January 1973. The timing of the land occupation—in an election year—suggests that, again, it was to pressure the government into accelerated reforms.

58. Hinds, 13. On the birth and development of the WPA, see Westmaas, "Resisting Ortho-doxy" and "1968 and the Social Foundations of the Working People's Alliance."

59. "Politics of the Gun Condemned," *Weekend Post & Sunday Argosy.*

60. "PNC Regime Steps Up Witch-Hunt Against ASCRIANS," *Mirror.*

61. Watani Stiner and Brown, 545.

62. Mayfield to Prime Minister Forbes Burnham, "US Publicity re Prime Minister," 14 August 1973; Lumumba and Umoja, "Viewpoint: Guyana Slave Trading 1973 Afro-Americans Charge"; Mayfield, "Divisive Blacks in Revolutionary Clothing"; Mayfield to Feeling, 5 June 1973.

63. Mayfield to Burnham, "Recent Visit to Los Angeles and San Francisco re US Opinion of Guyana," 25 May 1973.

64. Mayfield, "Political Refugees and the Politics of Guyana," 33–35. See also his two-part article "Divisive Blacks in Revolutionary Clothing," in the Julian Mayfield Papers.

65. Mayfield, "Divisive Blacks in Revolutionary Clothing."

66. Mayfield, *Burnham of Guyana* manuscript, 157, 158, the Julian Mayfield Papers.

Bibliography

"3 Black Power Disciples Shot at 'Scheme' Meeting," *Guyana Graphic*, 14 January 1969.

American Embassy Georgetown to Secretary of State, Washington DC, "ASCRIA Influence," 15 March 1971, "Government of Guyana Statement on Squatting Issue and Editorial Reaction," 24 January 1973, Reg. 59, Central Foreign Policy Files 1970–73, Box 2344, Pol. 13-10 (Guyana), NARA II, Maryland.

American Embassy Georgetown to Secretary of State, Washington DC, "Black Power in Guyana," 3 April 1969, Telegram, 27 May 1969, Reg. 59, Central Foreign Policy Files, 1967–69, Box 2169, Pol. 13–10 (Guyana), NARA II, Maryland.

American Embassy Georgetown to Secretary of State, Washington DC, "Support for Black Power Demonstrations in Trinidad," 9 March 1970, "Reaction to Trinidad Disturbances," 16 March 1970, "Burnham Urges Halt to Canadian Prosecution WI Students," 25 March 1970, "Williams Request for Guyanese Assistance," 22 April 1970, Box 2630, Pol. 23-8; "Reaction to Trinidad Developments," 23 April 1970, Box 2631, Pol. 23-9 (Trinidad and Tobago), Reg. 59, Subject-Numeric Files, 1970–73, NARA II, Maryland.

"ASCRIA Has Definitely Broken with the PNC," *Sunday Graphic* (Guyana), 24 June 1973.

"ASCRIA's Cultural Revolution," *Guyana Graphic*, 1 October 1968.

"ASCRIA's Plan for Guyana," *Sunday Graphic*, 23 March 1969.

British High Commission Georgetown to Foreign and Commonwealth Office, Telegram No. 241, 22 April 1970, Telegram No. 245, 24 April 1970, FCO 63/463 "Black Power in Guyana," TNA, London.

Central Intelligence Agency, *Central Intelligence Bulletin*, 8 April 1970, CIA-RDP79T00975 A015900110001-3, NARA, Maryland.

Central Intelligence Agency, Directorate of Intelligence, Intelligence Memorandum "Black Radicalism in the Caribbean," 6 July 1970, NARA, Maryland.

Feeling to Mayfield, 22 April 1971, the Julian Mayfield Papers, Schomburg Center for Research in Black Culture, New York.

Gaines, K. "From Black Power to Civil Rights: Julian Mayfield and African American Expatriates in Nkrumah's Ghana, 1957–1966" in Christine Appy (ed.), *Cold War Constructions: The Political Culture of United States Imperialism*, Amherst: University of Massachusetts Press, 2000, 257–330.

Hinds, D. *Ethnopolitics and Power Sharing in Guyana: History and Discourse*, Washington DC: New Academia Publishing, 2011.

"In High Places," *Weekend Post and Sunday Argosy* (Guyana), 6 December 1970.

Jagan, C. "ASCRIA's Balancing Act," *Mirror* (Guyana), 22 March 1970.

Knowles, Y. "Guyana: Black Power?" in Brian Irving (ed.) *Guyana: A Composite Monograph*, Puerto Rico: Inter-American University, 1972.

Kwayana, E. "ASCRIA's Plan for Guyana," *Sunday Graphic*, 23 March 1969.

———. "The Masterminds Have Made Buxton-Friendship a Human Wasteland," http://www.guyanacaribbeanpolitics.com/kwayana/kwayana_040603.html.

———. *The Morning After*, Georgetown: Guyana-Caribbean Politics Publications, 2005.

Latin America Bureau, *Guyana: Fraudulent Revolution*, London: Latin America Bureau Ltd., 1984.

Lewis, G. *Gather with the Saints at the River: The Jonestown Guyana Holocaust of 1978*, Rio Piedras: Institute of Caribbean Studies, 1979.

Lumumba, M. and Umoja, S. "Viewpoint: Guyana Slave Trading 1973 Afro-Americans Charge," *Caribbean Express*, 1973, in Julian Mayfield Papers, Schomburg Center for Research in Black Culture, New York.

Manley, R. *Guyana Emergent: The Struggle for Non-Dependent Development*, Boston: G. K. Hall, 1979.

Mayfield, J. "Political Refugees and the Politics of Guyana," *The Black Scholar*, Vol.4, No.10, July-August 1973, 33–35.

Mayfield, J. The Julian Mayfield Papers, Schomburg Center for Research in Black Culture, New York.

Mayfield to Burnham, "Recent Visit to Los Angeles and San Francisco re US Opinion of Guyana," 25 May 1973, the Julian Mayfield Papers.

Mayfield to Feeling, 5 June 1973, the Julian Mayfield Papers.

Mayfield to Prime Minister Forbes Burnham, "US Publicity re Prime Minister," 14 August 1973, the Julian Mayfield Papers.

Mayfield to Minister McDavid, "African-Americans Employed by Ministry of Information and Culture and Ministry of Education," [undated memo] the Julian Mayfield Papers.

Mayfield, *Burnham of Guyana* [manuscript, no date], the Julian Mayfield Papers.

Mayfield, "Divisive Blacks in Revolutionary Clothing" [no date], the Julian Mayfield Papers.

Mayfield interview with Forbes Burnham, Box 32, Folder 32/9, [no date] the Julian Mayfield Papers.

Morrison, A. "Birds of a Feather—Burnham and the Rabbi" in his *Justice: The Struggle for Democracy in Guyana, 1952–1992*, Georgetown: Red Thread Women's Press, 1998.

Naipaul, V. S. "Michael X and the Black Power Killings in Trinidad" in his *The Writer and the World*, London, Basingstoke and Oxford: Picador, 2003.

Omo, S. Telephone interview with author, Georgetown, Guyana, 9 September 2002.

Oxaal, I. *Race and Revolutionary Consciousness: A Documentary Interpretation of the 1970*

Black Power Revolt in Trinidad, Cambridge, Massachussetts: Schenkman Publishing, 1971.

"Pan-Africanists Pledge Support for Burnham," *Sunday Graphic*, 1 March 1970.

"PNC Regime Steps Up Witch-Hunt Against ASCRIANS," *Mirror*, 14 November 1973.

"Politics of the Gun Condemned," *Weekend Post & Sunday Argosy*, 10 October 1971.

Richie, K. G., British High Commission, Georgetown, to Sewell, T. R. M., Caribbean Department, Foreign and Commonwealth Office, 14 March 1970, 25 April 1970, 2 May 1970, 8 May 1970, 9 May 1970, FCO 63/463, "Black Power in Guyana," TNA, London.

"Riding the Tiger of Black Power," *Islamic Guardian*, 19 January 1969.

Watani Stiner, L. and Brown, S. "The US Panther Conflict, Exile and the Black Diaspora: The Plight of Larry Watani Stiner," *Journal of African American History*, (92:4) 2007, 540–52.

West, Michael O., William G. Martin, and Fanon Che Wilkins, (eds), *From Toussaint to Tupac: The Black International Since the Age of Revolution*, Chapel Hill: University of North Carolina Press, 2009.

Westmaas, N. "Resisting Orthodoxy: Notes on the Origins and Ideology of the Working People's Alliance," *Small Axe*, 15, March 2004, 63–81.

———. "1968 and the Social Foundations of the WPA," Conference Paper, 39th Annual Conference of the Association of Caribbean Historians, Kingston, 6–10 May 2007, 1–24.

"What the PM Thinks about Black Power," *New Nation*, 22 March 1970.

7

An Organic Activist

Eusi Kwayana, Guyana, and Global Pan-Africanism

NIGEL WESTMAAS

In *Holding Aloft the Banner of Ethiopia: Caribbean Radicalism in Early Twentieth Century America* (1998), Winston James wrote of Caribbean Pan-Africanism,

> It is no accident that the Caribbean, being the area that has historically produced the most peripatetic of all African peoples, has also thrown up an extravagantly disproportionate number of Pan-Africanist political activists and intellectuals. Edward Wilmot Blyden, H. Sylvester Williams, J. Alembert Thorne, J. Robert Love, Theophilus Scoles, Antenor Fermin, René Maran, Hubert Harrison, Marcus Garvey, Claude McKay, Una Marson, J. A. Rogers, Jean Price Mars, Ras Makonnen, C.L.R. James, Aimé Césaire, Leon Gontran Damas, and, perhaps the most under rated of them all—the great George Padmore of Trinidad . . . [1]

Significantly absent from James's list is Eusi Kwayana (Sidney King) of Guyana.[2] Despite its more far-reaching embrace of relatively unknown Pan-Africanists, Hakim Adi and Marika Sherwood's collection, *Pan-African History: Political Figures from Africa and the Diaspora since 1787* (2003), similarly fails to cite Kwayana.[3]

The dimensions, impact, and outcome of Eusi Kwayana's connections with Pan-Africanist causes and organizations, along with his curious exclusion from the Pan-African and Black Power storyline, are the chief focus of this chapter. It is a curious thing that Kwayana—a colleague of the late Walter Rodney and someone who engaged with Pan-Africanist titans like Kwame Nkrumah, and who contributed inestimably to black culture in Guyana and the Caribbean—somehow manages to escape official texts and narratives of the Pan-African and Black Power record. Even where he is acknowledged, his contribution to Pan-Africanist outlook and organization is given relatively short shrift. Unlike his regional counterparts, including Stokely Carmichael (Kwame Ture), Aimé Césaire, George Padmore, Walter Rodney, and others, Kwayana, in spite of his substantial literary, moral, philosophical, cultural, and political contribution to the Pan-Africanist project over decades, is underrepresented in Pan-African or, indeed, more general political profiles of the region and further afield.

But how to account for this under-recognition of Kwayana, whose towering contribution extends from the mid-1940s to modern times? Was it his preferred residence for over fifty years, in the village of Buxton, and the rural mythology that this inspired that hindered his adoption by the mainstream?[4] Was it his observant and critical outlook toward certain African leaders that is responsible for his relative absence from the limelight? Or is it the way that the traditional Pan-African narrative is ordered and prioritized that is at the crux of Kwayana's general absence? This chapter will assess Kwayana's contributions as a Pan-Africanist, and suggest reasons why he has not received the recognition he richly deserves.

The immediate challenge is to define Kwayana's placement within the Pan-African paradigm. To do so, it is first necessary to define what is meant here by the term "Pan-Africanism," and second, to sketch out Kwayana's own understanding of, or identification with, the concept. Most scholars and activists concur that the precise definition of Pan-Africanism is elusive, arguing that it "has always manifested a multidimensional character, which has included the use of political, economic, religious, and cultural approaches in the struggle to rehabilitate Africa and its people."[5] As Imanuel Geiss outlines in his work *The Pan-African Movement* (1968), Pan-Africanism can be defined "in both a narrower and a broader sense." The narrow sense ("Pan-Africanism") tends to be confined to "the political movement for the unification of the African continent"; the broader sense ("pan-Africanism") can include a wide range of cultural, intellectual, and political struggles broadly seeking the emancipation of, and invoking solidarity between, the peoples of Africa and its diaspora. For the purposes of this chapter, pan-Africanism is to be understood in its broadest sense, recognizing the flexibility and variety in historical and contemporary usages of the term. This broad definition here encompasses Black Power, which is seen as a particular manifestation of pan-Africanism in the context of the mid-twentieth century. As such, in this chapter the terms "pan-Africanism" and "Black Power" are used interchangeably.

Kwayana's own position on labels indicates a similarly flexible approach to the concept. Responding to a critic in a Guyanese newspaper, he stated that he had no objection to the pan-Africanist label, "although for myself I know that there must be at least twenty varieties of Pan-Africanists. My emphasis in Pan-African circles over the last two decades at least has been how to share power in multi-ethnic societies and how to help women's emancipation . . ."[6] Elsewhere he argued that pan-Africanism ought to be understood "as a body of thought and action shared but not uniform or dogmatic. A dynamic movement continually transforming itself and gaining new ideological perspectives in light of changing circumstance. Flowing from masses, groups and occasionally leaders of governments. Tending to the goal of restoration of freedom and dignity at home and abroad."[7] As will be argued in this chapter, this heterodox and expansive approach may partly explain Kwayana's unwarranted absence from the pantheon of pan-Africanist figures recognized in recent scholarship.

Formative Background and Stirrings: Emergence of the Organic Activist

Kwayana's embrace of pan-Africanist causes did not happen overnight. There were several formative phases on his journey to activism in this sphere. These include his youth; political activism in the burgeoning nationalist movement from 1946 to 1957; the period of breakup of political and ethnic unity in 1957 in Guyana; his founding and involvement with the African Society for Racial Equality (ASRE) and later the African Society for Cultural Relations with Independent Africa (ASCRIA)—both organizational assertions of African independence and ideology in the face of a divided Guyana in the early 1960s; the formal parting with the ruling People's National Congress party by 1971; and finally his involvement as a founding member of the Working People's Alliance (WPA) in 1974 and membership in the party to the present day. Kwayana's formative experience as an African Guyanese substantially influenced his global outlook and not the other way around. In fact, he was determinedly a "stay at home" pan-Africanist, a fact that augments the working definition here of Kwayana as an organic activist. Indeed, his relatively light overseas travel for the purpose of promotion and/or contact with pan-Africanist or Black Power organizations and his immersion in Guyanese national and village life help explain his unconventional associations with the black and pan-Africanist world.

Eusi Kwayana was born in Lusignan, but grew up in Buxton, one of the key independent villages pioneered by slave descendants of Africans from the continent. British Guiana, a colony of Britain since 1803,[8] was at the time of Kwayana's birth one of the biggest producers of sugar in the Caribbean. The burden of hard living was severely felt among the masses—in this instance the Africans, East Indians, native Amerindians, Portuguese, and other groups. The peculiarities of the Guyanese context, and in particular its multiethnic makeup, are central to understanding Kwayana's ideological formation and the shaping of his political consciousness. Two elements in Kwayana's youthful formation will be highlighted here: (1) his personal experiences of growing up in a multiethnic context and (2) the broader development of ethnic organizations and ethnic consciousness among both Afro- and Indo-Guyanese communities in the first decades of the twentieth century.

Kwayana attributes his own initial sense of global Africa and ancestry to a humble source, that is, to a comment made by an elder woman called "Gang-Gang" from Lusignan in the early 1930s. She told the five-year-old Kwayana: "Congo a' high nation, picknie, Congo a' high nation." By his own admission, this proud aphorism had a lasting impact on his own articulation of African cultural expression. Indeed, the strength of African cultural tradition in West Coast Berbice, where Kwayana grew up, was such that the area was known as "little Africa," famed for its skillful drummers and other cultural reserves in the African tradition. In such rural areas, the influence of the Anglican Church was negligible, thus allowing some African-Guyanese communities to develop their African cultural roots. As a lay reader in the local Anglican church in Buxton, Kwayana was particularly sensitive to its colonial moorings, observing that it "brought its own culture, not worrying to tell the congregation of the part played by Africans in the growth of the Christian religion."[9]

Reflecting on interactions with his Indian neighbors, Kwayana wrote that he "became curious about Muslims when at about six in Lusignan a school mate told me about his fast, which later I learned was Ramadan."[10] He also escaped from home one night to "peep through the schoolhouse window to see a Hindu classic play Indar Sabha."[11] Later, in the 1940s, Kwayana supported the Indian independence movement and served at one time as an associate member of the Indian National Congress of British Guiana (then located in his native Buxton). He also clashed with the Anglican church over the 1948 shooting of striking Indian sugar workers by the colonial authorities at Plantation Enmore, East Coast Demerara. The Buxton sage "attacked the Church leadership . . . from the lectern" for accepting a donation from the Bookers' corporation "to help build the Convent of the Good Shepherd . . ."[12]

The broader history of African-Guianese development and transformation after emancipation in 1838 is crucial to assessing the uncommon environment from which Kwayana's political and organizational support and struggle for African consciousness emerged. In the post-emancipation era from 1838, a number of prominent African-led associations were active through to the twentieth century. The Guiana African Association, founded in 1842, was one such organization. Composed of an embryonic black and colored middle class that sought to break the British colonial stranglehold over the civil service, the group was condemned by the then Governor Henry Light for its "mischievous agitation among the black population."[13] A second organization, the British Guiana Afro-Improvement Association was established in 1901, but little information on its activity is available in the public record. In 1919, the Garveyite Universal Negro Improvement Association (UNIA) was launched in Guyana. At maximum strength, it possessed seven groups scattered geographically across the colony with a combined average membership of two hundred. The local Garveyites were instrumental in organizing annual dinners for the "poor of all races," sent messages of solidarity to the Indian anticolonial movement (directly to Mahatma Gandhi), and publicly defended the state of Abyssinia (Ethiopia) when the Italians invaded in 1935. The high point of the Guyana UNIA was the much-publicized visit of Marcus Garvey to British Guiana in 1937.

By the early 1920s, the influence of middle-class African-Guyanese had become apparent in organizational form in the colony. In 1922, the middle-class-led Negro Progress Convention (NPC) was established, developing at its height forty branches throughout Guyana, followed in 1924, a year before Kwayana's birth, by the founding of the African Development Association.[14] In 1937, one of Guyana's most significant African-Guyanese organizations, the League of Colored Peoples (LCP), was founded. Claiming to be nonpolitical, the LCP self-identified as a "social organisation which in so far as it caters for the needs of the people of African descent in this country endeavours to take a recognisable place beside such useful and long established racial organisations as the British Guiana East Indian Association."[15] In 1950, the LCP sponsored a visit to British Guiana by Eze Ogueri II, a Nigerian paramount chief and the "first African dignitary to visit Guyana publicly and be exposed to the descendants of Africa and the general public."[16] As Kwayana recalls in *No Guilty Race,* the Ogueri stopover had a transforming effect on the local black population, and citizens turned out in the thousands as the Nigerian chief visited towns and villages throughout British Guiana.

The first decades of the twentieth century also saw a parallel organizational movement among the Indian Guyanese, as groups and prominent individuals began to assert themselves in what Clem Seecharan terms "a nationalist temper," strongly influenced by the anticolonial movement and ultimately by independence in the Indian subcontinent. This process simultaneously challenged British colonial hegemony and provoked competition with their African-Guyanese counterparts, who, Seecharan notes, viewed Indians as "predatory interlopers and usurpers of their ancestral lands."[17] This competition was especially prevalent around issues such as the Colonization Scheme or the effort to populate British Guiana with Indians.[18]

The cumulative effect of these personal experiences and broader Guyanese political mobilization impacted the youthful Kwayana. African-Guyanese, in spite of the restriction and repression of colonial rule, enjoyed a deep history of organization for economic independence and cultural solidarity. Colonial domination did not prevent African (and Indian) resistance and cultural assertion of all forms at both the rural and urban levels. The early experience of anticolonialism and ethnic organization are thus important dimensions in Kwayana's subsequent gravitation to pan-Africanism, his self-critical reflection on his role in supporting the ruling regime in the 1960s, and his open support for multiracial unity from the 1970s.

Nationalism, Pan-Africanism, and Ethnic Division

Kwayana's formal political career began in the 1940s, when he joined the multiethnic and nationalist Political Affairs Committee (PAC) established by Cheddi Jagan and others in 1946. PAC's emergence and development coincided with the rise of a global movement of anticolonialism reflected in events such as the important 1945 Pan African conference in Manchester, the Mau Mau rebellion in Kenya, and African anticolonial and liberation struggles that brought figures like Kwame Nkrumah, Sekou Toure, Jomo Kenyatta, Tom Mboya, and others to the forefront of pan-African consciousness. These causes were strongly supported by the PAC and by its successor, the People's Progressive Party (PPP), of which Kwayana was a founding member and in whose short-lived 1953 administration he served as Minister of Works and Communications.[19] In spite of the early unity of the PPP, which had coalesced around the independence agenda, by 1957 the national movement had split along ideological and, later, distinctly racial lines. One result of the dissection of the national movement was Kwayana's association with Forbes Burnham's wing, the PPP(B) or Burnhamite PPP (later called the PNC). According to Thomas Spinner, "the mercurial, incorruptible, but temperamental Sidney King [Kwayana] had been a marvelous prize for Burnham when he collared the young activist after his departure from the PPP in 1957."[20] Kwayana became first Vice Chairman in 1957 and later General Secretary of the new People's National Congress (PNC).[21] In 1958, the PNC led the country in organizing Ghana Day (after the first anniversary of Ghanaian independence), and Kwayana was active in the mobilization of the event in Guyana villages.

Kwayana's participation in Guyana's formal party politics of the pre-independence period has been the source of two diametrically opposed critiques of his political positions and presumed ethnic allegiances. For some, his early work with the Indo-Guyanese and participation in the Jaganite PPP raise questions about his commitment to his fellow Afro-Guyanese, particularly in the sensitive context of Guyana's volatile interethnic relations and party politics as they evolved from the late 1950s. It has also been a source of concern for supporters of pan-Africanism in its more mainstream variant. For others, his association with what became the Burnhamite PNC and his response to the interethnic violence of the early 1960s has seen him painted as an ethnic separatist. On the latter concern, the assertion that "Kwayana called for partition" has dogged him since the 1960s, and for all intents and purposes to the present day. The rudiments of the allegation of "partition" lie in the statement by leading members of the African Society for Racial Equality, including Kwayana, H. H. Nicholson, and C. K. Mercurius, in response to the ethnic antagonism of the early 1960s between African and Indian Guyanese.[22] In summary, the plan, in the face of extreme racial division, called for negotiations to consider a settlement; a joint and equal partnership of the leaders of the African and Indian people; a constitutional committee for the rights of the minorities with power to review legislation; and finally, partition as a last resort. In his own defense, Kwayana claims that it was only when the PPP and the PNC and "their leaderships and elites rejected the proposal that the 'last resort of partition' became a talking point."[23]

ASCRIA and Local and Global Pan-Africanism

Kwayana is also credited with pioneering modern Caribbean Black Power by taking up the issue in earnest from as early as 1961. His black-nationalist

African Society for Racial Equality (ASRE) and African Society for Cultural Relations with Africa (ASCRIA) were formed in 1961 and 1964, respectively—well before similar organizations that comprised the Caribbean Black Power Movement.[24] In 1961, ASRE, according to Kwayana, "did what no other force was doing at the time. It defined the basis of the conflict in Guyana as racial . . . all other forces in Guyana defined the problem as ideological . . ."[25]

Kwayana's popularization of the African contribution and his work among rural and urban Africans brought range and focus to the historical linkages between Africa as mother continent and Guyanese and Caribbean Africans. During Kwayana's time at the helm of ASCRIA, the organization displayed a strong Pan-Africanist identity and support for its global causes and events. In July 1966, amid civil rights struggles in the United States, Kwayana cabled the U.S. Ambassador in Georgetown to protest the American government's "dispatch of troops against Chicago's blacks and failure to send troops against southern whites."[26] ASCRIA likewise protested human rights violations in the United States and supported a day of solidarity for the release of black prisoners.[27] In 1968, the organization published "The Teachings of the Cultural Revolution," an explicit proto-African nationalist document. In a heated response to critics of the "Teachings," Kwayana said at a forum of ASCRIA: "those people who attack us, call us racist, accuse us of dividing the nation . . . are the people who enjoy the spectacle of the sleeping African, sleeping with a smile on his face, a smile directed to all the world, a nice chap offending no one but himself by over sleeping and over smiling." He added that "If Black Power means the overthrow of white power by non whites, by black men and brown men and yellow men on a world scale, we identify ourselves with it completely and without reserve." In this missive Kwayana also congratulated the Burnham government for steering clear of the "anti black power hysteria" that gripped Jamaica, Trinidad, and Surinam, stating that "We do not regard the ideas of Malcolm X, Stokely Carmichael, Elijah Muhammad or Walter Rodney or Muhammad Ali as subversive to our cause."[28]

ASCRIA's other activities included proactive participation in African Liberation Day celebrations.[29] In fact, Kwame Ture (Stokely Carmichael) once credited ASCRIA with inspiring the idea of African Liberation Day.[30] There is a basis, in fact, for the accreditation. A circular from the "Pan-African Secretariat" signed by Kwayana in 1970 stated that the "Pan-African Secretariat with a branch in New York, has decided in consultation with various liberation movements based in Zambia and Tanzania, to name May 25, 1971 as the world wide day of solidarity with the armed liberation movement of Africa."[31] The circular indicated high-level support from officials, including the "Prime Minister of Guyana and the Presidents of Zambia, Uganda, Tanzania, Kenya and Guinea."[32] When Kwayana visited Ghana (on the second of his three visits) in 1970, he took a cash collection for the MPLA of Angola that ASCRIA had initiated to "aid their struggle."[33]

Kwayana and ASCRIA were consistent supporters of Afro-Guyanese culture. The forms of this contribution vary in scope and emphasis and collectively include the encouragement of agricultural development; the popularization of African-derived local food; the use of the African drum; the teaching of African history in schools; the adoption in ASCRIA of positions such as the Akan "Chief of Recitations"; the encouragement of wearing dress like the dashiki; general community work; the establishment of respect for creolese and attendant proverbs and folk wisdom; and agitation on political issues, even when it became troubling for the regime that expected guarantees of African racial solidarity. ASCRIA also "campaigned for the Africanisation of symbols with slogans such as 'give black dolls to your children' and 'no snow in December.'"[34] ASCRIA was also in "close touch with" Black Power groups in Barbados, Dominica, St. Lucia, and Trinidad and Tobago,[35] and over time, Kwayana met and held discussions with key regional pan-Africanists and statesmen, including Eric Williams, C.L.R. James, Tim Hector, and Stokely Carmichael (Kwame Ture). Kwayana and Sase Omo, another member of ASCRIA, represented their organization in meetings in Trinidad and Tobago and Barbados for the preparatory committee of the Sixth Pan-African Congress.

Kwayana and Modern Guyanese Politics

By 1970, Kwayana and ASCRIA had become "progressively disgusted" with the People's National Congress.[36] Previously, a significant proportion of Kwayana's political and cultural work in ASCRIA had overlapped with his political support for the ruling party. After his public break with the PNC in 1971, Kwayana, along with his counterpart in IPRA (the Indian Political Revolutionary Associates), Moses Bhagwan, initiated dialogue and work with prominent Indo-Guyanese political and cultural groups and individuals. This induced criticism from within ASCRIA, other African-based organizations, and the PNC itself. Later, ASCRIA's official response came from its bulletin:

> ASCRIA's mistake was to lead the African people to believe, that once the problem of African solidarity was solved, a people's political line would be followed. Again, we, especially our leadership, trusted too much in the platform declarations of the elite and our leadership was slow to believe rumours of corruption among ministers. It did not exercise the vigilance necessary always, and especially when dealing with opportunists. ASCRIA therefore, unwilling to risk a "split," remained silent at the PNC doings and accepted rather weak excuses for the failure of the government to develop a mass line, to inspire the people and give them a right to govern.[37]

After his formal split with the PNC, Kwayana, along with others, helped to initiate and shape the multiethnic Working People's Alliance (WPA)[38] from its official pre-party formation in 1974. Thenceforth, in contrast to his previous association with proto-black organization and political practice, Kwayana resumed advocacy of what the WPA consistently termed "the multi-racial power of the working people." The structure and ideology of the WPA, flexible and accommodating as it presented itself, was not restrictive to Kwayana's pan-Africanist outlook, however "inert" it appeared to be, given his immersion in WPA philosophy and practice.

As with ASCRIA publications, Kwayana contributed significantly to the WPA's news sheets, including the *Dayclean* and *Open Word*. Established in 1986, *Open Word* attempted to broaden the range of *Dayclean*'s focus in both format and content. Kwayana excelled again, not only writing the news and analyses but also featuring in the news. A typical case was his 1987 fast against kerosene lines—an incident in which famed Caribbean novelist George Lamming was arrested while providing solidarity to Kwayana. As Lamming later observed,

> I went to see him outside the Parliament building, first out of concern for his health and general welfare, and also because Kwayana is a unique figure in our cultural and political history. There is, in all probability, no Guyanese or Caribbean political personality of comparable stature and with a similar record of personal integrity and political morality over the last three decades . . . I never anticipated the events which would follow—least of all my own arrest . . . when I was taken away with three others to the Brickdam Police Station . . . [39]

Kwayana's fight against a ruling party whose primary constituents were African Guyanese cut him off from some pan-Africanist movements and governments, which supported Forbes Burnham and the PNC. Given that the Burnham regime supported Cuba's military role in Angola in the 1970s, was at the forefront of the antiapartheid movement, and was a core member of the Non-Aligned Movement, it is no surprise that he was positively regarded in Pan-Africanist and radical Third World circles, especially in the 1970s. This created a curious situation, in which the WPA and the government it opposed were simultaneously in support of these same causes. However, those movements and countries that were given support by the PNC had to tread carefully with relation to Guyanese opposition groups, especially with the WPA, which had no "national front" ambitions with the governing PNC as the PPP did. This provides another explanation for the exclusion of Kwayana and the WPA from the Pan-Africanist or socialist pantheon at the time.

Kwayana's "Absence" from Formal Pan-Africanism

With this overall cumulative setting of agitation, personal involvement, and prose over several decades, what then is it about Kwayana's activity and legacy that precludes a wider recognition of his pan-Africanist history in official and international circles? Given the organic nature and context of his work and activity over time, there are in sum three predominant explanations for the relative silence on Kwayana in the Pan-African narrative and printed word. The first cluster of reasons broadly relate to the politics of knowledge production, including how history is recorded and how pan-Africanism is designated and framed. Arguably, the figures most commonly treated in the now fairly substantial body of work on pan-Africanism are those who have been made visible through their activism in international circuits, congresses and controversies (for example, Ras Makonnen, Claudia Jones, Kwame Ture); their positions as holders of state power or as figureheads of movements (Kwame Nkrumah, Julius Nyerere, Marcus Garvey); and their contribution to knowledge through internationally circulated publications (Walter Rodney, W.E.B. Du Bois, Sylvester Williams). Others, like Malcolm X, have sadly been made visible through paying the ultimate sacrifice for their endeavors. Thus, for example, Kwayana's colleague, Walter Rodney, who fits all of these criteria, has been widely recognized for his outstanding contribution to the theory and practice of black liberation. His activity in the region and further afield, and his physical and ideological contact with a number of groups and individuals in Africa, the Caribbean, and the United States have been well chronicled. He is widely recognized for two major academic contributions to African historiography, *A History of the Upper Guinea Coast 1545–1800* (1970) and *How Europe Underdeveloped Africa* (1972), and his *Groundings with my Brothers* (1969) remains a foundational text of Caribbean Black Power. These works place Rodney in the tradition of scholarship forged in the previous half century by pan-African academic titans such as W.E.B. Du Bois, George Padmore, and Sylvester Williams. Rodney's scholarship, however, had a unique ingredient, which was its conscious linkage to political and social activism. This would dramatically lead to a political explosion in Jamaica in 1968, a direct consequence of this fusion of politics and professional history. Curiously, one of the reasons why Walter Rodney was widely appreciated in Guyana was because of his ability to stay clear of "taking sides" in Guyana's racial politics in the 1960s, while embracing a multiracial philosophy. His assassination in Guyana on 13 June 1980 caused international outrage, prompting some who had perhaps turned a blind eye to the failings of the Burnham regime on the grounds of pan-African solidarity to reconsider their position.

Where then does Kwayana, who struggled alongside Rodney, fit in this schema? As this chapter has argued, Kwayana was determinedly a "stay at home" pan-Africanist whose relative lack of international travel to promote and engage with pan-African organization, and whose immersion in Guyanese village and national life help explain his relative lack of visibility when measured against the standards of pan-African recognition that have been based on attendance at international conferences and formal organizational output.[40] Ironically, ASCRIA's "biggest international achievement"[41] was in fact the organization of a conference of Pan-Africanists and Revolutionary Black Nationalists held in Georgetown in 1970; however, as a closed conference, it did not leave behind a wealth of public statements or manifestos that might have found their way into mainstream academic research. Kwayana himself, however, has produced a massive prose output chronicling the African-Guyanese contribution to the development of colonial and postcolonial Guyana, and engaging with the broader historical legacy of Africans elsewhere in the world. His pan-Africanist assessments, like his political and cultural practice, are largely homegrown, but are no less deep than the more "recognized" African academics and activists. Among dozens of other works, he published a text on African-Guyanese proverbs, a long history of the African cultural presence in Guyana, and scores of other articles, public lectures, letters, pamphlets, and opinion pieces on the African contribution to Guyana, the region, and the world. In spite of the quantity and quality of his prose and activity, Kwayana's record remains outside of the reach of an international scholarly and popular audience. There are two main reasons for this. First, because the bulk of his published work has been restricted to Guyana, it has fallen victim to the manner in which circuits of knowledge are conducted in the "developing" world. Second, on account of his own personal modesty and in concert with the fragmentation, lethargy, and lack of resources affecting archival upkeep in Guyana, his work has not been preserved in any coherent form.[42]

Relatedly, Kwayana's apparent lack of recognition by official pan-Africanism is linked to his concern for local black problems in his village politics and cultural activity and the corresponding disconnect with media-savvy Pan-Africanism. Again we note the impressive concern and attention Kwayana gave throughout time to his native Guyana. One of these areas was his lifelong concern with the African village and its history and development in Guyana. He explained his own "unpublished argument" that the "village movement constituted a democratic break out of the new plantation system and something of an economic revolution."[43] He was also an early proponent of African self-organization from the village to the national level, and, like many other pan-Africanists and socialists, was impressed with Nyerere's *ujamaa* experiment between 1967 and 1970.

The second area that has potentially stymied Kwayana's official reception in the pan-Africanist world is that, with the exception of the period between 1961 and 1970 when he focused on a "separate" ethnic response to Guyana's divisions, he consistently developed and argued for multiracial culture and action peculiar to Guyana's needs. Thus while Kwayana has been criticized for the "error" of one-race organization, linked to his sojourn with ASCRIA, he has been equally criticized for bypassing "the specificity of needs" of the ethnic groups that made up the multiethnic WPA.[44] Kwayana's support for multiracialism and his critique of ethnic defensiveness on the part of both Indians and Africans is captured in his important and self-critical *Racial Insecurity and the Political System* (1978). This talk constituted the foundation of a critical assessment of racial troubles in Guyanese society, a fundamental of the WPA's general multiracial philosophy. Whether or not this is acknowledged, Kwayana's input has retained a legacy in current political and race debates in Guyana. He continued to pursue the theme of racial insecurity years later in two separate and wide-ranging analyses of the cultural contributions of Indians and Africans in the Genesis of a Nation Conference held at the Pegasus Hotel in Georgetown in 1988. Kwayana's instinct for critique—and self-critique—has marked his assessment of the pan-Africanist process in any location. In an article in *Caribbean Daylight* in 1992, he explained that his "habit of looking critically at [his] own actions had provided other actors with a shield": "[this] habit . . . provides others with cover and all they do is add more and more to their storehouse of non-responsibility to win some quick short-lived advantage: whatever is not founded on truth will fall apart because reality has no supports on which falsehood can rest."[45]

It is in this critical stance that we might locate the third set of reasons for his unwarranted absence from the pan-Africanist pantheon. Kwayana has not shied from identifying cracks in the pan-Africanist edifice, whether condemning the oppression of Africans by Africans or in identifying its exclusions, most notably in the area of gender:

> Pan-Africanist thought and action must seek to establish in these impatient and restless times the fact that Africa was the source of civilization and culture of the highest order; that Africans will no longer stand at the end or near the end of the lowest queue in the world; that Africans must empower themselves by themselves or jointly with groups willing to share power, in and out of Africa, to overcome the social and economic evils of the day to promote human development; that oppression of Africans by Africans must not be tolerated; that there must be an international jury to consider the human wastage in Angola, Rwanda and in any other divided country to resolve the situation; that in addition to the traditional respect for elders we must raise up a new tradition, respect for young people also; that Africans must lead the world in the use of all means to assist African women and girls (and all women) to their rightful place in the family and society.[46]

This assessment of the global African situation signifies Kwayana's longstanding solidarity with the African continent and diaspora together with the criticism implicit in the passage, and expansion of the concept of pan-Africanism to include holistic empowerment inclusive of gender equality in Africa. Gender is an acknowledged area of some weakness historically for the Pan-Africanist movement, and Kwayana has been a frequent critic of this shortcoming. In another broadside, he notes, "[The] cultural constitution of Africa in relation to women and in relation to youth is in need of revision. And this cannot be done behind the backs of the youth and the women. Pan-Africanism will have validity only when it seeks to solve the fundamental problems of social injustice among Africans and supports every human community in its efforts for justice, freedom and development."[47]

During his long gestation in the multiracial WPA, he still articulated his passion and concern for the continent. Kwayana's invitation to visit Ghana in 1992 was a follow-up to his previous Ghana visits and a "personal one. . . . we were in touch in the sixties and Dr Kwame Nkrumah had responded to my concerns about ethnic disagreement."[48] In 1992, Kwayana's visit to Ghana indicated wider concerns: "the mission I am about to undertake should serve not only to reassure Afro-Guyanese of belonging to a world of vastness and depth, but to inform citizens of all backgrounds who have interest in the matter."[49]

The final consideration for Kwayana's apparent omission from the pan-African world is his many personal idiosyncrasies. His candid tussle with convention can be seen in his eating habits, sartorial outlook, inflexible stance against corruption, and nontraditional thinking. His strict vegan diet, asceticism, soft-spoken speech, and modesty, the latter a leitmotiv of Kwayana's persona, to put it mildly, are all part of his mystique. More importantly, his defiance of traditional office-seeking is an additional source of his comparative reclusion from fame seekers in the politics of not a few global pan-Africanists.

In sum, while sacrifice, dedication, and published work in the arena of Africana studies are all very notable in Kwayana's historical repertoire, he did not readily fall into the compatible or comfortable "assertions" of Pan-Africanism. From what we witness, Kwayana is a sensitive pan-Africanist with a public "cover." The cover is not a manipulation and/or deceit, but a protective shield derived from past criticism and political misstep, including associations and affiliations that were contentious. In great measure he expended in multiple ways in and for the pan-Africanist spirit without seeking favor. The fault of omission lies then in the keepers of the Pan-African record. Scholars such as Micere Mugo have noted these restrictions and urged not only a more self-critical approach but also a call for Pan-Africanism to be understood beyond the "congresses and proclamations with which it has come to be exclusively defined."[50]

Misunderstood and underrated over time, Kwayana continues to be one of the most difficult political figures to evaluate in the Anglophone Caribbean and the pan-African world. The key to understanding his omission from the pan-African narrative can only be understood from the position of his Guyanese rootedness and subsequent engagement of the black world from the race-class dialectic, and by his independence. A fuller appraisal of Kwayana's contribution to the pan-Africanist world, together with other work to fill other lacunae in his life and work, is long overdue for this organic African-Guyanese cultural, political, and intellectual figure.

Notes

1. James, 71.

2. "Eusi Kwayana" is Swahili for "black son of Guyana." Kwayana made the name change from Sidney King by deed poll in 1968, at the height of the activity of ASCRIA (African Society for Cultural Relations with Independent Africa).

3. Among the few examples in the scholarship on Pan-Africanism in the Caribbean that do not elide Kwayana's contribution are the books and articles of Horace Campbell and Rodney Worrell. See Campbell and Worrell, *Pan-Africanism, Pan-Africanists and African Liberation*.

4. Kwayana now lives in San Diego, California, but lived most of his life in Buxton, a village on the east coast of Guyana.

5. Williams, 169.

6. Kwayana, Letter, *Stabroek News*.

7. From an unpublished lecture given by Kwayana in 1993, cited in Campbell and Worrell, *Pan-Africanism, Pan-Africanists and African Liberation*, 40.

8. Formerly called British Guiana, the colony became independent in May 1966. "Guyana" will be used to describe both periods.

9. Kwayana, *Buxton-Friendship in Print and Memory*, 210.

10. Kwayana, E-mail response to Andaiye, May 2008.

11. Ibid.

12. Personal e-mail communication from Kwayana to Westmaas, 30 January 2012.

13. Westmaas, "A Profile of African and East Indian Ethnic Associations in British Guiana."

14. Ibid.

15. Harris, "The League of Coloured Peoples."

16. Kwayana, *No Guilty Race*, 17.

17. Seecharan, 335. Some of the Indian groups included the British Guiana East Indian Association, the British Guiana Ladies Guild, and the Hindu Society, alongside a plethora of individuals.

18. The Colonization Scheme, also known as the Nunan-Luckhoo Scheme, was adopted by the British government in 1919 with the motive of providing labor immigration into Guyana. The scheme met with very limited success and was terminated by 1928. According to Seecharan, "the basis of the scheme was the promotion of agricultural families as a unit . . . and land grants to immigrants who wished to embark on independent cultivation immediately on arrival." Ibid., 135.

19. Martin Carter, national poet of Guyana and leading light in the PPP of the 1950s, wrote poems about the African anticolonial and liberation struggles, including the antiapartheid movement. While the PPP leaders were in detention, they held a hunger strike protesting the use of heavy bombers in Kenya against the Mau Mau.

20. Spinner, 79.

21. Kwayana became General Secretary of the PNC in 1961 and was editor of the *New Nation*, the party's newspaper. He is also famous for authoring, courtesy of the creative use of certain English hymns, the party songs of three Guyanese political parties, the PPP, PNC, and WPA.

22. In a later assessment of the period, Kwayana states that he personally did not support the use of the phrase "partition" advocated by other leading members of ASRE but agreed to it out of loyalty to the collective. See Kwayana, *The Morning After*, 114.

23. Kwayana, *The Morning After*, 115

24. Hinds, "This Confounded Nonsense Must Stop."

25. Kwayana, "African Society for Racial Equality."

26. "Sidney King Protests," *Weekend Post & Sunday Argosy*, 17 July 1966.

27. Hinds, "African Society," 38.

28. "Many Guyanese Are Taking African Customs," *Sunday Chronicle*, 16 March 1969.

29. While Kwayana was General Secretary of the PNC, the political party officially established Ghana Day, in celebration of Ghana's independence from Britain.

30. Conversation with Eusi Kwayana, 14 December 2011.

31. Kwayana, "Let Us Pass from Words."

32. Ibid.

33. Hinds, "African Society," 37.

34. Ibid., 32.

35. Kwayana e-mail to N. Westmaas, 25 January 2008.

36. Spinner, 79.

37. *ASCRIA Bulletin*, 1 April 1973.

38. The WPA (Working People's Alliance) was established in 1974 with the collation of independent social and cultural organizations, including ASCRIA. The WPA became a formal political party in 1979. The disagreement arising from ASCRIA's absorption into the WPA (along with other constituent groups) meant that some members of the organization stayed with the WPA entrants while others continued to support the PNC.

39. Lamming, "Lamming's Statement." Lamming was referencing here his solidarity sit with Kwayana in front of Guyana's Parliament to protest the suffering, including electricity blackouts, brought on by a fuel shortage. Lamming was later released without charge.

40. Indeed, Kwayana notes that he never attended a Pan-African conference, though he "supported the one in 1974 and the one in 1994" (E-mail to N. Westmaas, 2008).

41. Hinds, "African Society," 37.

42. In an effort to remedy the bibliographic deficit of Kwayana's work, I have undertaken a bibliographic compilation of his work. Started in the 1990s, it is intended for future publication and popular access. See the appendix to this chapter for a list of some of his work.

43. Kwayana, *More than Survival*, 60.

44. Andaiye, "Black Power Organizing."

45. Kwayana, "Guyana's Race Problems and My Part in Them," *Caribbean Daylight*.

46. Unpublished lecture (1993), cited in Campbell and Worrell, 40.

47. Ibid., 37.

48. Statement on Kwayana Mission to Ghana, 25 June 1992.

49. Ibid. Kwayana had also reviewed Kwame Nkrumah's *Consciencism: Philosophy and Ideology for De-Colonization* (1964) in the early 1960s.

50. Mugo, 239.

Appendix: Eusi Kwayana: Samples from His Pan-Africanist Bibliography

"Weep for Biko" (undated poem).

"Right of Colonial Peoples to Self-Determination," *Thunder*, 7 September 1957.

Next Witness: An Appeal to World Opinion, first published 1962 by Labour Advocate (republished 1999 with new introduction by the author).

"Revolution . . . Torch of Liberty Hoisted by Slaves: Berbice Slave Rebellion," *Sunday Chronicle*, 3 March 1963.

"Damon Taken to Task" *Guyana Graphic*, circa 16 July 1963.

Review of Nkrumah's *Consciencism*, in *The Spark*, Ghana, 1964.

"African Ideology on the Continent," *New World*, 1965.

"Glimpses of Kwame Nkrumah," *Guyana Star*, 9 March 1966.

Teachings of the Cultural Revolution. Georgetown: ASCRIA, 1968, folleto.

Review of Kwame Nkrumah's *Consciencism: Philosophy and Ideology for De-Colonization* (1970s).

"Birth of Freedom," *Sunday Chronicle* Republic Issue, 22 February 1970.

"ASCRIA Chides Dr. Lewis on Black Power Issue—Eusi Kwayana," *Sunday Graphic,* 19 December 1971.

"Racial Insecurity and the Old Politics" (long essay, 1975).

Cable sent to Martin Luther King Day Celebrations (USA) following invitation to co-chair event. *Dayclean*, Vol. V, No. 13, 16 January 1981.

"Walter Rodney Lives: An Analysis of Walter Rodney's Contribution to National and International Struggle for Bread and Justice" in *Sign of the Times* (booklet), 1981.

Walter Rodney, Booklet, 1985.

Preface to Horace Campbell, *Rasta and Resistance: From Garvey to Rodney,* Africa World Press, 1987.

Paul Robeson: Constant Star. WPA booklet, 1988.

"More Than Survival: The Afro-Guyanese and the Nation," Genesis of a Nation Conference, University of Guyana and Guyana Commemoration Commission, Georgetown, 29–31 July 1988.

Statement of Eusi Kwayana on Mission to Ghana, 25 June 1992.

"Kwayana's Mission to Ghana Is Cultural," Report in *Dayclean*, 4–18 July 1992.

"Columbus (to Nkrumah), to Castro (to Winnie Mandela)," Excerpt from address—July 25, 1992, to the African Resource Center, NY. *Dayclean*, 1–15 August 1992.

"Guyana's Race Problems and My Part in Them," *Caribbean Daylight,* 16 August 1992.

"African Guyanese Should Have No Problem with an Indian Monument," *Stabroek News,* 22 April 1993.

"The Caribbean Pan-African Record," *Southern African Political and Economic Monthly*, December/January 1993/94.

"African-Guyanese Proverbs" in *Emancipation* No. 2, 1994.

"Fast Supports Haitian Call for 'Liberty or Death,'" *Caribbean Daylight,* 1 May 1994.

Celebrating Black History Month: The Story of a Fearless Civil Rights Fighter. Bob Moses: Full Circle. *Caribbean Daylight*. Part One and Part Two, 12 February 1995.

"Songs of the Folk," *Dayclean*, 26 June 1995.

"After Farrakhan," Part 1, *Dayclean,* Vol. 18, No. 4, 1996.

"Gang Gang": Thirty African Proverbs. Georgetown: Red Thread Press, 1997.

"Wisdom of the Africans," *Emancipation*, 1997–98.

Buxton-Friendship in Print and Memory. Georgetown: Red Thread Press, 1999.

Review of "Themes in African-Guyanese History," Winston McGowan, James Rose, David Granger (eds). Georgetown: Free Press, 1998, in *Emancipation Magazine* 1999–2000.

"On Walter Rodney: A Political Mission," *Sunday Stabroek*, 11 June 2000.

"African Society for Racial Equality (ASRE)" *Emancipation Magazine*, 2001–2.

Scars of Bondage (with T. Kwayana), Georgetown: Free Press, 2002.

"African Religious Survivals in Guyana," *Stabroek News*, 2 March 2002.

Book Review: Horace Campbell, "Reclaiming Zimbabwe: The Exhaustion of the Patriarchal Mode of Liberation, August 2003.

"Black Jacobins, by C.L.R. James: Revisiting a path-breaking book, with reference to other texts" (Malcolm X library e-mail, May 2004).

Afterword: "Tim Hector, Humanist, Political Values, and National Reconstruction" in Paul Buhle, *Tim Hector: A Caribbean Radical's Story*. Jackson: University Press of Mississippi, 2006.

(with Horace Campbell) "Pan-Africanists Cannot Ignore Where Zimbabwe Is Heading," *Stabroek News*, 22 June 2008.

"The Late Ms. Stella Williams Was an Oral Historian," *Stabroek News*, 11 April 2010.

"Letter: Emancipation Must Mean a New Level of Freedom and Security for All," *Stabroek News*, 5 August 2011.

Bibliography

Andaiye. "Black Power Organizing and the Multiracial Challenge in Guyana: Lessons from ASCRIA." Paper presented at the Centre for Caribbean Thought, University of the West Indies, Mona, Jamaica, 21 February 2008.

ASCRIA. *ASCRIA Bulletin*, 1 April 1973.

Campbell, H. and Worrell, R. *Pan-Africanism, Pan-Africanists and African Liberation in the 21st Century*, Washington DC: New Academia Publishing, 2006.

Harris, J. "The League of Coloured Peoples" in *African Guianese Achievement*, No 1. 1993, 29.

Hinds, D. "The African Society for Cultural Relations with Independent Africa (ASCRIA): A Short History" *Emancipation* No. 4, 1996–97, 32–38.

———. "This Confounded Nonsense Must Stop: Eusi Kwayana and Political Contrariness." Paper presented at the Guyana Folk Festival 2007 Symposium, Columbia University, New York, 2 September 2007.

James, W. *Holding Aloft the Banner of Ethiopia: Caribbean Radicalism in Early Twentieth Century America*, London: Verso, 1998.

Kwayana, E. "Let Us Pass from Words of Support to Deeds of Support." Statement by Eusi Kwayana for Pan-African Secretariat, Georgetown (Guyana), June 1970.

———. "More than Survival: The Afro-Guyanese and the Nation," Genesis of a Nation Conference, University of Guyana and Guyana Commemoration Commission, Georgetown, 29–31 July 1988.

———. Letter, *Stabroek News*, 20 January 1999.

———. *Buxton-Friendship in Print and Memory*, Georgetown: Red Thread Press, 1999.

———. *No Guilty Race*, Georgetown: Guyana Review, 1999.

———. "African Society for Racial Equality" *Emancipation*, 2001–2, 38–39.

———. *The Morning After*, Georgetown: no publisher listed (BOOKLET 128 pp.), 2005.

———. "Guyana's Race Problems and My Part in Them" *Caribbean Daylight*, 16 August 1992.

———. Conversation with Nigel Westmaas, 14 December 2011.

———. E-mail to Andaiye, May 2008.

———. E-mail to N. Westmaas, 25 January 2008.

———. Personal e-mail communication from Kwayana to Westmaas, 30 January 2012.

Lamming, G. "Lamming's Statement," *Open Word*, 16 November 1987.

"Many Guyanese Are Taking African Customs," *Sunday Chronicle*, 16 March 1969.

Mugo, M. "Re-envisioning Pan-Africanism: What is the role of gender, youth and the masses" in *Pan-Africanism and Integration in Africa*, Ibbo Mandaza & Dani Nabudere (eds.), Harare: SAPES Books, 2002, 239–62.

Nkrumah, K. *Consciencism: Philosophy and Ideology for De-Colonization*, New York: Monthly Review Press, 1964.

Seecharan, C. *Mother India's Shadow over El Dorado: Indo Guyanese Politics and Identity 1890s to 1930s*, Kingston: Ian Randle Publishers, 2011.

"Sidney King Protests," *Weekend Post & Sunday Argosy*, 17 July 1966.

Spinner, T. *A Political and Social History of Guyana, 1945–1983*, Boulder: Westview Press, 1984.

Westmaas, N. "A Profile of African and East Indian Ethnic Associations in British Guiana," *Stabroek News*, 13 May 1999.

Williams, M. "The Pan-African Movement" in Azevedo, M. *African Studies: A Survey of Africa and the Diaspora*, Durham: Carolina Academic Press, 1998.

PART II

Black Power in Colonial Contexts

8

Black Power in the Political Thought of Antigua and Barbuda

PAGET HENRY

In their classic 1967 volume, *Black Power*, Kwame Ture (Stokely Carmichael) and Charles Hamilton established and systematized the concept of Black Power as a challenge to white power. The latter was the power that reigned over the internal and external colonial situations around the world, in which people of African descent had been enslaved, racialized as "negroes," and ruthlessly exploited. Ture and Hamilton suggested that, to overcome this racialized exploitation, people of African descent needed to acquire Black Power. To generate Black Power, they suggested that "we must first redefine ourselves. Our basic need is to reclaim our history and our identity from what must be called cultural terrorism."[1] They also went on to suggest that the production of Black Power would require that we "struggle for the right to create our own terms through which to define ourselves and our relationship to the society [in which we live] and to have these terms recognized."[2] These ideas were distillations of strivings by oppressed people of African descent across the globe: in the United States, Canada, the United Kingdom, the Caribbean, Latin America, and Africa. Together this global cry for Black Power came to define in a very profound and indelible manner the decades of the 1960s and 1970s.

However, this dramatic appearance of Black Power in the 1960s was not an eruption out of a sociohistorical vacuum, and consequently, it was not unprecedented. As Cedric Robinson reminded us in his 1983 classic, *Black Marxism*, it is best to see the rise of Black Power as another erupting of the volcanic dimensions of what he called "the Black Radical Tradition." This tradition was not a well-recognized one. Robinson notes that "before the African and New World Black liberation movements of the post–Second World

War era, few Western scholars of the African experience had any conception of the existence of an ideologically based or epistemologically coherent tradition of Black radicalism."[3] Rather, these movements were seen as discontinuous events that were brought on by the pressure of specific circumstances. In contrast to this view, Robinson proceeded to show that this Black Radical tradition was not only of long standing and possessed of a persistent vision of black liberation, but also that its great architects have come from Africa and the major regions of the diaspora—including the Caribbean.

Before the 1960s, the quest for Black Power can be seen in the many slave revolts of the early colonial period, and most clearly in the case of the Haitian Revolution of 1791. It can also be seen in the uprisings of the post-slavery period, such as the Morant Bay rebellion in Jamaica, the Harlem Renaissance and Garvey movements of the 1920s, the Caribbean peasant movements of the 1930s, and, finally, the nationalist movements of the 1940s and 1950s that set the stage for the eruptions of the 1960s. In none of these major periods were specific eruptions of the quest for Black Power isolated events. Wherever they occurred—in Antigua and Barbuda, Trinidad, Guyana, the United States, Ghana, or Nigeria—they were connected to this vital, if poorly recognized, stream of Black Radical Thought.

It is impossible to understand the role of Black Power in the political thought of Antigua and Barbuda without reference to this powerful subterranean stream of thought. Thus it is against this larger background that I will develop the profile of Black Power in Antigua and Barbuda, discuss its great proponents, its contributions to the larger tradition, and the challenges with which both are currently confronted. In particular, I will argue that Black Power in Antigua and Barbuda—like much of the Caribbean—is confronted by new forms of white power that we, the advocates of Black Power, are not resisting very effectively at the present moment.

The Two George Westons: The Return of Nationalist Visions of Black Power

If, in general, the Black Radical Tradition is not very well known, then its manifestations on the tiny Eastern Caribbean twin island state of Antigua and Barbuda can only be described as thickly obscured by the dust of history. Yet, like the larger tradition of which it is a part, the roots of Black Power in the political thought of Antigua and Barbuda in the eighteenth and nineteenth centuries can be found in the efforts to resist the European enslavement of Africans on the sugar plantations of its colonial economy;

in the proto-nationalist slave conspiracies of 1729 and 1736; in the formation of maroon communities as a strategy of anticolonial resistance; and in the slave narratives of Rebecca Freundlich Protten and Mary Prince. All of these mark crucial moments in the formation of an emerging Afro-Creole political subject.[4]

To grasp the impact of the Black Radical Tradition on the Black Power struggles of the 1960s and 1970s in Antigua and Barbuda, it is necessary to take a few steps back and look at three figures whose political activism in the twentieth century constituted both a crucial background for the struggles of the 1960s, as well as sites of opposition and difference. These three figures are George Weston of the Point, George Weston of Gray's Farm, and V. C. Bird from Ovals—all distinct areas of the capital city of St. John's.

In any account of the return of a nationalist framework to the demands for Black Power in Antigua and Barbuda, the two George Westons must occupy a prominent place. One was very much the insurrectionist in the tradition of the maroons and King Court, the famous leader of the well-documented 1736 Conspiracy. This George was physically a very big man and was from the Point section of St. John's. The other was small of frame and much more the theorist—a Garveyite, to be more specific—and was from the Gray's Farm section of St. John's. The first George gave us what Tim Hector has called the "Weston Challenge."[5] In this 1918 uprising, Weston, along with Sony Price and John Furlonge, were the key nodes triggering and sustaining a course of insurrectionary collective action that had much in common with the earlier revolts against the plantation order. The challenge to white colonial power was back on the agenda and very much in the foreground of this uprising. Unfortunately, like the other revolts of its kind, the Weston Challenge was also put down by the forces of colonial state, its Black Power goals left unrealized, and Weston was forced to join the many others who had migrated to the United States in search of better opportunities.

As George Weston from the Point was making his black challenge to white colonial power in Antigua and Barbuda, Marcus Garvey's Pan-African movement was making its way into Antigua. The Garvey movement was the major eruption of Black Power after the Haitian Revolution. The movement began in Jamaica and came to full flowering after Garvey relocated to New York, joining other leaders of a growing Caribbean diaspora, such as Hubert Harrison, W. A. Domingo, and Richard Moore. Many Antiguans and Barbudans joined the Garvey movement and brought its message to Antigua and Barbuda as they returned home or established a branch of the organization there. Among the most prominent of these were George Weston of Gray's

Farm, who rose rapidly in the movement to become a vice president of the New York branch, and Bishop George McGuire, one of the chief architects of the religious life and theological thinking of the Garvey movement. Here our focus will be on George Weston from Gray's Farm.

The importance of Weston for the political thought of Antigua and Barbuda is twofold. First, as a seaman, he was among that group of brave souls who use their traveling positions to transport black radical literature across the black world, bringing them into ports where they were banned. In particular, he helped to keep Antigua and Barbuda supplied with Garvey's paper, *Negro World*, and also *The Golden Age* and *The Voice of Ethiopia*. In 1938, the planters and the colonial political elites attempted to stop this flow of radical black literature into Antigua and Barbuda by passing the Sedition and Undesirable Publications Act. This act was vigorously opposed by the leading journalist of the period, Harold Wilson, the publisher of *The Magnet*. In spite of this legislation, Weston and others maintained this important supply of black radical literature from abroad. He was a very good friend of my parents and a frequent visitor to our home.

The second reason for Weston's importance is his attempts to outline and implement a vision of Antigua and Barbuda with Black Power in control of the state and the economy. In the late 1930s and early 1940s, Weston envisioned an economy of medium-size independent peasants, who would be capable of making a decent living off the land, and an agro-industry that would grow out of peasant-based agricultural production. This was the core of his alternative to the plantation system. In the political arena, Weston supported an independent Antigua and Barbuda, free of racist colonial rule. The form this new government would take was not exactly clear from my conversations with him or from his writings; however, his model of a political leader was Marcus Garvey, and he envisaged the new political leadership of Antigua and Barbuda along the lines of a strong, almost monarchical leader, who at the same time would be limited by a constitution. As in Haiti, a creole political culture developed in the eighteenth and nineteenth century that was a peculiar mix of European republicanism and African monarchism that was also held together by an Afro-Christian discourse, as Weston's African Orthodox Christianity clearly indicated. But in spite of its incompleteness, these political formulations by Weston were clear indicators of upward movements in the recovery and re-formation of the earlier nationalist outlook and capabilities of the public (political) personas of Antiguans and Barbudans.

V. C. Bird, Socialism, and Black Power

The collapse of the Garvey movement in the 1930s marked an important turn in the history of the quest for Black Power in Antigua and Barbuda. It would lead to new theoretical accounts of the relationship between class and race oppression and thus to new dialectical mixes between race discourses and class discourses such as revolutionary Marxist socialism and Fabian democratic socialism. The trigger for this shift was the onset of the devastating economic effects of the Great Depression of the 1930s. As economic hardships increased, the need for constructive responses also grew. The planters had their solution: increase worker unemployment. But as the bread lines grew longer, the insurrectionary responses of the political personas of Antiguans and Barbudans began to coordinate and rise to the surface with their characteristic intensity. As in the past, this bubbling up of hidden public personas threw up a new set of leaders to be the crucial nodes of this new emerging eruption of negated and suppressed political subjectivities. Among the leaders who emerged were Reginald Stevens, Luther George, V. C. Bird, Douglas (Kem) Roberts, Novelle Richards, Edward Mathurin, and others. These leaders were different from the Westons. They had all been touched by the global workers movement of the 1930s, and were profoundly influenced by its socialist discourses. In short, they were part of a larger 1930s Left movement in ways that their earlier counterparts had not been. Here we will focus on V. C. Bird, as he would become the larger-than-life figure of this labor movement in Antigua and Barbuda.

In January 1939, Reginald Stevens, Norris Allen, Berkley Richards, and others formed a trade union, the Antigua Trades & Labour Union (ATLU), following a historic lecture by the general secretary of the British Trade Union Congress, Sir Walter Citrine. V. C. Bird, a former Salvation Army captain, joined the ATLU and within a few years replaced Stevens as its president. Bird was a very tall, handsome, charismatic young man and a gifted speaker, with roots in the poor sections of St. John's. He knew well the passions of the public personas of his fellow Antiguans and Barbudans, as they also lived in him. He also had an excellent sense of the strengths and weaknesses of these personas and also how they needed to maneuver within the colonial public arena of Antigua and Barbuda. Bird was very aware of the political philosophy of George Weston from Gray's Farm and other Garveyites, and had himself been profoundly influenced by Garvey's political philosophy. But in the context of the depressed 1940s, he sensed that something more was needed.

In response to this need, Bird fashioned a homegrown black democratic socialism—homegrown in the sense that, unlike Norman Manley in Jamaica or Eric Williams in Trinidad, Bird was not educated abroad but remained in the region while he was developing this political philosophy. Bird's black democratic socialism was a synthesis of his Garveyite leanings, his solidarity with workers, and his reading of socialist literature from England, particularly from the British Labour Party. The scribe of the black democratic socialism of this labor movement was Novelle Richards, whose book, *The Struggle and the Conquest*, is still the best insider account of the rise of the ATLU.

This black democratic socialism called for political independence, the full democratization of the state, nationalization of the sugar industry along with the key utilities, an end to practices of racial discrimination in hiring, and the placing of the workers—the vast majority of whom were black—at the center of concern for the state. Black Power in the 1940s thus asserted itself in a new dialectical relationship with class, in which black liberation and empowerment were articulated and addressed in terms of a class discourse. This strategy made it less racially confrontational than earlier expressions of black subjectivity; however, this did not mean that it was less insurrectionary in its thrusts.

Putting this philosophy into practice, Bird and his supporters captured the colonial state from the white planters and made it into a black postcolonial proletarian state, in which white and black middle-class elements had to justify their presence. He socialized education and the public utilities, and started a number of agro-industries that drew on the Weston model. However, he had a much more difficult time trying to nationalize and socialize the plantation economy.[6] To be brief, with the internal and external pressures he encountered, the only way in which he was able to counter the power of the planters was by allying with a new group of white entrepreneurs—primarily from the United States—who were interested in exploring the tourist possibilities of Antigua and Barbuda. Thus by 1966, when he was finally able to capture the entire plantation system, the new tourist entrepreneurs were very much in control of the economy, as sugar production was no longer its dominant sector.

Not surprisingly, in spite of his bold start, the primary lesson to be learned from Bird's long political career is not how to achieve Black Power through a democratic socialist strategy. Rather, the lessons to be learned concern the internal and external compromises, adjustments, and strategic reversals that a small peripheral country is forced to make in its socialist efforts to establish Black Power in a global context still dominated by white imperial power. For example, in 1968 there was a major split in Bird's party, as one of his most charismatic supporters, George Walter, broke away and formed a new party. This new party, the Progressive Labour Movement (PLM), would become a major opposition party and unseat Bird's Antigua Labour Party (ALP) between 1971 and 1976. Adjusting to this major split in his working-class base significantly changed Bird's outlook and practice. The survival of his party— "ALP-ism"—then became the primary concern.[7]

By the late 1960s, as a result of internal pressures and the earlier compromises with Western capitalism, Bird markedly abandoned socialist principles and embraced a system of state capitalism. In this new politico-economic order, the primary entrepreneurial initiative was to be supplied by the new white capitalists in the tourist sector. In this new setting, Bird's political philosophy could now be described as black laborism, as he remained committed to making the uplift of the black laboring masses the second central concern of his administration after the survival of his party. Needless to say, this goal was contradicted by the method of white capitalist power, through which he hoped to achieve this black goal.

This dramatic transformation of Bird's black democratic socialism into a white-dominated state capitalism offers some important clues for understanding the near-universal transformations of socialist states into state-capitalist or market-socialist formations that have been occurring since 1989, or even earlier, in the case of China. For example, Bird's state-capitalist turn could be read as a precedent for these later transformations. It also raises questions about problems inherent in central planning, the capabilities that states must have, and also the productive capabilities of workers needed for a viable proletarian state. We will meet some of these issues again with the New Left socialism of Tim Hector.

Tim Hector, Socialism, and Black Power

Long before the neocolonial contradictions inherent in Bird's state-capitalist turn reached maturity, they had become the objects of sharp criticism from several groups in Antigua and Barbuda. These criticisms would, by the late 1960s, become the sources of two important new formulations of the issue of Black Power. One reformulation developed out of a group led by Mali Olatunji and Robin Bascus, while the other grew out of a group led by Barry Stevens and Lestroy Merchant. The first was more culturally oriented and emphasized engagements with the African heritage of Antiguan and Barbudan culture. They are still best remembered for their introduction of African dashikis, their Afro hairstyles, and the adopting of African names. The second group was more scholarly and emphasized the writing and recovering of the history and thought of Antigua and Barbuda, and, more broadly, people of African descent. Their journal, *Outlet*, was very Pan-African in orientation. In addition to critiquing the racial implications of Bird's state-capitalist turn, *Outlet* featured the writings of the great figures of the Black Radical Tradition—particularly those of Marcus Garvey, W.E.B. Du Bois, and Frantz Fanon. It was this latter group that Tim Hector joined on his return to Antigua and Barbuda after studying in Canada.

Hector was an extraordinary speaker, a brilliant thinker, and a gifted writer. His Fan the Flame column in *Outlet*, which he had transformed into a newspaper, earned the Antigua Caribbean Liberation Movement (ACLM) international recognition. At the time of his return to Antigua and Barbuda, he had been deeply influenced by the political philosophy of C.L.R. James[8] and by the Black Power Movement that had erupted in the United States and subsequently spread to Canada and the Caribbean. When Hector joined Stevens and Merchant's Afro-Caribbean Movement (ACM), this neo-Garveyite ideology of Black Power was very much its dominant discourse. Not long after joining the ACM, Hector became its leader.[9]

The impact of his leadership was clearly visible after 1973. First, he brought new people into the organization—in particular Conrad Luke, Ellorton Jeffers, Jerome Bleau, Arah Weeks, Radcliffe Robins, and Harold Lovell. Second, he took the organization in a Jamesian socialist direction, and later renamed it the Antigua Caribbean Liberation Movement (ACLM). This alternative socialist order was not the democratic socialism of the early Bird, but a genuinely worker-controlled form of socialism. Third, with the help of Arah Weeks (later Arah Hector) and other women in the organization, the issue of gender equality was put high on the agenda. Hector's great contribution to the ACLM was to provide it with a political philosophy that not only critiqued Bird's state capitalism but also brought together the issues of class, race, and gender liberation in a new socialist discourse that drew heavily on the works of C.L.R. James.

The ACLM's critique of Bird's state capitalism, which they often referred to as the "tourist plantation," and of George Walter's failure to change it between 1971 and 1976, was clear and direct. Hector and his colleagues saw Antigua and Barbuda, a young, black nation in the making, as standing at a critical crossroads,

> . . . because in this last quarter of the twentieth century we can and must decide to end the 300 year-old system by which and through

which foreign capital remorselessly bleeds this 108 square mile island of all means of development as it exports profits from tourism, agriculture, commerce, banking, manufacturing and insurance. . . . At the crossroads because we can and must bring to an end, a complete end, the senseless division and useless strife fostered and promoted by two bankrupt parties, one in blue and white rags (the PLM) the other in red and white tatters (ALP).[10]

This was not a critique of the old plantation order, but of Bird's neocolonial state capitalism, and of the failure of the PLM to change it when they were in power between 1971 and 1976. Nor was it the democratic socialism of Bird, but the face of a New Left in Antigua and Barbuda, and also across the region. This difference emerges quite sharply when this and other Hector texts are compared to Richards's *The Struggle and the Conquest*.

The socialist alternative proposed by Hector and the ACLM developed in two phases. In its first phase, it combined Black Power discourses of race with C.L.R. James's insurrectionary socialism, particularly the political economy of the text *Facing Reality* (1958). The distinct Black Power elements of this socialist alternative were manifested in such things as support for the struggles that were taking place in Southern Africa and Angola. Every year the ACLM organized a massive African Day Parade to demonstrate this solidarity with Africa. These marches were huge and contributed a lot to the raising of black consciousness at the time.

The distinct socialist elements of this new synthesis were drawn primarily from two Jamesian texts, *Facing Reality* (1958) and *Modern Politics* (1960). In these two texts, James explored on a global scale the upward trend in the development of the revolutionary capabilities of the public personas of a number of different working classes. In particular, James referred to the 1956 Hungarian Revolution to demonstrate the high level of economic self-organization of which workers were capable. The unprecedented eruption in Hungary strongly supported James's claim that workers were now ready and able to take control of production, and thus to be economically self-governing. Worker self-organization in factories was thus the main lesson that James read in the 1956 eruption of the public personas of the Hungarian workers.

Like James, Hector and the ACLM read the self-organizing capabilities of the public personas of the workers of Antigua and Barbuda through the lens of the Hungarian workers. Assuming that it was now possible for workers throughout the world to carry out feats similar to those carried out in Hungary, they came to see the workers of Antigua and Barbuda as possessing public personas with similar coordinating capabilities. Thus the first formulation of Hector's insurrectionary socialism was one that called not only for popular democracy but also for worker self-organization in economic production. This meant going beyond the practices of both representative democracy and capitalist production. The reliance of Bird's state capitalism on foreign investors was thus seen as obsolete and an unnecessary exposure to continued racial domination by white power.

At the level of practice, this meant that the nature of ACLM as an organization was that of a small revolutionary group and not electoral party. Thus it would come to power not via an election but on the crest of another insurrectionary upsurge of the public personas of workers. Upon being swept into power by such an upsurge, the ACLM would then assist the workers in setting up systems of popular democracy and of self-organization in production. With regard to the latter, the ACLM advocated a model of development in which locally owned agricultural cooperatives would be the basic units of production. Industrialization would then flow from and serve the needs of rural transformation. Mindful of Bird's failure with similar projects and drawing on the economic work of Nobel laureate Sir Arthur Lewis, Hector called for the creation of "agricultural institutes" to educate farmers so that they could increase both their productivity and the scale of their operations.[11] To concretize this socialist idea of economic development through worker-controlled cooperative farming, the ACLM established its East Antigua Co-operative Farm. This would be the new way to the realizing of Black Power.

By the time of this formation of its first phase, the ACLM was not an isolated New Left occurrence on the Caribbean scene. In Trinidad and Tobago, there was NJAC and New Beginning; in Jamaica, Abeng; in Guyana, ASCRIA; and in Grenada, the New Jewel Movement. These were some of the new organizations of the Caribbean New Left, and they and their leaders were in similar oppositional relations to the Eric Williams, Hugh Shearer, Forbes Burnham, and Eric Gairy regimes as the ACLM was with the Bird regime. This was the specific regional configuration of political forces that was the basis for this classic period in the history of Black Power in the region. Indeed, when most people hear the words "Black Power," this is period that they associate with it.

However, as noted previously, the ACLM went through a second phase of internal transformation. As in the case of Bird's democratic socialism, this was in response to a number of internal and external pressures. Here I will focus on three crucial ones that will help us to understand the changes. First was the inaccuracy in the reading of the public personas of Antiguan and Barbudan workers produced by the use of the Hungarian lens. Second was the stronghold that the two-party system had secured over the public personas of the workers. Finally, there were the pressures that the latter exerted on the ACLM to become a political party and join the stream of electoral politics.

The adaptations that the ACLM made in order to accommodate these pressures were reflected quite clearly in the changes it made in its ideological outlook. These shifts were systematized in a new synthesis of Black Power ideas on race with a revised reading of the self-organizing capabilities of the Antiguan and Barbudan workers. This new reading made use of a Trinidadian lens, provided by a later James text, *Party Politics in the West Indies* (1962). In this book, James developed more systematically the differences between the self-organizing capabilities of different working classes as a result of his experiences in Trinidad with the People's National Movement, Eric Williams's party.

Watching Williams in action, his turn to state capitalism, and the response of the masses forced James to draw a clear distinction between the self-organizing capabilities of workers in developing countries like those in the Caribbean and the more advanced ones like the United States, England, or Hungary. This in turn led him to distinguish between the meaning of state capitalism in the advanced countries and developing ones, such as Antigua, Barbados, or Trinidad. In the latter cases, in the early 1960s, and even after his violent break with Williams, James argued that state capitalism was a progressive formation rather than the regressive one that it had been in the advanced countries. In the Caribbean context, James saw state capitalism as the social order that was overseeing the demise of the plantation system and serving as an interim replacement. It was not, as in the case of Poland, something that blocked the rise of a proletarian order that was well formed in the public personas of workers. One reason why state capitalism and not socialism was replacing the plantation system was the actual level of self-organization of which Trinidadian and other Caribbean workers were in fact capable. In James's view, Caribbean workers had demonstrated that they were capable of political self-organization and were thus more than ready for a system of popular democracy. However, these workers had not produced any concrete insurrectionary demonstrations of a high capability for economic self-organization. For James this had to come from deep within, a creative expression of the public personas of Caribbean workers. It could not and must not be imposed from above. Thus the policy prescriptions on the nature of the mass party in *Party Politics in the West Indies* are all about what can and must be done to facilitate the growth of an inner capacity for economic self-organization among Caribbean workers.

This shift in the analysis of *Party Politics in the West Indies* became crucial for the second phase in the life of the ACLM. Its immediate goal was no longer proletarian socialism, but a "national democratic phase" that in Antigua and Barbuda had to precede the transition to socialism. Thus in the organization's 1980 manifesto, *Towards a New Antigua*, Hector and his colleagues declared:

> ACLM is clear that what is required now in Antigua is not a socialist economy for which Antigua does not have the pre-conditions. ACLM is loud and clear that what is required is a NATIONAL ECONOMY with the Public Sector working along with the Private Sector, with the Cooperative Farm working in alliance with the Private Farmer, Foreign capital in partnership with national capital. However, and this is crucial, ACLM will plan the economy, stabilize the cost of living and accumulate capital for National Development.[12]

From a small revolutionary group, the ACLM would attempt to transform itself into a Jamesian mass party. But, in spite of his great skills as a speaker, thinker, and writer, Hector did not have the kind of personality onto whom the vast majority of the workers could project their public personas and thus trigger chains of spontaneous collective action. Compared to Bird and Walter, Hector might have been too middle class for workers to spontaneously identify with him. Consequently, the ACLM did not do very well at the polls. As a party, it contested the 1980 and 1989 general elections, and in both cases did not win any seats. In short, the ACLM was more of a challenge to Bird's social order as a small revolutionary group than it was as a party.

Moving still further away from its early roots, the ACLM in 1999 made the highly divisive move of allying with the new opposition party, the United Progressive Party (UPP), which had replaced the PLM. Some members joined in this alliance, while others did not. This left the ACLM deeply divided, and also failed to defeat the ALP. Further, Hector soon broke with the UPP; Harold Lovell stayed, however, and is today the Minister of Finance in a ruling UPP government.

At the same time that he was fighting these battles with the ALP, Hector was also in a difficult battle with heart disease. This battle had taken him to Cuba more than once for treatment. In early November 2002, to the great shock of his family, friends, nation, region, and diaspora, Hector departed this life, leaving a political, journalistic, and intellectual vacuum in Antiguan and Barbudan society that still has not been filled.

Black Power in the Post-ACLM Years

The period following Hector's death has been marked by three crucial de-velopments that have significantly affected the "we," or the collective iden-tity, of Antiguans and Barbudans. First is the aging of Bird's state-capitalist system and the inability of subsequent ALP leaders or the UPP adminis-trations to reinvigorate or move beyond it. Thus, from both a Black Power and a development perspective, this has not been a very innovative period. Consequently, a feeling of not knowing where we are going, as a nation, has certainly become a part of the Antiguan and Barbudan "we."

Second, in spite of this inability to transform our aging state-capital-ist system, the post-Hector years have seen little or no loss of strength in the grip that the two parties continue to have on the public personas of Antiguan and Barbudan workers. The strength of this grip is the prom-ise of a middle-class consumer lifestyle that both parties have made to the masses of workers. As neither party has really been able to deliver on these promises, the pattern of out-migration continues, with the resulting spaces being filled with workers from Guyana, Jamaica, Dominica, and the Dominican Republic. These new ethnic additions are among some of the biggest changes in the life and composition of the working class of Antigua and Barbuda. But in spite of the consumer promises and the new immigrants, the red and blue split in the capacity of workers for concerted collective action, produced by this two-party capture, continues unabated. Partyism—ALP-ism and UPP-ism—have become defining frameworks of immigrant and nonimmigrant public personas and thus of the Antiguan and Barbudan "we."

Third, the persistence of this partyist capture of the creativity of public personas has been accompanied by other changes in the creative expressions of the larger "we," of which the public persona is only a part. In addition to the public persona, the Antiguan and Barbudan "we" also has ludic and re-ligious dimensions. The ludic persona has expressed itself and its creativity primarily through our Christmas celebrations and, later, our annual carni-val; for a long time, in the theaters, this ludic persona dramatized the aspects of itself that it was unable to express in the course of everyday life. As a result, distinct characters and events—John Bulls, clowns, ghosts, highland-ers, calypsonians, drunks, the slave past, etc.—became the center of dramas performed on the streets or onstage. In these "mases," the full life (hidden and open) of this ludic persona was on spectacular display.

Particularly as of the last ten years, significant changes can be observed in the creative expressions of this ludic persona. In its hot soca music and new carnival "mases," these creative expressions have undergone an extreme eroticization that has given the celebrations a distinct Las Vegas look. Some, indeed, refer to them as "bikini mases." Whatever the label, the decline of the older mases and the rise of the new point to important shifts in the nature and creativity of our ludic personas. At the same time that this eroticization of our ludic personas has been increasing, our religious personas have been moving in more fundamentalist directions. Together these changes in our religious, ludic, and public personas suggest that the "we" that supports the "I" of Antiguans and Barbudans has undergone, and is still undergoing, dramatic changes. Consequently, as a people and a nation, we are changing. However, we are very unsure of where these changes are taking us.

Conclusion

What do these changes mean for the long and historic quest for Black Power? How will the creativity of our changing collective subjectivity, our transitioning "we," reformulate the historic demands for Black Power? So far they have pushed us into a period in which the demands for Black Power have and will be made at lower levels of intensity. Absent from the current scene is any sense of impending collective upsurges like the ones that produced and sustained the demands of the 1960s. Present are a number of new organizations in which issues of race, Africa, Afro-Caribbean identity, Afro-Antiguan and Barbudan creative arts, and black economic empowerment are of central concern; these include the Antigua and Barbuda Reparations Support Commission, the African Slavery Memorial Society, and the Antigua and Barbuda Studies Association. Among the goals of the Reparations Support Commission are "national reflection on the institution of slavery" and to "foster deeper ideological, social and economic connections with people of African descent in the Diaspora and continental Africa."[13] Among the African Slavery Memorial Society's goals are "the preservation of our African Heritage and the memory of our African Ancestors who were enslaved in Antigua and Barbuda."[14] The Antigua and Barbuda Studies Association has made its primary goals the creation of the field of Antigua and Barbuda Studies and the publication of the journal *The Antigua and Barbuda Review of Books*.

Finally, it is important to mention some recently published books that have addressed very directly the issue of Black Power and, in so doing, have made significant connections with many of the earlier authors of the Black Radical Tradition. By far the most important of these is Charles Ephraim's 2003 treatise, *The Pathology of Eurocentrism*.[15] Using the notion of *ressentiment*, this is a highly original study of the existential foundations of white power and its impact on black identities. This text can only be compared to *Bad Faith and Anti-Black Racism* (1995), the outstanding work by the Jamaican existential philosopher Lewis Gordon.[16] Also important is Akia Gore's book *Garrote* (2009), a detailed study of the experiences of Antiguan and Barbudan migrants to the American colony of St. Thomas, their stereotyping as Garrotes, and the race/ethnic subjugation and exploitation that it produced.[17] One cannot read this text and not think of Rebecca Protten and the many others who migrated to St. Thomas between her and Akia Gore.

This quick sampling of the current configuration of political and cultural forces in Antigua and Barbuda clearly indicates that the demands for Black Power and the quest for social justice inherent in them are not dead. On the contrary, these forces suggest that concerns with Black Power are continuing to stir in the creative domains of our public persona. While powerful counterforces are arrayed against these subdued stirrings, we cannot know today where these stirrings will lead us tomorrow.

Notes

1. Ture and Hamilton, 34.

2. Ibid., 35.

3. Robinson, 72.

4. On maroon communities and the Conspiracies of 1729 and 1736, see D. B. Gaspar, *Bondmen and Rebels*. On Rebecca Freundlich Protten, see Jon Sensbach, *Rebecca's Revival*. Rebecca, as she has come to be known in the literature, was kidnapped in Antigua around the age of seven and sold to the Van Beverhaut family in the then-Danish colony of St. Thomas. Because of the exceptional nature of her faith, and the manner in which she ministered to other slaves, Rebecca Protten was manumitted. She would go on to be a major force in early black Christianity on St. Thomas, as well as a missionary in Europe and Africa. Mary Prince, who was a slave of the Wood family in Antigua for sixteen years, records her life in *The History of Mary Prince* (2000). In 1829, while on a trip to England, she contacted the Anti-Slavery Society in an effort to gain her freedom.

5. The term was used frequently in Hector's speeches and acquired popular currency in Antigua and Barbuda in reference to the uprising.

6. Henry, *Shouldering Antigua and Barbuda*, 132–38.

7. Ibid., 170–71.

8. On the influence of C.L.R. James on the Antiguan Left, see Henry, "C.L.R. James and the Antiguan Left."

9. Henry, *Shouldering Antigua and Barbuda*, 239–41.

10. Hector, *Independence: Yes! The Old Mess: No!*, 5.

11. Ibid., 4.

12. Hector, *Towards a New Antigua*, 6.

13. Antigua and Barbuda Reparations Support Commission, *Mandate*, 2.

14. African Slavery Memorial Society, *Aims and Objectives*, 1.

15. Ephraim, *The Pathology of Eurocentrism*.

16. Gordon, *Bad Faith and Anti-Black Racism*.

17. Gore, *Garrote*.

Bibliography

African Slavery Memorial Society. *Aims and Objectives*, St. John's: ASMS, 2012.

Antigua and Barbuda Reparations Support Commission. *Mandate*, St. John's: ABRSC, 2011.

Ephraim, C. *The Pathology of Eurocentrism*, Trenton: Africa World Press, 2003.

Gaspar, D. B. *Bondmen and Rebels*, Baltimore: Johns Hopkins University Press, 1985.

Gordon, L. *Bad Faith and Anti-Black Racism*, New York: Humanities Press, 1995.

Gore, A. *Garrote,* New York: Wadadli Press, 2009.

Hector, T. *Independence: Yes! The Old Mess: No!* St. John's: ACLM, 1976.

———. *Towards a New Antigua*, St. John's: Outlet Publishers, 1980.

Henry, P. "C. L. R. James and the Antiguan Left," in Henry, P. and Buhle, P. (eds.) *C.L.R. James's Caribbean*, Durham: Duke University Press, 1992, 145–73.

———. *Shouldering Antigua and Barbuda*, London: Hansib Publications, 2009.

James, C. L. R., and Dunayevskaya, R. *Facing Reality*, Detroit: Correspondence Publishing Company, 1958.

———. *Modern Politics*, Port of Spain: PNM Publishing, 1960.

———. *Party Politics in the West Indies*, San Juan: Vedic Enterprises, 1962.

———. *The Black Jacobins*, New York: Vintage Books, 1989.

Prince, M. *The History of Mary Prince, A West Indian Slave, Narrated by Herself*, London: Penguin, 2000.

Richards, N. *The Struggle and the Conquest*, New York: Seaburn, 2004.

Robinson, C. *Black Marxism*, Chapel Hill: University of North Carolina Press, 2000.

Sensbach, J. *Rebecca's Revival*, Cambridge: Harvard University Press, 2005.

Ture, K. and Hamilton, C. *Black Power*, New York: Vintage Books, 1992.

9

I & I Shot the Sheriff

Black Power and Decolonization in Bermuda, 1968–1977

QUITO SWAN

Black Power was a global, Pan-African phenomenon. Across the West Indies, the movement largely reflected youth discontent with an array of political, cultural, economic, and social contradictions that bound the region to current, former, and new colonial masters. Black Power sought to address the unfulfilled socioeconomic and cultural promises of political independence. In the British colony of Bermuda, Black Power was an anticolonial, revolutionary youth movement that aimed to dismantle British colonialism and the latter's support of the island's white oligarchy. British, American, and Canadian security forces saw Black Power in Bermuda as a threat to their geopolitical interests and beleaguered the movement via collaborative, international networks of intelligence and repression. Black Power was attacked via legal persecution, police brutality, infiltration, surveillance, and an extensive propaganda campaign. Furthermore, between 1968 and 1977 British troops were sent to Bermuda on at least four different occasions to suppress Black Power–related incidents.

This chapter explores Black Power in Bermuda, in particular, the activism of Pan-Africanist Roosevelt Brown (Pauulu Kamarakafego); Bermuda's Black Power Conference of 1969; the revolutionary Black Beret Cadre; the 1972 and 1973 assassinations of Bermuda's British Police Commissioner and Governor; and the transnational suppression of Black Power in Bermuda. It demonstrates the need for more studies to examine the Black Power movement across the African diaspora outside of the United States, as the works in this volume do for the Caribbean. It strongly suggests that the systematic, international attacks on Black Power need to be incorporated into the narrative of the movement's repression, which understandably tends to focus on the U.S.-based FBI Counter Intelligence Program (COINTELPRO).

Forty Thieves and a British Governor

Bermuda is Britain's oldest existing colony. This relatively flat archipelago, lying 570 miles east of the U.S. Carolinas, spans merely 21.5 square miles. The island takes its name from a Spanish slave trader, Juan de Bermudez, who, in 1505, spotted the island during a transatlantic expedition, in which he carried sixteen enslaved Africans from the Guinea coast to Hispaniola.[1] Bermuda's socioeconomic foundation was based heavily upon African enslavement and became a significant node for the smuggling and transshipment of enslaved Africans across the Atlantic. Enslaved blacks, mostly from West and West Central Africa, cultivated primarily tobacco and toiled in activities such as domestic labor, agriculture, shipbuilding, deep-sea fishing, privateering, smuggling, piracy, salt raking, stonecutting, and carpentry.

Enslaved Africans in Bermuda resisted slavery in a myriad of ways, including revolts, absconding, appropriation or smuggling of goods, insolence, poisoning, petit and maritime marronage, and cultural retentions (such as the Gombey tradition). In the aftermath of chattel slavery, blacks built independent communities and formed mutual aid societies. In the twentieth century, blacks created a division of the Universal Negro Improvement Association (UNIA) and built a vibrant labor movement. Such political activism informed 1960s Black Power.

With its large white minority elite, Bermuda has often been labeled as the South Africa of the West Indies. In 1970, blacks made up approximately 59 percent (30,897) of Bermuda's population of 52,330, while whites totaled 40 percent (21,375). While blacks were a demographic majority, race relations and the relative visibility of "whiteness" and white power (i.e., large white population, white American tourists, colonial administrators and civil servants, British police force, segregation, tourism, colonialism) were similar to those of the United States as opposed to other West Indian countries with minute white populations. Hence, black protest in Bermuda often reflected a symbiotic fusion of black political struggle typically associated with both the wider West Indies (unionized labor struggles and nationalist movements) and the United States (boycotts and other tactics of the civil rights movement), the latter also being encouraged by Bermuda's proximity to the U.S. mainland, as well as the wider diaspora. Furthermore, this visibility of white oppression and colonialism perhaps explains the intensity of the island's Black Power movement.

Simultaneously occurring with African, Asian, and Caribbean independence and liberation struggles, and U.S. civil rights and Black Power movements, a decade of intense political activism directly preceded the emergence of Black Power in Bermuda. Such activism included an island-wide theatre boycott and dockworkers strike that desegregated Bermuda's hotels and restaurants (1959); the growth of the Black Muslims (Nation of Islam); the movement for universal adult suffrage; the formation of the Progressive Labor Party (PLP); and a violent clash between predominantly black strikers of the Bermuda Electric Light Company and the British Police Force (February 1965). Collectively, these struggles challenged a number of issues, such as segregation (which the white government deemed necessary to draw white elite North American tourists to Bermuda), colonialism, racism, job discrimination, police brutality, poverty, the disenfranchisement of Bermuda's majority-black population, increased cost of living, housing shortages, and the persistence of a white oligarchy.

This white oligarchy (known colloquially as the "Forty Thieves") was buttressed by a fraudulent electoral system whose constitutional boundaries boosted the white vote. For example, in 1960, Pembroke, the most densely populated working-class and black parish, averaged 3,534 inhabitants in each of its four constituencies. Meanwhile, the predominantly wealthy and white parish of Smith's contained two constituencies of 1,151 inhabitants each, yet had the same voting power as Pembroke. Furthermore, until 1963, only those persons owning land assessed at a certain value could vote. In 1963 a parliamentary act allowed all those above the age of twenty-five to vote, but those meeting the property requirements were given an extra vote.[2]

In the same year as the new parliamentary act, the Progressive Labor Party (PLP) was formed. From its inception, it was viewed as the party of the black working class. It consistently advocated national independence and the revision of voting acts and districts. It directly challenged Bermuda's 1966 constitution, which stipulated that a British-appointed Governor would have jurisdiction over Bermuda's external affairs, defense, and internal security, as well as function as the head of the Bermuda Regiment and Police Force and appoint the Chief Justice.[3]

In response to the PLP, in 1964 the "Forty Thieves" formed the United Bermuda Party (UBP) to protect its interests.[4] According to the PLP, the "pirate-ancestored aristocrats" of the UBP "sought the enlargement of their own economic empire and personal fortune to the detriment of the Bermuda working man." This "present power structure" maintained a "vile attitude of segregation" in schools, golf courses, tennis courts, and jobs, while advancing the "selfish interests of their outrageous oligarchy." Its parliamentary acts economically suppressed those who were not a part of the Forty Thieves or their "Uncle Tom allies."[5]

In 1967, the PLP's political platform included calls for compulsory government hospital insurance; full employment and effective training programs for Bermudian workers; an end to the retrogressive system of taxation; a low-cost housing program; a fully integrated education system; economic equality for businesses through the creation of antimonopoly laws; government boards to reflect Bermuda's racial demographics; full political independence; the establishment of an arts council and fund to help develop local creative arts; and a system of socialized medicine and free medical care. Appealing to black working-class Bermudians, it promised to use social legislation to give "economic power to the people of Bermuda."[6] Based upon these positions, the party had an intricate yet complicated relationship with Black Power.

Pauulu Kamarakafego and the 1969 Black Power Conference of Bermuda

Black Power in Bermuda emerged in a period of token desegregation. In April 1968, after being racially discriminated against and denied entry into a fair, youths from the "Back-a-Town" area of the capital, Hamilton, spontaneously clashed with the majority-British police force. This clash swiftly escalated into a weekend-long organized uprising against segregation, racism, police brutality, and colonialism. To suppress the rebellion, the British government sent a company of Royal Inniskilling Fusiliers. Among those involved in the disturbances, many affirmed that they were influenced by and supportive of Black Power; some self-identified as Black Nationalist.[7]

Subsequently, PLP member of Colonial Parliament Roosevelt Brown (hereafter Pauulu Kamarakafego), who had taken to the streets during the clashes, mobilized the PLP Youth Wing to help organize these Back-a-Town and other black youth. Kamarakafego, whose life story reads like a Pan-African epic, was well prepared for such an undertaking. Born in Bermuda in 1932, he grew up amid the island's staunch segregation and colonialism. Informed by the labor struggles of black Bermudians and their association with Garveyism, Kamarakafego's sojourn throughout the African diaspora included participating in a United Fruit Company demonstration in Cuba's Oriente (where he also learned to fly a plane); being a student-athlete at

New York University (1951–1954); fighting the Ku Klux Klan while studying at South Carolina State College (1954–1955); obtaining a PhD in ecological engineering from California Tech–Pasadena (1956–1959); teaching at the University of East Africa in Tanzania, Kenya, and Uganda (1961–1966); participating in Bermuda's suffrage movement; working with Pacific islander indigenous communities as an engineering consultant; pioneering the sustainable development movement; assisting in the decolonization of countries such as Vanuatu (New Hebrides); and leadership in the Pan-African movement.[8] Kamarakafego formed relationships with a number of African diasporic scholars, activists, and revolutionaries, such as Sylvia Hill, Acklyn Lynch, Sonny Carson, James Turner, John Bracey, Joseph Harris, Kwame Nkrumah, and Joseph Jordan.

Along with other PLP leaders, Kamarakafego attended the major Black Power conferences in New Jersey (1967) and Philadelphia (1968). After being informed by Malcolm X about Kamarakafego's work in Africa, Benjamin Wright, Nathan Wright, and Chuck Stone asked him to speak at the Philadelphia conference.[9] Addressing a primarily African-American audience, Kamarakafego suggested that a Black Power conference needed to be held outside the United States, as Black Power was internationally relevant to the black world. With the aim of formally launching the movement in the West Indies, in early 1969 it was announced that the next Black Power conference would be held in Bermuda in July of that year.

In Bermuda the public response to this announcement was divided along race lines, reflecting preexisting race relations on the island. It was strongly supported by Bermuda's black youth, as well as older individuals, such as African-American Rev. John Brandon, a minister of a local African Methodist Episcopal Church. The *Bermuda Recorder*, a newspaper formed by Garveyites, gave the conference positive coverage.[10] In contrast, the *Royal Gazette*, reflecting the views of the white elite, supported a ban on the conference, arguing that the meeting would bring "animosity" to the races and threaten law and order in Bermuda. Both its editorials and letters pages reflected the view that Black Power was a form of "reverse racism" synonymous with Hitler's ideals—poisonous, evil, horrific, and an "imminent danger" to the colony. Black Power, it was argued, would force whites to leave and destroy tourism, transforming Bermuda into an impoverished West Indian island.[11]

Led by Government Leader Henry Tucker, the UBP intended to ban the conference. However, the British government argued that a ban would help to legitimize Black Power, increase support for the PLP, and create more security threats by driving Black Power underground. This position, articulated within the Foreign and Commonwealth Office (FCO), was supported by British Prime Minister Harold Wilson. Aiming to implement "informed" countermeasures to thwart the conference, the FCO's Information and Research Department (IRD) requested information from the British Security Service (MI5), Secret Intelligence Service (MI6), and U.S. officials about the "operation and . . . finances of Black Power organizations, advocates and activities in the Caribbean and US" and on potential conference attendees.[12] FCO officials extensively documented Kamarakafego's canvassing across the Americas for the conference, even as he was denied entry into a number of countries. For example, FCO officials were aware that he had contacted several African-American nationalists and supposed U.S.-based "subversive" elements.[13] They also noted that while in Guyana he met with Janet Jagan, a prominent member of the leftist People's Progressive Party, and Eusi Kwayana, head of the Black Power–oriented African Society for Cultural Relations with Independent Africa (ASCRIA).[14] Charles Manning, U.S. consul to Bermuda, reported that Kamarakafego had a large following among Bermuda's black youth and had been recruiting many "known militants" in the United States. He recalled that the FCO documented about forty of his presumed contacts located in the Washington DC area and others in California.[15]

In the months leading up to the conference, immigration controls were tightened, with the explicit (though not publicly stated) intention of obstructing the entry of North American and West Indian Black Power activists to Bermuda. At the behest of the British, the UBP implemented a Race Relations Act that criminalized verbal and in-print racial slurs and incitements of "race hatred"; British troops were stationed on the island, and Canada placed two warships in Bermuda's waters. Lord Shepherd, British Minister of State for Foreign and Commonwealth affairs, informed the Governor of Bermuda, Lord Martonmere, that the British Defense Department would happily "arrange" for a vessel to have "engine trouble" off Bermuda during the conference.[16] The FBI and British officials collectively created an immigration stop list, and several would-be conference participants were denied entry into Bermuda (such as Omar Ahmed, Paul Boutelle, Trevor Munroe, and the bodyguards of Mulana Karenga). The CIA noted that about eleven hundred persons attended the conference, but only about one hundred were from outside Bermuda, including some forty from United States. It felt that these numbers would have been higher without the imposed immigration controls.[17]

However, several critical activists did manage to attend, among them C.L.R. James (Kamarakafego's mentor), Queen Mother Moore, Flo Kennedy,

Yosef Ben-Jochannan, and Acklyn Lynch. Local participants reasoned with these political stalwarts about Black Power (including future Berets Eliyaht-soor Ben Aaharon, Michelle Khaldun, and Sinclair Swan). James led a workshop on politics and gave the opening address at a packed football stadium. Moore and Kennedy led workshops on women and youth, and Ben-Jochannan on religion and history.[18]

Aiming his message directly at the black youth, James contextualized Black Power within a global, revolutionary framework of a "mighty struggle against the forces of American imperialism," the world of "Vietnam, Cuba and Tanzania" and continued colonialism in the Caribbean. For James, it was not neocolonialism, but the same old colonialism that had increased in strength after political independence in the Caribbean. He challenged the black youth not to "play with revolution," arguing that mobilization of the masses was the only way to successfully resist imperial intervention after a revolution.[19]

Although there were clear ideological differences among the delegates, a unifying thread was the identification with Pan-Africanism, anticolonialism, and other global struggles. Officially sponsored by the PLP Youth Wing, the conference workshops included economics, politics, religion and history, culture, technology, and communications. It dealt with local, regional, and international issues related to African people, including the negative impact of colonial education on blacks; police brutality; the irrelevance of black capitalism for black liberation; and Pan-Africanism, history, and political struggle. On a regional level, it addressed how West Indian leaders were beholden to foreign economic and political interests while their countries had yet to move beyond their plantation structures. Local issues discussed included economic discrimination against blacks (often to the benefit of Bermuda's Portuguese community), the government's use of West Indian police officers to police black Bermudians, the local media's negative attitudes toward black people, and the government's suppression of revolutionary literature.

Resolutions were passed regarding black nationhood, solidarity with Black Power globally, African liberation struggles and the West Indian student-led Black Power protests at Montreal's Sir George Williams University, the creation of independent black schools, media and global black communication networks, the need for the black church to adopt policies of black self-determination and for public education systems across the West Indies to increase access to literature related to the global black experience, and for Bermuda's government to release its ban on progressive black materials. A boycott of the *Royal Gazette* was also proposed, along with the creation of an alternative Black Power publication, *Umoja, the Bermuda Voice of the Black Power Conference.*[20]

The conference received messages of solidarity from numerous organizations and individuals, such as the Palestinian Liberation Organization, the Japanese Red Army, Antigua's *Worker's Voice*, Guyana's People's Progressive Party, the Black Panther Party, the South African National Liberation Front, North Korean and North Vietnamese revolutionary groups, student organizations from Haiti, Ethiopia, the Caribbean, and the United States, and indigenous peoples of the French Polynesian islands, New Caledonia, and the Solomon Islands.[21] Kwame Nkrumah extended "revolutionary greetings" to the "historic Black Power meeting" as part of "the world rebellion of the oppressed against the oppressor." For Nkrumah, this was a fight against colonialism, neocolonialism, and racism, and blacks should unify in armed struggle "against the common enemy."[22] Stokely Carmichael, who was then Nkrumah's political student, also submitted a statement, proclaiming that: "Black Power is the struggle for the possession of economic, cultural, social and political power which [black people] in common with the oppressed of the earth must have in order to . . . overthrow the oppressor."[23]

On a regional level, FCO officials suggested that the conference was a catalyst for the increase of overt Black Power activity in the Caribbean over the following year. They documented a list of groups in the region openly affiliated with Black Power, including Antigua's Afro-Caribbean Movement; Barbados's People's Progressive Movement; Bermuda's Black Beret Cadre; Dominica's Black Socialist Party; Guyana's ASCRIA; Montserrat's Black Power Party; St. Vincent's Educational Forum; and Trinidad and Tobago's Black Panther Party and National Joint Action Committee (NJAC).[24] U.S. President Richard Nixon called for an investigation into the relationship between Black Power in the United States and the Caribbean. A subsequent CIA report, "Black Radicalism in the Caribbean," described Caribbean Black Power as a "homegrown phenomenon" with developing ties to militant U.S.-based groups. The report contended that concrete contacts across the Americas had been established during the organization of the Bermuda Black Power Conference, as had serious efforts to establish a regional grouping of West Indian radicals.[25]

While the conference signified a critical moment for Black Power in the West Indies, it was not the beginning of the regional movement. The region's black youth were already waving the transnational banner of Black Power; for example, Trinidad's NJAC had already been founded in 1969, partly in response to the Sir George Williams University protests.[26] As Black Power fists were clenched, outstretched, and raised across the West Indies, the move-

ment questioned the class and racial structures of the island's "pigmentocra-
cies" and simultaneously wrestled with the legacy of Eurocentric cultural
boundaries in the Caribbean. One of the more challenging questions posed
by the movement in the region was to ask what Black Power meant in societies with demographically majority-black populations.

The lessons of Black Power in the West Indies and the wider diaspora can
offer much to the field of Black Power Studies. For example, James's opening
of the conference and mentorship to a new generation of global Black Power
activists highlights the relationship between pan-Africanism and Black
Power (Nkrumah saw Black Power as "the daughter of Pan-Africanism").
Such an analysis calls for a truly global narrative of the movement, as opposed to approaches that seek out the transnational dynamics of Black Power
only to fit these into a U.S. context. For example, Cedric Johnson's analysis of
the Bermuda Black Power Conference asserts that it was a "fiasco," as it was
"derailed" by the local government's refusal to allow a number of African-
American activists to attend. This, he asserts, is evidenced by the fact that
the conference resolutions primarily dealt with local issues. Furthermore, no
"viable organizational form" materialized from the conference, which "offered little—ideologically, strategically, or organizationally—that was novel
to the Black Power Movement in the US."[27] Johnson's U.S.-centric perspective is problematic. Firstly, the conference aimed to address the relevance
of Black Power beyond the United States, and for this reason it was held
precisely *outside* of the U.S. context. Its international significance (and that
of Black Power) was clearly demonstrated by the collaborative efforts of the
British, Canadian, U.S., and Bermudan governments to thwart it. In Johnson's analysis, the fact that the conference addressed concerns relating to
Bermuda and the wider diaspora, as opposed to domestic U.S. issues, is implicitly viewed as a limitation. That this was the case is unsurprising, but also
speaks to an inherent strength of Black Power; that is, that in emphasizing
self-determination it was flexible enough to allow advocates to apply Black
Power to local concerns.

According to Kamarakafego, the conference significantly impacted the
political education of blacks in and outside Bermuda.[28] For example, in the
immediate aftermath of the conference, he was interviewed by an Australian
radio station, and subsequently invited to Australia by the Aborigines Advancement League to help the indigenous Koorie in their Black Power struggle, which referred to indigenous land rights, self-reliance, and economic
and political independence.[29] Furthermore, the PLP Youth Wing embraced
a significant portion of the resolutions of the conference, and *Umoja* became

its official paper. Eventually, these Youth Wingers formed the Black Beret Cadre as a means to push forward the agenda of Black Power. This was due to their recognition that "fundamental differences existed between themselves and the PLP," such as middle-class aspirations within the PLP's leadership, as opposed to the Cadre's embrace of a total revolution in Bermuda.[30] Nevertheless, Kamarakafego remained an advisor to the Cadre, often reminding them of the need to establish a wider political base among Bermuda's masses (as James had called for) as opposed to direct military action against the state. In addition, the PLP publically continued to support the Cadre.

The Black Beret Cadre

The Black Beret Cadre was formed within months following the Black Power Conference. Some members had been involved in the 1968 uprising as well as the PLP Youth Wing. Its first Chief of Staff, John Hilton Bassett Jr., came from a Garveyite family and had studied in the United States (majoring in aeronautical engineering at the Aerospace Institute of Chicago). Several experiences abroad aided his political awareness, including being assaulted by police officers during the 1968 National Democratic Convention anti-Vietnam protests. Bassett practiced martial arts with Panthers of the Illinois chapter and attended Panther rallies. He was a close friend of Fred Hampton and Mark Clark, and their 1969 assassinations by the Chicago Police Department strengthened his resolve as a revolutionary.[31]

To Bassett, the black experience in Bermuda and the United States were part of the same Pan-African global struggle against oppression. In 1969 he began to organize the Cadre along with Ben Aaharon and other politically minded youth, initially studying Bermudan history with local elders. Predominantly between the ages of 18 and 30, Berets were often biologically related, raised in the same neighborhoods and attended the same schools and social organizations. While primarily working class, some studied at universities abroad. The Cadre was comprised of between forty and fifty "hard-core members" and less than one thousand associates; its membership included Black Nationalists, Socialists, Pan-Africanists, and Marxist Leninists.[32]

The Cadre was strongly influenced by the U.S. Black Panther Party. Bassett had brought a substantial amount of Panther materials to the island, and both groups visited and communicated regularly with one another. Berets received and contributed to the *Intercommunal News Service*, the Panthers' weekly periodical. The Panthers' influence was evident not only in the Cadre's uniform (black beret with an Africa insignia, black leather jacket, and red, black, and green button), but also in its ideology. The Cadre's manifesto, the "10–10 Program," was modeled on the Panther's "Ten Point Program," calling for freedom, land, decent housing, education, political independence in Bermuda and full employment for black people. The Cadre demanded that blacks be tried by juries of their peers, police harassment be eliminated, Bermuda cease to support racist regimes, and all public facilities be put in the hands of the people. They aimed to maintain a community news service and information center, political education classes, liberation schools, public meetings, a legal center and defense fund, day care centers, exchange programs to Africa, Asia, Cuba, and the United States, community work, and assistance for blacks on trial.[33] They called for the elimination of male chauvinism, the heightening of revolutionary consciousness and culture, the elimination of "religious escapism" and the return to blacks of the lands that were taken from them unfairly by whites. Staunchly anti-integrationist, they maintained the position that once blacks had closed ranks, coalitions with whites could be created (reflecting similar views to those expressed by Kwame Ture and Charles Hamilton).[34] However, one wonders what this would have meant in Bermuda, where a supportive "white Left" did not exist.

While there were internal debates regarding the balancing of revolutionary violence with community work, the Cadre generally saw itself as leading a revolutionary war against Bermuda's British colonizers and identified itself with continental African liberation struggles (including South Africa's anti-apartheid movement) and the Cuban Revolution. They had witnessed their own uncles, brothers, and elders clash with Bermuda's local British Police Force in previous rebellions (1959 and 1965), and had themselves experienced the deployment of British troops to suppress the 1968 rebellion. They also held that political independence would not be granted as long as the UBP controlled the local government, as the ruling party viewed British military support as essential to maintaining power over Bermuda's majority-black population. As such, the Cadre aimed to take political control of Bermuda via an armed revolution, sever ties with imperialism and establish an independent, self-determining, and egalitarian society. Explicitly arguing that "[the] only way to total freedom in Bermuda is through armed struggle," its *Black Beret Manifesto* (1971) called for a Black Revolution to "take whatever steps . . . necessary to protect the interests" of black people, who were being visibly exploited by British colonialism and Bermuda's local white elite.[35] Through low-scale urban guerrilla warfare, Berets clashed with the island's security forces. They conducted military, martial arts, and first aid training, and established an Information and Security Unit that was responsible for operations such as gathering photographs, license plates, personal information, and logistics about police officers. Defense units of small cell groups were formed, and performed security, intelligence gathering, and weapons maintenance. Berets were able to obtain weapons via a number of sources, including the Bermuda Regiment, while others were smuggled in via Berets strategically employed in Bermuda's post office. This was a risky and complicated process, as firearms were illegal on the island. Women were highly active in these units.

Despite this embrace of armed struggle, the Cadre primarily sought to further most of its aims through political education and programs such as its liberation schools, survival programs, karate demonstrations, Congo drumming, community service, publications, rallies, and anti-drug program (based on a Panther model that included interfering with drug sales and exposing suppliers in their writings). Berets were also encouraged to be drug and alcohol free. Their newspaper, the *Black Beret*, was published biweekly; other publications included a pamphlet called *Invisible Government*, which asserted that Bermuda was controlled "invisibly" by Britain. At the Cadre's headquarters, on Court Street, Hamilton, classes were held on local and international history, politics, economics, and law. Berets studied a variety of international movements such as South Africa's African National Congress, Angola's MPLA, the Young Lords, Nation of Islam, Japanese Red Guard, and the Republic of New Afrika, as well as political figures, including Kwame Nkrumah, H. Rap Brown, Samora Machel, Marcus Garvey, Stokely Carmichael, Malcolm X, Julius Nyerere, Martin Luther King Jr., Mao Tse-Tung, George Padmore, Carlos Marighella, and Albert Cleage. Fanon's *The Wretched of the Earth* was central to the Cadre's study of political theory, as were Che Guevara's writings on guerrilla warfare and Castro's on socialism. Berets employed at the post office covertly brought such prohibited literature into the island.[36]

The Cadre's longest-lasting program was its Liberation School, which peaked in 1971 with about forty-five students. Coordinated by female Berets (such as Jeanna Knights), it focused on black history and culture through tools such as liberation songs and "ABCs of . . . liberation."[37] Governor Lord Martonmere claimed that its students were being taught "racial and violent songs."[38] Student groups also invited the Cadre into schools to encourage faculty to embrace Black Studies. However, school officials firmly resisted Black Power within their institutions. The headmaster of the Winston Churchill School, for example, seized the *Black Panther Intercommunal News Service*, which an African-American teacher, Booker Quattlebaum, had given to a student for circulation.

The Education Department removed Quattlebaum from the school, and FCO officials recommended that this "menace to society" be deported. Led by a Beret, Churchill students held a sit-in protest on the school field. They also staged protests at the Secondary School Athletic Championships, calling for Black Studies classes and Quattlebaum's reinstatement. Thirty-two students were suspended, and the *Intercommunal News Service* banned.[39] Many Berets were members of the island-wide Black Union of Students (BUS), which encouraged students to enter historically black institutions such as Howard University. The local Berkeley High School Student Association also boycotted Berkeley's school sports day in a demand for Black Studies. Berets Michelle Khaldun and Ottiwell Simmons Jr. organized the boycott.[40]

Viewed as a threat to Bermuda's national security, the Cadre was systematically targeted by the colonial authorities as Black Power began to flourish along class lines.

The Empire Strikes Back

The government's campaign against the Cadre was orchestrated by an Intelligence Committee, which included Bermuda's Attorney General John Summerfield; Police Commissioner George Duckett; the head of Special Branch; a leading member of the Bermuda Regiment; an army intelligence officer; Governor Martonmere; A. J. Fairclough (head of the FCO's West Indian Department); and UBP leader Henry Tucker.[41] The committee attacked the Cadre through legislation (such as the Prohibited Publications and Offensive Behavior Bills and Seditious Intentions Act), surveillance, infiltration, police harassment, and anti-Beret propaganda. Berets were beleaguered in the United States, England, and Canada by the respective authorities.

These tactics reflected FCO concern with the spread of Black Power across the West Indies, where its strength lay in its concentration among the Caribbean's "unemployed, discontented and unfulfilled youth" and was principally directed against "overseas White control of . . . local economies" and local politicians who had failed to sufficiently reduce socioeconomic disparities in the region. Black Power transcended national boundaries and envisioned a Caribbean led by Black Power sympathizers backed by popular support.[42]

FCO officials believed that if Black Power in the Caribbean was "coherent and moderate," it could help to bring about unity in the region and reduce class privilege. However, Black Power possessed a "sinister" "racist base" and had "grown in a year from practically nothing to be a force to be reckoned with." Its spread as a threat to constitutional government or as a "movement in favor of the nationalization of foreign enterprises" would be "inimical" to British interests in the region. Of the dependent territories—where Britain was directly responsible for maintaining internal security—they believed the threat of Black Power was most evident in Bermuda, where the island's racial divisions and white-dominated minority government supplied "easy target[s]." Hence, since the 1969 Black Power Conference, it had placed the island's black youth organizations under close surveillance.[43]

In January 1970, local FCO officials noted that the Youth Wing was becoming more "militant," reporting that at one meeting members had discussed the possibility of "splitting into cadres . . . trained to carry out tactical maneuvers." At a subsequent gathering, there was "considerable talk of violence," with one young female reportedly stating that she was "prepared to sacrifice her own life to eliminate a prominent member of Government."[44] By September, the Special Branch reported that it had infiltrated a number of Black Power organizations. It felt that the "tightly controlled" and "security conscious" Black Berets had been "modeled on the lines of the Black Panther Party." The Cadre had become "more militant" than the Youth Wing, even as Berets remained as its leaders. As Bassett was "the cohesive driving force lacking among young militants," the Cadre was considered the "greatest threat to internal security."[45] Of particular concern was the danger of "hard core" Berets situated in "sensitive areas," such as the Regiment, the police force, and the post office. According to intelligence reports, one Regiment corporal had been seen distributing Cadre literature, and claimed to have only joined the Regiment so that he could learn to "fight when the revolution came." Officials were also alarmed that the Cadre had "infiltrated" youth centers, and had redecorated one with red, black, and green colors and slogans.[46]

Government responses to manifestations of Black Power activism in this period included the March 1970 deportation of Dominican student leader Rosie Douglas who, along with others involved in the Sir George Williams University protests, had been invited to Bermuda by Kamarakafego.[47] In April 1970, the British stationed a frigate in Bermuda's waters in anticipation of a proposed demonstration planned by Kamarakafego and the Berets to take place outside City Hall. The demonstration, planned in response to the trial of H. Rap Brown in the United States, did not take place. While the authorities stepped up security, the conflict between Black Power and the state appeared to shift in more confrontational directions. During Easter weekend, an eighteenth-century Anglican church was bombed, and arson attempts occurred at the House of Assembly and, in June, the Smith's Parish Vestry. Officials loosely linked these incidents to the Cadre.[48]

According to Fairclough, this "radical and dangerous movement" was "expanding in size and influence with alarming rapidity." Black Power could not be "eradicated but its evil influences" needed to be "retarded."[49] However, the Intelligence Committee felt that direct action against the Cadre was unwise, because it was unsure of how the black community would respond to its open suppression. Hence, the FCO's Information and Research Department was employed to mount professional "sustained counter propaganda" against the Cadre.[50] E. Wynne, an IRD officer, reported that with the advent of Black Power and the Cadre, "distinct attitudes of permanent protest" were "part of the everyday philosophy" of many black youth. He noted that the ruling UBP refused to address obvious genuine issues affecting blacks, such as police harassment, legal and economic discrimination, cost of living, and the grossly imbalanced distribution of Bermuda's wealth. The UBP needed to isolate the "extremists" by stating that Black Power was not relevant to Bermuda and repeatedly warn the black community that the movement would have negative consequences for them. Officers were to be sent to the United States to study how to handle race relations, and the UBP was advised to employ a public relations firm experienced in handling racial conflicts. He also suggested that a highly publicized public forum with government leaders be created to mediate racial disputes. It did not matter, he proposed, if the forum did not work; it just needed to be *seen to be* in existence and action.[51]

Fellow Intelligence Committee member, Attorney General Summerfield, felt that the "doctrine of violent revolution" had firmly taken root in the Berets, whose minds were "poisoned with hate." One local television program had "made a first class job of discrediting" the Berets. Known "trouble spots," such as schools, "were to be kept under observation" by police officers in the hope of capturing such "gangs of intruders" for violating laws such as the Race Relations Act. Summerfield called for all officers ranked at inspector or above to be armed with .38 revolvers. Duckett was instructed to recruit extra officers trained in riot control only from Britain or ex-colonial sources, as they were "more experienced" and "efficient" than "colored" West Indians.[52]

The UBP's powers of deportation were increased to keep out "agitators," and visits to Bermuda by "moderate and suitable outstanding Blacks" were arranged. As part of the counterpropaganda campaign, profiles of successful young Bermudians, denouncements of violence, and letters attacking Black Power placed in the *Royal Gazette* by IRD propaganda experts posing as black Bermudians (and then responding to themselves), were disseminated through the media. These also included anti–Black Power political speeches (constructed with IRD advice).[53] In a televised speech in April 1970, for example, Government Leader Henry Tucker denounced "incidents of lawless-ness," threats of violence, invasions of private property, meetings "where rac-ist propaganda" was "preached," the harassment of tourists, and the public distribution of "racist literature." He claimed that racist groups orchestrated these "evil" activities to stir up racial hatred and fear and to unlawfully "dis-rupt society . . . to create chaos." They aimed to disrupt the education system and destroy Bermuda regardless of innocent suffering. One hard-core group was "militant, disciplined and wore uniforms," while "a gang of outsiders" had wrecked Berkeley's sports day and threatened teachers with weapons. The government's duty was to "stamp out this evil" and to "take all neces-sary steps to ensure that this cancer . . . was eradicated" and expected "all responsible" community leaders to do likewise.[54] It is clear that these state-ments were made in reference to the Cadre, but such threats only seemed to strengthen their resolve.

There's No Black in the Union Jack

During an August 1970 rally on the steps of Hamilton's City Hall, the Cadre burned the British flag to protest Britain's sale of arms to South Africa, to commemorate the 1960 Sharpeville Massacre and highlight the connections between South African apartheid and colonialism in Bermuda. The police later arrested Bassett under charges of breaking the recently implemented Offensive Behavior Act. Bassett did not burn the Union Jack, but was targeted due to his leadership. The Crown's key witness was a British police officer who stated that he had not seen Bassett burn the flag, but would have been "offended" if he had. Bassett was sentenced to six months imprisonment.[55]

The following months were ripe with clashes as black youth protested Bassett's arrest and other injustices. In October 1970, after the police made arrests during a demonstration days before Bassett's incarceration, major public unrest ensued. Arson and sniper attacks spread across the island, tar-geting only nonblack-owned establishments.[56] As the Bermuda Regiment moved to subdue the uprising, a Regiment corporal, Derrick Binns (who was also a Cadre field marshall), instructed a company of soldiers not to oppose "the struggle for our future going on in Court Street." Having encouraged other soldiers to disobey an order, he was incarcerated for six months. Fifty-nine other soldiers were discharged amid concerns that they possessed Beret aims and high antiwhite feeling.[57] Subsequently, the Cadre issued a com-muniqué condemning Bassett's "unjust imprisonment" by Bermuda's "fascist kangaroo circus."[58] Bassett, Ben Aaharon, and Phil Perinchief were charged with contempt of court and imprisoned, as they were listed as the *Beret*'s editors and writers.[59] While incarcerated, they politically impacted Bermuda's prison system and formed a relationship with Erskine "Buck" Burrows.[60]

By 1972, government attacks on the Cadre had significantly diminished its overt activities. As a result of the 1970 arrests, a new leadership, represented by Ottiwell Simmons Jr., Calvin Shabazz, and Jerome Perinchief, had emerged. Also, Ben Aaharon and Simmons Jr. expressed interest in going to Cuba, Tanzania, or Zaire for guerrilla training, but lacked the funding to do so. The Cadre continued to try to further relationships with the black community through community projects.[61]

In September 1972, Police Commissioner Duckett, who had enforced the crackdown on Black Power in Bermuda, was killed in a shooting at his home. Several Berets were detained and questioned. Bassett fled the island amid concerns that he might be falsely charged for the murder, and never returned to Bermuda. He lived in exile in the United States until his suspicious death in 1995.[62] In March 1973, Governor John Sharples, his aide-de-camp, and his dog were shot and killed at Government House. Weeks later, two shopkeepers of the Hamilton Shopping Centre were murdered. With the assistance of the FBI and the Royal Canadian Military Police (RCMP), Scotland Yard launched a major "killer hunt" for suspects.[63] The U.S. State Department cited "Black Power, anti-colonialism and terrorism" as primary motives for the murders, remarking that the Cadre—an anticolonial, terrorist organization that was "Che Guevara at his most militant"—was a prime suspect.[64] During the ensuing state of emergency, Berets were once again detained. The police were "reasonably certain" that Simmons Jr. was involved. However, he quickly escaped to the United States disguised as a woman. He continued to Toronto, where the RCMP kept "tabs" on him.[65]

"Buck" Burrows, a Beret associate, was eventually implicated in the murders. The black community saw Burrows as a "Black Robin Hood," who stole from the rich to give to the poor. When captured, he was in possession of a ransom note demanding $150,000 in cash and air passage to Africa and suggesting that he had intended to kidnap the premier.[66] Governor Ted Leather stated that the motive for the murders "pointed to Black supremacy" and that those involved "may have been infected with the same [malignant disease] as the Palestinians." Leather described Burrows as a "single, lone, simple-minded young crook" and was convinced that the Berets had encouraged him to commit the assassinations. Driven further underground, some Berets joined the Nation of Islam, while Ben Aaharon and Simmons joined the African Hebrew Israelites and moved to Israel and Africa.[67]

Despite local and international protest, Burrows (age 33) and Larry Tack-yln (for the Shopping Centre murders) were convicted and executed by hang-ing on 2 December 1977. As an island-wide uprising ensued, a company of the Royal Regiment of Fusiliers and the British garrison in Belize were sent to Bermuda to suppress the uprising.[68] Acting Governor Ian Kinnear called for the UBP to consider independence as a step toward "curing" the "cancer" of black militancy. However, the UBP, concerned about the political challenge of black militancy, valued British military support. This led to the "unnatural anachronism" of a "highly prosperous community remaining a colony."[69]

What then were the legacies of this intense period of Bermudan history? On the one hand, Black Power pushed the government to employ integra-tionist reforms intended to quell further black "militancy" and maintain power. This increased the black middle class and served as a moderating influence on revolutionary black activism. The long-term propaganda cam-paign against black protest continued through police visits to schools, re-cruitment of local officers, youth outreach, television programs, and pub-lications.[70] The education system continued to perpetuate a myth of black privilege under British colonialism.

On the other hand, Black Power also helped to usher in an African-centered cultural renaissance. Politically conscious music (such as reggae) and artists such as the Ital Foundation grew in popularity. Its contemporary legacy can be seen via grassroots and African-centered cultural and religious organizations, such as Rastafarians, Gombeys, and the Nation of Islam. The PLP won its first national elections in 1998, and former Black Power leaders, Berets, and associates (such as former Premiers Ewart Brown, and Jennifer Smith and Phil Perinchief) have served in its government. Such develop-ments have only served to highlight a number of lingering social, political, cultural, and economic contradictions that Black Power sought to address. For example, the PLP named Kamarakafego, who passed away in 2007, as a "national" hero, but Bermuda remains a British colony (defined as a Brit-ish Overseas Territory). Furthermore, ask the average Bermudian "Who is 'Buck' Burrows," and the answer will probably reveal that Bermuda is per-haps just as politically polarized by race as it has ever been, and has yet to collectively deal with the implications of the Black Power movement and the subsequent political assassinations of the 1970s.

In closing, the narrative of Black Power in Bermuda offers much to the historiography of the Black Power movement in general. Kamarakafego's 1968 call for a Black Power Conference to be held outside of the United States reflected his understanding of the movement's emergence across the African diaspora, and its relationship to issues of colonialism, neocolonialism and "Third World" liberation struggles. This for him was due to his years of global activism and experience within Pan-African circles across the world, such as in Cuba, the United States, Liberia, and Kenya. Indirectly, this chapter suggests that analyses of the international dynamics of the movement should further explore the relationship between Black Power, the Pan-African movement, and Africa. This phenomenon could perhaps be best explored by the relationship between the 1968 Black Power Conference and the 1974 Sixth Pan-African Congress. In fact, Kamarakafego and James first began to hold talks about organizing the Sixth PAC in Bermuda in the aftermath of the 1968 Conference. As Black Power in Bermuda was also attacked by American, British, Bermudian, and Canadian governments, this chapter also suggests that explorations of the suppression of Black Power be internationalized and expanded beyond the FBI's COINTELPRO to include examinations of other governments and agencies; it also raises critical questions about the use of immigration control as a major tool of political repression.

Notes

Note on archival references: The archival references refer to the Columbia University Archival Collection, New York; the Foreign and Commonwealth (FCO) Records of the National Archives (TNA), London, England; the Bermuda National Archives, Hamilton, Bermuda; and the Department of State Records at the National Archives (NARA), College Park, Maryland.

1. Barreiro-Meiro, 9.
2. British Government, 20–23.
3. Ibid., 2.
4. Williams, 56, 97, 331.
5. *Bermuda Recorder*, 27 January 1967.
6. Ibid.
7. See Wooding Commission, *Bermuda Civil Disorders.*
8. Kamarakafego, *Me One*, 113–23, 141, 145.
9. Kamarakafego met Malcolm X when he was teaching in Kenya in 1964 ("Visitors of Black Power to Bermuda," 11 August 1967).
10. See, for example, coverage in the *Bermuda Recorder*, January to July 1969 and 10 October 1969.
11. *Royal Gazette*, 14 January, 11 February, 13 April, and 12, 23, and 25 June 1969.
12. Price to Sir Edward Peck, 14 March 1969.
13. West Indies and Caribbean Area, Monthly Intelligence Summary, July 1969.
14. "Bermuda, Black Power Activities in Bermuda," 14 March 1969.
15. Manning to U.S. Department of State, 9 May 1969.
16. "Bermuda: Black Power Conference," 16 May 1969.
17. CIA, "Black Radicalism in the Caribbean," 6 July 1970.
18. See Quito Swan, 77–95.

19. James, "Open Statement to Black Power Conference."

20. West Indies and Caribbean Area: Monthly Intelligence Summary, 15 August 1969.

21. Kamarakafego, *Me One*, 160, 189.

22. Nkrumah to Black Power Conference West Indies, 11 July 1969, reprinted in Kamarakafego, *Me One*, 190.

23. Carmichael to Black Power Conference West Indies, 11 July 1969, reprinted in Kamarakafego, *Me One*, 191.

24. Quito Swan, 90.

25. CIA, "Black Radicalism in the Caribbean," 6 July 1970.

26. See Austin, 513–36.

27. Johnson, 255–56, endnote 82.

28. Kamarakafego, interview by author, 12 October 2004.

29. Kamarakafego, *Me One*, 161.

30. Khaldun, interview by author, 10 October 2004; Quito Swan, 102–4.

31. Bassett, interview by author, 12 October 2004.

32. Record of Meetings in Mr. J. C. Morgan's Room, 19 August 1969; Ben Aaharon, interview by author, 10 May 2002.

33. "10–10 Program," 39–40.

34. *Bermuda Sun*, 26 November 1995; Ben Aaharon, interview by author, 10 May 2002; Sinclair Swan, interview by author, 14 October 2004; Bermuda Intelligence Committee Report, April 1971; Robin Swan, interview by author, 15 October 2004.

35. Intelligence Report, December 1970; Ben Aaharon, interview; Robin Swan, interview.

36. See Quito Swan, 95–113.

37. Khaldun, interview.

38. Intelligence Report, March 1971.

39. Quito Swan, 110–11.

40. Ben Aaharon, interview; Khaldun, interview.

41. Intelligence Report, 5 November 1973.

42. Kerr, D. M. to Sewell, T., 22 May 1970; "Black Power in the Caribbean," April 1970; Draft for PUS monthly letter, 27 April 1970; "Black Power in Trinidad and Tobago and elsewhere in the Caribbean," April 1970.

43. Bermuda to FCO, 1 April 1970.

44. Intelligence Report, March 1970.

45. Intelligence Report, February 1970.

46. Summersfield to Sykes, 13 April 1970; Ben Aaharon, interview; Robin Swan, interview.

47. Martonmere to FCO, 30–31 March 1970; *Royal Gazette*, 1 April 1970.

48. Bermuda Intelligence Committee Report, April 1970; Martonmere to FCO, 5 February 1970; *Royal Gazette*, 1 April 1970; Bermuda Intelligence Committee Report, June 1970.

49. Fairclough, A. J. to FCO, 17 April 1970.

50. Summersfield to Sykes, 13 April 1970, FCO 44/408.

51. Wynne, "A Note on the Structure of Society in Bermuda and Some of Its Peoples."

52. Summersfield to Sykes, 13 April 1970; Bermuda Intelligence Committee Report, March 1970.

53. Fairclough to FCO, 14 April 1970.

54. *Royal Gazette*, 18 April 1970.

55. See Quito Swan, 138–40.

56. Martonmere to FCO, 9 October 1970; *Royal Gazette*, 12–14 October 1970.

57. Ben Aaharon, interview; Summersfield to Sykes, 13 April 1970; Robin Swan, interview; Martonmere to FCO, 14–15 October 1970; *Royal Gazette*, 15 October 1970.

58. *Royal Gazette*, 7 October 1970.

59. Ben Aaharon, interview.

60. Fairclough to Morgan, 17 April 1970; Bermuda Intelligence Committee Report, January, April–June 1971; Perinchief, interview by Shané Simon, 2001.

61. See Quito Swan, 160–66.

62. Governor's Dispatch, 15 September 1972; Bermuda Intelligence Committee Report, October 1972; Basset, interview; Robin Swan, interview; Ben Aaharon, interview.

63. Pitt Commission, 4; *Royal Gazette*, 12 March 1973; *Daily Telegraph*, 22 March 1973.

64. Donald McCue to U.S. Department of State, 22 March 1973.

65. See Quito Swan, 169.

66. Sedgwick-Jell, F. to FCO, 12 October 1973; Leather to Watson, 23 October 1973.

67. See Quito Swan, 171–72, 175, 181.

68. Pitt Commission, 4–6; *Royal Gazette*, 29 November, 2–3 December 1977.

69. Kinnear, I. to FCO, 1 May 1973.

70. Quito Swan, 184–87.

Bibliography

"10–10 Program," *The Black Beret: Voice of the Black Community*, 1971.

Austin, D. "All Roads Led to Montreal: Black Power, the Caribbean, and the Black Radical Tradition in Canada," *Journal of African American History* 92:2, 2007, 513–36.

Barreiro-Meiro, R. *Las Islas Bermudas y Juan Bermudez*, Madrid: Instituto Histórico de Marina, 1970.

Bassett, L. Interview by author, Bermuda, 12 October 2004.

Ben Aaharon, E. Interview by author, Bermuda, 10 May 2002.

"Bermuda, Black Power Activities in Bermuda," FCO 44/196, 14 March 1969.

"Bermuda: Black Power Conference," FCO 44/199, 16 May 1969.

Bermuda Intelligence Committee Report, January 1970, March 1970, April 1970, June 1970 (FCO 63/379), January 1971, March 1971, April–June 1971 (FCO 44/541), October 1972 (FCO 63/946).

Bermuda to FCO, FCO 44/406, 1 April 1970.

"Black Power in the Caribbean," FCO 63/380, April 1970.

"Black Power in Trinidad and Tobago and elsewhere in the Caribbean," FCO 63/380, April 1970.

Bermuda Recorder, 27 January 1967.

Bermuda Sun, 26 November 1995.

British Government. *Report of the Bermuda Constitutional Conference*, London: Her Majesty's Stationing Office, 1967.

CIA. CIA Memorandum, "Black Radicalism in the Caribbean," 6 July 1970.

Daily Telegraph, 22 March 1973.

Draft for PUS monthly letter, FCO 63/380, 27 April 1970.

Fairclough, A. J. to FCO, FCO 44/408, 14 and 17 April 1970.

Fairclough, A. J. to Morgan, FCO 44/408, 17 April 1970.

Governor's Dispatch, 15 February 1971 (FCO 44/541), 15 September 1972 (FCO 63/946).

Intelligence Report, February 1970, March 1970, June 1970 (FCO 63/369); December 1970 (FCO 44/541); 5 November 1973 (FCO 63/946).

James, C.L.R. "Open Statement to Black Power Conference," C.L.R. James Papers, 1933–2001, Columbia University Archival Collection, New York.

Johnson, C. *Revolutionaries to Race Leaders: Black Power and the Making of African American Politics,* Chicago: University of Minnesota Press, 2007.

Kamarakafego, P. *Me One: The Autobiography of Pauulu Kamarakafego*, Canada: P.K. Publishing, 2001.

———. Interview by author, Bermuda, 12 October 2004.

Kerr, D. M., to Thomas Sewell, FCO 63/380, 22 May 1970.

Khaldun, M. Interview by author, Bermuda, 10 October 2004.

Kinnear, I. to FCO, FCO 63/1103, 1 May 1973.

Leather to Watson, FCO 63/1100, 23 October 1973.

Manning to U.S. Department of State, 9 May 1969, file A-29, CFPF 1967–69; POL 23 BER.

Martonmere to FCO, 5 February 1970 (FCO 63/379); 25, 30–31 March; 9, 14–15 October 1970 (FCO 44/406).

McCue, D. to U.S. Department of State, 22 March 1973, NARA, RG. 59, POL 19 BER; SNF 1970–1973.

Perinchief, P. Interview by Shané Simon, transcript in "Bermudian Literature: A Theory and Evaluation of the Social Laws that Govern the Belated Attention Given to Literature Produced in the British Colony, Bermuda." M.A. Thesis, University of Kent at Canterbury, 2001.

Pitt Commission. *Report of the Royal Commission into the 1977 Disturbances*, London: Her Majesty's Stationary Office, 1978.

Price, L. to Sir Edward Peck, FCO 44/203, 14 March 1969.

Record of Meetings in Mr. J. C. Morgan's Room, FCO 44/202, 19 August 1969.

Royal Gazette, January–June 1969, April 1970, October 1970, March 1973, November–December 1977.

Sedgwick-Jell, F. to FCO, FCO 63/1094, 12 October 1973.

Summersfield to Sykes, FCO 44/408, 13 April 1970.

Swan, Quito. *Black Power in Bermuda: The Struggle for Decolonization*, New York: Palgrave Macmillan, 2009.

Swan, Robin. Interview by author, Bermuda, 15 October 2004.

Swan, Sinclair. Interview by author, Bermuda, 14 October 2004.

"Visitors of Black Power to Bermuda," FCO 44/195, 11 August 1967.

West Indies and Caribbean Area, Monthly Intelligence Summary, FCO 44/202, July 1969, 15 August 1969.

Williams, J. R. *Lois: Bermuda's Grand Dame of Politics*, Bermuda: Camden Editions, 2001.

Wooding Commission. *Bermuda Civil Disorders, 1968: Report of Commission and Statement by the Government of Bermuda*, London: Her Majesty's Stationary Office, 1969.

Wynne, E. "A Note on the Structure of Society in Bermuda and Some of Its Peoples," FCO 44/408, 13 November 1970.

10

Youth Responses to Discriminatory Practices

The Free Beach Movement, 1970–1975

DERICK HENDRICKS

For several generations, the beaches of the U.S. Virgin Islands were utilized without restraint as a place for meditation, relaxation, and, through fishing the waters, survival. From the mid-1950s to the late 1960s, both visitors and residents swam in the sea and used the natural resource for other economic and recreational purposes.[1] However, as tourism increased in St. Thomas during the 1960s, numerous mainland North American developers purchased a significant amount of beachfront property and, by the early 1970s in both St. Thomas and St. John, prohibited the general public from using the beaches adjacent to their property.[2] As a result, from 1970 to 1975, activists in the islands organized the Free Beach Movement, holding public rallies, staging swim-ins, and conducting a letter-writing campaign to protest the fact that Virgin Islands beaches were no longer freely accessible to all. This chapter examines the Free Beach Movement as an example of black mobilization in a colonial Caribbean context. This campaign, with its emphasis on cultural self-determination and black solidarity, reflected elements of black nationalist ideology familiar to the mainland United States, and made a significant contribution to the struggle against discrimination in the highly unequal social context of the islands. Strongly influenced by the civil rights and Black Power movements in mainland North America, the Virgin Islands campaign helped to forge a sense of black consciousness and pride in a context where the growth of a predominantly foreign-owned tourism industry served materially and symbolically to underline the disparities between black local islanders and white American mainlanders, reenacting the unequal relationships of power between the United States and its "unincorporated" Caribbean territory.

It should be noted that by the early 1970s, the Virgin Islands had been a colony of the United States for more than fifty-five years. Purchased from Denmark in 1916, the Virgin Islands—consisting of the main islands of St. Croix, St. Thomas and St. John—shared the ambiguous political status of their Puerto Rican neighbors: as an unincorporated territory of the United States, its people acquired U.S. citizenship in 1927 but were unable to vote in U.S. presidential elections; their representative in Congress had a voice but no vote; and their local Governor was, until 1970, appointed by the U.S. President. The benefits and disadvantages of this ambiguous relationship were reflected in the local economy. In 1950, the islands were mainly agricultural, impoverished, and characterized by a slow pace of life, with a primarily native-born population. However, by the late 1960s and early 1970s, the economy was tourism-oriented and industrial-based, the native-born population was no longer a majority, and the islands had the highest per capita income in the Caribbean region and the third highest in the Western Hemisphere, exceeded only by the mainland United States and Canada.[3]

The dramatic demographic and economic transformations of the 1960s are linked to U.S. foreign policies in the aftermath of the Cuban Revolution. Prohibited from traveling to or investing in Cuba after 1959, North Americans increasingly visited other Caribbean destinations, primarily the Bahamas, Puerto Rico, and the U.S. Virgin Islands. As Boyer argues, the repercussions of the Cuban Revolution resulted in a major expansion of the Virgin Islands tourism industry, unchecked infrastructural growth in the islands, and a sizable number of foreigners relocating to the islands.[4] From 1960 to 1965, the population of white Americans in the islands nearly doubled, from thirty-nine hundred to sixty-five hundred. By 1974, the white American settlers—known colloquially as "continentals"—made up 15 percent of the Virgin Islands' population.[5] This group played an integral role in the rapid socioeconomic and infrastructural transformation of the islands, spearheading the launch of the modern tourism industry. The expansion was astonishing. The number of hotels and guesthouses quadrupled, from twenty-eight in 1950 to one hundred sixteen by 1975, while visitor numbers shot up from approximately twenty-six thousand to over one million in the same period. Visitor numbers per annum soon exceeded the population of the islands: for example, in 1970, there were 631,924 visitors to St. Thomas, which had a population of just 28,960.[6]

Inequalities were also reflected in the economy. Mainland firms and white transients owned the most sizable tourist facilities, as well as the majority of the large construction firms (the second-largest employer after tourism), while black Virgin Islanders operated taxis, managed small guesthouses, and worked for the local government.[7] In 1970, while white residents accounted for only 22 percent of the total labor force in the territory, they occupied 41 percent of all white-collar jobs and only 9 percent of blue-collar positions. Black residents accounted for just 52 percent of white-collar jobs while comprising 83 percent of blue-collar employment positions.[8] Some sectors, such as communications, the boating sector, radio and television stations, and the food sector (with one exception) were completely controlled by white settlers.[9]

The increasing number of "continentals" had significant social ramifications for the islands. Shopping districts such as Main Street in St. Thomas's capital, Charlotte Amalie, once the social focal point for locals, were transformed, as "continental" ventures catering to the tourist sector displaced and priced out native-owned small stores catering to the local community.[10] The "continentals" also brought with them culture and behaviors that clashed with the islanders' traditional ways of life, creating nostalgia for past times when friendly greetings and familiar faces were common, and leaving islanders increasingly feeling like foreigners in their own home.[11] This situation was exacerbated by the social, residential, and especially educational segregation that developed on the islands. The establishment of racially exclusive private schools with tuition fees beyond the reach of even middle-class "native" families, the creation of white residential districts (often in prime beachfront and scenic hillside locations), incidents of exclusion of black islanders from what were effectively racially segregated private member clubs, and discriminatory employment practices all contributed to a sense of resentment, marginalization, and increasing race consciousness among the native-born Virgin Islanders.

Like white Americans, Puerto Rican and West Indian immigrants settled in the U.S. Virgin Islands in meaningful numbers during the decade following the Cuban Revolution. Puerto Ricans who relocated to the Virgin Islands after 1959 moved there primarily to work in the agricultural industry of St. Croix. In 1974, Puerto Ricans made up 40 percent of St. Croix's population,[12] but while they contributed to development, they also helped to increase social pressure in the competition for living space, health care, education, social services, and other necessities for daily survival. The third major newcomers to the American territory—West Indians—had by far the greatest impact on the region. Beginning in the early 1960s, large numbers of West Indians migrated to the Virgin Islands in search of work, primarily providing the manual labor required by the booming tourism industry. Within five years, the population of Caribbean immigrants in the territory had more than quadrupled, from two thousand in 1960 to ten thousand in 1965. By 1973, following the passage of laws that allowed Caribbean immigrants to bring their family to the U.S. Virgin Islands, they made up 25 percent of the total population.[13]

These demographic changes, the introduction of "unfamiliar" cultures, and the fact that native-born islanders were no longer the majority in their own homeland, created a type of xenophobia among the "native" group toward the West Indian migrants, as it did toward the "continentals."[14] At the same time, the U.S. Virgin Islands experienced a growing racial polarization among Caribbean guest workers, Puerto Ricans, native-born Virgin Islanders, and newly arrived white Americans. This ever-increasing division between the black and white residents of the insular community amplified the race consciousness of many native-born Virgin Islanders. By 1965, no one ethnic group constituted a majority (50 percent or more),[15] and the processes resulting in the marginalization of the native-born islanders were well under way.

The Free Beach Movement

The right of Virgin Islanders to freely use the beaches was unrestrained under Danish rule and continued for fifty years after the United States purchased the islands from Denmark.[16] The Danish Crown held the land not as private property but in trust for the people. The 1916 Danish treaty with the United States stipulated that after the islands were transferred to the United States on 31 March 1917, all the beaches and shorelines of the Virgin Islands were to remain free and open to all Virgin Islanders.[17] Additionally, the Organic Act of 1936 placed the lands under the control of the insular government, and by law anyone could approach a beach by water and not be considered a trespasser. The Organic Act of 1954 also supported the notion of free and accessible beaches in the territory.[18] These historic and legal rights to free access began to be threatened in the middle of the twentieth century by the growth of mass tourism and the intensive development of hotels across greater swaths of the islands' shorelines. Black islanders, primarily in St. Thomas, which had been specifically developed as a tourist destination,[19] began to be confronted by hostile beachfront property owners, who chased them from beach areas and accused them of trespassing. In some instances, guard dogs or other security measures were used to keep the local population off of the beaches.[20] As Bingley Richardson recalls, Virgin Islands fishermen and fisherwomen frequently complained of being confronted by

brother of Free Beach Committee co-chairperson Marva Sprauve Brown and Black Power advocate Gaylord Sprauve.[38] Sprauve's testimony, which called for black solidarity and cultural autonomy to resolve the Free Beach issue, criticized private beach owners in St. John for using guns to drive people off the beaches, declared that natural resources were one of the few remaining birthrights of Virgin Islanders, and demanded that the politicians take steps to guarantee free public access to the beaches. Despite the chair's request for silence, the speech was greeted with loud applause from the public gallery.[39] This response suggests that Sprauve's message had given a voice and hope to the masses of marginalized St. Johnians. Not only had he publicly exposed the practice of white American beach owners in St. John using guns to terrorize black Virgin Islanders off the beaches, he had also challenged the territory's political leadership, a group comprised predominantly of native-born Virgin Islanders, to address the problem of white residents marginalizing the majority-black population.

Among the spectators, several beachfront property owners and persons with an interest in the hotel industry opposed any changes that would have allowed free and open beaches to the general public. The testimony of Lily Harthman Chen of Peter Bay, for example, resolutely opposed free beaches on the grounds that she was experiencing problems with people camping on her beach and smoking illegal drugs. Others argued that free public beaches would result in an increase of garbage, pollution, and ecological damage to the natural resources. A number of private owners and hotel interests warned repeatedly of the high costs to the Virgin Islands government that open beaches would entail, arguing that private beaches were in the best interests of tourism and that tourists visited the beaches to enjoy them away from public intrusion.[40] While all of these points can be challenged, the most nefarious was surely the open declaration that in the interests of the economy beaches should be reserved for visiting tourists who should be spared the "intrusion" of the majority-black population. Thus segregation was linked to the continued economic development of the islands and integration linked to their economic ruin—a position that was not only discriminatory but also failed to consider any alternatives to development beyond the dominant tourist sector.

Following a lengthy political debate in the Virgin Islands Senate, in May 1971, the legislature passed Bill No. 4849, which asserted that the public had the right to use and enjoy the shorelines and beaches throughout the islands. The committee, however, felt that the bill had failed to distinguish between the right to use beaches upon payment of a fee to a private individual, and the right to use beaches free of any such charge. They further objected to the bill's silence on the practice of selling alleged beach rights, which left open the possibility of developing exclusive enclaves around desirable beach real estate. As such, the committee outlined its objections in a letter to Governor Evans and the editor of the Virgin Islands *Daily News,* requesting that the bill be returned to the legislature for inclusion of the recommendations made by the people's petition and of testimony given by citizens at public hearings.[41] In June 1971, Governor Melvin H. Evans allowed Bill No. 4849—subsequently known as the Open Shorelines Act—to become law without his signature.[42] Dissatisfied with what they viewed as a weak compromise, the committee continued to lobby to persuade legislators to redraft and strengthen the law to favor the ordinary people of the Virgin Islands.[43] Ultimately, the local government did not exercise its total political authority to ensure free beaches. However, the very fact of government compromise between the interests of the lobbyists for and against free beaches is evidence of the influence the movement was able to exert through its strenuous campaigning. If they had not achieved their full aims, they had at least forced a compromise and placed the issue of equal access at the center of political debate.

Testing the Waters: The Sapphire Beach and Bolongo Bay Campaigns

Thus far we have focused primarily on the essentially traditional methods (petitions, lobbying, presenting testimonials) used by the committee to press for legislative reform. However, the movement also deployed a number of other strategies to execute its campaign, drawing on both local protest traditions and methods absorbed from the civil rights and Black Power movements in the mainland United States. Of particular note is the use of calypso to popularize the message of the Free Beach campaign. Corey Emanuel, a St. Thomian poet (and brother of Black Studies professor Lezmore Emanuel), wrote a "calypoem" that became a popular theme of the movement. Written in the local vernacular and with a melody that found a positive response among the islanders, the calypso was effectively used by the committee to engage Virgin Islanders from all walks of life with the free beach issue.[44] While the calypso drew on deeply rooted oral and satirical traditions of the Caribbean, other means of mobilization were externally inspired, drawing on the direct-action and civil-disobedience methods witnessed by many of the Free Beach campaigners during their time in the United States.[45] Such methods—swapping sit-ins for swim-ins—invigorated in particular two mobilizations in the early 1970s that tested the provisions of the Open Shore-lines Act, discussed here as the Sapphire Beach and Bolongo Bay campaigns.

On 12 February 1972, members of Girl Scout Troop No. 301, their leaders, and their chaperons were prevented from swimming at Sapphire Bay by the management of Sapphire Beach Resort, unless each person paid an entrance fee of $3.[46] As related to the St. Thomas *Home Journal* by Ellen Washington, a parent of one of the scouts, on seeing the entrance fee of $3, approached the reservations clerk and explained that the group of girls wished to use the beach and not the hotel's facilities. As the clerk told her they would not have to pay the registration cost, they proceeded toward the beach, where they were confronted by the manager, who insisted that each person would have to pay the fee.[47] Washington emphasized that the encounter took place in the presence of the juveniles, and that it illustrated the everyday contempt and mistreatment of Virgin Islanders by those who held an interest in the hotel industry. While they would have gladly paid 15 or 25 cents per child, she concluded, the $3 was designed to prohibit them from using the beach, and it did.[48] While Washington's letter does not elaborate on this, within the social and economic climate of the period it is highly likely that the reservations clerk was a black Virgin Islander, and the manager a white American. Their difference in attitudes to the beachgoers, then, is not surprising.

In solidarity with the scouts, the Free Beach Movement organized a swim-in at Sapphire Bay in March 1972. The activists traveled with their own tradi-tional Quelbe music, and food was brought from home as well as bought at the Sapphire Beach Restaurant. This beach-in, like many others, was a festive affair, and it took on the aura of a family picnic. No one paid to swim, and no one from the resort management approached any of the beachgoers. A scout from troop No. 301 and her family were among the movement's sup-porters, and the local press reported that the demonstration was successful.[49] The negative publicity in the local press around the Sapphire Beach inci-dent undoubtedly influenced the resort's sudden change in policy. While the original incident may have been the result of poor communication between the scouts and the proprietors, it is worth noting documented accounts of the Beach Club's questionable record of race relations—in late December 1968, for example, accusations of unjustified discharges, discrimination, and harassment of Sapphire's employees were made to the Virgin Islands Depart-ment of Law by three former hotel workers.[50] Swim-ins such as the Sapphire Bay campaign, as Richardson and Darwin Newton recall, attracted the par-ticipation of large numbers of St. Thomians, and were conducted at several beaches without any harassment from private owners. These swim-ins and rallies served to enhance the political consciousness of the participants as well as celebrate the local way of life, as beachgoers sang and danced to calypso music and listened to motivational speeches. Early successes of such campaigns included announcements by individual hotels (such as the Lime Tree Beach Hotel, which was located on the east end of the island, in St. Thomas) that they would subscribe to a policy of free access for all.[51]

A second campaign centered on the Bolongo Bay Beach Hotel, another east-end establishment. In April 1974, Charles C. Hull, a resident of St. Thomas, wrote an open letter to the Attorney General, published in the Virgin Islands *Daily News,* to express his concerns about the Bolongo Bay Beach Hotel's installing fences on its beachfront property, dividing the beach into three sections. Two approximately nine feet high barbed-wire chain fences were mounted along the eastern and western sides of the property, extending thirty feet into the sea on one side and fifty feet into the sea on the other. As a result, the barriers had entirely enclosed the hotel property, and beachgoers were denied access to the beach even from the sea along the shore. Hull stated that persons who wished to walk the entire span of the beach would have to walk into the water and either walk—if it was not too deep—or swim around the fence. In his opinion, the barriers were ugly, illegal, and contrary to the norms of the Virgin Islands.[52]

In April 1974, a meeting was held between Attorney General Verne Hodge, representatives of the Bolongo Bay Beach and Tennis Club, and Richard Doumeng, a white American who was vice president and general manager of the resort. The conference was the first step toward a test court case of the Open Shorelines Act. Doumeng contended that the fences were installed for security purposes against thefts, assault, and incidents of harassment of guests and employees of the resort by the island's young people, not to prevent the general public from using the beach. Thus, he claimed, he would be happy to remove the fences once the Department of Public Safety put in place measures to secure the beach area, or when conditions improved.[53] Doumeng's position failed to address the real issues: the threat to the local population's way of life; and the obstruction of access to the oceanfront (few black Virgin Islanders at the time would have owned a boat they could have used to transport themselves to the beachfront). Secondly, by informing the police department that he would remove the fences once the agency began to perform its job effectively, the general manager demonstrated his disregard for the competence of the local government and the character of the local people.

On 2 May 1974 the Virgin Islands government filed for an injunction against the Bolongo Beach Hotel corporate owners, St. Thomas Beach Resorts, Inc., in the U.S. District Court. The complaint against the hotel owners formally requested the removal of the fences installed across each end of its beach area and an injunction to prevent further obstructions. Subsequently, the federal government joined as a party to the suit.[54] Shortly thereafter, a group of citizens affiliated with the Free Beach Committee held a swim-in at the Bolongo Bay beach. After they refused to pay the entrance fee, Doumeng and a police officer approached the activists. The beachgoers reminded the general manager of the provisions of the Open Shorelines Act. Doumeng's reply—that the Virgin Islands Code had no authority over the islands—again illustrated his disregard for the mandate or jurisdiction of representatives of the Virgin Islands to decide their own affairs.[55] The Bolongo Bay case, hence, was about more than matters of access to the beach or the provisions of the Open Shorelines Act: it tested the very authority of local government in the context of the ambiguous colonial relationship with the United States.

The Virgin Islands government made it clear that it was not challenging the right of the hotel to keep the islands' residents off the hotel's property, nor was it contesting the resort's right to prohibit access to the beach through its property. Based mainly on the provisions of the Open Shorelines Act, the plaintiffs' case was limited to the question of access from the sea or adjacent beaches.[56] In December 1974, the case ended in the U.S. District Court in St. Thomas when Judge Almeric L. Christian ruled in favor of the plaintiffs. Upholding the authenticity of the Virgin Islands Open Shorelines Act, Judge Christian ordered that Bolongo Bay Hotel was in violation of the law and, therefore, it had to remove the fences.[57] After a number of failed appeals brought by the resort, the barricades were finally removed in December 1975.[58]

Whether or not the erection of the fence on the property of Bolongo Bay Hotel and the hotel's entrance fees were really intolerable is not important. Even if the islanders could have gained access to the beaches by successfully avoiding the fence and the registration costs, the dilemma would have remained. The barriers were symbols of white supremacy, the denial of the rights of black citizens, and the continued dominance of corporate interests in the Virgin Islands. By organizing and demonstrating to remove these symbols, the Free Beach Committee and its affiliates challenged the persistence of social inequality and the racist system embedded in the society of the Virgin Islands.

Conclusions

The Free Beach Movement focused on the single issue of gaining free and open access to the beaches of the U.S. Virgin Islands. This single-issue approach allowed for a focused campaign that achieved significant successes. Access to the beaches, however, had a broader symbolic significance in a context in which many native-born Virgin Islanders felt overwhelmed by the radical transformations that had left them feeling marginalized in their own land. It would seem that the leadership and supporters of the Free Beach Movement felt that Virgin Islands beaches were the sole remaining birthright that they could struggle to retain. In campaigning to reclaim the beaches, the movement was making a stand both against the local politicians who they felt had sold the indigenous possessions of the islanders to foreigners in the name of progress, and against the visible manifestations of discrimination that the new tourist economy had so sharply brought into relief.

It is important to note that the leadership of the Free Beach Movement, an educated middle-class group of Virgin Islanders, never advocated changing the islands' political status or their colonial economic structure. Unlike Mario Moorhead and the United Caribbean Association of Black People, which called for the end of American colonialism and Yankee economic domination of the islands, the agenda of the Free Beach Movement was not to challenge the territory's political status and economic ties to the United States. It should be noted that Marva Sprauve Brown and other leaders of the Free Beach Movement came out of an era of civil-rights activism, and this philosophy guided their ideology and actions, as opposed to a more militant nationalistic agenda. Nevertheless, the Free Beach Movement was a significant part of a wider attack on the broader inequalities so clearly manifest in the U.S. Virgin Islands.

By far the most important achievement of the Free Beach Movement was the creation of the Open Shorelines Act. This legislation asserted that the public has the right to use and enjoy the shorelines and beaches throughout the islands, and is still a part of the Virgin Islands Code. However, because of the decree's vagueness and lack of authority, even in present-day Virgin Islands society, there are still instances when hoteliers and private beachfront property owners attempt to block the general public's access to the islands' shores. Nevertheless, the Free Beach Movement succeeded in placing issues of access and discrimination at the center of public debate. Through persistent lobbying and direct action, they made a number of significant gains: pressuring the government into legislative reform; influencing individual hotels to change their access policies; and dismantling the (literal and symbolic) barriers erected by those who continued to pursue discriminatory practices around access to the natural resources of the islands. The pivotal Bolongo Bay case was a victory for the community, dismantling an overt expression of social bigotry and economic discrimination and reasserting the authority of the insular government. It is possible that without such campaigns, a de facto policy of beach segregation may have continued in the islands.

But the significance of the movement lies in more than these tangible gains. In confronting the issue of access to the beaches, the movement exposed the broader inequalities in a society dominated by U.S. capital and the imperatives of the tourist sector. They forcefully rejected the treatment of local islanders as second-class citizens and asserted the principle of equality in an unequal society. The Free Beach campaigns represent a significant example of black mobilization for the benefit of the local community and in defense of their cultural values and way of life. Through this mobilization, the Free Beach Movement helped to foment a sense of black pride, solidarity, and political consciousness among the islanders that can be considered an important exemplar of black empowerment.

Notes

1. *Daily News* (Virgin Islands), 16 September 1963 and 11 December 1975.

2. Adeyemi, 68.

3. The personal income per capita in the U.S. Virgin Islands was $625 in 1960; however, it increased to $3,204 in 1972. As a comparison, the 1972 personal income per capita on the U.S. mainland was $4,513 (McElroy, "The Virgin Islands Economy," 8; Krigger, 341; Paiewonsky, 416).

4. Bishop, 96; Boyer, 237; Hill, 139.

5. Willocks, 373, 383; Eastern Caribbean Center, "2002 Statistical Digest"; *The New York Times*, 10 February 1974, sec. X, 17; Harrigan and Varlack, "The US Virgin Islands and the Black Experience"; Boyer, 255–56.

6. Krigger, 349, 449, 450; V.I. Department of Commerce, Annual Economic Review, 1980, 34–35, 68; V.I. Department of Commerce, Visitors Bureau Annual Reports, 1969; Orlins, 102, 106.

7. Krigger, 341; *Daily News* (Virgin Islands), 28 December 1973; Orlins, 108; Cheechi and Company, 14.

8. Krigger, 362, 363; *Daily News* (Virgin Islands), 5 July 1952; *Daily News* (Virgin Islands), 7 July 1952; Cheechi and Company, 33, 37; V.I. Department of Commerce, 1980, 5; McElroy, 72.

9. Krigger, 563–64; McElroy, "Business Ownership," 5–6.

10. *Daily News* (Virgin Islands), 13 January 1972; *Daily News* (Virgin Islands), 4 October 1972; Krigger, 348.

11. *Daily News* (Virgin Islands), 13 January 1972; *Daily News* (Virgin Islands), 4 October 1972; Krigger, 350.

12. Eastern Caribbean Center, "2002 United States Virgin Islands Statistical Digest"; *The New York Times*, 10 February 1974, sec. X, 17.

13. Eastern Caribbean Center, "2002 United States Virgin Islands Statistical Digest"; *The New York Times*, 10 February 1974, sec. X, 17; Willocks, 373.

14. Boyer, 256.

15. Ibid., 256.

16. *Daily News* (Virgin Islands), 11 December 1975.

17. "Denmark and the United States: Convention for the Cessation to the United States of the Danish West Indies, and Declaration by the United States," 1916, *Statutes at Large*, vol. 39, pt. 2, art. 6.

18. *Daily News* (Virgin Islands), 28 December 1970; *Daily News* (Virgin Islands), 25 January 1971.

19. St. Croix was not developed as a tourist island and did not have a sizable number of hotels or condominiums. The chapter will therefore focus primarily on St. Thomas, where the Free Beach Movement first emerged. Nonetheless, Harold Willocks notes that in 1971 protests and marches over beach access did take place in St. Croix. They were led by Darwin King of the St. Croix Youth Councils (Willocks, 386; Richardson, interview by Derick Hendricks, 22 December 2005; Davis, interview by Derick Hendricks, 27 December 2005; Isaac, interview by Derick Hendricks, 22 December 2005). It should be noted that in Puerto Rico, a U.S. territory, which is located forty miles west of the U.S. Virgin Islands, beach access was also limited, because, generally speaking, white Americans who relocated to Puerto Rico often brought with them elements of racial prejudice against the Puerto Ricans (Lewis, 19; *Daily News* [Virgin Islands], 16 September 1963). It was also common for white North Americans and other foreigners who settled throughout the British West Indies to restrict public access to beaches and discriminate against the black islanders (Lowenthal, 120; Parry, Sherlock, and Maingot, 277–78).

20. Willocks, 385.

21. Richardson, interview. Richardson, a St. Thomian, was a boat owner and a member of a fishing and diving club. A founder and member of the Free Beach Committee, he played a leading role in the Free Beach Movement.

22. *Daily News* (Virgin Islands), 28 December 1970; *Daily News* (Virgin Islands), 11 March 1971; Krigger, 413.

23. Morgan State University, *Alumni Directory of Morgan State University*, 1985; Morgan State University, "Academics" in *Promethean*, 1967, 1969–74; Fleming, G., James Fleming Papers, "NT," Box #4, Folder #15, 11 October 1971, Beulah M. Davis Special Collection; Glaude, 1.

24. *The Morgan State College Spokesman*, March 1968.

25. Oswin Sewer, telephone interview by Derick Hendricks, 14 September 2008. It should be noted that dozens of Virgin Islanders attended Morgan State and other historically black colleges and universities (HBCUs) beginning in the 1940s and continuing thereafter for several decades.

26. Adeyemi, 68–69.

27. Richardson, interview; Davis, interview; Isaac, interview.

28. Terborg-Penn and Benton Rushing, 306, 311.

29. Moorhead, interview by Derick Hendricks, 6 January 2006; Willocks, 407.

30. Hendricks, 70; Memorandum to the Director of the FBI from SAC, 30 October 1974.

See Ryan and Stewart (eds.), *The Black Power Revolution 1970*; Moorhead, interview. *The Panther Speaks* was a newsletter of the Black Panther Party (BPP). *Muhammad Speaks* was a newsletter of the Nation of Islam, a religious organization as well as a black nationalist organization that was led by Elijah Muhammad from 1934–75.

31. Richardson, interview; Davis, interview; Isaac, interview.

32. Isaac, interview; Richardson, interview; Davis, interview.

33. *The New York Times*, 18 April 1971, 109.

34. Willocks, 385.

35. Richardson, interview; Davis, interview; Isaac, interview.

36. Krigger, 413. I made attempts to find the five-point petition at the Virgin Islands Senate and from other sources. However, I was unable to locate the document.

37. *Daily News* (Virgin Islands), 15 March 1971.

38. Ibid.

39. Ibid.

40. *Daily News* (Virgin Islands), 15 March 1971; Krigger, 414; Willocks, 385.

41. *Daily News* (Virgin Islands), 4 June 1971; Krigger, 414.

42. I contacted the Virgin Islands Government House and the Enid M. Baa Public Library several times for information on Governor Evans's personal papers. However, on each occasion, I was told that the primary data has not been catalogued as yet.

43. On 24 January 1972, approximately twenty-four committee affiliates gathered at the Senate to present their case. Among them was Marva Sprauve Brown, who admonished senators for recommending that there be first-class beaches for tourists and second-class beaches for locals, thus reflecting the segregationist proposals emanating from parts of the tourist industry (*Home Journal* [St. Thomas], 21 January 1972, 6).

44. Richardson, interview; Krigger, 415.

45. Richardson, interview; Darwin Newton, interview by Derick Hendricks, 28 December 2005.

46. *Home Journal* (St. Thomas), 19 February 1972, 6; Krigger, 415.

47. *Home Journal* (St. Thomas), 19 February 1972, 6.

48. Ibid.

49. *Daily News* (Virgin Islands), 10 March 1972.

50. *Daily News* (Virgin Islands), 24 December 1968.

51. *Daily News* (Virgin Islands), 22 March 1972.

52. *Daily News* (Virgin Islands), 18 April 1974; *Daily News* (Virgin Islands), 15 June 1974. Hull's accusations are corroborated by Free Beach member Barbara Isaac, who recalls that Virgin Islanders who visited the beach had to swim on either sides of the fences, but could not swim or relax on the sand in front of the hotel property. In her view, nonguests of the resort were left to swim in the most rocky and inconvenient areas of the beach (Isaac, interview).

53. *Daily News* (Virgin Islands), 29 April 1974.

54. *Daily News* (Virgin Islands), 15 June 1974.

55. Ibid.; Krigger, 419.

56. Krigger, 419.

57. *Daily News* (Virgin Islands), 30 December 1974.

58. *Daily News* (Virgin Islands), 24 January 1975, 11 December 1975, and 30 December 1975.

Bibliography

"A Look at Business Ownership in the Virgin Islands," *Virgin Islands Forum*, Vol. 2, No. 7, August 1974.

Adeyemi, S. *Engaging Freedom's Journey: Virgin Islands Africans' Struggle for Self Determination and Empowerment (1644–1993)*, Richmond: Djenne Publishing House, 2006.

Afro American (Baltimore), 23 March 1968–21 May 1970.

Bishop, M. *Maurice Bishop Speaks: The Grenada Revolution and Its Overthrow, 1979–1983*, New York: Pathfinder Press, 1983.

Boyer, W. *America's Virgin Islands: a History of Human Rights and Wrongs*, Durham: Carolina Academic Press, 1983.

Cheechi and Company. "Significance of Tourism to the US Virgin Islands," Mimeographed Report to the V.I. Department of Commerce, 1974.

Daily News (Virgin Islands), 10 April 1961–2 May 1995.

Davis, Glen. Interview by Derick Hendricks, St. Thomas, U.S. Virgin Islands, 27 December 2005.

"Denmark and the United States: Convention for the Cessation to the United States of the Danish West Indies, and Declaration by the United States, US-Den," 4 August 1916, *Statutes at Large*, vol. 39, pt. 2, art. 6., December 1915–March 1917.

Digitization for Access and Preservation. Database on-line. Available from http://webpac.uvi.edu/imls/project2002/2000/.shtml.

Dookhan, I. *A History of the Virgin Islands of the United States*, Essex: Caribbean University Press, 1974.

Eastern Caribbean Center. "2002 United States Virgin Islands Statistical Digest," Eastern Caribbean Center of the University of the Virgin Islands, St. Thomas, U.S. Virgin Islands, 2004.

Fleming, J. G. "Papers of G. James Fleming," Beulah M. Davis Special Collection, Morris A. Soper Library, Morgan State University.

Glaude, E. S. Jr. *Is It Nation Time? Contemporary Essays on Black Power and Black Nationalism*, Chicago: The University of Chicago Press, 2002.

Harrigan, N. and Varlack, P. I. "The US Virgin Islands and the Black Experience," *Journal of Black Studies*, 7:4, 1977, 387–410.

Hendricks, D. "Black Awareness and Social Unrest in the US Virgin Islands: a Case Study of Black Nationalism, 1968–1986," Ph.D. diss., Morgan State University, 2009.

Hill, V. A. *Rise to Recognition: an Account of Virgin Islanders from Slavery to Self-Government*, St. Thomas: St. Thomas Graphics Inc., 1971.

Home Journal (St. Thomas), 14 May 1968–16 December 1972.

Isaac, Barbara. Interview by Derick Hendricks, St. Thomas, U.S. Virgin Islands, 22 December 2005.

Krigger, M. "A Quarter-Century of Race Relations in the US Virgin Islands: St. Thomas, 1950–1975," Ph.D. diss., University of Delaware, 1983.

Lewis, G. K. *Notes on the Puerto Rican Revolution: an Essay on American Dominance and Caribbean Resistance*, New York: Monthly Press, 1975.

Lowenthal, D. "Black Power in the Caribbean Context," *Economic Geography* 48: 1, January 1972, 116–34.

McElroy, J. "A Look at Business Ownership in the Virgin Islands," Prepared for the V.I. Planning Office, Office of the Governor, St. Thomas, 1974.

———. "The Virgin Islands Economy: Past Performance, Future Projections, Planning Alternatives," Prepared for the V.I. Planning Office, Office of the Governor, St. Thomas, 1974.

Moorhead, Mario. Interview by Derick Hendricks, St. Croix, U.S. Virgin Islands, 6 January 2006.

The Morgan State College Spokesman, 23 March 1968–17 May 1970.

Morgan State University. "Academics" in *Promethean*, Winston Salem: Hunter Publishing Company, 1967, 1969–74, January 1972, 116–34.

———. "Alumni Listings: Geographical" in *The Alumni Directory of Morgan State University 1985*, New York: Bernard C. Harris Publishing Company, 1985, 240–88.

Moses, W. J. *Classical Black Nationalism: from the American Revolution to Marcus Garvey*, New York: New York University Press, 1996.

Newton, Darwin. Interview by Derick Hendricks, St. Thomas, U.S. Virgin Islands, 28 December 2005.

Ogbar, J.O.G. *Black Power: Radical Politics and African American Identity*, Baltimore: The Johns Hopkins University Press, 2004.

O'Neill, E. *Rape of the American Virgins*, New York: Praeger Publishers, 1972.

Orlins, M. "The Impact of Tourism on the Virgin Islands of the United States," Ph.D. diss., Columbia University, 1969.

Paiewonsky, R. M. *Memoirs of a Governor: a Man for the People*, New York: New York University Press, 1990.

Parry, J. H., Sherlock, P., and Maingot, A. *A Short History of the West Indies*, London: Macmillan Publishers Ltd, 1987.

Rennert, R. *Elijah Muhammad: Religious Leader, Black Americans of Achievement*, Los Angeles: Melrose Square Publishing Company, 1993.

Richardson, Bingley. Interview by Derick Hendricks, St. Thomas, U.S. Virgin Islands, 22 December 2005.

Ryan, S. and Stewart, T. (eds), *The Black Power Revolution 1970: A Retrospective*, St Augustine, University of the West Indies Press, 1995.

Sanders, C. L. "Struggle for Paradise" *Ebony*, (ND), October 1970, 72.

Sewer, Oswin. Telephone interview by Derick Hendricks, Baltimore, MD–St. John, U.S. Virgin Islands, 14 September 2008.

Terborg-Penn, R. and Benton Rushing, A. *Women in Africa and the African Diaspora: a Reader*, Washington DC: Howard University Press, 1996.

Times (New York), 10 February 1924–10 February 1974.

U.S. Bureau of the Census, Census of Population: Virgin Islands of the United States, 1917–80.

U.S. Department of Justice. Federal Bureau of Investigation, Memorandums, *Lezmore E. Emanuel*, Washington D.C.: Government Printing Office, 1974.

U.S. Department of Justice. Federal Bureau of Investigation, Memorandums, *Fountain Valley Massacre*, Washington D.C.: Government Printing Office, 1972–77.

U.S. Department of Justice. Federal Bureau of Investigation, Memorandums, *United Caribbean Association for Black People*, Washington, D.C.: Government Printing Office, 1970.

Virgin Islands Department of Commerce. Annual Economic Review, 1980.

Virgin Islands Department of Commerce. Visitors Bureau, Annual Reports, 1950–75.

Willocks, H.W.L. *The Umbilical Cord: the History of the United States Virgin Islands from the Pre-Columbian Era to the Present*, St. Croix: Harold W. L. Willocks, 1995.

Willocks, H. and Allick, M. *Massacre in Paradise: the Untold Story of the Fountain Valley Massacre*, St Croix: Harold Willocks, 1997.

X, Malcolm. *Ballots or Bullets,* First Amendment Records 100, 1964 Phonorecords.

11

Black Power, Popular Revolt, and Decolonization in the Dutch Caribbean

GERT OOSTINDIE

Two crucial moments in the history of the decolonization of the Dutch Caribbean lie at the heart of this chapter. On 30 May 1969, black rioters set fire to the city center of Willemstad, Curaçao, bearing such slogans as "*Nos lo sinja nan respeta nos*" ("We will teach them to respect us"). On 25 November 1975, Suriname became an independent republic, a triumph for the overwhelmingly Afro-Surinamese coalition government. Ideals of Afro-Caribbean liberation certainly contributed to both events, and, in hindsight, connections can be drawn between the Curaçao disturbances and the achievement of independence in Suriname. However, this relationship does not conform to a simple heroic narrative of emancipatory Black Power in the Dutch Caribbean.

This chapter opens with a summary of Dutch decolonization policies in the Caribbean, followed by an analysis of the state of affairs in Suriname and the Netherlands Antilles in the late 1960s, including the position of the Afro-Caribbean population in the two countries. The next part details the dramatic events of the May 1969 revolt in Curaçao. The closing sections offer some observations on the long-term legacy of this revolt for the constitutional development of the transatlantic Kingdom of the Netherlands and for Afro-Caribbean empowerment in the former Dutch colonies.[1]

Dutch Decolonization Policies in the Caribbean and the 1954 *Statuut*

The core of Dutch colonialism was not situated in the Caribbean, but in the Dutch East Indies. Here classical colonialism—based on economic and geopolitical interests combined with administrative zeal—was abruptly ended through a classical decolonization struggle marked by bloody battles and protracted negotiations, subsequently poisoning postcolonial relations. Within just seven years—framed by the Japanese occupation in 1942, the unilateral proclamation of independence in 1945, and the transfer of sovereignty in 1949—the Netherlands lost the Dutch East Indies, which were, many thought, both the cork that kept the Dutch economy afloat and the Dutch ticket to being a serious political player on the world stage.[2] In the end, the loss of Indonesia did not turn into an economic drama, but it did indeed reduce the Netherlands' significance in the international political arena.

Concurrent with this arduous process, the Hague developed a decolonization policy for its Caribbean colonies. The outcome was the *Statuut*, or Charter of the Kingdom of the Netherlands, proclaimed in 1954. The charter defined the kingdom as a voluntary relationship between three equal and internally autonomous countries: the Netherlands, Suriname, and the six Caribbean islands that formed the Netherlands Antilles. This definition of the relationship between the metropolis and its former colonies represented a middle path between two extremes that were not seriously discussed at the time by any of the partners involved: full sovereignty for the former Caribbean colonies or, conversely, complete integration into the metropolis as provinces.

As the charter's preamble stated, the three countries would "take care of their own interests autonomously, manage communal affairs on an equal footing, and accord each other assistance."[3] The charter defined foreign policy, defense, citizenship, and the safeguarding of a proper governmental administration as matters of common interest to be governed by the Kingdom of the Netherlands. This kingdom government was simply delineated as the ruling Dutch cabinet expanded to include one plenipotentiary minister for each of the two Caribbean territories. The initial idea to inaugurate a kingdom parliament to which this expanded government would be accountable was eventually abandoned by all parties. At some point during the long-winded negotiations, all parties agreed that this structure would be too complicated and place too much strain on the limited Caribbean political and administrative elites. The simpler variation was chosen for pragmatic reasons, thereby producing the democratic deficit of a kingdom government without a corresponding kingdom parliament.

The charter rested on notions of "equality" and "reciprocal assistance," which, because of the asymmetrical balance of power, were (and are) utterly fictitious. This was already obvious in 1954. The initial formulas were not, in fact, invented with a view to Caribbean decolonization, but during World War II by the Dutch cabinet in exile in London in the hope of convincing the Indonesian nationalists to remain within a modernized postwar Kingdom of the Netherlands. When we consider the demographics, we find a double irony at play here. In 1940, the Netherlands had about nine million inhabitants, while Indonesia had seventy million. The Hague was, therefore, offering "equality" to a population many times bigger than its own. At the same time, Suriname had only 140,000 inhabitants and the Dutch Antilles 108,000. During the negotiation process that led to the charter, West Indian politicians capitalized on the accommodations the Hague had originally devised specifically for the Dutch East Indies. Hence, the fictitious "equality" of two Caribbean nations was, in reality, dwarfed by their metropolis.

The Dutch Caribbean in the Late 1960s

In 1954, the charter was hailed as a substantial achievement by all the parties involved. Antillean and Surinamese politicians were satisfied with local autonomy and the promise of substantial Dutch development support. After the fiasco in Indonesia, the Hague was relieved that Dutch decolonization this time was met with the explicit approval of the United Nations. But there was no clear vision as to where to go from there. For the first fifteen years, the Dutch in the Caribbean prided themselves on the charter and the way the newly structured transatlantic kingdom functioned in practice. However, this early optimism was increasingly more difficult to sustain in light of developments in the region in the first decades of the new relationship.

In the late 1960s, the Netherlands Antilles (now comprising some 225,000 citizens) had been weakened by uneasy relations between the six islands and in particular by a separatist movement on Aruba, the second-largest island in terms of population. Formal democracy had been installed on all the islands, but in practice the dominance of predominantly light-skinned insular elite cartels and the complexities of six-island coalitions elicited justified criticism of the quality of governance and its results for the local populations.

"Race" was a subject not discussed much in political debates, but strongly present in everyday life. With the exception of Aruba and the tiny island of Saba, all Antillean islands had an overwhelmingly Afro-Caribbean population. Anti-Curaçaoan sentiments in Aruba, the second-largest island, originated not only in dissatisfaction with the central role of Curaçao in national governance, but had barely hidden racial undertones. This would become only more explicit after the May 1969 revolt in Curaçao.

On Curaçao itself, the segment of African origins amounted to over 90 percent of the total population. Traditionally, economic power had been in the hands of the local white Protestant and Jewish elites. Over the centuries, Curaçaoans of mixed origins had become part of this light-skinned elite. The establishment of Royal Shell in the 1920s had attracted highly skilled Dutch personnel, both for the industry and governance, but also labor immigrants from the Caribbean, including Suriname, and even from Portugal and Eastern Europe. From the 1920s through the 1950s, there had been unprecedented economic growth, to the advantage of all. But prosperity was not evenly spread, and the low-skilled Afro-Curaçaoan population lagged behind not only the European but also the Caribbean immigrants. This created resentment, all the more so when, in the 1960s, the economic boom came to an end.

While the Antilles were characterized by insularity and socio-racial divides within populations of African and European origins, Surinamese society, and hence politics, were determined by ethnic plurality. In 1970, roughly half of Suriname's 350,000 inhabitants were of African descent, the other half of British Indian or Javanese descent. Political parties and affiliations reflected the fragmentation of the nation. Issues of racial empowerment had little to do with the European element in the population, which was insignificant. The real issue was the balance of power among the various ethnic groups.[4] Among Afro-Surinamese politicians, there was some interest in future independence, even if only one small party, the *Partij Nationalistische Republiek* (PNR), led by the charismatic lawyer Eddy Bruma, advocated an immediate transfer of sovereignty. Hindustani and Javanese leaders voiced no interest in independence whatsoever, opting for empowerment of their ethnic constituencies within the framework of their non-sovereign state instead.

The absence of a strong pro-independence movement in either of the two non-sovereign states does not indicate a lack of nationalist feelings or racial pride. In the Antilles, identity discourse was predominantly insular, based on loyalty to a particular island. In Aruba, mestizo insular nationalism served to set the island apart from "black" Curacao, often at the cost of denying the Afro-Caribbean immigrant population full access to the imagined community of the Aruban nation.[5] The prevalence of insular nationalism would lead to the separation of Aruba in 1986 and ultimately, in 2010, to the dismantlement of the Netherlands Antilles. But in this process, "race" was never the issue. Much of this is reminiscent of the previous failure of the West Indian Federation. But of course, the former Netherlands Antilles remained exceptional in refusing to choose sovereignty to this very day.

Suriname has a stronger tradition of anticolonialism, mainly articulated by the Afro-Surinamese. In this regard, the life and works of Anton de Kom (1898–1945) and Otto Huiswoud (1893–1961) in particular provided inspiration to postwar nationalists. Both men were engaged with international anticolonialism and socialism. De Kom was active in radical left-wing and anticolonial circles in the Netherlands; during the Nazi occupation, he joined the resistance, was arrested, and died in a concentration camp. His 1934 book, *Wij slaven van Suriname* (*We slaves of Suriname*), still stands as the quintessential expression of Surinamese nationalism. Referring mainly to Suriname's African roots and the experience of slavery and slave resistance, the book nevertheless allowed for a truly pan-ethnic struggle against colonialism. Otto Huiswoud was mainly active in the United States and Suriname, only moving to the Netherlands after the war. He was among the founders of the Communist Party of the United States and an active agent of Comintern in the Caribbean and Europe. After the war, he counseled young Surinamese students in the Netherlands. Both men were of African origin, but neither advocated a nationalism centered primarily on notions of blackness. In his writings, though, de Kom was clearly more focused on race than Huiswoud, a hard-core Communist who valued class over race struggle.[6]

In the spirit of de Kom and under the direct guidance of Huiswoud, Afro-Surinamese students in the Netherlands began in the 1950s to define a political program aimed at independence. Among these was Eddy Bruma, the later leader of the PNR. Their ideals were also inspired by a wider engagement with issues characteristic of later Black Power movements, from local black empowerment to decolonization in Africa and the Caribbean to the struggle against apartheid in South Africa. Ironically, upon their return to Suriname, these nationalists found that their ideals met with more resistance among their compatriots than in the metropolis, where interest in the remnants of empire was rapidly shrinking.[7]

Curaçao, trinta di mei

On 30 May 1969, Curaçao's capital, Willemstad, was in flames. A labor conflict that erupted into a revolt ended with the deployment of Dutch marines to restore order. Once the smoke had cleared, part of the historical city lay in ruins. The long-term consequences of this revolt were to be far-reaching.[8]

In the 1960s, Curaçao was forced to say farewell to a period of strong economic growth, which had not only made the island one of the wealthiest in the wider region, but had also raised living standards above those of the distant "mother country." The Shell oil refinery, which from the 1920s on had brought the island a prosperity that was as turbulent as it was unstable, completely transformed Curaçao within the space of a few decades. The shrinking of this same industry rang in a gradual decline, which, in the 1960s, translated into increasing unemployment, growing frustrations linked to unfulfilled expectations of getting a "piece of the cake," and dissatisfaction with a political system that could not or would not address these grievances. In this context, labor conflicts became more frequent, while, in a parallel development, a youth group uniting young educators and recent returnees from studies in the metropolis began to express themselves through "inflammatory" publications and demonstrations against clientelism, the local light-skinned elites, and also Shell. Their weekly journal *Vitó*, which was filled with the writings of the teacher Stanley Brown and other young Antilleans, expressed such views in increasingly aggressive terms as early as 1965.

A few individuals, like the progressive priest Amado Römer, had warned of a possible outburst. "Latin America isn't far away [. . .] great changes still need to come through a peaceful revolution, because, if this doesn't happen peacefully, the day is not far off when the oppressed [. . .] will rise up."[9] Local businesspeople too, like the young banker Lio Capriles, believed that things could not go on as they were.[10] Yet despite such warnings and recurrent demonstrations organized by the *Vitó* group, the revolt of 30 May came as a complete surprise to almost everyone on the island. The local government seemed to believe that a gradual improvement of the economic situation would resolve the discord, and hence tended to downplay its significance. In the Netherlands, only a few were concerned with the Caribbean parts of the kingdom at all and even those had no idea what was brewing. Even the Antillean and Dutch security forces were taken completely off their guard by the revolt.[11]

Consequently, 30 May came like a thunderbolt out of the blue. For some it was a liberating explosion, for others a deplorable caesura in Curaçaoan history. The less than pro-government newspaper, *Amigoe di Curaçao*, which was linked to the diocese, wrote a devastating commentary the following day under the headline "End of a Myth": "In less than a day the leaden mask of a carefree, untroubled life in the Caribbean Sea was ripped from part of Curaçao, perhaps forever." The *Amigoe* identified the cause of the outburst as "the festering feeling of uncertainty [. . .] of the ordinary man, the—misplaced or otherwise—realization that he is no more than a ball being tossed around by the lucrative arbitrariness of impersonal powers, which keep on growing as he becomes disproportionately smaller."[12]

The run-up to and course of the revolt can be summed up concisely. An employment conflict at Wescar, a subcontractor to Royal Dutch Shell, led to rising tensions, work stoppages, and solidarity strikes. Once a relatively generous employer, Shell was resorting to automation and outsourcing, creating much local resentment. If the Dutch were a target in the revolt, it was not as much the Hague but rather this Dutch company and its elite employees living in secluded, luxurious, and mainly white parts of Willemstad. The Dutch government, respecting the autonomy of the Antillean government, was not inclined to interfere in this local issue at all.

Despite being asked to intervene, the Antillean government refrained from adopting a mediatory role in what had still seemed to be a labor conflict only. This led to embitterment among union leaders and striking workers: the government, it was felt, was taking sides. On the morning of 30 May, a protest march left the Shell site for the center of Willemstad. Youths, mainly unemployed, who had nothing to do with the strike, joined the march. These were, on the whole, young *men* (men still dominating the public domain in this era), partly oil workers, partly unemployed, mainly lower class. The march ended in looting and burning. Stolen alcohol inflamed spirits even higher. In the meantime, the slogans became more political and provocative: *Ta kos di kapitalista, kibra nan numa* and *Tira piedra. Mata e kachónan di Gobièrnu. Nos mester bai Punda, Fòrti. Mata e makambanan* ("These are possessions of capitalists, just destroy them. Throw stones. Death to the government dogs. Let's go to Punda, to the fort [Fort Amsterdam, seat of government]. Death to the whites/Dutch.")[13] In spite of the strong wording of the slogans, there was no real political program. Most of the looting affected locally owned shops.

As fights broke out, the police fired shots; two people were killed; several others were wounded. One of the leaders of the march, the trade union leader Papa Godett, was hit by a bullet and carried off seriously wounded. After that, the leaders lost all control of the march. Arsonists and looters moved through two areas of the old city, Punda and Otrabanda. With the police totally losing control of the situation, the Dutch Navy based on Curaçao was called upon to intervene. The march of striking workers had turned into the raging fire of an uncontrollable crowd.

The raging fire—the people, the city—provoked the most diverse reactions. Eyewitness reports present a range of emotions, from pride that finally the blacks of Curaçao had dared to stand up for their rights, to rage and incomprehension. Almost all expressed bewilderment. In the heat of the moment, curious observers had become active participants as frustration, greed, grudges, and opportunism fueled the arson and looting. The day was also dominated by the absurd, by humor, play, and a cat-and-mouse chase between police and looters. Sorrow and shame soon followed. "Everyone was crying," said Capriles later, referring to the mood in the days following the 30th as people gazed upon the rubble of the smoldering city center. Shame that it could have come to this, but shame too, perhaps, for having taken part in the plundering—stolen artifacts were to be found in many a home. And still there was anger, of all kinds: at the looters and at the police, who did not respond adequately, but equally anger directed at Shell and the government, which did not or could not prevent the march. And running through it all, anger about a Curaçaoan society that was the way it was, with all its inequalities. The blind rage of 30 May had not ebbed away.

On 5 June, under threat of a general strike and new outbursts, the *De-mokratische Partij* (DP), which dominated the Antillean government, stepped down. It looked like the end of fifteen years of DP hegemony. In the run-up to the elections, trade union leaders Amador Nita and Papa Go-dett and *Vitó* editor Stanley Brown founded a new party, the *Frente Obrero i Liberashon 30 di mei 1969*. In defiance of expectations, the elections once again brought victory for the DP, but also for the newly formed *Frente*. The formation of the coalition led to a remarkable result: the DP "establishment" and the "revolutionaries" of the *Frente* met each other on the governmental plush—a remarkable entente between the establishment party and its erstwhile mortal enemy indeed.

Partly in response to Dutch pressure, the Antillean government appointed a commission of inquiry, which reported back in May 1970. The commission emphasized the "unexpected character" of 30 May. It found no evidence of a "premeditated, organized, mass march to the city center" nor of "a plot to bring about large-scale arson and plundering or to overthrow the Government of the Netherlands Antilles." However, it did explicitly indicate that it had found a direct link between Brown's actions and one or two other radical union leaders and the escalation of the strike, through the march, into looting.[14] With the benefit of hindsight, the events of 30 May were no longer viewed as a bolt from the blue.

How, then, is the Curaçao rebellion to be understood in comparison with similar disturbances elsewhere in the Caribbean in the same period? How did the protesters themselves articulate their grievances? To what extent can it be considered a racial conflict, as many in the international press believed it to be?

As elsewhere, the underlying factors that led to the revolt clearly stemmed from the particular socioeconomic and closely associated racial divisions operating in the society. In contrast to the surrounding (is)lands, and even the Netherlands, Curaçao was not poor in the 1960s. The riotous growth of the forties and fifties, however, had come to an end, and unemployment had greatly increased. The high expectations of continued prosperity disappeared as life in the 1960s got harder for most Curaçaoans. In addition, the inequality of income distribution and thereby access to political and social circles was clear for all to see, as was the unmistakable racial dimension to this inequality. Even though increasing numbers of Antilleans from the black working classes were able to climb the social ladder, thanks in part to a government-led scholarship program, the stratification of society stemming from the colonial era remained largely intact: the higher, the whiter, and vice versa. Clearly, for many at the end of the 1960s, disaffection with the status quo weighed more heavily than belief in gradual development that would lead to larger circles of Curaçaoans, including the black working class, being able to benefit from the fruits of economic growth and modernization.

Dissatisfaction with the way Antillean politics functioned also fundamentally contributed to the revolt. In May 1969, the Netherlands Antilles had been self-governing for around twenty years. There was universal suffrage, but the parties were predominantly white. The dominant *Democratisch Partij* had put its white Curaçaoan leader Efrain Jonckheer forward for election four times in a row. In his fourth cabinet he handed over the premiership to his party colleague, Ciro Kroon, who was also white. He left for the Hague to take up the position of plenipotentiary Minister for the Netherlands Antilles in the kingdom, which was intended as a step toward being made Governor of the Netherlands Antilles. On 2 May 1969, the Council of Ministers indeed decided to advise the queen to appoint him as such. Disaffection with the hegemony and policies of the DP, in particular, and the functioning of Curaçaoan politics in general, increased. But there was no breakthrough. The government in power had little to fear from its loosely organized political challengers.

Remigration made a crucial difference. In the second half of the 1960s, displeasure regarding the political chicaneries of the established elite grew among young Antilleans returning from studying in the Netherlands. The 30 May Commission correctly identified that this group was to play an important role in the creation of a social climate in which the revolt could take place. In a sense, this group, via a postcolonial detour through the Netherlands, brought to Curaçao the spirit of the sixties that was alive in the universities of Europe and the United States: a mixture of politics and cultural

resistance; from socialism, anarchism, and Maoism to a call for sexual liberation and "flower power." This youthful element and its immersion in political
struggles outside the island resonates with the experiences of movements
elsewhere in the Caribbean, where graduates (returnees and locals) played
a significant part. Ironically, this radical wave included light-skinned Antilleans such as Stanley Brown as well.

Moreover, a new dimension of the zeitgeist emerged at this time, which
held a strong appeal, especially on Curaçao and elsewhere in the Caribbean:
the radicalism of the Black Power movement. Things African—hairdos,
clothing, music, and of course references to the island's past of slavery and
slave revolts—were publicly "rediscovered" and glorified; white racism was
unequivocally attacked; and so on. But there was no tightly organized Black
Power movement in Curaçao, and even among the radicals there were young
white Antilleans. The binary racial conditions of the United States simply did
not apply to Curaçao. The colorful mix of forms of protest, often fashioned
on the Dutch Provo movement,[15] found a certain core in the magazine *Vitó*
and the meetings that were held from 1967 onward in Da Costa Gomesplein,
Willemstad, which became notorious among the white or light-skinned
elites. But a central figure in all of this was Stanley Brown, himself a light-
skinned Antillean.

A decisive link between the disaffection of these young people and the
trade union movement was forged in the period prior to May 1969, when
close cooperation between Brown and the black union leaders Godett and
Amador Nita took shape. Nita, the leader of a number of small unions, also
published various comparatively radical political treatises. The larger unions
were led by more experienced and, moreover, moderate figures like Ewald
Ong-A-Kwie and Reggie Venloo. Brown argued that the triumvirate strategy
was expressly aimed at taking over the reins of power in the labor unions;
shortly after the 30 May events, the directors of Shell and Wescar confirmed
that there had indeed been a struggle for power, which had been settled to
the disadvantage of the moderates.[16]

The more the union conflict around Wescar escalated and the more the
government kept its distance, the more radical the leadership became. Initially, the various union leaders formed a united front with the same demands, which were aimed at solving what in essence was a labor conflict. But
as the march to the city advanced and got out of hand, the initiative seems
to have shifted toward Godett and Nita, who in turn were partly inspired
by Brown. The latter, remarkably, was not present at the march. The slogans
became increasingly political, eventually demanding the resignation of the

government, and 30 May gradually developed into a revolt. When, on the eve of 30 May, a hesitant Ong-A-Kwie read a declaration over the radio on behalf of the union leaders announcing an agreement with Wescar and postponement of the strike, an impatient Nita snatched the paper out of his hands and read out the new demand himself: the government was to step down or else there would be a new general strike. This move pushed Nita and his supporters into the ascendancy and brought with it the political battle Ong-A-Kwie had sought to avoid.

While the international climate of the 1960s, via the Netherlands, undoubtedly had an impact on the buildup to May 1969, it cannot be said that the outside world was preoccupied with Curaçao; it was, after all, just a small island in the Caribbean and still widely regarded as undisputed Dutch territory. The 30 May Commission found no evidence of an active foreign role in the revolt, and with the information we have today, there is little reason to dispute this. The obvious candidates for foreign interference would have been Cuba, Venezuela, and the American Black Power movement. Only Brown maintained serious contact with radical union leaders in Cuba in the run-up to 30 May, although fairly vague notions about the Cuban revolution did circulate on the island. It was not until after the revolt that interest grew; however, this was mainly Curaçaoan interest in Cuba rather than the other way around. The military-style outfits of the *Frente* leadership were certainly inspired by Fidel Castro. Venezuela, with its traditional claim on the Leeward Islands, made military preparations during 30 May, which could have been interpreted as moves toward intervention. However, the government of the Kingdom of the Netherlands had already let it be known directly to Venezuela—and the United States—that foreign assistance was neither necessary nor desirable. In Democratic Party circles, it was pointed out that some of the union leaders had been educated in Caracas. However, it is difficult to maintain the argument that these apprenticeships were aimed at causing disruption on Curaçao in order to provoke a Venezuelan intervention—even if simply because the most radical union leader was not trained in Venezuela. The fact is that, although Venezuelan interest in the Leeward Islands remained undiminished after 30 May 1969, there were never any demonstrable or strong ties between Curaçaoan radicals and any power of any kind (guerrilla, army, political parties) in Venezuela.

In the immediate aftermath of May 1969, there emerged conflicting interpretations of the racial dimensions of the revolt. While the establishment in Curaçao preferred to minimize any suggestion of a racial conflict—referring instead to irresponsible rioters, communists, and radical agitators—the international press, at least in part, sought explanations precisely in this realm. As a result, there was a relatively large amount of attention, including in the Dutch press, for the supposed "Black Power frontman" Benjamin Fox, who, on exactly that day, had flown from the United States to the island of his birth, Curaçao, only to be arrested on Aruba. Fox indeed emphasized his links with Black Power in later interviews. However, there do not seem to have been earlier ties to the Curaçaoan revolt, and even afterward the relationship between Fox and men such as Brown or Godett never became close. There are no serious indications of any kind of interference in the Curaçao Revolt by either the North American or the Anglophone Caribbean Black Power movements. This did not change in any appreciable degree after May 1969.

In sum, then, "revolt" may be too broad a term for what happened in May 1969, and revolution was certainly never at stake. *Trinta di mei* originated from deep resentment within the Afro-Caribbean majority on a specific labor conflict, on the continuing preponderance of the local lighter-skinned elites, and on the lack of visible progress of black empowerment. Frustrations were also directed at the Royal Dutch Shell and particularly the Dutch living luxurious lives in splendid isolation, but did not target the Dutch government or Dutch (neo)colonialism per se—indeed, in accordance with the *Statuut*, the Dutch role in Antillean politics was at an unprecedented low in these years.

By definition, given the socio-racial structure of society, class struggle had a racial dimension in Curaçao. But there was no integrated political program, nor an integrated leadership, nor clearly defined links to outside movements or organizations, whether Black Power in the United States or the Anglophone Caribbean, the Cuban Revolution, or even international labor union organizations. Surely something was brewing prior to 30 May 1969, but it might just as much have happened a bit later, a bit earlier, or possibly not at all. Coincidence was as important as loose planning. But all this, of course, does not diminish the fact that the *trinta de mei* was a watershed in Dutch Caribbean history.

Decolonization in the Aftermath of the Curaçao Revolt

On 3 June 1969, the Dutch parliament held emergency consultations on the Curaçaoan revolt. Few words were wasted on procedures. Both coalition and most opposition parties agreed that no other response had been possible. Much was said about the dilemma of having a constitutional relationship that obliged the Netherlands to offer military assistance, but that denied any scope for remedying the source of possible tensions in advance. However, to avoid the impression that the Netherlands was about to let its Antillean partners down at a time of crisis, the coalition parties felt it was inappropriate to raise the issue of the future of the charter itself. Among the left-wing parties, reactions were considerably more critical. Not only was criticism directed at the granting of assistance to a regime that apparently enjoyed little support among the local citizenry, but also at underlying constitutional factors. The outdated nature of the charter was highlighted in every way possible. There was particularly severe criticism of the paradoxical obligation of the Kingdom of the Netherlands to guarantee good governance in the countries concerned, while leaving the responsibility for the quality of government as much as possible to the countries themselves. The left now urged for an end to transatlantic ties to be placed at the top of the political agenda.

While Dutch coalition parties initially responded rather approvingly to intervention, the response in the press was unequivocally critical and more consistent with the left-wing position, calling for a thorough revision of the kingdom's relations. After all, it was not only in Curaçao that trouble was brewing. Latent resentment had been made more than apparent earlier that year in Suriname, where large-scale demonstrations had led to the fall of the Surinamese government. The views in the press later gained ground within the government, fueled in part by concerns about the image of the Dutch. The belief that the Dutch intervention had been understood by the outside world as a neocolonial act played an increasingly important role. Images of Dutch Marines patrolling the smoldering ruins of Willemstad, machine guns at the ready, had been broadcast worldwide. With little understanding of the kingdom's relations and the nature of the charter, the world inevitably read this as colonial intervention. In hindsight, this concern could be understood as a typical overestimation of foreign interest in the way the Netherlands acted within its own sphere of influence. Yet this concern was to be crucial to the Netherlands' new approach to the kingdom's relations.

Chance took care of the rest. In the same period as military assistance was sent to Curaçao, a debate on earlier military actions in Indonesia had flared up in the Netherlands in response to revelations about excesses committed there in the dying days of colonialism. The link was all too easily made. No more excesses and no more "colonial actions" had to be the new resolution. Had the wrong party once again been granted military assistance? Would the conclusion later be drawn that in the Antilles too the Dutch had misunderstood public sentiment? The answer clearly lay in a concerted effort to find a definitive solution to the postcolonial issue: the dismantling of the transatlantic kingdom. In the months and years that followed the Curaçaoan revolt, this new view found wide support within Dutch politics. A new debate now began, which would result in the independence of Suriname six years later.

A fundamental change in Dutch policy became apparent in its response to *trinta di mei*: the Hague no longer categorically refrained from political intervention. The Dutch reassessment of the appointment of a new Governor to the Antilles was symptomatic of this. The appointment of the white DP leader Ephraim Jonckheer as Governor was now regarded as ill advised. This had become increasingly apparent during the heated protests of 30 May—insofar as the revolt had been a political protest, it had mainly been aimed at the hegemony of the Democratic Party. Thus Jonckheer's appointment, decided upon by the kingdom government just a few months before, was repealed, and in his place came the first black Antillean to hold the office of governor, the Afro-Curaçaoan Ben Leito. In so doing, the Netherlands supported "progressive" development—the emancipation of the Afro-Antillean population—while at the same time taking a "regressive" step—breaking with the custom of accepting the candidate proposed by the Caribbean government. Not without reason, the Democratic Party experienced this as a significant attack on its autonomy and felt that, by intervening in this way, the Hague had placed itself between the parties, whereas its intention had been to distance itself from Antillean politics.

Believing it was now time for political action, the government of the Netherlands initiated renewed consultations on the kingdom, which recommenced in Willemstad in January 1970. However, both the Antillean and Surinamese MPs categorically refused to discuss early independence, as they worried about losing the tangible rewards of the postcolonial arrangements of the *Statuut* and correctly assumed that a majority of their electorate would oppose a parting with the Netherlands. The Dutch minister responsible assured them that the Netherlands would not unilaterally attempt to change the charter. In contrast, the left-wing parties maintained their standpoint, which was critical of government policy, and urged for preparations to be made for a transfer of sovereignty. In July 1971, with the inauguration of a new center-right administration in the Hague, the emphasis shifted. The new government stated that the Netherlands "could also take the initiative to amend the constitutional status of the countries."[17] Later that year, the Second Chamber of the Dutch parliament announced for the first time its support for the transfer of sovereignty to both Caribbean countries—and by an overwhelming majority. Within this new setting, the Netherlands had moved to advocating the transfer of independence not only as a logical and, indeed, inevitable step in the process of decolonization, but also as both a right and an obligation for Suriname and the Netherlands Antilles. Behind such rhetoric hovered a new pragmatism. The Hague had shifted to the position that its relationship with the Caribbean parts of the kingdom did not bring significant, positive benefits for the Netherlands, but rather bore many inconvenient liabilities.

There were—and, in terms of the Antilles, still are—three main considerations behind metropolitan reluctance to continue relations with the kingdom territories in their existing form. Initially, the most important concern was that the charter entrusted the responsibility for guaranteeing good governance in the overseas territories to the kingdom's government, while at the same time provided little opportunity for the government to take preventive action because of the domestic autonomy provided for in the same charter. Hence, from a Dutch perspective, the Hague had little to do with the root causes of the local discontent that sparked the 1969 riots, yet it was obliged to intervene and ended up being criticized for neocolonial behavior. Dutch policy, consequently, needed to disentangle itself from the risk of similar obligations in the future, either by simply terminating the postcolonial relationship or, conversely, by becoming even more interventionist in order to prevent new, potentially embarrassing situations from developing. The first line dominated until about 1990; the second ever since.

The second consideration lay in the realm of economics. The expectation expressed in the charter that mutual assistance would help to narrow the gap in living standards between the various parts of the kingdom proved illusory. Parliament and the media became increasingly wary of the relatively generous Dutch development aid, claiming that it led to "aid addiction," rather than promoting genuine economic development and self-reliance. Over time, a third, mainly domestic, concern would grow in significance for Dutch politicians: unease about unrestricted migration from the Dutch Caribbean to the metropolis. By the early 1970s, only forty thousand people from the Antilles and Suriname had settled in the Netherlands, but Surinamese migration was on the rise. This factor certainly inspired the Dutch willingness to bring the constitutional relationship to an end. But, as it turned out, the hasty transfer of independence only served to trigger a massive exodus. Today there are around 350,000 citizens with Surinamese backgrounds living in the Netherlands, compared with half a million in Suriname itself. By 2000, the continuation of unrestricted access for Antilleans to the Netherlands would become one of the most hotly debated issues in the kingdom's relations—the

Antillean community in the Netherlands now stands at 135,000, compared with 300,000 on the six islands.

Suriname indeed became independent in 1975 in a highly unusual and fast-track political process, which undermined any claim the kingdom's government may have had to being a patron of good governance. There was certainly a nationalist, pro-independence movement in the country, which mainly catered to the Afro-Surinamese in a society that was deeply divided along ethnic lines. The new, mainly Afro-Surinamese government, led by Prime Minister Henck Arron, would celebrate the transfer of sovereignty as if it had been a hard-won victory, which was definitely not the case. In fact, Arron's coalition had worked reasonably smoothly with a Dutch government that had been prepared to make many concessions to secure the transfer of sovereignty.

The dominant sentiment in the Hague was no less anticolonial, but the government there was particularly concerned about the effect on the Dutch image and the balance between costs and benefits. One might cynically characterize this as a strange brew of self-interest and paternalism dressed up as progressive policy. The cabinets in the Hague and Paramaribo managed to accomplish the transfer of sovereignty in just twenty months. The population of Suriname was never directly invited to give its opinion on this transfer of sovereignty. Neither of the two governments had any interest in staging a referendum: both sides assumed, probably correctly, that a majority would oppose independence.

During these twenty months of negotiations, the mainly Hindustani opposition had little faith in either the process or its outcome. Meanwhile both governments watched helplessly as one third of the population of Suriname voted with their feet, choosing to live in the cold, European motherland rather than stay on in the new republic. In the end, the transfer of sovereignty was only achieved because, at the critical moment, there was a majority of just one vote in the Surinamese parliament in favor of independence. The Dutch parliament agreed wholeheartedly with this wafer-thin majority, while the Antillean assembly did not object as long as there were no implications for its own, non-sovereign status.

Dutch policy now shifted to encouraging the Netherlands Antilles to take the same step, which would mean complete withdrawal from the Caribbean. However, Antillean politics was ruled by pragmatism, and there was virtually no support for political independence. Antillean aims were, therefore, diametrically opposed to Dutch decolonization policies throughout the 1970s and 1980s. Backed by the newly appointed black governor, Ben Leito, subsequent Antillean governments resisted Dutch pressure and bluntly rejected independence in any foreseeable future. By 1990, the Dutch parliament had no choice but to accept this unanticipated and unwelcome outcome of the decolonization process. Since then, the agenda of the transatlantic kingdom has been marked by struggles over the limits of Caribbean autonomy, accusations of "recolonization" by the Dutch, migration issues, and the disintegration of the former six-island country. In 2010, the former Antilles was carved up into six islands, each with its own direct relation to the Netherlands and with a more direct Dutch administrative presence than anyone could ever have predicted on the eve of the May 1969 revolt.

Afro-Curaçaoan Empowerment?

What did *trinta di mei* bring to Curaçao? In retrospect, the revolt was regarded as a decisive moment in the emancipation of the Afro-Caribbean population and thereby the growth into maturity for Curaçao. But is this correct?

The grievances of 1969, the links between skin color and socioeconomic opportunities, cannot be regarded as belonging to a distant past. From May 1969, there was a gradual flow of black Curaçaoans into the island's elite. The *Frente Obrero y Liberacion 30 di Mei* (FOL) and the more intellectual-leaning *Movemento Antiyas Nobo* (MAN) were black parties emerging directly from the 1969 revolt urging for Afro-Curaçaoan empowerment, but soon all other parties took such issues aboard and included black Curaçaoans in their leadership. In political and civil-servant circles, Afro-Curaçaoans now occupy a majority of managerial positions, in significant contrast with the period prior to 1969. But there has been no power shift in the world of business. In terms of entrepreneurs especially, newcomers to business tend to come from new generations of immigrants, rather than from the Afro-Curaçaoan population.

But meanwhile, a large part of the Afro-Curaçaoan population has remained excluded from the country's prosperity, despite the emancipation of a black middle class and, influenced in part by *trinta di mei*, the gradual buildup of a social safety net. This is linked to the unsatisfying economic development of the island over the last few decades, which has structurally pushed unemployment to an extremely high level. The government budget has become increasingly unbalanced, successive governments have proved incapable of restoring the situation, and more and more Dutch aid has been needed, bringing with it increasing Dutch involvement. This can, to a degree, be attributed to an unfavorable economic constellation, which affects almost all, equally small and vulnerable, Caribbean economies. However, critics claim that many of the serious economic problems are directly attributable to what are considered the "successes" of 30 May, in particular the growth of an inefficient yet very costly civil-service apparatus.

The functioning of the political and public administrations in Curaçao has been analyzed elsewhere in similar terms. The domination of the administration by the white elite is over; the island and country has had an almost unbroken succession of black prime ministers, ministers, and governors since 1969. But have these politicians operated any differently, any better, with more integrity? Have they been any more beneficial to the Afro-Curaçaoan majority? This is a serious question indeed. May 1969 created room for a new, black political elite. A part of this new political elite quickly adopted the mechanisms of the detested "old" politics. It was precisely the "revolutionary" *Frente* party under Papa Godett, and later his son Anthony, that on several occasions became entangled in lawsuits involving accusations of corruption and abuses of power.

What can be stated is that *trinta di mei* provided the impetus for a reassessment of Curaçaoan identity. Where Dutch, or Western culture in general, had been regarded as normative, Curaçaoan culture now lost the stigma of inferiority. Often supported by new government policy, culture in the narrow sense of the word (music, painting, literature) underwent a strong development, in which the "mother country" was less of a model than ever before. In education, attention shifted toward the local, for instance through the introduction of Antillean and Caribbean history. And there was, of course, the further emancipation of the local creole language, Papiamentu, in almost all realms of the society. This is all frequently understood within the context of an *Afro*-Curaçaoan emancipation that expressly aimed to separate itself from the aesthetic values of the "old" colonial world. In the background resonated the phrase "Black is beautiful," which had been so clearly audible in the 1960s. The informal 1980s movement *Di nos e ta*—roughly, "This is ours"—with its conscious glorification of Afro-Curaçaoan culture, is the embodiment of the spirit of resistance that may indeed be regarded as the direct legacy of 30 May 1969.

However, critical comment is appropriate even with this legacy. To start with the most basic, supposedly emancipatory legacy of 30 May: Does "Black is beautiful" truly apply in Curaçao today? Does local culture really provide direction for the youth, or for the pre-1969 generation? It is impossible to give an unequivocal answer; what is striking, though, is that such questions are hardly ever asked in public. In extension to this, one might ask where, after 1969, the core of Curaçaoan identity should be sought. Is it only, or primarily, in *Afro*-Curaçaoan culture, or precisely in the mutual cross-fertilization between all the different cultures that assert themselves on Curaçao? And how should the appealing aspects of promoting a local culture—for instance, by introducing Papiamentu as the official language of instruction—be offset against practical and fundamental objections, and against resistance from many sections of the Curaçaoan population? Why have Antillean governments—autonomous, free to establish their own policies since 1954 and, since 1969, with the ideological encouragement to embark on cultural renewal—never been able to develop a consistent and decisive policy on language and education, to the extent that the devastating criticism of Curaçaoan education standards expressed today is almost identical to comments about education on Curaçao made by the inquiry commission in 1970?[18]

It is still difficult to establish what 30 May meant for the Curaçaoan population and the Afro-Curaçaoan working class in particular. *Since*, but not necessarily *because of,* May 1969, a process of emancipation has taken shape, and there is without a doubt more scope for personal improvement for working-class individuals and groups. Ten years after 1969, Papa Godett called "the most beautiful result" of the previous decade the acknowledgment and "respect" that black Curaçaoans and the trade union movement had acquired.[19] Insofar as one can speak of a structural change to Curaçaoan society, this does not really square with slogans of the past. Cries for respect and greater opportunity can still be heard, but now they are also aimed at a local and predominantly Afro-Curaçaoan political elite, which has evidently been unable to develop substantially different or effective policies. This partly is why 45 percent of the Curaçaoan population lives in the Netherlands. Meanwhile, despite Black Power and *trinta di mei*, the view from Curaçao, more than ever, is directed toward the Netherlands, at the expense of its Caribbean surroundings.

Is this likely to change? There are some indications it might, politically at least. On the "magical" date of 10 October 2010 (hence 10/10/10), the non-sovereign island nation of the Netherlands Antilles was dismantled. Henceforward, the transatlantic Kingdom of the Netherlands has four countries: the Netherlands (including the three Caribbean pseudo-municipalities of Bonaire, St. Eustatius, and Saba), Aruba, Curaçao, and St. Maarten. In the negotiations leading up to this restructuring, the Hague offered support for this dismantlement and debt servicing to the amount of 1.7 billion Euros, but requested a stronger involvement in the maintenance of law and in financial governance in the Dutch Caribbean in return.

In the years of negotiation leading up to this constitutional rearrangement, strong protest arose against what the opposition on the islands qualified as Dutch "recolonization." The first post-10/10/10 coalition government of Curaçao consisted mainly of opponents of the concessions made to the Dutch government. The most vociferous anti-Dutch party, *Pueblo Soberano* (PS), played an anticolonial card with racial overtones—all of this reminiscent of the rhetoric of May 1969, but with a much stronger anti-Dutch element to it. *Pueblo Soberano* even briefly appointed one of the protagonists of the *Di nos e ta* movement, anthropologist René Rosalia, to the position of Minister of Culture.[20] Indeed, 2011 has seen many official statements stressing the value of Afro-Curaçaoan culture and the need for full emancipation. But there is little indication that the black majority of Curaçao is leaning toward more radical politics, much less to a severing of the rewarding lifeline with the Netherlands—if only because nearly half of the Curaçaoan community now lives in the metropolis.

Notes

1. This contribution draws extensively on Oostindie (ed.), *Dromen en littekens*; Oostindie, *Paradise Overseas* and "Dependence and Autonomy in Sub-National Island Jurisdictions"; and Oostindie and Klinkers, *Het Koninkrijk inde Caraïben* and *Decolonising the Caribbean*. Please consult these publications for more detailed analysis of the decolonization of the Dutch Caribbean, the 1969 Curaçao revolt, and contemporary politics within the transatlantic Kingdom of the Netherlands.

2. The transfer of Papua New Guinea was postponed until 1962 and caused further deterioration of bilateral relations.

3. Cited in Oostindie and Klinkers, *Decolonising the Caribbean*, 84–88.

4. Dew, *The Difficult Flowering of Surinam*.

5. Alofs and Leontien, *Ken ta Arubiano?*

6. Meel, "Anton de Kom and the Formative Phase of Surinamese Nationalism"; Boots and Woortman, *Anton de Kom: Biografie 1898–1945*; and van Enckevort, *The Life and Work of Otto Huiswoud*.

7. On Afro-Surinamese (proto-) nationalism and Anton de Kom, see van Stipriaan, "July 1: Emancipation Day in Surinam"; and Meel, "Towards a Typology of Surinamese Nationalism" and "Anton de Kom and the Formative Phase of Surinamese Nationalism." For a comparison of identity discourse in the two Dutch Caribbean countries, see Oostindie, *Paradise Overseas*, 111–35.

8. Two English-language analyses of the revolt are Anderson and Dynes, *Social Movements, Violence and Change* and Verton, "Emancipation and Decolonization," 88–101.

9. Cited in Oostindie, *Dromen en littekens*, 11.

10. Ibid.

11. Ibid.

12. Ibid.

13. Cited in Commissie, 74–75.

14. Commissie, 5, 66–67, 189; about the leaders: 95, 110, 118, 121–22.

15. "Provo," shorthand for "provocation," was a loosely organized 1960s antiestablishment movement in Amsterdam. Provo hardly aspired for, and never attained, direct political influence, but was instrumental in stimulating a move toward the left of Dutch politics at large.

16. KITLV, Collection "30 mei 1969."

17. Oostindie and Klinkers, *Het Koninkrijk inde Caraïben*, 104.

18. Commissie, 87–88, 170, 177, 193.

19. Cited in de Sola, 7.

20. His term did not last long, as PS leader Helmin Wiels withdrew him as a consequence of intraparty quarrels.

Bibliography

Alofs, L. and Leontien M. *Ken ta Arubiano? Sociale integratie en natievorming op Aruba*, Leiden: KITLV, 1990.

Anderson, W. A. and Dynes, R. *Social Movements, Violence and Change. The May Movement in Curaçao*, Columbus: Ohio State University Press, 1975.

Boots, A. and Woortman, R. *Anton de Kom. Biografie 1898–1945, 1945–2009*, Amsterdam: Contact, 2009.

Commissie. *30 mei 1969. Rapport van de Commissie tot onderzoek van de achtergronden en oorzaken van de onlusten welke op 30 mei 1969 op Curaçao hebben plaatsgehad*, Oranjestad: De Wit, 1970.

de Sola, J. H. *De Nederlandse Antillen en met name Curaçao sinds 30 mei '69*, Berlicum: Stichting ABC Advies, 1994.

Dew, E. *The Difficult Flowering of Surinam. Ethnicity and Politics in a Plural Society*, The Hague: Nijhoff, 1978.

KITLV, Collection "30 mei 1969," Box 3, Interviews E. Ong-A-Kwie, R. Venloo, J. Isphording, and J. J. Vos.

Meel, P. "Towards a Typology of Suriname Nationalism," *New West Indian Guide* 72, 1998, 257–81.

———. "Anton de Kom and the Formative Phase of Surinamese Nationalism," *New West Indian Guide* 83, 2009, 249–80.

Oostindie, G. (ed.) *Dromen en littekens. Dertig jaar na de Curaçaose revolte, 30 mei 1969*, Amsterdam: Amsterdam University Press, 1999.

Oostindie, G. *Paradise Overseas. The Dutch Caribbean: Colonialism and its Transatlantic Legacies*, Oxford: Macmillan, 2005.

———. "Dependence and Autonomy in Sub-national Island Jurisdictions: The Case of the Netherlands Antilles and Aruba," *The Round Table* 95(386), 2006, 609–26.

Oostindie, G. and Klinkers, I. *Het Koninkrijk inde Caraïben: een korte geschiedenis van het Nederlandse dekolonisatiebeleid 1940–2000*, Amsterdam: Amsterdam University Press, 2001.

———. *Decolonising the Caribbean: Dutch Policies in a Comparative Perspective*, Amsterdam: Amsterdam University Press, 2003.

———. *Gedeeld Koninkrijk. De ontmanteling van de Nederlandse Antillen en de vernieuwing van het trans-Atlantische Koninkrijk der Nederlanden,* Amsterdam: Amsterdam University Press, 2012.

van Enckevort, M. *The Life and Work of Otto Huiswoud (1893–1961). Professional Revolutionary and Internationalist.* Dissertation, University of the West Indies, Mona, 2000.

van Stipriaan, A. "July 1: Emancipation Day in Suriname. A Contested *lieu de mémoire,* 1863–2003," *New West Indian Guide* 78, 2004, 269–304.

Verton, P. "Emancipation and Decolonization: The May Revolt and Its Aftermath in Curaçao," *Revista/Review Interamericana* 6(1), 1977, 88–101.

Conclusion

Black Power Forty Years On—An Introspection

BRIAN MEEKS

> Do you know what it is to have a revolution?
>
> DENNIS BROWN, *REVOLUTION*

Looking back across these forty-something years, what is most striking about the Caribbean Black Power movement is the steepness of the curve of its rise and fall and yet the significant impact that it has had on subsequent social and political events in the region. In the narrow definition, Caribbean Black Power flourished for a mere six years. Inspired in name by Stokely Carmichael's 1966 rallying cry in Mississippi and really taking flight with the demonstration, riot, and events surrounding Walter Rodney's expulsion from Jamaica in 1968, Black Power rose to a crescendo in "the 1970 Revolution" in Trinidad and Tobago and then was rapidly eclipsed with the crushing of the National United Freedom Fighters (NUFF) in Trinidad. The rise of the New Jewel Movement (NJM) on a Marxist-Leninist footing and the Grenadian Revolution of 1979–83 can be viewed as the tragic epilogue to this period. There is, of course, as captured in many of the chapters in this volume, a longer genealogy that reaches back into the history of resistance by people of African descent against Caribbean societies built on stifling race and color hierarchies and is captured in the history of the Universal Negro Improvement Association (UNIA) and Garveyism, the Negritude movement, Rastafarianism, and the numerous riots, protests, and demonstrations that punctuated the century after emancipation. Yet there is always the evident danger of conflating the specifics of the movement with the general history of resistance, which, inevitably, will obscure its contribution to the longer process.

Another critical dimension, missed too often by the existing, if limited, commentaries on the period, is that it was a far more pan-Caribbean movement than any of the contemporary participants genuinely understood. Thus, while one could arguably make connections between the emerging movement in the Anglophone Caribbean, with its evident linkages to the 1969 Sir George Williams University protests in Montreal and with ready-made connections through the New World Group[1] and the student and faculty of the University of the West Indies (UWI), similar organic connections did not exist with the Dutch Caribbean, and there were only limited linkages to the U.S. Virgin Islands and Bermuda, to mention two other instances. Yet, as this volume vividly illustrates, the movement emerged and flourished for a time in all of these jurisdictions and beyond.

To appreciate its scope, then, one has to move beyond the specific concerns that fed the Caribbean movement in order to locate it within the broader global wave of resistance of the late 1960s. From such a purchase, Black Power was the peculiarly African Caribbean response to an international revolutionary *abertura* that was captured, *inter alia,* in the Czechoslovakian Spring; the student uprisings in Mexico that were brutally suppressed preceding the Olympics; the tumultuous, revolutionary French student and worker strikes; the Tet offensive in Vietnam; the flourishing of the peace movement in the United States and Europe; and, of course, the North American Black Power movement. All were focused around that remarkable year, 1968. The rise of the Caribbean movement from this perspective was only part of an irrepressible wave of anti-systemic insurrection, questioning the authority of dominant states and systems and threatening, though unsuccessfully in the short run, to overturn them. Such moments, as Immanuel Wallerstein et al propose, are rare.[2] While national and international events conspire to produce on a more regular basis the conditions for local revolt, it is a rare moment when there is a global alignment—the 1848 European revolutions being, in Wallerstein's accounting, the only prior example. It is this overarching zeitgeist that must necessarily be introduced into the calculation to grasp the moment. The anti-systemic moment of 1968, as a virtual force of nature, battered traditions, tossed social mores around, and demanded that individuals caught up in the maelstrom take a position on one or the other side of the ramparts. I can best try to explain this, with my own little narrative as a high school student coming to maturity at the cusp of the moment.

I was fortunate, indeed, privileged, to live for extended periods in three nodal points in the Caribbean, looking at the region from the perspective of the consolidation of a radical politics, beginning with the Rodney events of

1968 in Jamaica.[3] I grew up and went to high school in Jamaica and was in sixth form in 1968, during the period of Walter Rodney's exclusion and the subsequent riots. I went to university in Trinidad and Tobago—my mother's country—as an undergraduate in late 1970 and stayed until graduation in 1973. This was the period of the state of emergency that followed the mass demonstrations and their aftermath,[4] when radical politics, despite the defeat of the street phase of the Black Power revolution, continued to have significant momentum in the Eric Williams–led twin island state. I returned to Jamaica in 1973 and spent the crucial years from then until 1980 as a graduate student at UWI–Mona and later as a television producer at the Jamaica Broadcasting Corporation (JBC) and partisan in favor of the Workers Party of Jamaica (WPJ) and Manley's People's National Party (PNP) during its radical, "democratic socialist" phase.[5] And I lived, at the invitation of the People's Revolutionary Government (PRG) in Grenada, from 1981 to 1983, returning to Jamaica only weeks before the collapse of the Grenada Revolution in October 1983.

Jamaica

I begin in Jamaica, somewhere around 1968, my first year as a sixth former at Jamaica College (JC), one of the premier high schools in Kingston, in order to suggest the outlines of what was, if only in retrospect, a prerevolutionary situation. The date of 16 October 1968 marked the occasion when the Guyanese historian Walter Rodney, who had been attending the historic Black Writers Congress in Montreal, was declared persona non grata and excluded by the government from returning to his home and job at the Mona campus of the University of the West Indies. It tossed us schoolboys and -girls headfirst into the hurricane of Jamaican politics. In its immediate prologue, Emperor Haile Selassie of Ethiopia had visited Jamaica in 1966, and part of his itinerary had taken him to Jamaica College. This close-up of the man revered by so many ordinary Jamaicans, but more so the sheer numbers and enthusiasm of the many Rastafarians who followed his every move, exposed us to Rastafari not simply as a religion, but a mass movement.[6] Rodney's banning on 16 October 1968, on his way back to Jamaica from the Black Writers Congress, suggested that the Jamaica Labour Party (JLP) government led by Hugh Shearer was arbitrary and capable of committing what seemed to us to be extreme calumny in its condemnation of Rodney and the students as dangerous subversives.[7] The tear-gas attacks on the students who marched in support of Rodney and the subsequent attempt to paint them—particularly those from other territories—as anarchists and terrorists elicited tremendous sympathy among students and young people like me.

We moved overnight from partial Black Power sympathizers to avid supporters. A year later, in upper sixth form, a small group of us would leave school without permission to support university students who had occupied the new Creative Arts Centre at UWI, arguing that its aims and purposes were not sufficiently oriented to black and African themes. Our little group eventually published a cyclostyled news sheet entitled *LIJ Youth Move*.[8] We had read somewhere that the Amharic word *lij* meant "sons of one mother," and this was our symbolic way of announcing our own blood brotherhood, albeit inadvertently reflecting the deeply gendered character of both our enterprise and the times in general. The content, as I recall (I have not been able to rescue an intact copy), varied between articles attempting to recover a lost African past, reflections on poverty in Jamaica, and calls to revolution expressed in fairly incendiary terms. Awareness of its publication and distribution was cause, I learned many years later, for an item at a board meeting of the school, and my parents were called in to warn them of their sixteen-year-old son's "dangerous" turn.

The Jamaican Black Power movement took the form of an intense popular process of consciousness-raising. Students demonstrated against those they considered to be colonial-minded principals, some of whom actually banned the Afro hairstyle in their schools. There was also, as developed in both Rupert Lewis's and Anthony Bogues's chapters, a proliferation of pamphlets, led by the iconic *Abeng* but including *Black Man Speaks*, *Bongo-Man*, and many others, among them *LIJ*.

Undoubtedly, the most important vehicle for consciousness-raising was popular music. If rocksteady, the beat of the rude boys, with its slow, deliberate rhythm was a portent of a broader, mass rebellion, then reggae, its far more famous successor, whose history is almost parallel to the rise of Black Power, was, from its origins, rebel music.[9] Bob Marley and the Wailers' 1969 *Babylon Burning* epitomized the new mood in its prophecy of the cleansing destruction of Babylon by fire: "Fire, fire, fire, fire, fire, fire, they have no water / Babylon burnin', Babylon burnin', Babylon burnin', they have no water."[10] This and scores of other similar 45 rpm recordings became the clarion call for a generation who came from varying social backgrounds, ranging from inner-city poverty to upper-middle-class comfort and privilege.

The remarkable feature of this phase of Jamaican politics, however, is how this broad river of young people, dedicated to a cause (even if the cause had not been sufficiently defined) chose, for the greater part, a channel that led into the mainstream political party system. By 1972, it was the youth, many inspired by Black Power, who had propelled Michael Manley up from his lower profile as a trade unionist and son of Norman to become Joshua, the charismatic leader who would march around the walls of Jericho and defeat the heathen in the 1972 elections.[11] Thus, aside from the profound street act of October 1968, Jamaican Black Power took the form of a broad, multifaceted process of consciousness-raising, of newspaper publishing and distribution, of street corner and backyard "reasonings," and of the utilization of popular music as a means of social and political education. Its ultimate effect was both profound (the election of a government and leader to power who could only have won because they promoted the cultural and some of the implicit political aims of the popular movement) and compromised (as the party itself, the vehicle of the victory was deeply divided between a commitment to the new politics and a rootedness in a traditional, relatively conservative two-party system that dominated the country's politics then, as it still does now).

Trinidad

I graduated from JC in the summer of 1970 and, despite gaining a letter of acceptance to .Columbia University, decided to study social sciences at UWI–St. Augustine in Trinidad and Tobago. The reasons were twofold. Trinidad was my mother's homeland, and growing up in Jamaica, it was a part of my own background that I felt I needed to understand. More importantly, word of the Black Power demonstrations had reached me just about the same time that I had to make decisions as to which college to attend. In my mind, there was no question, as Trinidad was the venue where the real action was taking place. I landed at Piarco International Airport in September 1970 as a seventeen-year-old youngster, with a very thin veneer of militancy derived from my sixth form experiences of marginal involvement in the publication of a newspaper, membership in a Rasta-oriented school band, and three weeks of teaching literacy in the Jamaican countryside in the summer of 1970. I came to a country in the middle of a revolutionary crisis. The leaders of the National Joint Action Committee (NJAC) had been imprisoned since April, but all over the place were second-level leaders, supporters and followers of the mass movement that had taken over the streets in the preceding months. The movement had not been cowed, but with the state of emergency had entered a new and more dangerous phase. Within a few months of being on the St. Augustine campus, I had been introduced to the *Anarchist's Cookbook*,[12] a truly subversive publication with recipes for manufacturing dangerous things. One evening I had been invited and visited some "brothers on the block" in Belmont on the outskirts of Port of Spain, who were talking insurrection and seemed to have close connections with others who actually had guns in the hills to the north of the city. Later, I would discover that they were actually not just talkers, but very serious. This was the beginning of the National United Freedom Fighters (NUFF) that carried out limited guerrilla action in various parts of Trinidad and Tobago between 1971 and 1974.[13] NUFF was indeed a small splinter from the mass movement that had gathered force between February and April 1970, but it also reflected, simultaneously, the extent to which the movement had moved beyond the parliamentary fabric of Trinidadian society and shifted focus on the more fundamental questions of state and power. As a post-1970 pamphlet of the NJAC—the leading Black Power organization—succinctly put it: *Conventional Politics or Revolution?*[14] The People's National Movement (PNM) government was attempting to recover authority in the wake of an army rebellion that had failed, and in the context of an urban, black population, many of whom, particularly among the young, were fully open to the possibilities of insurrectional politics. When a group of students, among whom I was a mere freshman participant, held a march in support of the detained NJAC leaders, we later discovered we were under intense surveillance. A policeman who was also a student on campus brought us a picture with neatly penned-in arrows and numbers pointing at me and a number of other marchers. He told us to be very, very careful. Trinidad Black Power operated within its own cultural and political confines. In the same way as the street phase of the movement was initiated during the 1970 carnival celebrations, Trinidadian social life never abated during the state of emergency, with fetes continuing sometimes until dawn, in order to avoid the curfew.

The Black Power movement, however, never brokered the unity between the divided African and Indian elements of the society that it aspired to achieve as one of its main and laudatory goals.[15] As a young Jamaican student without the same cultural patterns of constraint that applied to Trinidadian society, I remember being advised by friends on both sides of the ethnic divide that too much friendliness might be inappropriate and Indian girls were off limits. Yet, with all the communally imposed constraints, small numbers of Indian Trinidadians were deeply involved in the movement, especially in urban areas like St. James, Curepe, and Tunapuna, sometimes in significant numbers.

Trinidad Black Power never recovered the momentum that it had on the streets in early 1970, before the state of emergency was declared. The decision of NUFF to wage guerrilla warfare was more a reflection of the extent of alienation among the young than it was a concerted and serious attempt to capture state power. But simultaneously, NUFF, by its engagement in armed warfare, intensified state repression against more peaceful mass organizations like NJAC and the leftist trade unionists like George Weekes in the Oilfield Workers Trade Union (OWTU) and Joe Young in the Transport and Industrial Workers Union (TIWU). The various factions, at any rate, were unable to forge a working alliance that might have countered the traditional base of the PNM, and despite the belated attempt to do so through the United Labour Front,[16] by 1973, with the Arab Oil crisis and the spike in the price of petroleum internationally, the popular foundation for the movement was mortally wounded as the Trinidadian state moved into a decade of rising incomes, state-sponsored jobs, and cost-of-living allowances that acted as a successful palliative against radicalism of whatever stream.

Back to Jamaica

Returning home to Jamaica in the seventies to pursue graduate studies at UWI–Mona, there was an entirely different situation. The radicals were in power, but then again they were not. I recall as if it were yesterday a meeting of the "anti-imperialist forces" in Cookhorne Lane in South West St. Andrew in 1973 hosted by Ben Munroe of the South West St. Andrew Citizens Association (SWSACA). Representatives came from among Mona students; the People's National Party Youth Organization (PNPYO), a Maoist faction; the Youth Forces for National Liberation (YFNL); the embryonic Marxist-Leninist Workers Liberation League (WLL); the Marxist but never clearly defined Movement for Social and Political Consciousness (MSPC); and the neo-Trotskyist/neo–C.L.R. Jamesist Revolutionary Marxist Collective (RMC). The proliferation of names and organizations alone—very few, if any, of which existed three years earlier—indicates the mushrooming of radical ideas that had taken place in the mere three years of my absence.

At the entrance of the dark lane off Spanish Town Road was our security detail—a single young man armed with a "bucky," a hollowed-out bicycle frame that was now the improvised barrel for a shotgun. Just after the meeting started, we heard the sound of automatic gunfire. It certainly was not the primitive weapon of our security detail, and the meeting dispersed as everyone ran for cover, scaling the fence of the yard and heading up Waltham Park

Road, or seeking cover wherever seemed adequate. What saved us that dark night was that one of the PNP comrades rang their party headquarters, and Tony Spaulding, then Minister of Housing and a leading figure on the left of the party, sent his personal security team, which, properly armed, dispersed the invaders in short order. This early indicator turned out to be the truest warning of the violence that was soon to come.

Michael Manley, in his somewhat hesitant and uncertain attempts to undermine the colonial undergirdings of Jamaican society, was entirely unprepared for outright class war. The history of this period has yet to be told in a determined and scholarly manner. My own experience suggests that the burnings and lootings—a sort of early ethnic cleansing practiced against partisan opponents—were first unleashed by the social and political opposition.[17] At first it was met with resistance, and aided by the state of emergency, Manley won the 1976 election with an increased mandate over that of 1972. However, when following the 1976 victory, open urban warfare was combined with economic destabilization, it proved to be overwhelming for the fledgling movement. Manley plunged from the heights of political success in 1976 to massive electoral defeat in 1980, though even then he was able to retain a solid 41 percent of the electorate, despite months of incessant violence, a prostrate economy, and at least eight hundred dead in the streets.

The election took place in late October, and by January, I, along with twenty other newsroom and current-affairs workers, had been made redundant by the Jamaica Broadcasting Corporation (JBC), the sole television station. The new Edward Seaga–led JLP government had accused us of partisanship and had kicked us out of our jobs—illegally, as it was later adjudged in court. Seaga was correct in his perception that there was little support for his party in the newsroom, but in dismissing the entire staff he had breached the statutory requirement that the station should provide a regular stream of news and current affairs. We were later to be compensated, though in the economic situation of a rapidly devaluing Jamaican dollar, it amounted to very little.

Grenada

I was unemployed from then until June, when I got a message from WPJ General Secretary Trevor Munroe that the People's Revolutionary Government in Grenada wanted me to help develop their work in the media. I dropped everything and left for Grenada. Salary was not a question, terms of employment not an issue. The revolution called and I left. Grenada was something new. The youthfulness of the movement, even from a Jamaican perspective, was palpable. Both Maurice Bishop and Bernard Coard, the top leaders, were in their thirties. The next tier of leadership was largely in its early twenties. The existence of a radical state power without a powerful, reactionary opposition seemed almost unreal and intoxicating coming from the near-civil-war trenches of Jamaica. There was much that was going on in the new situation that was positive. The work in education and the formulation of a new curriculum for primary and secondary students was rich and ahead of much of the Caribbean.[18] The annual budget debate, carried out through popular discussions surrounding the economy that took place across the length and breadth of the island, was rich and still provides a template for alternative approaches to a more participatory economic democracy.[19] However, there was a darker side to all this. I remember being at a political education meeting in 1983, chaired by Maurice Bishop at his home, when I mooted that I might be going back to Jamaica to pursue graduate studies. Someone said, jokingly, "Comrade, it is easy to come to Grenada, but not so easy to leave. Remember, we control immigration." Of course, it was a joke and one that I later discovered was oft repeated to visiting supporters of the "Revo." It nonetheless reflected the reality that, after 1979, power and almost absolute power belonged to the People's Revolutionary Government (PRG). The United States had genuinely failed to anticipate revolution in Grenada,[20] and in the face of Caribbean resistance to its intervention, had no concerted plan as to what to do. Further, there were the bigger geopolitical problems of Iran and Nicaragua, with both of these revolutionary overthrows occurring in the same year. This temporary window of opportunity enhanced the PRG's virtual monopoly and helped encourage various abuses of power. Long before the crisis of 1983, there was the excessive detention of so-called "counters" (counterrevolutionaries) and the brutalizing of some of them by senior officers. While there are disputed figures as to the number of persons detained during the tenure of the PRG, there is little disputing now that many instances were unwarranted.[21] There is a certain logic to governments that come to power by insurrection, and that is that they must protect themselves against imminent counter-insurrection. Certainly, among the leading failures of the PRG was the failure to recognize that in a country in which its support had been built on popular opposition to Eric Gairy's authoritarian tendencies, then if support was to be consolidated it would have to be on a foundation of enhanced democracy and not a new authoritarianism supposedly justified by the act of revolution.

The New Jewel Movement (NJM) also evolved a particularly rigid and mechanical version of Marxism Leninism, very evident in the stolen party documents that still reside in Washington, D.C.[22] Thus the party recognized that Grenada, with fewer than one hundred thousand largely rural people, did not have a proletariat. A conscious proletariat was seen to be a prerequisite for socialism. So, since socialism was desirable, the PRG would have to build a proletariat, which meant building factories—a daunting task at best, in a country with a working population of fewer than fifty thousand persons. This mechanistic, one-size-fits-all, building-block approach to politics and socialism signaled the doom of the nascent process. It is inappropriate here to reprise the crisis of 1983,[23] except to say that the death of Maurice Bishop and his associates at the hands of some of his closest comrades, closely followed by the United States–led invasion, signaled not only the end of the Grenadian Revolution, but the rapid demise of an entire political movement that spanned the region and that had been born some fifteen years earlier in the moment of popular efflorescence that followed Walter Rodney's banning from Jamaica.

By Way of Conclusion

Caribbean Black Power was a movement for radical change of the social and economic system in the Caribbean. It borrowed critical elements from American Black Power, in some of its symbols and styles, as well as the militancy that came to be identified with the mature North American movement, through formations like the Student Non-Violent Coordinating Committee (SNCC) and, later, the Black Panther Party.[24] Caribbean Black Power, however, possessed its own autonomy rooted in indigenous movements for black self-assertion, such as Rastafari, and was sparked by a new generation of radicalized youth who keenly felt the failure of the states across the region to fulfill the immense expectations invested in the nationalist and independence movements, including an end to racial privileging, real economic and social improvement, and a more meaningful, democratic politics.

Caribbean Black Power operated in the world of the sixties and seventies, a time of unprecedented international uprising. Thus the icons of that era—Guevara and Ho Chi Minh, Huey Newton, Angela Davis, and Malcolm X—were all inscribed on its masthead, along with other images of Marcus Garvey and Haile Selassie, Trinidad's (and Grenada's) Tubal Uriah "Buzz" Butler, and, of course, the iconic figure of their generation, Walter Rodney.

However, among its many flaws, Caribbean Black Power was a male-centered movement, as evident in the paucity of female names among the icons of the era and their virtual absence at the top leadership levels of the various organizations throughout the Caribbean territories. Women were everywhere present in the "struggle," but they were almost everywhere subordinate to male leadership.[25]

It also borrowed substantially the styles, strategies, and tactics of its own generation of insurgents—the Black Panthers and the French and Mexican students—in notions of frontal confrontation, of guerrilla warfare, and of revolutionary overthrow as primary moves in any political engagement, as opposed to the more moderate notions of struggling for trade union rights, universal adult suffrage, and general elections that occupied the attention of an earlier generation. The idea that all of these tactics, each deployed appropriately, depending on the overall national and international conditions, could be woven into a more complex and nuanced political strategy, was largely alien to the generation of 1968. This political immaturity and, indeed, naiveté, was the Achilles heel of the movement. It contributed to the failure of the Trinidad contingents to overcome minor differences and build a potentially winning coalition; the failure of the Jamaican movement to consolidate as an autonomous political force; and the egregious failure of the Grenadian movement (albeit in its post–Black Power Marxist-Leninist garb) to maintain political unity at all costs in the face of daunting international opposition from the United States and conservative countries in the region.

Finally, the impact of the Black Power movement on the course of the region is, at best, ambiguous. On the one hand, the overt and exclusive hierarchies of color that characterized the colonial and immediate postindependence eras have largely retreated. The discriminatory employment of lighter-skinned persons in banks and businesses, which Acton Camejo saw in his early-1970s study of Trinidad, is no longer immediately evident.[26] But has this changed the more fundamental underlying reality of ethnic minorities dominating Caribbean economies? The answer is undoubtedly no. The Black Power movement heralded an era of black pride and identity, most evident in the Rastafari movement, which gained worldwide popularity in the seventies and continuing into the present era. But the irony of the moment is that, while wearing the once denigrated dreadlocks hairstyle has become a fashion statement, skin bleaching in inner-city communities in Jamaica has proliferated, with practitioners arguing that lighter-skinned persons have better chances at employment and even attracting a mate.[27] And at the macro level of Caribbean political economy, it is sobering to note how the more things change, the more they remain the same. In October 1980, the Michael Manley government, which came to power on the wave of the Black Power movement, was defeated in elections in part because of the strangulating effect of one of the earliest International Monetary Fund (IMF) structural adjustment agreements that it was forced to implement.[28] Four decades later, in December 2012, another PNP government, headed by a black Jamaican woman from humble, rural origins, Portia Simpson Miller, is entangled in negotiations with the IMF in order to hammer out an agreement that some suggest will inevitably undermine her popularity and everyone recognizes will impose new hardships on the backs of the long-suffering Jamaican working people.

Notes

Epigraph source: Dennis Brown, "Revolution" from the album Revolution, Yvonne's Special, LP YS4, 1985.

1. For a crisp description of the New World Group, which functioned throughout the Caribbean and the diaspora in the 1960s and early 1970s, see Norman Girvan, "The New World Group: a Historical Perspective" in Brian Meeks and Norman Girvan (eds.).

2. Wallerstein, Hopkins, and Arrighi, Antisystemic Movements.

3. See Lewis, chapter 5 in Walter Rodney's Intellectual and Political Thought.

4. See Ryan and Stewart (eds.), The Black Power Revolution 1970.

5. See, for instance, Stephens and Stephens, Democratic Socialism in Jamaica.

6. See Bogues, 189, and Lewis, 91.

7. See Girvan, "After Rodney."

8. Rupert Lewis speaks eloquently to the variety of publications that were emerging in this period in his Small Axe interview. See Scott, "The Dialectic of Defeat: an Interview with Rupert Lewis."

9. See Bogues, chapter 7 in Black Heretics, Black Prophets.

10. Bob Marley and the Wailers, Fire, Fire, 1969.

11. See Senior, The Message Is Change.

12. Powell, The Anarchist's Cookbook.

13. See Millette, "Guerrilla War in Trinidad 1970–1974" in Ryan and Stewart (eds.), and Brian Meeks, chapter 2 in Narratives of Resistance.

14. National Joint Action Committee, Conventional Politics or Revolution?.

15. See John La Guerre, "The Indian Response to Black Power: a Continuing Dilemma," in Ryan and Stewart (eds.).

16. For a discussion of Trinidadian politics in the period of the rise of the United Labour Front, see Ryan, Revolution and Reaction.

17. For a reading of this period closer to my own, see Manley, Jamaica: Struggle in the Periphery. For an opposing perspective, see Seaga, My Life and Leadership Vol. 1.

18. See Ann Hickling-Hudson, "Grenada: Education and Revolution."

19. See, for instance, Meeks, Social Formation and People's Revolution: a Grenadian Study, and Coard, Grenada: Village and Workers, Women, Farmers and Youth Assemblies During the Revolution.

20. This is evident in the post-invasion, post-mortem conference hosted in part by the

United States Naval Postgraduate School, which arrives at similar conclusions. See Jiri Valenta and Herbert Ellison (eds.), *Soviet/Cuban Strategy in the Third World after Grenada*.

21. See, most notably, former Deputy Prime Minister of the PRG Bernard Coard's interview in the *Journal of Eastern Caribbean Studies*, in which he admits that many people were detained unnecessarily. See Grenade, "Retrospect: a View from Richmond Hill Prison: an Interview with Bernard Coard."

22. See, for a partial selection, Departments of State and Defence, *The Grenada Documents: an Overview and Selection*.

23. See Meeks, "Grenada, Once Again: Re-Visiting the 1983 Crisis and Collapse of the Grenadian Revolution."

24. See Joseph, *Waiting 'Til the Midnight Hour,* especially 132–275.

25. See Pasley, *Gender, Race, and Class in Urban Trinidad.*

26. See Camejo, "Racial Discrimination in Employment in the Private Sector in Trinidad and Tobago."

27.See Nettleford, 41–111, and "Skin Bleaching a Growing Problem in Jamaica," *Jamaica Observer,* 11 April 2011.

28. See Girvan, Bernal, and Hughes, "The IMF and the Third World: The Case of Jamaica."

Bibliography

Bogues, A. *Black Heretics, Black Prophets: Radical Political Intellectuals,* New York and London: Routledge, 2003.

Brown, D. "Revolution," *Revolution,* Yvonne's Special, LP YS4, 1985.

Camejo, A. "Racial Discrimination in Employment in the Private Sector in Trinidad and Tobago: A Study of the Business Elite and the Social Structure," *Social and Economic Studies,* vol. 20, no. 3, September 1971, 294–318.

Coard, B. *Grenada: Village and Workers, Women, Farmers and Youth Assemblies During the Revolution,* London: Caribbean Labour Solidarity and the NJM, Karia Press, 1989.

Departments of State and Defence, *The Grenada Documents: an Overview and Selection,* Washington DC, 1984.

Girvan, N. "After Rodney: the Politics of Student Protest in Jamaica," *New World Quarterly* vol. 4, no. 3, 1968, 59–68.

———. "The New World Group: a Historical Perspective" in Brian Meeks and Norman Girvan (eds.), *The Thought of New World: the Quest for Decolonisation,* Kingston and Miami: Ian Randle Publishers, 2010, 3–29.

Girvan, N., Bernal, R., and Hughes, W. "The IMF and the Third World: The Case of Jamaica," *Development Dialogue,* No. 2, 1980, 113–55.

Grenade, W. "Retrospect: a View from Richmond Hill Prison: an Interview with Bernard Coard," *Journal of Eastern Caribbean Studies,* vol. 35, nos. 3 and 4, Sept.–Dec. 2010, 108–39.

Hickling-Hudson, A. "Grenada: Education and Revolution," in Rupert Lewis (ed.), *Caribbean Political Activism: Essays in Honour of Richard Hart,* Kingston and Miami: Ian Randle Publishers, Caribbean Reasonings Series, 2012, 227–53.

Huber Stephens, E. and Stephens, J. D. *Democratic Socialism in Jamaica: The Political Move-*

ment and Social Transformation in Dependent Capitalism, Basingstoke and London: Macmillan, 1986.

Joseph, P. *Waiting 'Til the Midnight Hour: A Narrative History of Black Power in America,* New York: Henry Holt and Company, 2006.

La Guerre, J. "The Indian Response to Black Power: a Continuing Dilemma" in Ryan and Stewart (eds.), *The Black Power Revolution 1970: a Retrospective,* St. Augustine: ISER, 1995, 273–308.

Lewis, R. *Walter Rodney's Intellectual and Political Thought,* Kingston: University of the West Indies Press, and Detroit: Wayne State University Press, 1998.

Manley, M. *Jamaica: Struggle in the Periphery,* London: Writers and Readers, 1982.

Marley, B. and the Wailers, *Fire, Fire,* Wail N Soul M, 45rpm, c. 1969.

Meeks, B. "Social Formation and People's Revolution: a Grenadian Study," PhD thesis, the University of the West Indies Mona, Kingston, 1988.

———. *Narratives of Resistance: Jamaica, Trinidad, the Caribbean,* Kingston: University of the West Indies Press, 2000.

———. "Grenada, Once Again: Re-Visiting the 1983 Crisis and Collapse of the Grenadian Revolution" in Rupert Lewis (ed.), *Caribbean Political Activism: Essays in Honour of Richard Hart,* Kingston and Miami: Ian Randle Publishers, 2012, 199–226.

Millette, D. "Guerrilla War in Trinidad 1970–1974" in Ryan and Stewart (eds.), *The Black Power Revolution 1970: a Retrospective,* St. Augustine: ISER, 1995, 625–60.

National Joint Action Committee, *Conventional Politics or Revolution?* Port of Spain: NJAC Publications, 1971.

Nettleford, R. "African Redemption: the Rastafari and Wider Society" in *Mirror, Mirror: Identity, Race and Protest in Jamaica,* Kingston: Kingston Publishers, 1998, (first published 1970) 41–111.

Pasley, V. "Gender, Race, and Class in Urban Trinidad: Representations in the Construction and Maintenance of the Gender Order 1950–1980," unpublished PhD dissertation, University of Houston, May 1999.

Powell, W. *The Anarchist's Cookbook,* New York: L. Stuart, 1971.

Ryan, S. *Revolution and Reaction: Parties and Politics in Trinidad and Tobago 1970–1981,* St. Augustine: ISER, 1989.

Ryan, S. and Stewart, T. (eds.), *The Black Power Revolution 1970: a Retrospective,* St. Augustine: ISER, 1995.

Scott, D. "The Dialectic of Defeat: an Interview with Rupert Lewis," *Small Axe,* no. 10, September 2001, 85–177.

Seaga, E. *My Life and Leadership Vol. 1: Clash of Ideologies,* Oxford: Macmillan, 2010.

Senior, O. *The Message Is Change: a Perspective on the 1972 General Elections,* Kingston: Kingston Publishers Ltd, 1972.

"Skin Bleaching a Growing Problem in Jamaica," *Jamaica Observer,* 11 April 2011.

Valenta, J. and Ellison, H. (eds.), *Soviet/Cuban Strategy in the Third World after Grenada: Toward Prevention of Future Grenadas,* Washington DC: The Wilson Center, 1984.

Wallerstein, I., Hopkins, T., and Arrighi, G., *Antisystemic Movements,* London: Verso, 1989.

Contributors

Anthony Bogues is Lyn Crost Professor of Social Sciences and Critical Theory and the director of the Center for the Study of Slavery and Justice at Brown University. He is also associate director of the Centre for Caribbean Thought. His books include *Empire of Liberty: Power, Desire and Freedom* and *Black Heretics and Black Prophets: Radical Political Intellectuals.*

Richard Drayton is Rhodes Professor of Imperial History at King's College London. He is author of *Nature's Government: Science, Imperial Britain and the Improvement of the World*, which was awarded the Morris D. Forkosch Prize by the American Historical Association in 2001. He was awarded the Philip Leverhulme Prize for History in 2002.

Derick Hendricks is lecturer in the Department of History and Geography at Morgan State University. His PhD, on *Black Awareness and Social Unrest in the U.S. Virgin Islands: A Case Study of Black Nationalism, 1968–1986*, was awarded by Morgan State University in 2009.

Paget Henry is professor of Sociology and Africana Studies at Brown University. He is the author of many works on the Caribbean, including *Shouldering Antigua and Barbuda: The Life of V. C. Bird* and *Caliban's Reason: Introducing Caribbean Philosophy*, which was awarded the 2003 Frantz Fanon Award for the best book in the field of Africana thought in the last five years. He is also editor of the *C.L.R. James Journal.*

Rupert Lewis is associate director of the Centre for Caribbean Thought and professor of Political Thought in the Department of Government, University of the West Indies–Mona. He has published extensively on Caribbean political thought, including two edited volumes on Marcus Garvey and a study of Walter Rodney: *Walter Rodney's Intellectual and Political Thought.*

Brian Meeks is director of the Sir Arthur Lewis Institute of Social and Economic Studies and former director of the Centre for Caribbean Thought, University of the West Indies–Mona. He has published extensively on radical and revolutionary politics in the Caribbean, including *Caribbean Revolutions and Revolutionary Theory: An Assessment of Cuba, Nicaragua and Grenada; Radical Caribbean: From Black Power to Abu Bakr;* and *Narratives of Resistance: Jamaica, Trinidad, the Caribbean.*

Gert Oostindie is professor of Caribbean History and director of the KITLV (Royal Netherlands Institute of Southeast Asian and Caribbean Studies) at the University of Leiden. He has published more than twenty books, including *Paradise Overseas: The Dutch Caribbean, Colonialism and Its Transatlantic Legacies; Decolonising the Caribbean;* and *Postcolonial Netherlands.*

Kate Quinn is lecturer in Caribbean History at the Institute of the Americas, University College London. She is coeditor with Professor Paul Sutton of *Politics and Power in Haiti* and has also published articles on postindependence Trinidad and on revolutionary Cuba. She is Chair of the Society for Caribbean Studies.

Brinsley Samaroo is senior research fellow at the University of Trinidad and Tobago. He has published extensively on the history of the Caribbean, including pioneering work on the Indian presence in the Caribbean. His edited collections include *India in the Caribbean* and *Across the Dark Waters: Ethnicity and Indian Identity in the Caribbean.*

Quito Swan is associate professor of African Diaspora Studies in the Department of History at Howard University. He is the author of *Black Power in Bermuda and the Struggle for Decolonization* and director of the Pauulu Project, a research initiative based on the work of Pauulu Kamarakafego.

Nigel Westmaas teaches in the Department of Africana Studies at Hamilton College, New York. His research and activist interests include social movements in Guyana and the Caribbean, the works of poet Martin Carter, and Marcus Garvey in British Guiana. He has published in a number of journals and newspapers, including *Small Axe,* where "Resisting Orthodoxy: Notes on the Origins and Ideology of the Working People's Alliance" appeared. Westmaas is a former political activist of the Working People's Alliance.

Index

www.ingramcontent.com/pod-product-compliance
Lightning Source LLC
Chambersburg PA
CBHW032011150725
29645CB00022B/424